Metaethics after Moore

Metaethics after Moore

EDITED BY

TERRY HORGAN

and

MARK TIMMONS

CLARENDON PRESS · OXFORD

OXFORD
UNIVERSITY PRESS

Great Clarendon Street, Oxford OX2 6DP

Oxford University Press is a department of the University of Oxford.
It furthers the University's objective of excellence in research, scholarship,
and education by publishing worldwide in

Oxford New York

Auckland Cape Town Dar es Salaam Hong Kong Karachi
Kuala Lumpur Madrid Melbourne Mexico City Nairobi
New Delhi Shanghai Taipei Toronto

With offices in

Argentina Austria Brazil Chile Czech Republic France Greece
Guatemala Hungary Italy Japan Poland Portugal Singapore
South Korea Switzerland Thailand Turkey Ukraine Vietnam

Oxford is a registered trade mark of Oxford University Press
in the UK and in certain other countries

Published in the United States
by Oxford University Press Inc., New York

British Library Cataloguing in Publication Data

Data available

Library of Congress Cataloging in Publication Data

Metaethics after Moore / edited by Terry Horgan and Mark Timmons.
p. cm.
Includes bibliographical references and index.
1. Ethics. 2. Moore, G. E. (George Edward), 1873–1958. Principia ethica.
I. Horgan, Terry, 1948– II. Timmons, Mark, 1951–
BJ37.M47 2006 170′.42—dc22 2005023277

Typeset by Newgen Imaging Systems (P) Ltd., Chennai, India
Printed in Great Britain
on acid-free paper by
Biddles Ltd., King's Lynn, Norfolk

ISBN 0–19–926990–4 978–0–19–926990–7
ISBN 0–19–926991–2 (Pbk.) 978–0–19–926991–4 (Pbk.)

1 3 5 7 9 10 8 6 4 2

PREFACE

Since its publication in 1903, G. E. Moore's *Principia Ethica* has continued to exert a powerful influence on metaethical enquiry. This volume contains sixteen essays that represent recent work in metaethics after, and in some cases directly inspired by, the work of Moore. Seven of the essays were originally presented at the 2002 Spindel Conference commemorating the one hundredth anniversary of the publication of *Principia Ethica* and in celebration of a hundred years of metaethics. They are reprinted here (some slightly revised) from the *Southern Journal of Philosophy*, 41 (2003). Our introduction situates the essays in relation to central themes in Moore's metaethics.

We are grateful to the *Southern Journal of Philosophy* for permission to reprint the papers that appeared in the 2003 supplement. We also wish to thank our editor at Oxford University Press, Peter Momtchiloff, for his guidance and support in our work on this anthology.

T.H. and M.T.

Tucson, Ariz.

CONTENTS

He scurried away.

"You think he did it?" I hissed to Erica.

"I dunno. He seemed to have a lot of hate in his demeanor."

Wolfie returned and dutifully recited his wife's phone number, which I scribbled on the cover of my notebook.

"Listen, make me look good in the paper. My business is already down because of Raina. I didn't kill her, even if I wanted her out of the picture. I mean, I wanted her out of the yoga picture. That's all."

"Understood." I squeezed his shoulder. "I'll be in touch."

He and Erica shook hands, and again he implored her to come to class.

We wandered out into the bright sun.

"I notice he didn't ask me to come to class," I joked.

"You should do a little stretching." She slipped on her sunglasses. "It would be great for you. I do yoga on my boat."

I fired up the car. "How does that work, exactly?"

"I have room on the bow. Really helps with my balance."

As I drove, Erica mused about the difficulties of practicing yoga on her sailboat. "It gets a little wobbly, but better for your equilibrium. You could join me sometime. Or we could go to a class together."

"Are you saying I'm inflexible?"

"Nothing a few mind-opening stretches can't cure." She smiled.

"There's an idea. We should take a class at Raina's studio to grab some other sources. I'll bet her students are still practicing there. That way I could get some color for the article. Look up the schedule for Dante's Inferno while I drive."

Erica fiddled with her phone. "Here we go. Candlelight yoga. Tonight at seven."

LIST OF CONTRIBUTORS

ROBERT AUDI is Professor of Philosophy and David E. Gallo Chair in Ethics at the University of Notre Dame. His books include *The Good in the Right* (2004), *The Architecture of Reason* (2001), *Religious Commitment and Secular Reason* (2000), and *Moral Knowledge and Ethical Character* (1997).

STEPHEN BARKER is Lecturer in Philosophy at the University of Nottingham. In addition to many articles, he is the author of *Renewing Meaning: A Speech-Act Theoretic Approach* (2004). He is currently completing a book on an expressivist theory of truth.

PAUL BLOOMFIELD is Assistant Professor of Philosophy at the University of Connecticut and in addition to many articles in metaethics he is author of *Moral Reality* (2001).

PANAYOT BUTCHVAROV is the University of Iowa Distinguished Professor of Philosophy. He is the author of *Resemblance and Identity* (1966), *The Concept of Knowledge* (1970), *Being qua Being: A Theory of Identity, Existence and Predication* (1979), *Skepticism in Ethics* (1989), and *Skepticism about the External World* (1998).

JONATHAN DANCY is Professor of Philosophy at the University of Reading and Professor of Philosophy at the University of Texas at Austin. He is the author of *An Introduction to Contemporary Epistemology* (1985), *Berkeley: an Introduction* (1987), *Moral Reasons* (1993), *Practical Reality* (2000), and *Ethics without Principles* (2004).

STEPHEN DARWALL is John Dewey Collegiate Professor of Philosophy at the University of Michigan. His books include *The British Moralists and the Internal 'Ought': 1640–1740* (1995), *Philosophical Ethics* (1998), and *Welfare and Rational Care* (2002).

JAMIE DREIER is Professor of Philosophy at Brown University. He has published numerous papers on a wide variety of subjects, most recently: 'Why Ethical Satisficing Makes Sense and Rational Satisficing Doesn't', in *Satisficing and Maximizing: Moral Theorists on Practical Reason* (2004), 'Relativism and Nihilism', forthcoming in *Oxford Handbook of Ethical Theory*, and 'Pettit on Preference for Properties and Prospects', forthcoming in *Philosohical Studies*. He is editor of Blackwell's *Contemporary Debates in Moral Theory* (2005).

ALLAN GIBBARD is the Richard B. Brandt Distinguished University Professor of Philosophy at the University of Michigan, and the author of *Wise Choices, Apt Feelings* (1990) and *Thinking How to Live* (2003).

BRAD HOOKER is Professor of Philosophy at the University of Reading. He is author of *Ideal Code, Real World: A Rule-Consequentialist Theory of Morality* (2002), editor of *Rationality, Rules, and Utility* (1993), and *Truth in Ethics* (1996), and co-editor of *Well-being and Morality* (2000), *Morality, Rules, and Consequences* (2000), and *Moral Particularism* (2000). He has also published a large number of articles, mostly in moral philosophy. He is currently working on a book about fairness and a textbook on moral philosophy and a history of twentieth-century moral philosophy.

TERRY HORGAN is Professor of Philosophy at the University of Arizona and author of many articles in philosophy of mind and metaphysics. He is co-author (with John Tienson) of *Connectionism and the Philosophy of Psychology* (MIT, 1996) and (with Matjaz Potrc) of *Austere Realism* (forthcoming) and is completing a book with David Henderson, *A Priori Naturalized Epistemology: At the Interface of Cognitive Science and Coneptual Analysis*. He and Mark Timmons have collaborated on many papers in metaethics and they are currently working on topics in moral phenomenology.

CONNIE S. ROSATI is Associate Professor of Philosophy at the University of Arizona. She specializes in ethics, philosophy of law, and social and political philosophy. Her ongoing research concerns the nature of personal good and the nature and normativity of constitutions. Recent publications include 'Agency and the Open Question Argument', *Ethics* (2003) and 'Some Puzzles About the Objectivity of Law', *Law and Philosophy* (2004).

RUSS SHAFER-LANDAU is Professor of Philosophy at the University of Wisconsin and author of *Moral Realism: A Defence* (2003), and *Whatever Happened to Good and Evil?* (2003). He is also co-editor of *Reason and Responsibility* (12th edition, 2004) and editor of *Oxford Studies in Metaethics*.

WALTER SINNOTT-ARMSTRONG is Professor of Philosophy and Hardy Professor of Legal Studies at Dartmouth College, where he has taught since 1981, after receiving his BA from Amherst College and his Ph.D. from Yale University. His newest book, *Moral Skepticisms*, will be published by Oxford University Press in 2006. He is currently working on empirical moral psychology and brain science.

MICHAEL SMITH is Professor of Philosophy at Princeton University and author of *The Moral Problem* (1994), *Ethics and the A Priori: Selected Essays on Moral Psychology and Meta-Ethics* (2004), and co-author (with Frank Jackson and Philip Pettit) of *Mind, Morality, and Explanation: Selected Collaborations* (2004).

PHILLIP STRATTON-LAKE is Professor of Philosophy at the University of Reading and author of *Kant, Duty and Moral Worth* (2000). He is editor of *On What We Owe to Each Other: Scanlon's Contractualism* (2004), *Ethical Intuitionism: Re-evaluations* (2002), and a new edition of W.D. Ross's *The Right and the Good* (2002).

SIGRÚN SVAVARSDÓTTIR is Assistant Professor of Philosophy at the Ohio State University. Her publications include: 'Objective Values: Does Metaethics Rest on a Mistake?' in *Objectivity in Law and Morals*, B. Leiter, ed. (2001), 'Moral Cognitivism and Motivation', *The Philosophical Review* (1999), and 'How Do Moral Judgments Motivate?' in *Contemporary Debates in Moral Theory*, J. Dreier, ed. (2006).

JUDITH JARVIS THOMSON is Professor of Philosophy at the Massachusetts Institute of Technology, specializing in ethics and metaphysics. She is the author of *Acts and Other Events* (1977), *Rights, Restitution, and Risk* (1986), *The Realm of Rights* (1990), and *Moral Relativism and Moral Objectivity*, with Gilbert Harman (1996). She has also authored many highly influential papers.

MARK TIMMONS is Professor of Philosophy at the University of Arizona and author of *Morality without Foundations* (1999) and *Moral Theory: An Introduction* (2002), and editor of *Kant's* Metaphysics of Morals: *Interpretative Essays* (2002). He and Terry Horgan are currently working on philosophical issues associated with the phenomenology of moral experience.

Introduction

Terry Horgan and Mark Timmons

Metaethics, understood as a distinct branch of ethics, is often traced to G. E. Moore's 1903 classic *Principia Ethica* (*PE*). Whereas normative ethics is concerned to answer first-order *moral* questions about what is good and bad, right and wrong, virtuous and vicious, metaethics is concerned to answer second-order *non-moral* questions, including (but not restricted to) questions about the semantics, metaphysics, and epistemology of moral thought and discourse. Metaethics, then, as a recognized branch of ethics, is part of the philosophical legacy of *PE*. Moreover Moore's own combination of metaethical views has continued to exert a strong influence on metaethical enquiry of the last hundred plus years, and forms another part of the rich legacy of *Principia*.

The papers in this volume represent recent work in metaethics that reflects the rich philosophical heritage of Moore's *PE*. They are organized in relation to central metaethical claims defended by Moore—claims that can be put into four main groups: the subject matter of ethics, moral semantics, moral metaphysics, and moral epistemology. In what immediately follows we will briefly summarize the papers, relating them to Moore's metaethical views.

The subject matter of Ethics

In the first chapter of *PE*, 'The Subject-Matter of Ethics', Moore spends the first four sections explaining his conception of the field of ethics. In these passages, he refers to an 'ideal of ethical science' (56) which he divides into two main parts. First, there are semantic and related metaphysical questions about the meanings of moral terms (and the concepts they express) and, second, there are questions about what sorts of items possess the properties which moral terms denote. What emerges from Moore's discussion of the subject matter of ethics are two theses. First is what we will call the *independence thesis*, according to which semantic and related metaphysical questions—questions of metaethics—can be pursued independently of and are properly prior to enquiry into substantive matters about the kinds of items that are good or bad, right or wrong, virtuous or vicious. Second, Moore holds a certain *primacy thesis*, according to which the concept of goodness (and badness) is more fundamental than and can be used to define the concepts of rightness (and wrongness) and virtue (and vice). Thus, for Moore, the study of ethics, properly conducted, should begin with an enquiry focused on the concept of goodness.

The papers by Stephen Darwall, Sigrún Svavarsdóttir, Jonathan Dancy, Robert Audi, Connie Rosati, and Michael Smith all have to do with one or another of these two theses. In 'How Should Ethics Relate to (the Rest of) Philosophy?', Darwall challenges both the claims of independence and priority. He argues that although metaethics and normative ethics are properly focused on different issues, they need to be brought into dynamic relation with one another in order to produce a systematic and defensible philosophical ethics. This mutual dependence, claims Darwall, is owing to the fact that issues of normativity are at the center of the concerns of both metaethics and normative ethics. In making his case, Darwall examines Moore's doctrine that an irreducible notion of intrinsic value is fundamental in ethics and argues that although Moore was correct in thinking that ethical notions are irreducible, he was incorrect in thinking that this is because they have a notion of intrinsic value at their core. Rather, according to Darwall, the notion of a normative reason is ethically fundamental, and a proper philosophical ethics that fully accommodates the normativity involved in ethical thought and discourse will require that metaethical issues and normative issues bearing on normativity be 'pursued interdependently as complementary aspects of a comprehensive philosophical ethics'. He illustrates this claim by explaining how certain debates within normative ethics over consequentialism and over virtue depend upon metaethical issues about the nature of normativity.

Darwall's paper reflects one important way in which contemporary metaethics differs in emphasis from Moore's position. In recent times, philosophers have come to recognize the importance of evaluations of normative reasons and rationality, not only in the field of ethics but in relation to the subject matter of such fields as epistemology, semantics, and philosophy of mind. The contributions of Svavarsdóttir and Dancy reflect this trend. Svavarsdóttir's 'Evaluations of Rationality' works from the guiding idea that rationality is the excellence of a rational agent qua rational and goes on to defend a neo-Humean conception of evaluations of theoretical and practical rationality, according to which such evaluations make essential reference to an agent's ends or goals in assessing the rationality of the agent's beliefs, actions, and intentions. Evaluations of theoretical and practical rationality differ according to the types of goals relative to which we make evaluations of rationality. Svavarsdóttir defends this view by appealing to intuitions about irrationality with respect to particular cases, which she claims are best explained by the neo-Humean—a defense which is neutral with regard to metaphysical issues about the nature of reasons. Svavarsdóttir's defense of her view is admittedly partial because it does not fully address questions about the justificatory force of rationality evaluations, leaving as she notes important tasks for the neo-Humean to tackle.

Moore held that considerations of intrinsic value grounded moral reasons to act. As we noted, according to Darwall, considerations of normativity are fundamental for both metaethical enquiry and normative ethics. Dancy's paper, 'What Do Reasons Do?' is focused on the issue of how we are to understand what he calls practical 'contributory reasons', particularly as they are related to oughts. Dancy begins by rehearsing six proposals for understanding contributory reasons in terms of an 'overall ought', and rejects them all. Dancy's own proposal is that a 'reason is something that favours action', where favoring is a normative relation in which a reason stands to a particular way of acting.

Since the contributory cannot be reduced to an overall ought (or any overall notion, such as goodness), Dancy proposes to go the other way and reduce overall oughts to the contributory. However, instead of attempting to reduce overall oughts to favoring reasons (which he doubts can be done), Dancy introduces the notion of a 'contributory ought'—'a monadic feature of an action which is consequent on, or resultant from, some other feature—the "ought-making" feature, whatever it is'. How are we to understand how an overall ought is related to the contributory ought? Here is where Dancy thinks that appeal to *fittingness*, a notion employed by the classical intuitionists, offers promise. In partially defending this claim, he argues that Michael Smith's 'Humean realism' and Allan Gibbard's expressivism lack the resources needed for adequately understanding practical reasons and oughts.

The papers by Audi and Rosati concern aspects of Moore's theory of intrinsic value. In 'Intrinsic Value and Reasons for Action', Audi sketches a theory of intrinsic value that aims to incorporate certain elements of Moore's theory, but which goes beyond it in important ways while also avoiding commitment to many of Moore's controversial normative and metaethical views. Moore held that experiences and non-experiential items such as artworks can be the bearers of intrinsic value. By contrast, Audi defends *experientialism*—according to which the bearers of intrinsic value are concrete experiences—partly by arguing that it is experiences that seem to have the kind of Aristotelian 'finality' and thus 'choiceworthiness' that is appropriate for anything's having intrinsic value. In order to accommodate the Moorean idea that items such as artworks are in some sense 'good in themselves' (and not merely instrumentally good), Audi introduces the notion of *inherent value*—a species of value that is possessed by something whenever an appropriate experience of it is instrinsically good. A painting, for example, can be inherently good because an appropriate aesthetic experience of that object is itself intrinsically good. The concepts of intrinsic and inherent value, along with a Moorean principle of organic unities (suitably broadened), provide the basis for a nuanced theory of value whose merits include the recognition and explanation of a wide range of intuitively plausible value judgments, as well as contributing to a general theory of practical reason.

While Audi's contribution attempts to build on some of Moore's ideas about intrinsic value, Rosati in her 'Personal Good' challenges one aspect of Moore's view. In his critical remarks about egoism as a theory of motivation, Moore argued that the notion of 'good for' that figures in claims about this or that activity or pursuit being (non-morally, intrinsically) good for an individual is incoherent.[1] Rosati argues that Moore is mistaken and defends an account of the good-for relation modeled on the interpersonal relation of successful loving. Success in an interpersonal loving relationship is characterized by the fact that such relationships support their participant's self-esteem, they are energizing, they provide comfort and feeling of security as well as providing an important element of a participant's identity and sense of direction in life, and such relationships tend to be self-perpetuating. The sort of relation involved in something's being good for an individual—part of her personal good—exhibit these same general sorts of features. According to Rosati, then, the property good-for is a second-order relational property that is realized in a person's life when she stands in the sorts of esteem-enhancing, energizing, and other just mentioned relations to some pursuit or activity. Rosati defends her view in two ways. First, she appeals to certain dualities of human nature and experience: we are partly biological creatures on the one hand who often discover our good, as when one discovers that she has a natural talent for music and proceeds to develop her musical talent so that playing music becomes part of her personal good. But we are also autonomous agents for whom our personal good is often partly a matter of one's own making—something invented rather than simply discovered. In order for playing music to be part of her personal good, the would-be musician must cultivate her talent and in this way she makes playing music part of her personal good. Rosati's account of personal good nicely accommodates such dualities in that the various relations involved in something's being good for oneself depend partly on facts about oneself that are beyond one's control but partly on what one does. The second way Rosati defends her view is by responding to certain possible Moorean objections.

---

[1] See Darwall's paper, section 3, for an illuminating explanation of Moore's reason for this view.

In chapter V of *PE*, 'Ethics in Relation to Conduct', Moore turns from questions about the definition of 'intrinsic value' generally and 'good' in particular to questions about right action. He defends two claims in this chapter. First, he defines right action in terms of intrinsic value: to claim that an action A (performed by someone S on some occasion O) is right means the same as claiming that S's performing A in O resulted in a greater amount of intrinsic value than would performing any alternative action open to S in O. In short, for Moore, right actions maximize intrinsic value. Ideally, then, what Moore calls 'Practical Ethics' aims to tell us which actions are right. But, as Moore explains, in light of severe epistemic limitations on our knowledge about which, from among alternative actions open to an agent, will maximize intrinsic value, there is some question about how a morally motivated person should make decisions on specific occasions. Such epistemic limits impose a 'humbler' task on Practical Ethics: one of determining which alternative action *likely to occur to an agent* on some occasion is *most likely* to maximize intrinsic value. This is the second of the claims about right action defended in chapter V. Frank Jackson has argued that there is good reason to reject both of Moore's claims.[2] In their place, Jackson proposes a conception of right action in terms of the *expected* intrinsic values of alternative actions, where the relevant expectation is from the agent's point of view on the occasion of action. According to Jackson, this conception of right action is not only immune from various counterexamples that beset both Moore's proposal for Practical Ethics as well his definition of 'right', but properly ties the rightness of actions to our critical practices of holding agents responsible for what they do.

In 'Moore on the Good, the Right, and Uncertainty', Michael Smith proposes a conception of Practical Ethics which, unlike Jackson's proposal, ties what epistemically limited agents are to do on some occasion not only to limits on their non-evaluative information about how much intrinsic value would result from various actions, but also to epistemic limits on their evaluative information about what has intrinsic value. This amounts to advising morally motivated agents that they are to maximize expected intrinsic value-as-they-see-it—advice that recognizes the double epistemic limits humans possess—an extension of Jackson's view. However, instead of following Jackson and defining a conception of right action in terms of the doubly constrained notion in question, Smith argues that we have good reason to accept Moore's definition and thus good reason to resist tying our primary notion of right action to the concept of what we can hold an agent responsible for. But adopting Moore's conception of right action might seem to be in tension with his modified

<hr>

[2] 'Decision-Theoretic Consequentialism and the Nearest and Dearest Objection', *Ethics*, 101 (1991).

Jackson-style conception of Practical Ethics. After all, if the rightness of an action depends on the comparative level of intrinsic value it would produce if performed, then won't a morally motivated agent be motivated by a desire to do what Moore's Practical Ethics recommends, namely, by a desire to do what will likely maximize intrinsic value? If so, the Moorean element of Smith's view is in tension with the Jackson-inspired element. But Smith denies the assumption about moral motivation featured in this challenge. Rather than thinking of moral motivation in terms of a desire to maximize intrinsic value, Smith claims that we should think instead in terms of having intrinsic desires for things one judges to be intrinsically valuable, such as pleasure, or knowledge, or autonomy, or whatever. Thus, according to Smith, Moore's conception of right action represents an appropriate idealization of a plausible account of rational decision making.

Moral semantics

Moore famously began the 100 years of metaethics with his open question argument—which he thought exposed the fallaciousness of all 'reductive' accounts of moral terms and concepts. On the basis of this argument, Moore concluded that the primary concept of ethics—goodness—is 'simple and indefinable'. The *indefinability thesis*, as we call it, is the cornerstone of Moore's moral semantics.

Moore's version of the open question argument works by taking some purported reductive definition of 'good' in terms of some nonnormative term or phrase (e.g., 'what we desire to desire') and posing two questions of the following kind (where 'X' is to be replaced by a term designating some item of evaluation):

X is good, but is it what we desire to desire?

And

X is what we desire to desire, but is X good?

Now if 'good' just means 'that which we desire to desire', then these questions ought to strike us as equivalent to:

X is something we desire to desire, but do we desire to desire it?

This latter question is closed in the sense that its answer is trivially affirmative. But the preceding questions are both open in the sense that they strike us as non-obvious and open for debate.

For Moore, the pair of questions have an 'open feel' to them which he explained in terms of our grasping of the meanings of the concepts involved.

Toward the end of the twentieth century, we find that the open question argument is alive and well. T. M. Scanlon uses a version of this argument in defense of his buck-passing account of value.[3] Scanlon claims that the 'open feel' of the Moorean questions comes from the fact that judgments about whether something is good express a practical conclusion about the reasons one has for caring about that thing. To judge that some item of evaluation has such and so natural properties does not involve judging that the item is good. Hence, even if the claim that it has natural properties a, b, and c is the ground for concluding that the item is good, it is a further step to draw the conclusion that it is good. Hence, the open feel between judging that some item has natural properties and judging that it is good. Whereas Moore concluded on the basis of the open question argument that goodness is an unanalyzable, simple, non-natural property, which itself (as distinct from the natural properties upon which goodness supervenes) provides reasons for action, Scanlon argues that a better account of the matter is that goodness is a formal, higher-order property which can be understood as a complex non-natural property: the property of there being base properties that provide practical reasons. For Moore, what has reason-giving power is the property of goodness itself—the reason-giving buck rests with this property. For Scanlon, the reason-giving buck is passed on to a thing's good-making properties. Scanlon argues in various ways for his buck-passing account, partly by explaining its superiority to the Moorean view and partly by giving two arguments—one appealing to considerations of parsimony, the other appealing to the plausibility of value pluralism.

In 'Scanlon versus Moore on Goodness', Philip Stratton-Lake and Brad Hooker offer a partial defense of Scanlon's buck-passing account of the relation between base properties, goodness, and practical reasons. Jonathan Dancy and Roger Crisp have both argued that even if Scanlon's buck-passing account is superior to the Moorean account, there are other contending accounts that Scanlon does not consider. Against Dancy and Crisp, Stratton-Lake and Hooker argue that these proposed accounts, although genuine alternatives to the Moorean and buck-passing accounts, are nevertheless deeply problematic and do nothing to harm the case for Scanlon's account. Regarding Scanlon's two arguments, the authors find that the parsimony argument, once clarified, does offer some support for the buck-passing view, but they conclude that the appeal to value pluralism does not aid the defense of this view. They finally defend Scanlon's account against an open question worry about the relation between the fact that something has reason-giving properties and its goodness.

---

[3] *What We Owe to Each Other* (Cambridge, Mass.: Harvard University Press, 1998).

Paul Bloomfield in 'Opening Questions, Following Rules' begins by noting that the twentieth-century beneficiary of the open question argument has been (rather ironically) the class of non-realist views, including non-cognitivism and expressivism. Bloomfield contends that Moore did not properly diagnose the openness of the relevant questions about goodness; it is not simplicity versus complexity, and it is not indefinability versus definability. Rather, Bloomfield contends, it is the normativity involved in moral judgments and concepts that keeps Moorean questions open and blocks definitions of 'good'—the same sort of normativity that keeps questions open in relation to concepts like 'plus', 'mass', 'triangle'. According to Bloomfield, then, the issue of normativity in semantics, epistemology, and ethics is basically the same which he puts as follows: 'How can features of the world establish conditions under which it makes sense for us to think that there are ways we ought to conduct ourselves (with regard to our actions, our speech, or our beliefs) and other ways which ought not to be followed?' A clear implication of Bloomfield's line of argument is that those working in metaethics have often labored under the mistaken assumption that moral terms like 'good' are *especially* problematic.

In addition to the semantic thesis of irreducibility, Moore took for granted the *descriptivist thesis* according to which moral judgments of the forms 'A is good' and 'A is bad' purport to attribute a property to some item and can thus be true or false in just the same way in which ordinary non-moral judgments about the empirical world can be true or false. Since Moore thought that such judgments sometimes successfully do what they purport to do, he was committed to certain metaphysical views to which we now turn.

Moral metaphysics

Moore held a version of moral realism—roughly the view that there are moral properties and moral facts (in which those properties figure) whose existence and nature are independent of the stances of individuals and groups. But perhaps the most puzzling doctrine in Moore's metaethics is his view that goodness is a non-natural property. Many have found this hard to accept, partly because the claim itself is so obscure. In his paper 'Was Moore a Moorean?', Jamie Dreier traces Moore's attempts, beginning in *PE* up though his 1922 'The Conception of Intrinsic Value',[4] to characterize the difference between

---

[4] This paper appeared originally in chapter VII of Moore's *Philosophical Studies* (Kegan Paul, Trench, Trubner & Co., 1922) and is reprinted in the 1993 revised edition of *PE* published by Cambridge University Press.

natural and non-natural properties, finding the most plausible characterization in terms of a distinctive kind of non-logical supervenience relation that links the property of goodness to the natural properties upon which it supervenes. The problem with the appeal to a kind of non-logical supervenience, according to Dreier, is that it does not really help us understand the idea that goodness is supposed to be non-natural: the property of being yellow does not logically follow from a characterization of those properties upon which it supervenes, but yellow is a paradigm natural property for Moore. Based on certain textual clues, Dreier proposes that Moore misdescribed the distinction he sought to capture in his natural/non-natural properties distinction. What Moore was after, claims Dreier, is more aptly put as a distinction between description and evaluation—a distinction central to expressivist views. So why wasn't Moore an expressivist? Expressivists generally agree with Moore that there is a conceptual gap between the descriptive and the evaluative. Dreier's conjecture is that for the Moorean, this gap is a gap between *properties*, while for the expressivist it isn't.

But despite Moore's difficulties in understanding this distinction, and despite the fact that many post-*PE* moral philosophers rejected Moore's non-naturalism, the view is now enjoying a revival.[5] In 'Ethics as Philosophy: A Defense of Ethical Nonnaturalism', Russ Shafer-Landau provides a partial defense of non-naturalism. He first provides an epistemological criterion for understanding the metaphysical thesis of non-naturalism and then proceeds to mount a defense of the view against two common objections: objections based on facts about ethical disagreement and on causal criteria for having ontological status. His strategy is to call attention to the close parallel between ethical enquiry and philosophical enquiry generally and argue that these parallels provide a basis for rejecting the lines of objection in question and also provide positive reasons to favor non-naturalism over its metaethical rivals. So first, just as disagreement in philosophy itself does not undermine (or should not undermine) thinking that there are objective truths about such matters, neither should disagreement in ethics undermine thinking that there are objective truths or facts or justified belief in such facts and truths. As for the causal efficacy criterion of ontological status, Shafer-Landau argues that even if moral facts do not possess causal efficacy, we need not be skeptics about their ontological status as objectively real. If one insists on the causal efficacy test, then it looks as if all putative normative facts fail the criterion and are not real. The implausibility of this implication, then, casts doubt on the causal argument against moral facts.

[5] See, for instance, Robert Audi, *The Good in the Right* (Princeton: Princeton University Press, 2004) and Russ Shafer-Landau, *Moral Realism: A Defense* (Oxford: Oxford University Press, 2002).

Arguably, the strongest challenge to any type of moral realism comes from what is now called expressivism, the heir apparent of non-cognitivism. Expressivists deny the semantic thesis of descriptivism and propose a different philosophical picture for understanding and explaining moral thought and discourse. According to Judith Jarvis Thomson ('The Legacy of *Principia*'), the legacy in question is that the force of the open question argument together with the rejection of the Moorean idea that there are non-natural properties motivate two related claims: the *no normative truth value thesis* according to which no normative sentences have truth value, and the *expressivist thesis* that in uttering or thinking a normative sentence what one does is express a favorable or unfavorable attitude toward the object of evaluation. Thomson explores two main sources of reason for rejecting the first thesis—appeals to minimalism about truth and the so-called Frege–Geach problem. She argues that appeals to minimalism about truth are ultimately circular. However, the Frege–Geach problem does represent a more serious challenge to those (particularly expressivists) who embrace the no normative truth value thesis. According to Thomson, the underlying insight of the Frege–Geach challenge is the idea that 'is good' functions as a 'logical' predicate so that sentences containing this predicate enter into logical relations with other sentences. But, so the challenge goes, if 'is good' is a logical predicate then there is such a property as goodness and (further) this means that if someone thinks or says a sentence of the form 'A is good', then she has said something that has a truth value. Hence, by this line of reasoning, the no normative truth value thesis is false.

Thomson argues that attempts, particularly by expressivists, to rebut this challenge falter, but rather than embrace the Moorean position (or any metaethical position that would countenance the property goodness, or rightness), she denies the claim that 'is good' is a logical predicate. Rather, according to Thomson, sentences of the form 'A is good' are semantically incomplete and thus 'is good' is not (in the requisite sense) a logical predicate. The main idea is that simply to say of something that it is good without also thinking that it is good in a certain way is not to attribute any genuine property to the item in question. Thus, there is no property that people attribute to something when they use this form of expression and so Moore's premise—that there is a property of goodness—is false. However, on Thomson's view, expressivists who deny Moore's premise are mistaken in what someone does in engaging in normative evaluation. Normative claims that predicate goodness or rightness *in a way*, as when someone claims that so and so is a good baseball player or that such and so move in chess was the right move to make, are predicating genuine properties and properties that are moreover arguably natural. If this is correct, then, as Thomson notes, Moore's open question argument has misled philosophers to fix upon the pseudo-property of goodness.

Recent developments of the expressivist position are represented in the papers by Terry Horgan and Mark Timmons, Stephen Barker, and Allan Gibbard. As already noted, metaethical expressivism is (broadly speaking) the view that moral judgments do not primarily function to report or describe moral facts or properties, but instead have an action-oriented expressive function. This primarily negative characterization leaves much open, including what sort of psychological state a moral judgment expresses, though it is often taken for granted that such states are not beliefs. And if one embraces what Horgan and Timmons call the *semantic assumption*—the idea that beliefs are necessarily descriptive in that they purport to represent or describe some state of affairs—then an expressivist must reject the idea that moral judgments are beliefs. Cognitivism in ethics is the view that moral judgments are beliefs and so, given the semantic assumption, expressivism is not compatible with cognitivism. Horgan and Timmons challenge the semantic assumption by arguing that moral judgments share enough of the phenomenological and functional features that are central to the notion of belief to count as genuine beliefs—a notion that does not require beliefs to be primarily descriptive. This, they claim, opens the door to a cognitivist version of expressivism. Horgan and Timmons sketch a version of cognitivist expressivism, including an account of logical embedding (meant to deal with the Frege–Geach problem), which they argue is prima facie more plausible than non-cognitivist and descriptivist alternatives in metaethics.

In 'Truth and the Expressing in Expressivism', Barker proposes a new framework for metaethical expressivism which involves a combination of several elements. First, Barker claims that evaluative sentences are used to make genuine assertions, and so there are at least two types of assertion: reportive and expressive. Second, and following from the first, assertions of both sort are truth-apt. These claims are embraced also by Horgan and Timmons. But unlike them, Barker argues that all assertions are representational in that they purport to represent or describe some state of affairs. So, how do merely reportive assertions differ from expressive assertions? In response, Barker proposes what he calls a pragmatic conception of truth according to which truth-bearers are sentences with representational content *that are also used with an assertoric purpose.* The idea is that the essential difference between reportive and expressive assertions concerns the purposes or intentions for which they are asserted: 'in reportive assertions, speakers defend commitments to representational intentions; in expressive assertions speakers defend commitments to states [cognitive or conative] whose possession they have in fact represented.

In uttering a value sentence, for instance, one is expressing a desire (or related motivational state) which, according to Barker's analysis, the speaker is prepared to defend. Barker explains how his form of expressivism can make sense of the various objectivist trappings of moral discourse including its truth-aptness, logical embedding, and being subject to rational debate.

Moore claimed that what he took to be the fundamental moral concept, *goodness*, is a non-natural concept from which, together with his premise that there is a property goodness, he inferred that this concept signifies a non-natural property. Gibbard ('Normative Properties') distinguishes properties from concepts. The concepts *water* and *H₂O* are different concepts though they in fact signify the same property: the property of being water is the same property as that of being composed of H_2O molecules. According to Gibbard, Moore was correct in noting an important difference between basic moral concepts and naturalistic concepts of the sort featured in scientific and everyday discourse about the empirical world. However, it is Gibbard's view that basic moral concepts in particular and normative concepts in general signify natural properties: some natural property *is* the property of being good. For Gibbard, the concept of good is a complex concept involving the concept of ought, and his main thesis in his paper is what he calls the thesis of natural constitution: *some broadly natural property constitutes being what one ought to do*. Gibbard's main argument for this claim begins with a traditional non-cognitivist (expressivist) theme that to understand what the word 'ought' means we need to say what it is to think or claim that someone ought to do something. Gibbard understands ought-statements in terms of the activity of planning and proposes that we can best grasp the content or meaning of such statements (both simple and logically complex) by understanding what it is to disagree in plan. The upshot of his argument (presented in section 1 of his paper) is that any planner is committed to the thesis of normative constitution. Gibbard's paper is concerned with exploring and defending the philosophical assumptions (e.g., about the nature of properties) presupposed in this argument. His overall metaethical view represents a blend of non-naturalism about moral concepts with a naturalist concept of moral properties.

Moral epistemology

In *Principia*, Moore's enquiry into the meaning of moral terms was intended to have a direct bearing on issues in moral epistemology. With respect to substantive claims involving predication of goodness, Moore held that 'no relevant evidence whatever can be adduced' (*PE*, 1st edition preface, 34), that such claims are self-evidently true, and that they can be known on the basis of intuition. The basic claim of the moral intuitionist is that it is possible for individuals to be epistemically justified in holding certain moral beliefs independently of whether they are able to infer those beliefs from other beliefs they hold. This is typically called 'non-inferential' justification. The twentieth century has seen the fortunes of moral intuitionism wax and wane. In the first half of the century, prominent moral philosophers such as H. A. Prichard, W. D. Ross, and A. C. Ewing defended moral intuitionism, but with the emergence, beginning in the 1930s, of non-cognitivist treatments of moral thought and language, intuitionism fell out of philosophical favor. It is only very recently that some moral philosophers have been interested in reviving intuitionism in ethics, and we now find Robert Audi and Russ Shafer-Landau among intuitionism's champions.[6]

Notice that moral intuitionism, so defined, is not committed to non-natural moral properties (as was Moore) or to some version of moral pluralism (as was Ross). Intuitionism, as here understood, is a purely epistemological position. Those who reject intuitionism, then, claim that it is not possible for people to be non-inferentially justified in any of their (non-trivial) moral beliefs. How might this dispute be resolved?

In 'Moral Intuitionism Meets Empirical Psychology', Walter Sinnott-Armstrong claims that any direct answer to this issue is likely to simply beg the question on one side or the other, and hence that some indirect strategy is needed in order to come to grips with the controversy. In particular, Sinnott-Armstrong claims that recent developments in psychology and brain science cast considerable doubt on moral intuitionism. In arguing for this claim, he first develops a set of six principles concerning when non-moral beliefs require justifying beliefs to back them up. In short, whenever a belief is important, partial, controversial, emotional, subject to illusion, or explicable by dubious sources, then that belief needs to be backed up by confirming beliefs if the believer is to be epistemically justified in holding it. By appealing to recent empirical work, Sinnott-Armstrong argues that moral beliefs of all sorts fall under one or more of his principles and thus they are in need of support from other relevant beliefs. If so, then, as he points out, moral intuitionism is incorrect: no moral beliefs enjoy the status of being non-inferentially justified. This is his strong claim. More cautiously, Sinnott-Armstrong claims that even if there may be some individuals who, in some contexts, have moral beliefs that do not require inferential support, still, for educated adults who are well aware

---

[6] See also the contributions in Philip Stratton-Lake (ed.), *Ethical Intuitionism: Re-evaluations* (Oxford: Oxford University Press, 2002).

of the various possible distorting factors affecting beliefs, no moral beliefs are non-inferentially justified. Even if moral judgments are not themselves claims that can be confirmed or disconfirmed entirely by empirical means, including the methods of science, it does not follow that developments in the sciences, including biology, psychology, sociology, anthropology, cognitive science, and brain science, are not relevant to whether a person's (or group's) moral beliefs are epistemically justified. To think they are is typically characterized as commitment to moral epistemology naturalized.

This last point returns us to what we have called Moore's *independence thesis*, which Darwall found reason to reject. But Panayot Butchvarov ('Ethics Dehumanized') advocates a return to Moorean independence. One dominant metaethical trend (which we have just seen in Sinnott-Armstrong's contribution) is moral epistemology naturalized. Another metaethical trend has been conceptual analysis, often called 'analytic ethics', which was preoccupied with analyzing the meanings of moral terms and the concepts those terms express. Butchvarov argues that both trends are philosophically misguided. Ethics naturalized, he claims, is unphilosophical in lacking the kind of supreme generality and abstractness that is distinctive of philosophical enquiry, taking human beings to occupy moral center stage, rather than the kind of cosmological ethics we find in Moore, whose views focused on the value of all things in the universe as a basis for ethical enquiry. Moreover, ethics naturalized lacks competence in that its scientific pretensions are at odds with how philosophers go about their business. Analytic ethics, which is explicitly concerned with armchair, intuitive judgments about meanings, cannot overcome lack of competence signaled by the philosophical lessons found in Kant, Quine, and Wittgenstein about conceptual analysis. In light of these failures, Butchvarov advocates returning to the cosmological orientation of Moore's ethics which, he thinks, can be properly understood as avoiding the traditional metaethical debate between realism and anti-realism, as well as avoiding the battery of objections to the effect that Moore's ethics is not relevant to action. Such a return to a Moorean view of ethics would represent a version of 'ethics dehumanized': cosmological in its focus and thus properly philosophical.

Conclusion: expanding metaethics

If we stand back far enough from the metaethical fray of the past one hundred or so years to see if we can view general trends or developments with this field, we notice some basic contrasts between metaethics as practiced throughout much of the twentieth century and metaethics now. In at least three ways metaethics has expanded: in its methodology, in the extent of its recognized philosophical import, and in the currently available metaethical options. First, whereas metaethical enquiry went through a phase of rather narrowly focused a priori linguistic or conceptual analysis, such enquiry today, while still very much concerned with how to understand the meanings of moral concepts, has expanded methodologically. Gone apparently is the search for analyses of moral terms and concepts in terms of necessary and sufficient conditions. Second, as many of the papers in this collection make clear, the concerns of metaethical enquiry really extend to all areas of philosophy in that issues concerning normativity are now being raised in philosophy of mind, philosophy of language, and epistemology. In his paper for this volume, Allan Gibbard suggests that metaethics is properly understood as a branch of what we might call meta-normativity, thus bringing into close connection the concerns of metaethics and other areas of philosophy. Finally, the options in metaethics have expanded at least in the sense that there is a growing 'centrist' trend among defenders of opposing metaethical views to find as much common ground as possible with their traditional adversaries. This is particularly evident in the papers by Horgan and Timmons, Barker, and Gibbard.[7]

Metaethics, appropriately expanded, continues to flourish.

---

[7] For a recent attempt to wed expressivist themes to moral realism, see David Copp, 'Realist-Expressivism: A Neglected Option for Moral Realism', *Social Philosophy & Policy*, 18 (2001).

1

How Should Ethics Relate to (the Rest of) Philosophy? Moore's Legacy

Stephen Darwall

1. Moore and metaethics

From our perspective a century later, *Principia Ethica* seems a revolutionary work. It didn't seem that way at the time, however.[1] Moore's claims about the irreducibility of good struck his contemporaries as familiar. And *Principia's* reviewers thought Moore's objections to naturalists like Mill and Spencer were 'the standard criticisms.'[2] In these respects and several others, Moore was, as Thomas Hurka has brilliantly shown, thoroughly within a tradition of moral philosophy that ran 'roughly from the first edition of Sidgwick's *Methods of Ethics* in 1874 to [W. D.] Ross's *Foundations of Ethics* in 1939.'[3]

Moore acknowledged that he wasn't original in insisting on an irreducible core of all ethical concepts. He didn't appreciate the roots of this thought in eighteenth-century intuitionists like Clarke, Balguy, and Price, not to mention sentimentalists like Hutcheson and Hume, but Moore did see himself as

---

[1] G. E. Moore, *Principia Ethica*, revised edition with the preface to the (projected) second edition and other papers, edited with an introduction by Thomas Baldwin (Cambridge: Cambridge University Press, 1993), initially published in 1903. References will be placed in the text and include section number along with page numbers to this edition, thus: (§ 14, 69). For a very insightful account of Moore's ideas in their context, to which I am much indebted, see Thomas Hurka, 'Moore in the Middle,' *Ethics*, 113 (2003): 599–628.

[2] Norman Wilde, Review of *Principia Ethica, Journal of Philosophy, Psychology and Scientific Method*, 2 (1905): 581–3, at 582. Bernard Bosanquet also termed Moore's criticisms of Mill 'not quite original' (Bernard Bosanquet, Critical Notice of *Principia Ethica*, *Mind*, 13 (1904): 254–61, at 261). And J. S. Mackenzie remarked that Moore's critical observations of Spencer, Mill, and Green 'have already been brought out by other critics' (J. S. Mackenzie, Review of *Principia Ethica*, *International Journal of Ethics*, 14 (1904): 377–82, at 378). I am indebted to Hurka's article for these references.

[3] Hurka, 'Moore in the Middle.' Hurka describes this tradition further as follows: 'Moore's principal predecessors in this sequence, alongside Sidgwick, were [Hastings] Rashdall, who began publishing on ethics in 1885; Franz Brentano, whose *Origin of Our Knowledge of Right and Wrong* appeared in 1889; and J. M. E. McTaggart, who discussed ethics in his 1901 *Studies in Hegelian Cosmology*. His successors included H. A. Prichard, C. D. Broad, W. D. Ross, A. C. Ewing, and later members of the Brentano school such as Alexius Meinong and Nicolai Hartmann.'

following Sidgwick. Sidgwick was, Moore said, the 'only . . . ethical writer' who had clearly seen the irreducibility of ethics' defining notion.[4]

Nevertheless, ethical philosophy of the last century looked considerably less to Sidgwick than to Moore.[5] This is partly due, no doubt, to *Principia's* radical self-presentation—the sense it gives of wiping the slate clean, exposing the fallacies of all prior ethical thought. But the main reason, I think, is *Principia's* exemplification of the emerging Russell/Moore program of *philosophical analysis*, which would prove so influential in twentieth-century philosophy. This brought ethical philosophy into dynamic relation with more general philosophical trends in metaphysics and the philosophies of language and mind in ways that would dramatically affect how ethics was conceived and practiced as a subject. Among other things, it gave *Principia* a readership that extended far beyond consumers of systematic ethical thought, including many who were relatively unfamiliar with *Principia's* place in the tradition Hurka has described.

Principia Ethica might fairly be called the first work in analytical ethical philosophy. As we've noted, other writers had considered and discussed the nature and content of central ethical ideas and terms. Perhaps most prominently for Moore's contemporaries, Sidgwick had claimed that 'ordinary moral or prudential judgments . . . cannot legitimately be interpreted as judgments respecting the present or future existence of . . . any facts of the sensible world.' Sidgwick believed this was because 'the fundamental notion represented by the word "ought" . . . which such judgments contain expressly or by implication,' is 'essentially different from all notions representing facts of physical or psychical

---

[4] Samuel Clarke, *A Demonstration of the Being and Attributes of God* (London: J. Knapton, 1705) and *A Discourse Concerning the Unalterable Obligations of Natural Religion* (London: J. Knapton, 1706). Both can be found in *The Works of Samuel Clarke*, 4 vols. (London: J. & P. Knapton, 1738), facsimile edition (New York: Garland, 1978); John Balguy, *The Foundations of Moral Goodness* (London: John Pemberton, 1728), facsimile edition (New York: Garland, 1976); Richard Price, *A Review of the Principal Questions in Morals*, originally published in 1758, ed. D. D. Raphael (Oxford: Clarendon Press, 1974). For a discussion of the relevance of earlier British intuitionists to Moore, see A. N. Prior, *Logic and the Basis of Ethics* (Oxford: Clarendon Press, 1949).

I mention Hutcheson and Hume because Hutcheson argued that the concept of moral goodness cannot be reduced to natural goodness (and so requires a special sense) and Hume held that moral judgments do not concern any matter of fact and that an 'ought' cannot follow from any 'is'. Francis Hutcheson, *An Inquiry into the Original of our Ideas of Virtue* (London, 1725), relevant passages in D. D. Raphael (ed.), *The British Moralists: 1650–1800*, 2 vols. (Oxford: Clarendon Press, 1969) and L. A. Selby-Bigge, *British Moralists*, 2 vols. (Indianapolis: Bobbs-Merrill, 1964), an electronic version is available through InteLex *Past Masters* (http://library.nlx.com); David Hume, *A Treatise of Human Nature*, ed. with analytical index by L. A. Selby-Bigge, 2nd edn. with text revised and variant readings by P. H. Nidditch (Oxford: Clarendon Press, 1978).

[5] The *Philosopher's Index*, which has catalogued philosophical articles since 1940, has 120 entries in which both 'Sidgwick' and 'ethics' appear, and well over 350 with 'Moore' and 'ethics' (subtracting those concerned with other Moores, like A. W. Moore, Asher Moore, etc.).

experience' (a claim to which we shall return in due course).⁶ Clear as he was about this, however, Sidgwick did not give analysis of ethical terms and ideas the *methodological* emphasis that Moore would.

The methodological priority of analysis is front and center in *Principia*. Moore begins the Preface by citing the failure to appreciate its importance as the major obstacle to progress in prior ethical thought.

[I]n Ethics, as in all other philosophical studies, the difficulties and disagreements, of which its history is full, are mainly due to a very simple cause: namely to the attempt to answer questions, without first discovering precisely *what* question it is that you desire to answer.(P, 33)

Moore took his own advice, devoting much of the first half of *Principia* to the analysis of ethical concepts and to illustrating how failures of analysis, specific-ally, what he called the 'naturalistic fallacy,' had confounded clear ethical thinking.

As the passage just quoted makes clear, Moore held the analysis of ethical terms and questions to be but one instance of a general philosophical program. The emergence of metaethics (also 'analytic' or 'critical' ethics) in the twentieth century was thus part of a general 'analytic,' later 'linguistic,' turn in anglo-phone philosophy that was itself due partly to Moore.⁷

Metaethics' development as a potentially freestanding area of philosophical enquiry can be traced to Moore, therefore, in a way that it cannot be even to such analytically minded predecessors as Sidgwick. After Moore, it became possible to pursue metaethical questions completely independently of issues of normative ethics and possible also to specialize in this area without any interest in normative issues whatsoever—or, at least, any philosophical interest. Charles Stevenson, for example, introduced *Ethics and Language* in 1944 by saying that he was concerned 'with a narrowly specialized part' of ethics, whose purpose is 'to send *others* to their tasks with clearer heads.'⁸ At one point the 'linguistic turn' became so dominant that a philosopher could expect to raise no eyebrows by introducing a book titled *Modern Moral Philosophy* as follows: '[A] moral philosopher . . . thinks and speaks about the ways in which moral

---

⁶ Henry Sidgwick, *The Methods of Ethics*, 7th edn. (London: Macmillan, 1967), 25. All of Sidgwick's chapter on 'Ethical Judgments' is worth noting in this connection.

⁷ Russell and Moore's analytic turn was in part a critical response to Idealism. On this, see Peter Hylton, *Russell, Idealism, and the Emergence of Analytical Philosophy* (Oxford: Clarendon Press, 1990). Particularly relevant here is Moore's 'The Refutation of Idealism,' *Mind*, 12 (1903): 433–53, which was published the same year as *Principia*.

⁸ Charles Stevenson, *Ethics and Language* (New Haven: Yale University Press, 1965), 1 (emphasis added). This was originally published in 1944. It is worth noting that Stevenson was initially attracted to philosophy by Moore and Wittgenstein when he was studying English literature at Cambridge in the early 1930s.

terms, like "right" and "good" are used by moralists when they are delivering their moral judgments.'[9] This not only proclaimed the legitimacy of metaethics as an independent philosophical area, it read normative ethical reflection out of the philosophical canon altogether.

That metaethical analysis should dominate ethical philosophy was hardly Moore's intention. It is consistent with *Principia*'s methodological principles, indeed, that metaethics' philosophical significance is entirely instrumental, a clarificatory preliminary to answering the normative ethical questions that give ethical philosophy its real task. *Principia* begins by distinguishing 'two kinds of question, which moral philosophers have always professed to answer': first, 'What kind of things ought to exist for their own sakes [alternatively: are good in themselves or "intrinsically valuable"]?' and second, 'What kind of actions ought we to perform?' (P, 33–4). Moore argues that, contrary to what many philosophers have implicitly believed, questions of the first kind can be ana- lyzed no further, that the concept of intrinsic good is simple and unanalyzable. And he argues that questions of the second kind *are* analyzable, specifically, in terms of questions of the first kind and empirical causal questions: 'To assert that a certain line of conduct is, at a given time, absolutely right or obligatory is obviously to assert that more good or less evil will exist in the world, if it be adopted than if anything else be done instead' (§ 17, 77). From this, Moore infers that in order to answer questions of the first, intrinsic value, kind, 'no relevant evidence whatever can be adduced' (P, 34). All we can do is to make sure that we have the question of value clearly before our minds and not some other naturalistic or metaphysical issue with which philosophers have mistakenly confused it. But since questions of right conduct are analyzable as a complex of an empirical causal question together with a question of intrinsic value, what a per- son ought to do does admit of evidence, namely, 'causal truths' regarding actions in the agent's power and 'ethical truths of our first or self-evident class' (P, 34).

This sets up *Principia*'s strategy after chapter I. In chapters II and III, Moore discusses earlier philosophers' misbegotten attempts to support normative intrinsic value claims with empirical naturalistic evidence, which he criticizes for committing the 'naturalistic fallacy.' Here Moore's diagnosis is that natural- istically minded philosophers like Mill and Spencer have simply failed to get the ethical question of intrinsic value they purport to be addressing clearly in view and confused it with naturalistic issues that are both distinct from it and incapable of shedding any light to answer it. In chapter IV, Moore pursues a similar strategy with regard to metaphysical ethicists like Kant and Green who, in his view, had been guilty of essentially the same error, this time confusing the

---

[9] W. D. Hudson, *Modern Moral Philosophy* (Garden City, NY: Doubleday, 1970), 1.

ethical question of intrinsic value with a distinct metaphysical issue, for example, one concerning a transcendental will. In chapter V, 'Ethics in Relation to Conduct,' Moore reaffirms his (agent-neutral) consequentialist analysis of right or ought to do, arguing that philosophers who have advanced fundamentally agent-relative normative principles of conduct, whether egoists or deontologists, have been guilty of conceptual confusion or incoherence.[10] He then draws out what he takes to be the practical consequences of an analytical consequentialism, arguing that, as a practical matter, individuals are nonetheless always best advised to follow commonsense moral 'rules which are both generally useful and generally practised' (§ 99, 213). Finally, in chapter VI, Moore sketches his normative theory of intrinsic value, according to which 'by far the most valuable things, which we know or can imagine, are certain states of consciousness, which may be roughly described as the pleasures of human intercourse and the enjoyment of beautiful objects' (§ 113, 237).

This left Moore with a remarkable normative position. On the one hand, he championed the unparalleled intrinsic value of friendship and aesthetic appreciation together with an analytical consequentialism of the right according to which 'it is only for the sake of *these things*—in order that as much of them as possible may at some time exist—that any one can be justified in performing any public or private duty' (§ 113, 238, emphasis added). These were the ethical ideas that thrilled Bloomsbury. On the other, Moore held that, practically speaking, everyone should always conform to commonsense morality. (This part, Bloomsbury quietly ignored.[11])

It is worth noting that Moore's premier intrinsic values were *organic wholes*. Moore calls them 'states of consciousness'—the 'pleasures of human intercourse' and 'enjoyment of beautiful objects'—but it is important to him (and to his critique of idealist accounts of the mind) that consciousness involves a relation between something mental and some object that is (in these cases, anyway) outside the mind. For Moore, the relevant conscious states are pleasures, but they are pleasures taken in the existence of something really existing outside the pleasurable experience itself. In order for the pleasure of human intercourse to exist, there must really be human interaction that the participants actually enjoy. Similarly, in order for someone to enjoy a beautiful object, it must be the case that there really exists such an object, that it is really beautiful, and that pleasurable experience comes from a rapport with that object and its beauty. Moore did not deny that either relatum by itself had some intrinsic value, but he held that whatever value unappreciated beauty or the pleasurable regard of

---

10 We will consider these claims of Moore's in more detail below.

11 Or so said Keynes. See John Maynard Keynes, 'My Early Beliefs,' in *The Collected Writings of John Maynard Keynes*, vol. x (Cambridge: Macmillan, 1972), 435.

'fool's beauty' might have is 'so small as to be negligible' in comparison to the complex whole (§ 113, 237). Moore's premier intrinsic values thus exhibit his 'principle of organic unities': '*The value of a whole must not be assumed to be the same as the sum of the values of its parts*' (§ 18, 79).

Hence Moore's normative theory of intrinsic value was organicist and pluralist. He held that there was more than one intrinsically valuable kind, and he thought that these included organic wholes, whose value substantially exceeded that of the parts of which they were composed. In value theory, Moore's took his major disagreement to be with monistic theories such as hedonism that held that *the* good was simple. Moore believed that value or *good*, as he called it, was a simple property, but he believed that *the* good, that is, the things that are good or have intrinsic value, is complex in the ways just indicated. One form of the naturalistic fallacy consisted in confusingly taking the simplicity of good for simplicity of the good. Some might mistakenly infer that the good is simple, say, that it is identical with pleasure, because they correctly saw that pleasure is simple (§ 12, 64) and mistakenly identified good with pleasure (perhaps dimly perceiving that good is simple, but failing to see that it is a distinct simple from pleasure).

In *Principia*, therefore, the main rationale for metaethical analysis is to prepare the way for accepting Moore's *normative* ethics by clearing away the main source of support for its competitors. Non-consequentialist theories of right (more precisely, non-agent-neutral consequentialist theories), such as deontology and egoism, are to be rejected for their failure to appreciate the conceptual tie rightness of action must have to intrinsic value. And monistic views of intrinsic value can be seen to lack support if they are advanced on the basis of mistaking some property that might characterize *the* good with good itself.

It is thus ironic that *Principia*'s main effect was to help create an environment in which metaethics could be pursued independently of normative ethics as a freestanding philosophical area, one which would even for a time at mid-century claim exclusive legitimacy as genuine ethical philosophy. At the same time, however, although in *Principia* Moore pursued metaethics in service of normative ethics, he did not think that normative ethics had anything *positive* to learn from metaethics. More precisely, he didn't think that its *purely ethical* part—normative theory of the good—could receive positive support from metaethical theory. He did believe that metaethics bears positively on normative theory of the right, since he thought that analysis reveals that the concept of right is a complex composed of empirical causal concepts and the concept of intrinsic value. This enables us to identify the empirical causal issues and issues of intrinsic value we are to look to as evidence of what a person should do *and* to rule out as incoherent agent-relative normative theories of right like egoism and deontology. But when it comes to theory of the good, the irreducible core of normative ethical theory according to Moore, metaethics can play no more than a destructive role, showing only how attempts to ground intrinsic value claims in putative analyses, or indeed, to give any justificatory reasons for intrinsic value claims at all, must always come to grief. Metaethical reflection can never count in favor of any (wholly) ethical claim. It can only properly count against attempts to count it in favor.

Now this picture is actually quite congenial to the philosophical environment that emerged *after* the heyday of analytic metaethics, during the great resurgence and expansion of normative ethical theory in the 1970s.[12] With, on the one hand, the linguistic turn and philosophical analysis on the wane owing to Quinean objections to the analytic/synthetic distinction, and, on the other, an impressive example of systematic normative theory in Rawls's *Theory of Justice*, an atmosphere emerged in which normative theory could be pursued without apology and independently of metaethical reflection. Rawls proclaimed the 'Independence of Moral Theory,' arguing that normative theory might proceed entirely on the basis of considered ethical judgments or intuitions and without concern about more general philosophical foundations, or connections to other areas of philosophy.[13] In retrospect, this attitude was not really so different from Moore's. It extended Moore's view that metaethics has no positive relevance to value theory or to normative ethical theory in general. Normative theories of the good, right, virtue, and so on could be constructed on a base of considered judgments without much of a glance at other, non-evaluative philosophical areas.

In another way also, the indifference of some normative theorists to metaethics in the 1970s was substantially similar to the 'that's not my department' view analytic metaethicists had earlier sometimes taken toward normative ethics, but from the other direction. Both believed that their part of ethical philosophy, normative ethics or metaethics, respectively, could be pursued successfully without any attention to the other.

12 For a short historical overview, see Stephen Darwall, Allan Gibbard, and Peter Railton, 'Toward Fin de Siecle Ethics: Some Trends,' *Philosophical Review*, 101 [1992]: 115–89. Reprinted in S. Darwall, A. Gibbard, and P. Railton (eds.), *Moral Discourse and Practice: Some Philosophical Approaches* (New York: Oxford University Press, 1997).

13 John Rawls, *A Theory of Justice* (Cambridge, Mass.: Harvard University Press, 1971); 'Independence of Moral Theory,' *Proceedings and Addresses of the American Philosophical Association*, 48 (1975): 5–22, reprinted in John Rawls, *Collected Papers*, ed. Samuel Freeman (Cambridge, Mass.: Harvard University Press, 2001), 286–302. Rawls's method in *Theory of Justice*, however, might better be viewed as a 'wide' reflective equilibrium that takes in, among other things, the sorts of broadly metaethical considerations Rawls presents in his 'Kantian Interpretation.' On the distinction between narrow and wide reflective equilibrium, see Norman Daniels, 'Wide Reflective Equilibrium and Theory Acceptance in Ethics,' *Journal of Philosophy*, 76 (1979): 256–82, also in Norman Daniels (ed.), *Reading Rawls* (Stanford, Calif.: Stanford University Press, 1989), 253–82.

2. Why should normative ethics be part of philosophy?

Why then should normative ethics and metaethics be in the 'same department'?
Or to put it another way, what reason, other than tradition, is there for normative ethical theory to be conducted in a philosophy department? Metaethics, the
philosophy *of* ethics, might seem to have roughly the same relation to
normative ethics that the philosophy of physics does to physics. And although
there was no way to sharply demarcate physics from metaphysics before the rise
of the experimental method, no one these days would argue for a merger
between the departments of physics and philosophy. So why should things be
any different with ethics?[14]

I believe that the case of ethics *is* different and that the practice of ethical
theory should reflect this fact. Unlike the natural and social sciences, ethics has
not spun off from philosophy, nor should it. The various sciences became
autonomous disciplines when the experimental method gained wide acceptance as the only reliable way of confirming theory about their respective subject
matters.[15] Disagreements in the philosophy of science or in metaphysics or
epistemology leave this consensus largely unaffected. Whether theories are
interpreted realistically, as the best explanation of observed experimental
results, or instrumentally, as the best device for predicting them, is mostly
irrelevant to scientific practice, which proceeds largely independently of these
philosophical disputes.

Nothing like this consensus has emerged in the case of ethics, nor is it likely
to. Unlike the sciences, ethics' subject matter is itself the focus of a lively philosophical debate to which we can envision no end. Cartesian skepticism
notwithstanding, there is sufficient consensus about the phenomena the
sciences are to explain that they can proceed without attention to fundamental
metaphysics and epistemology. In my view, however, this is not the case with
ethics. As I shall attempt to illustrate in the final section, there is no consensus
regarding the *normativity* of (various) ethical propositions and judgments (nor
even about what normativity or normative judgment itself is). These are matters of metaethics—of the 'metaphysics of morals,' ethical epistemology, and
the philosophy of language and mind as they relate to ethical talk and ethical
states of mind. And once they are brought in, other philosophical issues and
areas come in their wake—for example, in the philosophy of action, concerning

---

[14] In the next several paragraphs I draw on my 'Why Ethics is Part of Philosophy: A Plea for Philosophical
Ethics,' in Klaus Brinkmann (ed.), *The Proceedings of the World Congress of Philosophy* (Bowling Green, Oh.:
Philosophy Documentation Center, 1999), 19–28.

[15] These are matters of degree, of course. Scientific questions are not *entirely* independent of issues in the
philosophy of science. My claim is that theoretical physics is independent of the philosophy of physics to a
larger degree than ethical theory is independent of metaethics.

the nature and freedom of the will and action. When these broader philosophical issues are in the background, I shall claim, it is impossible to completely seal them off from intelligent normative discussion and debate. My conclusion will be that, although metaethics and normative ethics focus on different issues, systematic ethical philosophy thrives when these areas are brought into dynamic relation and pursued in an integrated way we might call 'philosophical ethics'—framing normative ideals we can accept in light of both the best normative reasons as we see them *and* an adequate philosophical understanding of their subjects and of the possibilities for knowledge or justified acceptance in this area.[16]

It is only in this century that we have come to distinguish sharply between metaethics and normative ethics. That, again, is Moore's legacy. Earlier systematic ethical thinkers pursued issues of both kinds, attempting to integrate them into a coherent overall view. The past hundred years has seen a sharpening of issues and insights in both areas but also a degree of specialization and compartmentalization that has sometimes closed off opportunities for mutually beneficial interaction and the development of more comprehensive philosophical ethical outlooks.

We are, of course, right to distinguish metaethics from normative ethics. It is possible to combine any given normative view with a variety of metaethical positions. Among consequentialists, we have non-cognitivist prescriptivists (Hare), theological voluntarists (Berkeley), naturalists (Mill), and intuitionists (Sidgwick and Moore). Nonetheless, there do seem to be affinities between metaethical and roughly corresponding normative ethical theories. Metaethical naturalists have almost always been consequentialists, for example, although, as we've noted, a consequentialist need not be a naturalist. Deontologists, on the other hand, require a metaethical account of moral obligation that can explain how the right can diverge from the beneficial, and the wrong from the harmful. Some deontologists have been theological voluntarists. Some have been rational intuitionists, holding, like Clarke, Price, Prichard, or Ross, that we can perceive the truth of fundamental deontological moral principles immediately by reflection. And some have followed Kant in maintaining that deontological normative principles are grounded in the structure of deliberation of a free rational agent. These associations seem far from accidental.

As I mentioned, a major reason that normative ethical theories can never completely dispense with metaethics is that the normativity of their subject matters is often in dispute, along with the character of their respective forms of

---

[16] For a more extended development of this idea, see my *Philosophical Ethics* (Boulder, Colo.: Westview Press, 1998).

normative judgment. In the next section, I will discuss Moore's views in this light and argue that, while Moore is right that ethical concepts all have an irreducible core, he is wrong to identify it with intrinsic value. Here, I shall urge, we really would do better to look to Sidgwick rather than Moore. The central ethical notion is that of normativity or normative reason, which we require to understand both the notion of good and that of right action. Moore held intrinsic value to be a normative notion, but I believe that he mislocated its normativity. Moreover, for Moore, intrinsic value is the only genuine normative notion. Although he was a normative pluralist in the theory of value, he was a metaethical monist. In this, I shall argue, Moore was dramatically mistaken. In principle, there are as many normative notions as items (action and attitudes) that can be normatively regulated—the desirable, the estimable, the dignified (that worthy of respect), and so on. Most regrettable here was Moore's failure to understand reasons for action and ought-to-do's, which he reduced to the ought-to-be's he identified with intrinsic value. This, it seems to me, is a metaethical failure whose consequences have been at least as serious as any of the 'naturalistic fallacy.' In the final section, I will move from Moore to the contemporary scene in order to illustrate how debates in a variety of areas of normative ethics cannot be settled independently of metaethical disputes about the normativity of their respective subjects.

3. Moore and normativity

By 'good', Moore says he means the 'unique object—the unique property' we have before our minds when we say that something has 'intrinsic value,' 'intrinsic worth,' or 'that a thing ought to exist' (§ 13, 68). For Moore, therefore, something's being intrinsically good is identical to its being such that, by virtue of its intrinsic nature, it ought to *exist*: '[W]hen we assert that a thing is good, what we mean is that its existence or reality is good' (§ 70, 171).[17] It follows that what most fundamentally possesses intrinsic value for Moore is a *state of affairs*. Or, to be more precise, the normative proposition entailed by a thing's having intrinsic value is that the state of its existing ought to be.[18]

Now there appear to be ways of valuing something intrinsically whose content does not reduce to, nor even arguably entail, that that thing ought to

---

[17] This is reinforced by Moore's famous 'isolation test.' A's being better than B amounts to its being the case that, as Moore put it in *Ethics*, 'it would be better that A exist quite alone than that B exist quite alone' (G. E. Moore, *Ethics* (New York: Oxford University, 1965), 39).

[18] In this and following paragraphs, I draw on my 'Moore, Normativity, and Intrinsic Value,' *Ethics* 113 (2003): 468–89.

exist. Kantian respect for a person as an end in herself seems a form of intrinsic valuation, but it cannot be reduced to the proposition that the person ought to exist, and it may not even entail it. It may not be surprising that respect is hard to fit into Moore's consequentialist framework but so also is the kind of intrinsic valuation involved in benevolent concern for a person (or other creature) for her own sake. In caring for someone we properly want her to exist *if, but only if,* existing is good *for her.*[19] The difficulties of accommodating these within Moore's scheme are some indication already of idiosyncrasies in his theory.

Moore says that what is intrinsically valuable is what 'ought to exist for its own sake.' But how are we to understand this? Oughts gain their sense from norms; only what can be regulated by norms can be subject to normative judgment.[20] True, we can say of some event that it ought to happen and simply mean that its happening follows from the laws of nature and initial conditions (as we believe them to be), as in, 'the car ought to start.'[21] But there is nothing normative in such a statement.

Now this doesn't mean that the only oughts are ought-to-do's. Normative guidance need not be voluntary, and there is much that we judge normatively and regulate by norms other than action, for example, reasoning, beliefs, choices, emotions, responses, feelings, intentions, and attitudes.[22] But it does mean that there cannot be a *brute* ought-to-*be* that is genuinely normative (unlike the ought in the 'car ought to start now'). The state of something's existence can be the object of various attitudes, and we can sometimes say that a state ought to be, thereby expressing a normative judgment about that attitude. Most obviously, one can desire that something exist. So we might say that that state ought to be, meaning that its obtaining ought to be desired, that it is desirable. Or we might mean that that state is worth caring about. Or that it is worthy of concern from a particular perspective, say, the moral point of view. In the final analysis, we must understand ought-to-be's as elliptical and underspecified, requiring completion by reference to something that can be normatively regulated: some attitude or agent-state.

[19] This is an important theme of Elizabeth Anderson's in *Value in Ethics and Economics* (Cambridge, Mass.: Harvard University Press, 1993), 26–30. I defend an account of welfare inspired by this insight in *Welfare and Rational Care* (Princeton: Princeton University Press, 2002).

[20] A fortiori, only what exists can be subject to normative judgment. This is, I think, what lies behind Prichard's somewhat curious remark that 'only something which is can be something which ought, or ought not, to exist. To say, e.g., that a feeling of generosity which I am not having "ought" to exist is to say nothing, just because ex hypothesi there is nothing here for "being something which ought to exist" to be attributed to' (H. A. Prichard, 'Moral Obligation,' in *Moral Obligation and Duty and Interest* (London: Oxford University Press, 1968), 163).

[21] On this point, see Roger Wertheimer, *The Significance of Sense: Meaning, Modality, and Morality* (Ithaca, NY: Cornell University Press, 1972).

[22] I am indebted here to Allan Gibbard, *Wise Choices, Apt Feelings* (Cambridge, Mass.: Harvard University Press, 1990).

If intrinsic value is to be a normative notion, then, it will have to be interpreted in terms of a normative connection to some valuing attitude or agent-state. The distinction between intrinsic and extrinsic value, between values that depend only on the intrinsic properties of what has it, and those that depend also on extrinsic properties, must consequently be drawn *within* such norms. When we say that something is intrinsically valuable solely because of, or in virtue of, its intrinsic nature, we should understand the relevant 'because' and 'in virtue of' *normatively*, that is, as asserting that its intrinsic nature provides reasons *for* so valuing it.[23]

There are good reasons for Moore to hold that intrinsic value is an explicitly normative notion, additional even to the obvious one that it is hard to see how it could be intrinsically relevant to ethics otherwise. The most important one was identified by Frankena, namely, that it is hard to see what else underlies the open question and other arguments Moore employs to argue that intrinsic value cannot be reduced to naturalistic or metaphysical notions. Frankena writes: '[T]o my mind, what makes ethical judgments seem irreducible to natural or metaphysical judgments is their apparently normative character.'[24] But if this is right, and there cannot be a brute ought, then, as Frankena also pointed out, intrinsic value must be, not a simple, but a complex notion that embeds the idea of normativity or ought within it. Roughly, to be intrinsically valuable must be to be something that ought to be valued (that there is reason to value) just in light of its intrinsic features.[25] And it will follow further that Sidgwick, not Moore, was right about the irreducible core of all ethical notions. The central idea contained in all ethical notions is not intrinsic value but normativity: 'the fundamental notion represented by the word "ought".'[26]

So although Moore was right that ethical notions are irreducible to non-ethical ones, he was wrong in thinking that this is because they all have the idea of intrinsic value as their irreducible core. If the concept of intrinsic value is to be normative, as it must be to make the open question argument (and the naturalistic fallacy) plausible, then it must include the idea of normativity or ought.

---

[23] We should say, as W. D. Falk puts it, that it is something that would be so valued on a *proper review* of its intrinsic properties (W. D. Falk, 'Fact, Value, and Nonnatural Predication,' in *Ought, Reasons, and Morality* (Ithaca, NY: Cornell University Press, 1986)). See also Wlodek Rabinowicz and Toni Rønnow-Rasmussen, 'The Strike of the Demon: On Fitting Pro-attitudes and Value,' *Ethics*, 114 (2004): 391–423.

[24] William Frankena, 'Obligation and Value in the Ethics of G. E. Moore,' in Paul A. Schilpp (ed.), *The Philosophy of G. E. Moore* (LaSalle, Ill.: Open Court, 1942), 102.

[25] Cf. Scanlon's 'buck-passing' account of value, according to which 'to call something valuable is to say that it has other properties that provide reasons for behaving in certain ways with regard to it.' That the relevant reasons must be for action, as opposed also to attitudes of other kinds, seems too narrow, but otherwise the ideas are quite similar (T. M. Scanlon, *What We Owe to Each Other* (Cambridge, Mass.: Harvard University Press, 1998), 96).   [26] *Methods of Ethics*, 25.

Moore was also wrong in thinking that the concept of right conduct, or what one ought to *do*, can be reduced to that of intrinsic value, or what ought to *be*. Moore believed, again, that to assert that a given action is right, something one ought to do, 'is obviously to assert that more good or less evil will exist in the world, if it be adopted than if anything else be done instead' (§ 17, 77). But if this were true, then deontological claims to the contrary, for example, that one should not torture even if it would bring about greater good, would not be false, so much as incoherent. And, indeed, this is what Moore claimed, arguing as follows.[27]

1. To say that an action at a time is an agent's 'absolute duty' is to say 'the performance of that action is unique in respect of value.'
2. A dutiful action cannot possibly be unique in respect of value in the sense of being the only valuable thing (since '*every* such action would [then] be the *sole* good thing, which is a manifest contradiction').
3. A dutiful action cannot possibly be unique in respect of value in the sense 'that it has more intrinsic value than anything else in the world' ('since *every* act of duty would then be the *best* thing in the world, which is also a contradiction').
4. Therefore, the only sense in which the performance of an action can possibly be unique in respect of value is 'that the whole world will be better, if it be performed, than if any possible alternative were taken' (§ 89, 197).

From 1 and 4 together, it follows that an action's being an agent's absolute duty is equivalent to its being the case that the world would be better were the action performed than if the agent were to do anything else she could. Any non-consequentialist duty or ought-to-do claim to the contrary is self-contradictory.

Moore's argument assumes that action's essence is instrumental, that a doing is simply the intentional bringing about of a state. Premise 1 is uncontroversial (at least in one direction) if we understand it as saying that if an agent has an absolute duty to do something then that means the action would be the best thing for her *to do*, that it is the best *act* of those available. In 2 through 4, however, most obviously, in 4, Moore slides to a different kind of evaluation—namely, his broader category of intrinsic value. In *this* sense, an act's having intrinsic value consists in its being true that the state of its being performed ought to *be*. Now 4 allows for the possibility that an act can have intrinsic value in this sense. But even if an act has intrinsic value *as an existent*, Moore's argument clearly assumes that its value *as an action* is purely instrumental. Its value

---

[27] In *Principia Ethica*. Moore changed his view in *Ethics* to hold that consequentialism is a synthetic a priori truth rather than an analytic one (G. E. Moore, *Ethics* (New York: Oxford University Press, 1966), 89).

as an action, the sense in which one's absolute duty is the *best available act*, is its instrumental value in bringing about intrinsically valuable states, including, perhaps, the state of the act itself being performed.

Moore's reduction of right to good, of ought-to-do's to ought-to-be's, thus depends upon a purely instrumental view of action. What action is *for* is the production of intrinsically valuable states. The concept of a reason for acting, therefore, reduces to an empirical part, which is concerned with the consequences of acts within the agent's power, and an ethical part, which is concerned with the intrinsic value of those consequences. On this picture, the ethical aspect of the question of what to do is entirely agent-neutral. It is the question of what states the world should contain, viewed as from nowhere. Even if the commonsense description of an act or an agent's reason is agent-relative, the question of whether the state of the act's being performed, or being performed for that reason, ought to exist is not itself agent-relative, but agent-neutral. If we ask, for example, whether someone's caring for her children, or benefiting a child because it is hers, ought to exist for its own sake, the grounds for answering *that* question will not themselves be agent-relative. If it is a good thing that Jesse helps his children then it will likewise be a good thing that Mervis helps hers.[28]

Moore to the contrary notwithstanding, however, 'What to *do?*' is in its nature an *agent-relative question*. It is the question of what *the agent* should do. Moore doesn't deny this in a sense. It is just that he holds that its agent-relativity is restricted to an *instrumental*, causal question concerning the consequences of all actions in the agent's power. These are not, however, normative issues. According to Moore, the only ethical issues that agents ever face are agent-neutral: what states *should be?*

Moore's analytic consequentialism can be shown to be mistaken by a version of the very same open question argument he himself uses to illustrate the naturalistic fallacy. When a deontological theorist of the right asserts that one ought not to torture another person even if that would have better consequences, she is not saying, incoherently, that, in the situations where torturing would produce better consequences, not torturing would actually have better consequences. Neither is she just saying that the state of someone's torturing has intrinsic disvalue. She is saying that even in the case where one could prevent, say, a morally equivalent torturing, it would be wrong, one ought not, to torture another *oneself*. But if this is a coherent claim, as it surely seems to be, then *analytic* consequentialism cannot possibly be right.

---

[28] This is not to deny that some evaluations of what should be are *evaluator*-relative or even that the agent's own evaluations of what should be are distinctively relevant to what he should do.

Of course, consequentialism might still be correct as a substantive normative theory of the right. However, I believe that it will appear so only so long as we are in the grip of the same instrumental picture of action that Moore plainly assumed. So long as we view the question of what to do entirely from the perspective of how it would be best for the world to be, consequentialism of some sort will seem inevitable. But agents are not simply producers of world states. Many of the most important practical questions concern how *to relate* to the world from within it, most especially how to relate to other agents. That this is a central feature of the ethical context has been stressed by deontological writers, like W. D. Ross, and it is an important part of the Kantian and contractualist pictures. Thus Ross's list of prima facie duties includes those we have by virtue of various special relationships we stand in to others (parent, trustee, etc.) and special relations arising from past actions (promise, contract, restitution, gratitude), as well as general relations of reciprocity, beneficence, and non-maleficence we can stand in to any person (or, in the latter two cases, to any sentient being).[29] Kant and contractualists, on the other hand, see standards of moral right and wrong as principles that define expectations moral persons rightly have of each other as mutually respecting free and equal agents.

The affinity between Moore's consequentialism, his instrumental conception of action, and his reduction of the right to the good is a deep feature of his philosophical ethics. Ultimately, Moore fails to appreciate the idea that really drives his arguments for the irreducibility of the ethical, including the open question argument—namely, the concept of normativity or ought. For any property that is characterized non-normatively, we can ask whether (or coherently deny that) things with that property are good because we tacitly assume that good is an explicitly normative property. And Moore fails to appreciate the implications of normativity for the instrumentalist picture of action that underlies his consequentialism. The concept of ought and explicitly normative notions that contain it are ideas we have use for because we are self-reflective beings who are capable of normative guidance. Only a being who can be aware of her own attitudes and take a critical perspective towards them can grasp the distinction between what she actually values and what she ought to value— what is valuable. Relatedly, as Butler pointed out, only a being who can distinguish between the strength of a motivational state and its authority—between how much she actually desires something and how much she *should* desire it— can be an agent.[30] Our finding the open question argument persuasive is thus

[29] W. D. Ross, *The Right and the Good* (Oxford: Clarendon Press, 1963).
[30] Bishop Butler, *Sermons*, ed. Stephen Darwall (Indianapolis: Hackett Publishers, 1983), II. 14, p. 39.

an expression of our own freedom.[31] As free agents, we cannot possibly accept the Moorean definition of action as simply *for* bringing about valuable states of the world. That would involve a kind of 'bad faith,' as though we weren't free even to consider whether there are agent-relative reasons for action, ought-to-do's (for example, those having to do with our relations to other persons) that cannot be given a Moorean reduction.[32]

Ultimately, then, Moore failed to grasp that ought-to-do's can be independent of ought-to-be's—that reasons for acting can be independent from reasons we have to desire or value states of the world—because he failed to appreciate the idea of normativity and its full implications for ethics. Intrinsic value cannot be the fundamental ethical notion from which all others derive. What makes it an ethical notion in the first place is its containing the idea of normativity or ought. But in this it is no more or less fundamental than the idea of right, what we ought to do; the estimable, what we ought to esteem; the desirable, what we ought to desire, and so on. Working out the relations between different normative notions is a complicated matter.[33] As I will suggest presently, some of this can be done at the metaethical level in a way that can fit with various normative claims. But it is also partly, no doubt, a substantive normative matter.

4. Philosophical ethics: why normative ethics should be part of philosophy

The foregoing discussion shows that the relation of metaethics to normative ethics is more complex than Moore thought. There are normative disputes about the right, for example, that cannot be settled without attention to metaethical issues about its normativity that Moore thought he had decisively settled. Indeed, much of the debate between consequentialists and their critics over the past two decades has had an important metaethical element, with consequentialists arguing that agent-relative restrictions can be given no philosophically satisfying rationale, and their opponents trying to do precisely that,

---

[31] That the appeal of the open question argument is deeply related to freedom is an important theme of Connie Rosati's 'Naturalism, Normativity, and the Open Question Argument,' *Nous*, 29 (1995): 46–70. See also, Stephen Darwall, 'Internalism and Agency,' *Philosophical Perspectives*, 6 (1992): 155–74, and 'Autonomist Internalism and the Justification of Morality,' *Nous*, 24 (1990): 257–68.

[32] In 'Moore, Normativity, and Intrinsic Value,' I defend the claim that we are only capable of a conception of ourselves as free agents by virtue of standing in second-personal relations to other free agents.

[33] See John Skorupski, *Ethical Explorations* (Oxford: Oxford University Press, 1999), 38–46, on 'bridge principles.'

for example, by grounding them in some form of contractualism.[34] As I have said, I think this is a very good thing. Both metaethics and normative ethics thrive when they are pursued interdependently, as complementary aspects of a comprehensive philosophical ethics. In this final section, I will try to illustrate some ways in which current matters of lively debate in normative ethics depend upon metaethical issues regarding the normativity of their subject matter. In these areas as in many others, I believe, solid progress can be made only when normative ethics and metaethics are kept in close contact with one another.

For example, critics often point out that act consequentialism is self-defeating in various ways. The overall consequences of publicizing the act-consequentialist theory of right, or even of each person's privately using act consequentialism as a deliberative standard, would be worse than either publicizing some other non-consequentialist doctrine or having individuals deliberate according to a non-consequentialist standard of choice, respectively. Many consequentialists accept that this is probably so, and some, indeed, follow Moore in holding that the standards for private or public choice should therefore be commonsense deontological rules (such as Ross's principles of prima facie duty). At the same time, however, many consequentialists argue that this is in no way an argument against their theory. Act consequentialism may be a correct theory of right even if it would not be practical in consequentialist terms to say so too loudly, whether to oneself or to others.

Now surely whether being self-defeating is an objection to act consequentialism depends significantly on metaethical issues concerning the nature and concept of morality and of moral right and wrong, as I will illustrate presently. In a somewhat different vein, critics sometimes argue that consequentialism is too 'demanding,' since it holds that agents act wrongly when they fail to do all they can to respond to unmet needs even at levels of sacrifice substantially beyond what commonsense morality would require. This may seem to be simply a disagreement in considered judgments, but here again it is difficult to contain the debate within normative ethical boundaries. Some consequentialists who hold that any non-maximizing act is wrong, nonetheless also say that it would often be mistaken to blame agents for such actions, and not just on strategic grounds but because such wrongdoing may not be blameworthy even when the agent lacks any standard excuse. Or again, they may hold that, although such conduct is wrong, and so something agents have the best *moral*

---

[34] See, for example, Samuel Scheffler, *The Rejection of Consequentialism* (Oxford: Clarendon Press, 1982); T. M. Scanlon, 'Contractualism and Utilitarianism,' in A. Sen and B. Williams, *Utilitarianism and Beyond* (Cambridge: Cambridge University Press, 1982), 103–28, and *What We Owe to Each Other*.

reason not to do, that doesn't mean that agents shouldn't so act, all things considered, in light of all the reasons that bear on the case.

These consequentialist judgments have metaethical implications. If someone dubs an action 'morally wrong,' but not something for which a person would be blameworthy lacking adequate excuse, she severs a connection between wrong and blameworthiness that others may think is part of the very concept of moral wrong. Thus Mill famously wrote that 'we do not call anything wrong unless we mean to imply that a person ought to be punished in some way or other for doing it; if not by law, by the opinion of his fellow creatures; if not by opinion, by the reproaches of his own conscience.'[35] If act consequentialists and their critics use 'wrong' in these different ways, they may simply be talking past each other. But how *should* we conceive of moral wrong? My own view is that Mill is right and that the usage he points to is part of a deep connection between morality and mutual accountability. What is wrong is not simply conduct that we have strong reasons of a certain kind for avoiding but conduct that we are responsible or accountable (to the moral community) for avoiding. More recently, writers like Gibbard and Skorupski have echoed Mill's thought, arguing that the concept of moral wrong must be understood in terms of such distinctive moral sentiments as guilt and blame.[36] In each case, the idea is that judging an action wrong is an aspect of holding the agent accountable. It is seeing the agent as rightly subject, lacking adequate excuse, to something, perhaps a sanction, perhaps some form of a self- or other-directed, second-personal 'reactive attitude,' like blame or guilt, that might help constitute holding him morally responsible.[37]

This metaethical issue has normative implications. If wrong is tied to accountability, then some position other than *act* consequentialism would seem the most sensible position for a consequentialist to take. Or again, the metaethical issue of morality/reasons internalism may be partly at issue in what

[35] John Stuart Mill, *Utilitarianism*, ed. George Sher (Indianapolis: Hackett Publishing Co., Inc., 1979), ch. 5, pp. 47, 48.

[36] Gibbard, *Wise Choices, Apt Feelings*, 42, and John Skorupski, *Ethical Explorations*, e.g. 142. This is also an important strain in Bernard Williams's thought. See his *Ethics and the Limits of Philosophy* (Cambridge, Mass.: Harvard University Press, 1985), and 'Internal Reasons and the Obscurity of Blame,' in *Making Sense of Humanity* (Cambridge: Cambridge University Press, 1995). See also Russ Shafer-Landau, *Moral Realism: A Defense* (Oxford: Oxford University Press, 2003).

[37] The term comes from P. F. Strawson, 'Freedom and Resentment,' in *Studies in the Philosophy of Thought and Action* (Oxford: Oxford University Press, 1968), 71–96. More precisely, Strawson calls these 'participant reactive attitudes' ('natural human reactions to the good or ill will or indifference of others towards us') (80). These attitudes are 'second-personal' in the sense both that they are felt in response to something second-personal (an attitude *directed* towards one) and that their natural expression is also directed toward their object. For example, both anger and fear have intentional objects, but anger is directed towards its object in a way that fear is not.

seem simply to be normative debates about consequentialism and 'demand-ingness.' Act consequentialists are frequently externalists on this issue, while their critics frequently take it to be a presupposition of moral debate that morality purports to be action- or feeling-guiding. Here again, it is impossible to isolate the normative moral disagreement and bracket philosophical reflection on the nature and source of morality's authority. My own view is that standards of moral right and wrong do purport to be authoritatively action-guiding, and that one way to see this is to reflect on the connection just mentioned between morality and accountability. Blame commits one to thinking there was a good reason for the person not to have done what she did. It would simply be incoherent to judge someone blameworthy while acknowledging there really was no reason whatsoever for her not to have acted as she did.[38] It seems incoherent, indeed, to blame while allowing that the wrong action, although recommended against by some reasons, was nonetheless the sensible thing to do, all things considered (supremacy). Part of what one does in blaming is to say that the person shouldn't have done what she did *period*. And accepting blame involves an acknowledgment of this proposition also. To feel guilt is, in part, to feel that one shouldn't have done what one did. If, however, supremely normative purport is internal to the very idea of moral standards of right and wrong, then this will have implications for considered moral conviction. It will mean that our judgments of right and wrong will be staked on their having authority, such that, if we come to believe they lack it in some case or area, we will have to withdraw them.[39]

To take another example in a very different area, consider the issue of how virtue ethics should be positioned within moral or normative ethical theory. That would seem analogously to depend on virtue's normativity. Sometimes virtue is understood as a distinctively *moral* goodness of the person or of character, as, for example, in Francis Hutcheson's virtue theory.[40] If we understand it in this way, then virtue's normativity will be related to morality's, but different from that of moral obligation. Hutcheson thought that morality, fundamentally moral goodness, was normative for distinctive feelings of moral approbation and condemnation. More usually, however,

---

[38] John Skorupski makes a similar point in *Ethical Explorations*, 42–3, as does Bernard Williams in 'Internal Reasons and the Obscurity of Blame,' in *Making Sense of Humanity*, 40–4. See also Russ Shafer-Landau, *Moral Realism: A Defense*.

[39] This thought underlies some of Samuel Scheffler's arguments in *Human Morality* (New York: Oxford University Press, 1992).

[40] Francis Hutcheson, *An Inquiry into the Original of our Ideas of Beauty and Virtue* (London, 1725). For selections, see *Moral Philosophy from Montaigne to Kant*, ed. J. B. Schneewind, 2 vols. (Cambridge: Cambridge University Press, 1990); and *British Moralists: 1650–1800*, ed. D. D. Raphael, 2 vols. (Indianapolis: Hackett Publishers, Inc., 1991).

virtue theories are put forward either as including good-making features of persons that extend beyond or intersect the moral or as an alternative to morality.[41] How are we to understand the normativity of this sort of goodness? It is impossible to know how virtue theory relates to other normative theories without taking a position, if only implicitly, on this metaethical issue.

Obviously, the virtues concern how we ought to be, in some sense. But in what sense? The virtues of a car are what make it a good thing of its kind, that is, relative to the standard purposes and expectations we have for cars, either in general or of a certain kind. Should we think about ethical virtues in the same way? Can we, without thinking human life serves a larger purpose? We might make use of broader functionalist notions, but even if we can, it is not obvious what normativity this would have for us as agents, since, in Moorean fashion, we could always sensibly ask why we should uphold the standards for a good thing of that kind, and it is not obvious what could provide a satisfactory answer.

Alternatively, the virtues are sometimes thought of as features of the person or character that are necessary for well-being, qualities without which, in Philippa Foot's words, a person does not 'get on well.'[42] Virtue's normativity here apparently derives from that of a person's good or well-being. But exactly what normative force welfare has for a person is itself controversial.[43] Or perhaps we should understand the virtues in relation to a kind of value that differs from goodness of a kind, from well-being, and even from moral goodness narrowly conceived, as more general worthiness of admiration or esteem.

In the final analysis, what normative judgments of virtue we are prepared to accept on reflection cannot be separated from these metaethical issues of virtue's normativity. So here again, it seems impossible to seal off the normative theory of virtue from philosophical reflection about the very phenomena that such a theory would hope to explain. Ultimately, a satisfactory theory of the virtues must be placed within a philosophical ethics that integrates these normative and metaethical issues.

The development of metaethics as a freestanding area was Moore's legacy, even if it wasn't his intent. For the past hundred years, metaethics and normative ethics have frequently had an agonistic, sometimes even an antagonistic,

---

[41] See, for example, Michael Slote, *From Morality to Virtue* (New York: Oxford University Press, 1992), and *Morals from Motives* (New York: Oxford University Press, 2001); and Rosalind Hursthouse, *On Virtue Ethics* (Oxford: Oxford University Press, 1999).

[42] Philippa Foot, 'Virtues and Vices,' in *Virtues and Vices* (Berkeley and Los Angeles: University of California Press, 1978), 2.

[43] In *Welfare and Rational Care*, I argue against the view that it entails agent-relative reasons for acting and for the claim that it is normative for care—that what is for someone's good is what one should want for that person for her sake, that is, insofar as one cares for her.

relationship. We have seen periods in which one was in the ascendancy and the other in eclipse, only to be followed by a reversal of roles. Perhaps this century can see a period in which we do not lose the substantial benefits that a specialist's sophistication in these areas can bring but also gain more of the interaction that a genuinely philosophical ethics requires.

2

What Do Reasons Do?*

Jonathan Dancy

1. Reason and reasons

When I talk in this paper about reasons, I will be focusing primarily on practical reasons, reasons for action; and I will talk mainly about what I call contributory reasons. A contributory reason for action is a feature whose presence makes something of a case for acting but in such a way that the over-all case for doing that action can be improved or strengthened by the addition of a second reason of the same sort. Also, a contributory reason on one side is not necessarily destroyed by the presence of a reason on the other side. This does happen sometimes, I agree, but it is far from the standard case. Contributory reasons are officially reasons capable of doing what they do either alone or in combination with others. But they can combine in peculiar and irregular ways, as we will see. There is no guarantee that the case for doing an action, already made to some extent by the presence of one reason, will be improved by adding a second reason to it. Reasons are like rats, at least to the extent that two rats that are supposedly on the same side may in fact turn and fight among themselves, so that the addition of the second reason makes things worse rather than better. Remember the old joke about a New York restaurant: there are two things wrong with this restaurant—the food is terrible and the portions are too small.[1]

Much of our talk of reasons is about contributory reasons in this sense, reasons on one side or on the other, reasons that stack up with others to make a better or worse case for an action. But as well as talking about reasons in this way, we also speak of what there is overall reason to do. There is nothing wrong with that, of course, but it should not delude us into thinking that there are such things as overall reasons in addition to the contributory ones. To talk of what there is overall reason to do (and note that 'reason' in this phrase is not a count noun) is to talk about where the contributory reasons come down—on

* The material in this paper has appeared, in substantially the same form, as parts of chs. 2, 3, and 4 in Dancy 2004*b*.

[1] Thanks to Jerry Dworkin for this and other jokes.

this side or on that. We can say we have more reason to do this than to do that, but most reason to do some third thing. These verdicts[2] do not themselves specify further reasons (of an overall sort), on pain of changing the very situation on which they pass verdict. So there are no overall reasons. All reasons, then, are contributory, unless we can find a further sort of reason that is neither contributory nor overall.

2. The role that reasons play

How are we to understand the role played by a contributory reason? This question is not often asked, and when it has been asked the answers given have tended to be a bit incautious. Those who have addressed the issue have mostly tried to explain the role of the contributory in terms of what happens at the overall level. Jean Hampton, for instance, knows perfectly well that there are contributory reasons. She mentions Ross's notion of the prima facie, though only with the now standard gripes about Rossian terminology (1998: 51 n.). But when she talks about reasons, she constantly uses terms that are, one would have thought, quite inappropriate for the merely contributory. She says that reasons are 'directive' (51, 85), have 'obligatory force' (99), have 'compelling rightness' (93, 99), are 'prescriptive' (87), are or express commands (88), concern the 'ought to be' (92), 'feel like orders' (106), and have a 'compelling quality' (91–2). All these remarks seem to be more appropriate at the overall level. An overall 'ought', we might say, is a directive; in a perfectly clear sense (at least for present purposes), it tells us what to do—what we should do. It expresses a command, maybe, it has a compelling quality, it has 'obligatory force' in some sense or other, it feels like an order and directs us to do this rather than that. The question then is whether contributory reasons do the same as the overall does. And the answer is surely that they don't. If an overall 'ought' commands, it cannot be that contributory reasons command as well; there is no such thing as a pro tanto[3] command. We have reasons on both sides of the question, often enough. Is it that each reason on either side commands and then that somehow the sum

---

[2] I get this term from Philip Stratton-Lake (2000: 14), who in turn owes it to Philippa Foot. Stratton-Lake also accepts Foot's contrast between the verdictive and the evidential. But I prefer the term 'contributory' to their 'evidential', since I do not identify reasons for doing an action with evidence that the action ought to be done, on the grounds that something can be evidence without being a reason.

[3] 'Pro tanto' means 'as far as that goes'. It has become common to prefer this term to Ross's term 'prima facie', because the latter looks as if it means 'at first glance'—which, in Ross's usage, it most definitely does not. In this paper I try to avoid both of them in favor of 'contributory reason'. But all these terms are trying to capture the same phenomenon.

total of them commands as well? I don't think this is a coherent scenario; there are too many commands floating about.

Hampton may have made a mistake in supposing that one can simply capture what reasons do by talking in terms that really apply only at the overall level. But this does not show that with a bit more subtlety we could not do better, while still appealing to some relation to an overall 'ought' to explain the role of the contributory. In what follows I consider a long list of suggestions of this sort and reject them all. But they are rejected not because there is reason in advance to say that no attempt of this sort can succeed. Each will be rejected for specific failings rather than for being of that general style.

The first and most common suggestion about the relation between contributory reasons and oughts is that to be a contributory reason is to be a consideration that would decide the issue (i.e. ground an overall 'ought') if it were the only relevant consideration. My own favorite version of this idea is in Ross, who wrote:

I suggest 'prima facie' duty or 'conditional duty' as a brief way of referring to the characteristic (quite distinct from that of being a duty proper) which an act has, in virtue of being of a certain kind (e.g. the keeping of a promise), of being an act which would be a duty proper if it were not at the same time of another kind which is morally significant. (1930: 19–20)

We can think of this as a functional definition or characterization of the role played by a reason: the characterization runs by appeal to something that such a thing would do in a certain circumstance. And this is supposed not just to get it right about which things are reasons and which are not, but to capture what is going on when a consideration is not alone, or defeated, but still making a contribution of the style that we are trying to understand. Now there can be no objection to functional definitions of this sort, I think, but there can be objections to instances—and there are to this one. I have four objections, in what I think of as increasing strength. The first is that the supposed definition makes essential appeal to the very concept it is trying to explicate. It does this because of the presence of the word 'significant' at the end, for this sort of significance is exactly what we are trying to understand, and the account appeals to that concept in a way that certainly looks viciously circular. It would be just the same if Ross had spoken of what is morally 'relevant'; what we are trying to understand is what it is to be 'relevant' to how to act, in the sort of way that a contributory reason is. So an answer that makes essential use of any such notion does not seem able to advance us very far. My understanding of functional explanations, however, is not good enough to tell me whether this objection is really important. So I pass to the second. This is that it is true of every feature whatever, whether relevant or not in the actual case, that it would decide the issue if it were the only relevant one. If so, the definition does not help us to distinguish those things that are reasons from those that are not. It has the consequence that everything is a reason for everything. The third problem is that the definition is trying to characterize something that a feature can do in concert with others by appeal to something that can only be done in isolation, and this is a peculiar procedure. I think of it as no better than trying to characterize the contribution made by a football player to his side's victory by talking only about how things would have been had he been the only player on the field. It is as if one tried to give an account of what a conversation is which ran entirely in terms of how things would have been if there had only been one participant. Finally, and perhaps most forcibly, the definition assumes that each relevant feature could be the only relevant feature. But this assumption seems not to be true. There can be, and are, some reasons that are only reasons if there is another reason present as well. The best example I know of this, which is contrived but still effective, I owe to Michael Ridge. Suppose that I promise to do something only if there is some other reason to do it. If there is no other reason to do it, my having promised gives me no reason either. The promise only comes into play as a reason if there is a second reason present. And this means that the definition we are considering fails to capture reasons of this sort. But such reasons are as much reasons as any other. So the definition is defective.

It is important to be clear what is going on here. There is something undeniable in the offing, namely that if there is a reason to φ, and no reason for doing anything else, and no reason not to φ, one ought to φ. At least, I think this is undeniable, though that does not mean that no philosopher has denied it.[4] But this undeniable truth should be distinguished from the falsehood that I exposed in the previous paragraph, namely that to be a reason to φ is to be such that if there is no reason not to φ, one ought to φ. Perhaps the problem really lies with the intermediate claim that if a feature is a reason to φ, then if there were no other reason in the case, one ought to φ. What is wrong with this claim is that there are some reasons of which the antecedent and the consequent of this conditional explication cannot both be true at once. The example of the promise to act only if there is some other reason is exactly of this sort. This being so, the intermediate claim cannot be held to be a full characterization of what it is to be a reason.

---

[4] John Broome denies it implicitly, I think, because he thinks that there can be some oughts that are not grounded in reasons. If so, there might be a reason around, and that the only reason, without that reason grounding an ought, because there is an opposing ought of the special Broomean sort already in play. See Broome 2004.

I now leave that attempt to capture the role of a reason, which we could call the 'isolation approach', for another equally down to earth attempt. Perhaps a contributory reason is a consideration in whose absence the relevant action would be less obligatory, or even not obligatory at all. This version requires us to make sense of the notion that obligatoriness can be a matter of degree. But I let that pass, for reasons that will emerge later. The problem, as I see it, with this definition is that sometimes a consideration is a reason, even though in its absence we would have more reason, not less. To see what I mean by this, consider a case in which I am thinking of doing something for a friend. My action, were I to do it, would be good, and partly good because it is an expression of our friendship. But now, if I were to be doing the action and not doing it for a friend, I would (let us suppose) be doing it for a stranger. And in such a case the action might be even better. Now one does not have to accept this actual example in order to accept the point it is trying to make. The point is that the sort of support we are trying to capture is not easily capturable in conditional terms. However we are to understand the matter, our friendship seems to be a reason to do the action even though if we were not friends I would have even more reason to do it. The contribution of a reason seems to be non-comparative, in this sense. (This is all very contentious, but there is more on the point below.)

A further and less contentious objection to this definition will emerge later, but I pass on to the idea that a contributory reason is a consideration on which we ought to act if it is stronger than other reasons. Here I could content myself with saying that the appeal to the notion of strength that is made here is viciously circular (and I think the charge of vicious circularity is this time more obviously effective than it was in the case of the isolation approach). But I have another suggestion to make at this point. This is that as well as the sort of peremptory reasons I have so far been discussing, which certainly do stand in some close relation to oughts (even if we are finding it hard to characterize them in terms of that relation), there are reasons of another style, which I call enticing reasons, and these do not stand in the same relation to oughts at all. Enticing reasons are to do with what would be fun, amusing, attractive, exciting, pleasant, and so on. They can be stronger and weaker, and they are often strong enough for action. But (as I understand the matter) they never take us to an ought; it is not true of an enticing reason that if one has one of them and no reason of any other sort, one ought to do what the reason entices one to do. One can do that; but one has the right not to. With peremptory reasons we could not say any such thing.[5]

---

[5] One might allow that there is a weak sense of 'ought' in which one ought to choose the most enjoyable way of spending the afternoon, where no considerations other than pleasure are at issue. But in this weak

Of course if there were enticing reasons, no attempt to define the general notion of a reason in terms of some relation to oughts could hope to succeed. We would have to restrict ourselves to the claim that peremptory reasons can be so understood. And this itself would not be insignificant. So it is worth continuing the chase, leaving the possibility of enticing reasons to one side.

My next suggestion is that a contributory reason is a consideration that ought to motivate one. The difficulty that I see with this is that it is hard to believe that the structure of motivation should match the profile of the reasons. It is not as if for every reason one ought to have a little bit of motivation (whatever that might mean), nor is it the case, so far as I can see, that one's overall motivation to do the action ought somehow to match the extent to which the reasons for doing it are stronger than the reasons against, or the reasons for doing something else. Note that the 'ought' in the present suggestion, as in all the others, is an overall ought. (At the moment we are supposing that all oughts are overall oughts.) It is not that there is some reason to be motivated by each reason for doing the action, but rather that all things considered one ought so to be motivated. And this seems to me to be false.

A somewhat similar idea is that a reason is a consideration that ought to affect how one deliberates. Again, the ought here needs to be an overall ought, for otherwise we are merely using the notion of a contributory reason to explain itself. And there would be a further defect in the present case, which is that we would be attempting to understand a reason for action by identifying it with a reason for deliberating in one way rather than another, and this seems to subvert the focus of the reason. The reason, we might say, is trying to get us to act in the way it wants; it would not be satisfied if we told it that we had fully recognized it by deliberating in the way it told us to. (Apologies for the anthropomorphism here.) But this complaint holds good even if we understand the ought involved as an overall ought; the focus of the reasons still seems to be subverted. What is more, there may be reasons (even overall reason) to deliberate in a certain way that are not matched by reasons for action. For instance, suppose that there is a feature that is very commonly a reason but is not a reason in the present case. We should, perhaps, bear the presence of this feature in mind when deliberating, but only so as to determine that it is not in fact here a reason. So being a reason for action is not the same as being a consideration that one ought to bear in mind when deliberating.

---

sense of 'ought', it might be both that one ought overall to choose this and that one is permitted not to choose it. And this is hardly a sense of 'ought' at all. I discuss enticing reasons in much greater detail in Dancy 2004*a*.

Finally, consider a remark by Jean Hampton: 'we speak of reasons using the language of obligation, as in "you ought not to drink that stuff because it is petrol" ' (1998: 80). The best way to take what Hampton is saying here, I think, if it is to be different from anything we have seen before and rejected, is that to be a reason is to be the sort of thing that leads to an ought. Now this is plausible, but there is a subtle problem with it. There is a presumption here that reasons are essentially 'ought-makers'. But it seems to me that we are in fact dealing with two normative relations rather than one. The first is the relation between reasons and ought-judgments; we specify the reasons and pass to the judgment that we ought to act. The second is a relation between reasons and action which is not necessarily mediated by any ought at all; it is the one that is in play when we engage in the sort of practical reasoning whose 'conclusion' is an action. Crucially, the relation between reason and ought-judgment is different from the relation between reason and action. And it is really the latter that we are after when we try to understand the notion of a reason for action— a practical reason. Ought-judgments are judgments, and reasoning to those judgments, however practical its purpose, is theoretical rather than practical, since it is reasoning to something that is accepted as true. It is compatible with this to suppose that people often reason to action by passing from reasons to ought-judgments, and only then to action. The point is only that the relation between the reasons and the action is different from the relation between the reasons and the ought-judgment. And we should also avoid supposing that the relation between the reasons and the action is the same as the relation between the ought-judgment and the action. For, as we said earlier on, an overall ought is not a reason. This, I think, is evidence (should any be needed) that the attempt generally to capture what a reason does in terms of some relation to an ought is looking in the wrong place. The relation that lies between reason and action is not going to be captured in ways that discuss only the different relation that lies between reason and ought-judgment.

3. Reasons as favorers

I have been arguing that there is no known way of understanding what a contributory reason does by appeal to some relation in which the contributory stands to the overall ought. Every suggestion we have come up with has fallen to one objection or another. I conclude that the notion of a reason is incapable of explication in this sort of way. Is there then nothing we can say to explicate the role played by reasons? The only thing left to say, I think, is that a reason is a consideration that favors action. Favoring here is a normative relation in which a reason stands to acting in a certain way. (Reasons for belief stand in the same relation to believing something.) But when we have been told this we do not seem to be very much further forward. Myself, I think that the focus on a normative *relation* is a positive step forward. But nonetheless we have ended up saying not a lot. One thing we have said, of course, is that the notion of a reason cannot be understood in 'other' terms. Here I see myself as saying something rather like what Moore said about value. Moore thought that every attempt to characterize value, the good, in other terms fell foul of the naturalistic fallacy. That has not been my argument; far from it. In fact I had no such general argument. I tried to deal with particular suggestions one by one rather than all together. But the end result is similar.[6]

If one cannot explicate a philosophically significant concept, there may however be other ways of giving people a sense that the concept is itself in good order and that they have a reasonably clear grasp on it. One way of doing this is to work through a range of examples, showing how the concept applies to them and showing that there is a graspable distinction between cases in which it applies and cases in which it does not apply. In this way one can hope to train people up in the use of a concept on which (we are supposing) they already have an implicit grasp. My experience is that, in the case of favoring, not too many examples are needed. Consider the following piece of practical 'reasoning':

(1) I promised to do it.
(2) My promise was not given under duress.
(3) I am able to do it.
(4) There is no greater reason not to do it.
(5) So I do it.

Note here that there is a similar train of thought that ends not with (5) as presented, but with:

(5*) So I ought to do it.

Think of (5) and (5*) as 'conclusions' of the reasoning presented in (1)–(4). This is a bit odd, because I intend (5) to be (or represent) an action undertaken in the light of the reasoning that leads to it, and it is hard to think of an action as the conclusion of anything (except a series of other actions, I suppose). If (5) is an action done in the light of (1)–(4), somewhere in (1)–(4) we should be able to find something that favors that action. And indeed there is; the only question will be how many favorers there are there. For ease of reference, I will

---

[6] Thanks to Walter Sinnott-Armstrong here.

call (1)–(4) the 'premises' of the reasoning, for the while at least. Later I will suggest that they are not premises at all, whether the conclusion is an action, as in (5), or an ought, as in (5*).

Premise (1) presents a clear favorer. That I promised to do it is (in this context at least) a reason in favor of doing it. I am not going to argue for this; it is an assumption of the example. What I am going to argue for is that none of the other 'premises' is a favorer. They play other roles; they are relevant, but not in the favoring way. Take (2). I want to say that the fact that my promise was not given under duress is not a second reason for doing the action, to be set alongside the first one. What is true here is that if my promise had been given under duress, I would have had no reason to keep it. What this means is that in the absence of (2), (1) would not have favored the action. In this sense, the presence of (2) *enables* (1) to favor (5). In my preferred terminology, (1) is a favorer, and (2) is an enabling condition or enabler.

Various people have suggested to me a rather different picture: that the favorer here is not that I promised, but rather that I freely promised—a combination of (1) and (2). I have no objection to this idea in principle; there will be many cases where a favorer is a complex of which no part is itself a favorer. The suggestion requires, then, that promising does not of itself favor acting, since we must be dealing now with a complex favorer which does not contain simpler favorers. (If promising itself favors, it is hard to think that freely promising also favors.) I would only object to all of this if it were premised on the idea that one can always put a favorer and an enabler together to make a more complex favorer. This does seem to me to be false; I say a little more about it later. The reason why I don't need to insist that (1) is an independent favorer is that the official purpose of my example at the moment is only to train people up in distinguishing favoring from other forms of relevance. Those who want to argue that the real favorer is really (1) + (2) are thereby showing that they don't need a lot of training.

Not but what it may be that their grasp on the notion of favoring could be improved. For I don't myself accept the idea that the real favorer is that I freely promised rather than that I promised, so that it is a mistake to think that promises only give a reason if they are freely made. I still hold that what favors my doing the action is that I engaged myself to do so. But it is hard to know how to tell whether this is correct or not. One clue is that those who recognize that their promise was deceitfully extracted from them often feel some compunction in not doing what they promised, even though they themselves recognize that in such circumstances their promise does not play its normal reason-giving role. I think their attitude would be different if what plays the reason-giving role were not that one promised but that one 'freely' promised (where to be free a promise must not be extracted by deceit). For on that hypothesis there would be no sign of a favorer in the case at all. Another example: that someone is asking you the time is a reason to tell them, a reason that would not exist if their purpose were to distract you so that their accomplice can steal your bag. I would not be very tempted to say that the reason is really that they are asking you the time for a genuine rather than a surreptitious purpose.

Now consider (3). That I am able to do an action is not often a reason in favor of doing it. There are unusual occasions, such as when I have been paralyzed for a while and the mere ability to flex my arm is a reason for me to do so (for a while). But this is not one of those, I am supposing. What then is the importance of (3)? Suppose we agree that (in some suitable sense) 'ought' implies 'can'. This tells us that (5*) cannot be true unless (3) is true. But we might also think that 'has a reason' implies 'can'—that one cannot have a reason to do an action that one is (in the relevant sense) incapable of doing. I have, perhaps, a reason to run as fast as I can but no reason to run faster than that. If so, then in the absence of (3), again (1) would give me no reason to act. What (3) does is to enable (1) to favor (5). It is another enabler, perhaps not quite of the same type as (2).

Are we sure that (3) is not a favorer? I think there is a conclusive reason for saying that it is not, which is that if it were, all favored actions would share one and the same favorer: that they are actions of which the agent is capable. But it is not the case that if an action is favored, we already know at least one of the reasons for doing it, namely that the agent is capable of doing it. The agent's capacity to act must therefore be playing some other role, and I suggest that the role that it is playing is that of a general enabler (unlike the role of (2), which we could think of as that of a specific enabler, one specific to the particular case, or at least to a limited class of cases).

Now consider (4). The presence of (4) does not enable (1) to favor (5). (1) would have favored (5), we may suppose, even if something else had more strongly favored not doing (5); that one promised can be some reason to act even if there is greater reason not to. What (4) does enable is the move from (1) to (5). In the absence of (4), that move should not be made. This is a different sort of enabling from what is done by either (2) or (3).

Are we sure that (4) is not a favorer? Again, there is a conclusive reason for saying that it is not. Judgments like (4) are verdictive; to assert (4) is to pass judgment on the balance of the reasons present in the case. If (4) was itself a further reason over and above those on which it passes judgment, we would be forced to reconsider the balance of reasons once we had asserted (4), in a way that would continue ad infinitum. Which is ridiculous. So (4) is not itself a favorer. We can add to this the sort of point I made about (3): that if (4) was a favorer, all actions that we have overall reason to do would have at least one common favorer, which I take to be intrinsically implausible. In saying this I don't mean to be appealing to any first-order theory, idiosyncratic or otherwise. What is implausible is that the structure of reasons alone should guarantee that all right actions share a common favorer, which it would if (4) were taken to be favoring rather then enabling.

So what we have in the present example is one favorer and three enablers, none of which is doing exactly what any of the others is doing. For a simpler example of a similar sort, consider Plato's suggestion in his *Crito* that agreements should be respected so long as they are just. The ordinary reason for respecting one's agreements is, I suppose, that one agreed to them. Plato's idea seems to be that this would be no reason if the agreement itself were unjust. But that the agreement is not unjust does not seem to be another reason for respecting it; that something is not unjust is not ordinarily a reason for doing it, and it does not seem to be one in this case either.

In addition to favoring and enabling as two different sorts of things that relevant considerations can do, there is a third role that a relevant consideration can play. To see what this might be, consider a rather different example:

1. She is in trouble and needs help.
2. I am the only other person around.
3. So I help her.

That she is in trouble and needs help is a consideration that favors my helping her. That I am the only other person around does not seem to be another reason, on top of the first one. It is not as if, even if she were not in trouble, that I am the only other person around would still favor my helping her. The reverse, however, is true; even if there were others around, I would still have a reason to help her, a reason given by the trouble she is in. But my being the only other person around does make a rational difference, all the same. I suggest that what it does is to intensify the reason given me by her need for help. Instead of two reasons, what we have here is one reason and an intensifier. Presumably there is the opposite of an intensifier, an attenuator. An example might be this:

1. She is in trouble and needs help.
2. It is all her own fault, and she got in this situation through trying to spite someone else.
3. But still I help her.

One might think that there is reason to help her even though it is all her own fault but less reason than there would otherwise be.

So far, then, we have identified three sorts of role that a relevant consideration can play: a relevant consideration can be a favorer/disfavorer, it can be an enabler/disabler for another favorer/disfavorer, and it can intensify/attenuate the favoring/disfavoring done by something else. All such considerations are relevant, but there is more than one way of being relevant.

These distinctions are important. Here I mention just two ways in which they matter. Consider again the third attempt to characterize reasons in terms of oughts. This was that a reason for action is a consideration in whose absence the relevant action would be less obligatory, or even not obligatory at all. We can now see a much stronger argument against this suggestion. This is that enablers are not reasons, but they are considerations in whose absence the relevant action would not be rendered even partly obligatory. Further, intensifiers are not reasons, but they are considerations in whose absence the action would be less obligatory than otherwise. And here we have an instance of the second, and more general, way in which our distinctions matter. They show that in the attempt to understand what reasons do, subjunctive conditionals are blunt tools. Every time we see an attempted explication that centers on a subjunctive conditional, we should be wary.

4. Some strategic considerations

It is worth confessing that the picture I am offering deprives us of two considerable advantages. If we had been able to understand contributory reasons in terms of some relation to the overall ought, we would have been handed on a plate answers to two important questions:

1. What makes the notion of a reason normative?
2. What makes the notion of a reason deontic?

We take it that the notion of an ought is both normative and deontic. It is deontic by definition, more or less. The normative realm is divided into two halves: the evaluative and the deontic. The former is concerned with what is good and bad, the latter with what is right or wrong, with what one ought to do, with duty and obligation and so on. The idea is that one can sense a sort of family resemblance between the different deontic concepts, even if one cannot do much to explicate that resemblance. Now which side of the divide would the notion of a reason fall on? Traditionally, it is shown to be both deontic and normative because of its definability in terms of an overall ought.

However, we have now decided that we cannot define a reason in that way, and I think we have also seen the possibility of non-deontic reasons. For enticing reasons, if indeed there are any such things, do not seem to be concerned with what we ought to do; they are more concerned with what it would be pleasant to do, without any suggestion that somehow one *ought* to take the most pleasant course (at least, not in any sense that is incompatible with one's being permitted not to). If so, these reasons don't take us to oughts, and it looks as if we are going to have to think of them as lying on the evaluative side of the evaluative/deontic distinction. They are more to do with what is best than with what one ought to do. This leaves us trying to say in what sense they are normative. But that issue also now arises for the non-enticing reasons, the peremptory ones, once we have accepted that they cannot be shown to be normative by simple appeal to the sort of definition we have rejected. If we want still to think of the notion of a reason as normative (or even as *the* basic normative notion, as I will be urging later), we will have to think of it not as extrinsically normative (i.e. as normative in virtue of some relation it bears to an intrinsically normative ought) but as intrinsically normative. We will, that is, have to appeal directly to the notion of favoring and maintain that it is itself normative, normative in its own nature. Perhaps this can be done, but there is a struggle ahead. We may find ourselves saddled with two styles of favoring: the more deontic style that is appropriate for the peremptory and the more evaluative style that is suited to enticers.

5. Two basic notions?

We have decided that we can neither understand the contributory in terms of some one relation to the overall nor do without the contributory altogether. This leaves us with a further strategic choice. One option is to take it that there are two basic notions, that of a contributory reason and that of an overall ought, neither of these being definable in terms of the other. Our other main option is to reverse our original direction and to try to define the overall in terms of some relation to the contributory. Of course to do this we will have to show how to define *all* overall notions in contributory terms, not just that of the overall ought; we will have to pull the same trick for the notions of goodness and rightness, which may not be so easy. Nonetheless the general program of reducing overall concepts to contributory ones is extremely attractive, for reasons that I now turn to investigate.

The matter can be brought out by considering the difficulties that Ross gets into when he tries to relate what he calls prima facie duty to what he calls duty proper. First, he says that 'the phrase "prima facie duty" must be apologized for, since it suggests that what we are speaking of is a certain kind of duty, whereas it is in fact not a duty, but something related in a special way to duty. Strictly speaking, we want not a phrase in which duty is qualified by an adjective, but a separate noun' (1930: 20). Second, he says that prima facie duty 'may be called a parti-resultant attribute, i.e. one which belongs to an act in virtue of some one component in its nature. *Being* one's duty is a toti-resultant attribute, one which belongs to an act in virtue of its whole nature and of nothing less than this' (1930: 28). Each of these claims causes problems.

The first one is awkward because by denying that prima facie duty is duty in any sense, Ross makes it impossible for himself to make sense of the idea that duty proper is in some sense the product of various normative pushes or forces coming up from below—from the various features that stand as reasons. Ross effectively maintains that there is nothing like duty at the contributory level, and so leaves nothing there that we can think of as contributing to duty. But this is to sever what he has to say about duty from its proper ground. To put the matter another way: we have to find some way of understanding right-making features so that the 'right' in 'right-making' is the rightness of duty proper, and Ross has prevented himself from doing that.

The second one is awkward because it reinforces the divide between duty proper and the things that contribute to it. If the ground for duty proper is really every feature of the relevant action, and the ground for prima facie duty is some particular feature or other, we have deprived the relevant right-making features (which occur at the contributory level) of the ability to be what make the action right. It is impossible to conceive how they can be what make the action right because we have been explicitly told that they play no special role in the construction of duty proper—no role, that is, that is not played by every feature of the action whatever.

It may be that there is some other resolution of these difficulties, but by far the easiest is to work with a contributory ought, which is a matter of degree. I think of this contributory ought as a monadic feature of an action which is consequent on, or resultant from, some other feature—the 'ought-making' feature, whatever it is. So oughts of this sort are not relations. But for them to be present there must be a certain relation between the ought-making feature and the action. One might suppose that this relation must be the favoring relation. Things are a little delicate here. I am still inclined to say that we are dealing with more than one normative relation. The monadic ought is reached by detaching from the ought-making relation. The train of thought here is 'Feature *F* ought-makes action *A*; Feature *F* is in place; so one ought (so far as that goes) to do action *A*'. This expresses the idea that the relevant relation is not favoring, but ought-making (or right-making, if you like—so long as 'right' does not mean only morally right). So we can stick to our intuition that favoring is a relation between a feature and an action, and ought-making is a making-the-case relation that holds between a feature and the (contributory) rightness/oughtness of an action.

6. Fitting and most fitting

Suppose, then, that we pursue this strategy. We are going to understand the overall in terms of the contributory. For this, we need a sound conception of what happens at the contributory level and a way of understanding the overall as some function of that. I want to suggest briefly that classical intuitionism is well placed to offer what is needed here, and I will end by trying to show that some other more recent positions are in much worse shape. The intuitionists tended to understand reasons and oughts in terms of what is fitting. The action which overall one ought to do, which one has most reason to do, is that action which best fits (or is most fitting to) the situation in which one finds oneself. An action that one has at least some reason to do is an action that fits the situation in some respects but not necessarily in others. It is this notion of being fitting in a certain respect, of partial fittingness, that is the crucial one here. If this notion makes as much sense as it seems to, intuitionism has the right strategic shape to capture the notion of a reason and to explain the overall ought in its terms. Can others claim as much?

7. Humean realism

Michael Smith (1994: 151 ff.) understands rightness as the property an action has of being such that one's most rational self would advise one to do it. Now if we converted this directly to yield an account of reasons, we would get something like this: for there to be a reason for me to φ is for my most rational self to advise me to do it, so far as that goes. But this is clearly wrong, for reasons that should now be familiar. The notion of advice is an overall notion. There is no such thing as partial or contributory advice. One cannot say 'To some extent (or in some respect) I advise you to do this, but overall I advise you not to do it.' So if Smith were restricted to the terms in which his official account is presented, he would be stuck at the outset. But there is a way of understanding advice in terms of desirability; it is not as if the actual act of giving and receiving advice is especially important here. We could try to re-express Smith's position thus: for an action to have the property of rightness is for it to be such that one's most rational self would judge it desirable that one do it. And now things are looking more promising, for there does seem to be some prospect of finding a suitable notion of what is desirable in a certain respect, but not overall.

If there is such a notion, we can use it in the following analysis of a reason: for there to be a reason for me to φ is for my most rational self to find it desirable in a certain respect that I φ. So far, then, things are going well for Smith. But what exactly is this notion of desiring or finding desirable in a respect? I know two ways of understanding this notion, and I do not think that either will work. The first is to construe desiring in a respect in terms of valuing that respect. The idea here is that I value honesty, integrity, kindness, and thoughtfulness. The action I propose to do will be dishonest and, to that extent, lacking in integrity, but it will be kind and thoughtful. I have reasons to do it and reasons not to do it. My most rational self, that is, desires honesty and integrity and kindness and thoughtfulness, and those independent desires for features are construed as partial desires for any action in which the features desired are present.

This conversion of the valuing of features one by one into a partial valuing— and hence desiring—of complexes in which they occur will not work, because of the organicity (or holism) of value. It is generally agreed that the value of a complex whole is not to be identified with the sum of the independent values of its parts. If that is so, we cannot move automatically from an independent evaluation of the parts to any judgment of how valuable/desirable they are in the whole. But our first way of making sense, on Smith's behalf, of a notion of desiring in one respect and not in another involved exactly that move. It involved the identification of desiring a part wholly and desiring a whole partly, and this is flatly at odds with the organicity of value (once we understand value as desirability).

There is however another way of working. To desire a whole partly might be to desire the whole more with the part than without it. There is a subjunctive conditional operating here: I desire *O* partially for being *F* iff I desire it as it is more than I would if it were not *F*. This subjunctive conditional should remind us of one of the failed definitions of what a contributory reason does. And I suggest that the problems we had with that definition are repeated here. The crucial point is that the following things are compatible:

1. Part of the value of the whole derives from the presence of feature *F*.
2. If it were not *F*, the whole would be even more valuable than it currently is.

The way to show these two compatible is to find a case where, if the whole had not been *F*, it would have been *G*—and being *G* is even more valuable than being *F*. In such a case, we can say that the whole is the better for the presence of *F*, but we had better not mean by this that it would be worse without *F*. Now let us see if such a case can be found. The simplest case of that sort is one where being not-*F* is even more valuable than being *F*. This sort of win-win situation does not seem unimaginable to me, and I have already suggested some examples. I might praise you for doing something nice for a friend and praise you even more fervently were you to do it for someone who is not a friend. But perhaps this suggestion appears fanciful. The first approach I mooted involves the thought that if the whole had not been *F*, it would (as things stand) have been *G*. Let us suppose that had Mary been at the party, her presence would have been one of the respects in which the party was enjoyable. But as things stood, her absence enabled a more intimate gathering that was even better than the party would have been had she been there. Now is this a relevant example? If it is, it is easily repeatable and will defeat any attempt to understand partial desirability in terms of an overall ranking of alternatives.

There seems to be only one effective objection to such examples, which is that they involve appeal to the wrong subjunctive conditional. Instead of appealing to how things would have been if they had not been *F*, it may be said, we should start from how they are, with feature *F* present, and create a contrast with *that very same situation minus F*. So in the case of the party with Mary, we should extract Mary from that party and then ask about the value of the resulting object, the actual party minus Mary. The greater value of the other party, the one we actually had, is irrelevant.

I do not think that this maneuver can possibly be got to work across the board; and it has to work across the board if it is to be the basis of a sound general understanding of 'desirability in a certain respect'. The idea had been that we are to rank alternatives, and alternatives have to be ways in which things might have gone. Now there are certainly two ways things might have gone, to pursue the party and Mary a little further. There was the larger party with Mary, and the smaller, more intimate one without her. What is not a way things might have gone is the ebullient party without Mary. Look at another example. Suppose that my wife and I hire a car and drive across the country to the West Coast, spend a day there, and then drive back. (I wrote this on the East Coast of New Zealand.) Now I want to assess the value of having a car to make the trip in. Do I compare the value of the trip with a car and without a car, leaving it somehow unspecified how we are to get from East to West Coast and back again? No, I compare doing it by car with doing it by bus, let us say—or by bicycle, perhaps. Do I compare doing it by car with the weighted average of doing it in the various alternative ways, or with doing it in no particular way, but in some way or other (shades of Berkeley on abstraction here)? No, again.

There really only seems to be one coherent comparison. And the same applies to Mary and the party; we need whole alternatives to compare for value, and the Mary party without Mary is no such thing. Or rather, if it is anything at all, it is the intimate party, not a less well-attended ebullient one.

Perhaps we could cope with this by supposing that context, rather than logic, should determine the appropriate subjunctive conditional. This is of course a wise sort of thing to say in general; the problem is how to apply it to the Mary case so as to get the right answer. The right answer is that Mary would have contributed to the value of the ebullient party but that 'it' would have been even better without her. So what might the 'it' be here? To fill out the context a little: the three of us who made up the intimate party would, with Mary, have had an ebullient rather than an intimate evening. We want to find something in between the incomplete ebullient party—that party but Maryless, as it were—which seems to be incapable of existing, and the intimate party, which could exist but gives us the wrong answer (that Mary did not contribute to the ebullient party). And I don't think that there is anything intermediate to be found here. So the tactic of allowing the subjunctive conditional to vary according to context does not seem to be even applicable to the present case.

All this seems to me to show that as things stand Smith is devoid of any suitable notion of 'desirability in a respect'. And if this is true, it is at best moot whether his general approach is capable of capturing the notion of a contributory reason. If it is not, the probable diagnosis is that it was constructed with only the overall in mind, in a way that turns out not to be as flexible as it needs to be if it is to cover all the normative ground.

8. Expressivism

For an expressivist attempt to capture what it is to be a reason or, perhaps better, what it is to take something to be a reason, we need to look at Allan Gibbard's *Wise Choices, Apt Feelings* (1990: 160–6). To see the problem from Gibbard's point of view, we need to ask what we might expect an expressivist to say about the notion of a reason. An initial suggestion might go something like this:

> To say that R is a reason for S to ϕ in circumstances C is to express acceptance of a system of norms that directs S to ϕ in C.

The trouble with an account of this sort is that it does not address the notion of a contributory reason. We want to know what it is to say that R is some reason for S to ϕ in C, and what we are told is surely located more at the notion of overall reason. After all, I might say that R is a reason for S to ϕ in C while actually adhering to a system of norms which forbids S to ϕ in C. What is required, then, is to find some other term than 'directs'. What then does Gibbard in fact offer? He writes: 'To say that R is some reason for S to ϕ in C' is to express acceptance of a system of norms that direct us to award some weight to R in deciding whether to ϕ in C' (1990: 163). Note that our initial suggestion supposed that the norms I sign up to in saying that there is a reason for S to ϕ in C are norms that require (or recommend) that S should be doing the ϕ-ing in C (or the deciding whether to ϕ in C). On Gibbard's account, by contrast, they require *me* to be doing something, not S. But that is by the by. The real weakness is that the account makes explicit use of some appropriate conception of weight—of normative weight, as one might put it—and that was pretty well exactly the thing we were trying to understand. Further, we should note the way in which the account is entirely in terms of 'awarding weight to R in *deciding* whether to ϕ in C'. But to award weight to R in one's decision is not the same as taking R to favor ϕ-ing in C. I might think, for instance, that I should always consider the question whether R if I am deciding whether to ϕ in C, but suppose nonetheless that on many occasions the question whether R or not will be in fact irrelevant to how I ought to act. This would happen if R was very commonly relevant, so that it is a consideration one ought always to bear in mind, even though sometimes its relevance is defused by other considerations. If, by contrast, awarding weight to R is another way of saying 'take R to count in favor or against' we are left grasping for an expressivist account of *these* notions, which were surely the ones the analysis was supposed to be grappling with in the first place.

We might therefore try the following slightly different version:

> To say that R is a reason for S to ϕ in C is to express acceptance of a system of norms that would lead one to approve of S's ϕ-ing, at least to some extent, in respect of R.[7]

The problem now is that, though one thinks there is indeed some reason for S to ϕ in C, it might well be that one also thinks that there is conclusive or overall reason for S not to ϕ in C at all. The difficulty is to make sense of the idea that one might approve of S's ϕ-ing to some extent while being entirely against it. But isn't there such a phenomenon as approving of an action in one respect and not in another? Let us say that the action is that of my son's buying a car

---

[7] Note that this suggestion could be turned into a non-Gibbardian one by dropping the explicit reference to the system of norms. This would give us:

To say that R is a reason for S to ϕ in C is to express approval of S's ϕ-ing, at least to some extent.

This version is more amenable to the general thrust of expressivism; it is something that Simon Blackburn, for instance, might espouse. But the criticism offered in the text applies to this simpler suggestion as well (or badly) as it does to the Gibbardian one in the text.

(a 1971 Citroën DS). The elegance of the car is some reason to buy it, I think, and its unreliability is some reason not to buy it; the unreliability wins, and there is overall reason not to buy it. One way to understand what is going on here is to say that I approve overall of the elegance (my approval of the elegance is unmixed, as it were) and disapprove overall of the unreliability. These will be two overall approvings, and we are going to try to construct a notion of contributory or partial approving of buying the car out of them. This should remind us of the previous discussion of Smith. The difficulty for Smith in this connection arose because of the organicity of value, and I suggest that the same problem arises now. Wholesale approvals of parts considered apart cannot be converted directly into focused approval of those same parts when they are parts of wholes, or of wholes in virtue of the presence of those parts, because a feature need not have the same value in every whole in which it appears.[8]

One can say 'I partly like him and partly dislike him; I like his wit and charm but I dislike his manipulativeness.' This is overall liking and overall disliking, directed at a part. Whether overall one likes him or not will be determined by the balance between these partial likings (likings of parts) in an organic way. What the expressivist needs here is a notion of overall liking whose object is the whole but which is somehow also focused on the part. I like *him* for his wit and charm; I dislike *him* for his manipulations. But so far we have not seen how to do this.

The second approach we might try on behalf of the expressivist tries to piggy-back on an expressivist conception of an overall 'ought'-judgment. We are, for present purposes, allowing that there is nothing wrong with the standard expressivist approach on *this* topic:

> To say that S ought overall to φ in C is to express acceptance of a system of norms that would require S to φ in C.

So we might try something like the following, for the contributory:

> To say that R is some reason for S to φ in C is to say that, if it had not been the case that R, S's φ-ing in C would have been less right than it is.

But this can hardly succeed, for reasons most of which we have seen too often before. First, our expressivist has not yet established a good sense for the notion of more and less right. We just have the notion of requiring that appears in the account of overall oughts, and we have not been shown any expressivist way of taking requiring to come in degrees of stringency. (Note that there is a difference between degrees of acceptance of a norm and degrees of stringency

---

[8] This is a tendentious version of organicity. I defend it in Dancy 2003.

of the norm accepted.) Second, the subjunctive conditional we are now considering is anyway incorrect as an analysis of the contributory. For this point, we can again appeal to the discussion of Smith; this sort of appeal to subjunctive conditionals does not work, because it can be the case both that this feature counts in favor of the action and that the action would have been better (more right) without it.[9]

Some will feel that this is all mere skirmishing. Suppose, then, that we try to capitalize on the approach to pro tanto or ceteris paribus preference considered earlier. What we are looking for, again, is a notion of approval of an act in virtue of the presence of some feature *F*, to take this as a model for taking the presence of *F* as a reason for doing the action. We could try to do this in terms of approving of the act with that feature more than one approves of 'the same' act without it. But we have already seen all sorts of difficulties with this approach. And what if the presence of a certain reason against doing the action was required for the presence or force of other stronger reasons in favor of it? For a formal example of this, what if I promise that even if there is some significant reason against doing this, I will still do it?

My conclusion is that the expressivists have failed to offer any effective account of a contributory reason and that they do not seem to have the resources to do better.

References

BROOME, J. (2004). 'Reasons.' In Wallace et al. (2004).

DANCY, J. (2003). 'Are There Organic Unities?' *Ethics*, 113: 629–50.

—— (2004*a*). 'Enticing Reasons.' In Wallace et al. (2004).

—— (2004*b*). *Ethics without Principles.* Oxford: Clarendon Press.

GIBBARD, A. (1990). *Wise Choices, Apt Feelings.* Cambridge, Mass.: Harvard University Press.

HAMPTON, J. E. (1998). *The Authority of Reason.* Cambridge: Cambridge University Press.

ROSS, W. D. (1930). *The Right and the Good.* Oxford: Clarendon Press.

SMITH, M. (1994). *The Moral Problem.* Oxford: Blackwell.

STRATTON-LAKE, P. J. (2000). *Kant, Duty and Moral Worth.* London: Routledge.

WALLACE, R. J., PETTIT, P., SCHEFFLER, S., AND SMITH, M., eds. (2004). *Reason and Value: Themes from the Moral Philosophy of Joseph Raz.* Oxford: Clarendon Press.

---

[9] Further, this analysis says of a reason something that is just as much true of an enabling condition that is not a reason.

3

Evaluations of Rationality

Sigrún Svavarsdóttir

I

One hundred years ago, G. E. Moore declared, 'how "good" is to be defined, is the most fundamental question in all Ethics'[1] and, then, proceeded to argue that 'good' is indefinable. The rest is history: the history of twentieth-century metaethics. That history is often recounted as a series of responses to Moore's open question argument for the indefinability conclusion and the further conclusion that goodness is a non-natural property accessible through rational intuition. New developments in the philosophy of language, metaphysics, epistemology, and the philosophy of mind have opened up new ways of diagnosing the fault in Moore's argument and new ways of understanding the semantics, metaphysics, and epistemology of ethical discourse. I will not recount the details of that history here.

Philosophical reflections on the nature and grounds of ethical judgment did not start with Moore. However, he set them on a new footing by turning attention to the analysis of ethical concepts. This marked the 'analytic turn' within moral philosophy and the advent of metaethics as a distinct philosophical enterprise. Nevertheless, the history of twentieth-century metaethics cannot be fully told as a series of responses to Moore. That leaves out an important part of the ongoing discussion about the nature and grounds of moral judgment: a

This is a revision of 'Evaluations of Rationality' as printed in the *Southern Journal of Philosophy, Spindel Supplement*, 41 (2003): 121–36. Aside from a new introduction, the changes are very minor. The original version was written while I was a Fellow in residence at the National Humanities Center. I gratefully acknowledge the Center's support. Lectures based on this article were given at the Spindel Conference 2002, at a conference titled 'Mikjálsmessa' held at the University of Iceland in March 2003, and at North Carolina State University, March 2003. A version of the article was also presented to the Triangle Ethics Group, North Carolina. I thank everyone who participated in the discussion at these four forums. Special thanks are due to Russ Shafer-Landau for fair and challenging comments presented at the Spindel Conference and published in the conference proceedings. Finally, I would like to thank Justin D'Arms for comments on the paper and Jenefer Robinson for a helpful discussion.

[1] G. E. Moore, *Principia Ethica* (Buffalo, NY: Prometheus Books, 1988), 5.

part that pertains to the nature of reasons for action, practical rationality, and the relation between morality and rationality. Many have thought that we can only understand the normativity of moral judgments, if we attend to such matters. This paper is a small contribution to this part of metaethics. I will not discuss the thorny notion of a reason for action nor the relation between morality and rationality. Instead, I focus attention on the evaluation of agents as more or less rational. How is it best to construe this type of evaluation?

I will not come to a final conclusion about this matter, although I offer a first approximation of a theory of rationality. This is a neo-Humean theory, since it relativizes evaluations of rationality to the ends or attitudes of the agent evaluated. Neo-Humeans about rationality often do little to defend their view. They take themselves to be offering a minimalist theory—minimalist in the sense that whatever they have to say about the nature of rationality has to be included in their opponents' theory of rationality. The neo-Humeans, then, challenge the anti-Humeans to defend the part of their theory that goes beyond its neo-Humean component, which is considered a common ground and, hence, beyond controversy. This will not be my strategy. Below, I motivate the idea that all evaluations of rationality are relativized to the agent's ends or attitudes as neo-Humeans maintain. Indeed, I argue that this is true for evaluations of both theoretical and practical rationality. This distinction should, I suggest, be drawn in terms of the types of goals that need to be taken into account in evaluations of rationality. I end the paper by discussing what shape a defense of my and other neo-Humean accounts of rationality has to take. In this context, I argue that the sort of relativity proposed here has no obvious metaphysical implications and should not be confused with the type of mind-dependence that has figured into metaphysical discussions of objectivity. I also broach issues concerning the connection between rationality and the pursuit of (or respect for) values as well as issues concerning the justificatory or critical force of verdicts of rationality.

II

It seems uncontroversial that only RATIONAL as opposed to arational beings are subject to evaluation in terms of rationality or irrationality. (In order to avoid confusion, I will use small capitals when using 'rational' to contrast with 'arational'.) Now, a natural thought is that *rationality is the excellence of a being qua RATIONAL being.* This will be my guiding idea. Notice that this approach makes rationality out to be a *virtue.* Of course, no one might instantiate this virtue perfectly. People are rational to a greater or lesser extent. At some point they are not merely lacking in rationality but are downright irrational. Moreover, there is both the issue of how rational an individual is overall and also the issue of the extent to which he displays rationality in having a specific belief or intention.[2] It is the latter type of evaluation that mostly interests me here.

Perhaps we can make some headway in thinking about rationality as a form of evaluation by getting clear on what it is to be a RATIONAL being. Minimally, it consists in having well-developed cognitive capacities—capacities for mental representation and reasoning. I will not attempt here to specify fully what these capacities must be like in order for their possessors to count as RATIONAL beings. Suffice it to say that the representational capacity must go beyond a mere disposition to register features of the environment in the way that a shadow of a tree may indicate the time of day. The representations must be able to feed into thought processes that amount to sound reasoning—sequences of mental states whose representational contents stand in relations such as *implies, is consistent with, explains, is a generalization of, is an instance of,* etc. There must also be room for failure: the representation may be inaccurate and the reasoning faulty.

These normative properties of representations and of reasoning invite the idea that the excellence of a being qua RATIONAL being consists in representing and reasoning well or correctly. But this does not give us a plausible conception of rationality, not even theoretical rationality. It is possible to represent something incorrectly without being guilty of irrationality. This might happen when the subject is so unfortunately situated in the world that he receives a misleading input into his cognitive system and is not in a position to discover the error however well he uses his cognitive capacities. A representation may also be poor though correct. This does not detract from the rationality of the cognizer if it is due to the poverty of the input available or the limits of his cognitive powers. Indeed, it is rational to leave out details, when they are irrelevant or distracting. Perhaps less obviously, it is possible to be rational even if one's reasoning does not quite measure up to the standards of inductive and deductive reasoning. As Gilbert Harman has noted, if it takes a genius to recognize that a triad of propositions imply a fourth proposition, the average Joe is not irrational in failing to draw the inference.[3]

---

[2] We also evaluate actions, intentions, beliefs, and possibly some other intentional states as rational or irrational. These evaluations, I submit, are best understood as derivative evaluations. A rational action or attitude is an action or an attitude that an agent would undertake or have if he were rational.

[3] Gilbert Harman, *Reasoning, Meaning and Mind* (Oxford: Oxford University Press, 1999), 18. It seems odd, however, to say that he is rational in failing to draw the inference. The verdict that someone is not irrational in doing something is not the same as the verdict that he is rational in doing it. The former verdict absolves the person from a certain type of criticism rather than commends him. The latter verdict commends him. The difference between these verdicts is illuminated by how the overall assessment of the agent's rationality is affected by his failing to draw the inference in question. Failing to draw the inference does not detract from the agent's overall rationality, although it does not bolster his rationality either.

These observations suggest that making an error and being irrational are not quite the same thing, even in the theoretical arena. Rationality is less about being free from error than about not making mistakes that could be avoided by exercising one's cognitive capacities well; thus, evaluations of rationality must be sensitive to the limits of the cognitive powers of the subject evaluated, as well as to any other feature of the subject, or his circumstances, that may affect his ability to exercise these cognitive powers to the fullest. (From now on, I will refer to these as his epistemic limits.) This leads to the suggestion that rationality—the excellence of a being qua RATIONAL being—consists in using one's cognitive capacities as well as possible given one's epistemic limitations.[4]

III

Something still seems amiss. It is irrational to clutter one's mind and waste one's time by teasing out all the trivial and uninteresting implications of one's beliefs or to weed out any inconsistency between them.[5] It seems also irrational to go off endlessly on tangents and explore at length insignificant side issues rather than continue a main line of enquiry, no matter how exquisitely one handles the tidbits. In these cases, one need not be making avoidable errors in representation or reasoning. One might, indeed, be using one's cognitive capacities superbly, at least in the sense that the reasoning is sound and the representation is both subtle and correct. So why do I fall short qua RATIONAL being if I spend my days teasing out trivial implications of my beliefs? A first stab at an answer focuses on my limitations: I have a finite mind and a finite amount of time. Spending them in this way diminishes my opportunity to grapple with matters more important than trivial implications of my beliefs. This raises the question of whether the excellence of a being qua RATIONAL being is in part constituted by not letting an enquiry into less important matters detract from one's enquiry into more important ones. If so, we could even save the suggestion that rationality—the excellence of a being qua RATIONAL being—consists in using one's cognitive capacities as well as possible given one's epistemic limitations. We would only have to add that it is possible to use one's cognitive capacities poorly, not only by falling into avoidable error, but also by using them on one subject matter at the cost of another, more important, subject matter.

I do not dispute that some subject matters are more important than others and that we may be using our cognitive capacities poorly if we concentrate on the less important at the expense of the more important subject matter. But it

---

[4] Of course, the notion of an agent's epistemic limits needs to be clarified. I leave that for the future. It also needs to be rendered more precisely how the agent's epistemic limits affect evaluations of his rationality.

[5] This observation is borrowed from Gilbert Harman. See his *Reasoning, Meaning and Mind*, 18–19.

does not seem as though this in itself amounts to irrationality. It seems more important to find the cure for cancer than design household equipment. Moreover, it seems a shame if a genius decides to use his formidable mental powers on designing household equipment rather than on finding the cure for cancer. Perhaps, it is also a moral failing. Certainly, it is not the best use to which the genius can put his cognitive capacities. But this hardly suffices for making the genius irrational. Imagine encountering the genius in his lab excitedly explaining to you the newest intricate design of the perfect bottle opener. You think of what he could have accomplished as a medical researcher. Alas, he was never able to develop interest in anything but the complex design of silly household equipment. Do you accuse him of irrationality for designing bottle openers rather than developing new drugs? That does not seem like the appropriate kind of criticism in this case.

Now imagine that the genius starts obsessively to work out all the implications of his beliefs. He gets to the point of tediously listing all the disjunctions that follow from his belief that snow is white, an endless task indeed. There are half-finished designs waiting on his drawing table, finished designs that need to be forwarded to the production department, unpaid bills, missed appointments. He neglects his friends, loses sleep, and forgets to eat. Calling him irrational is at best an understatement. This is a descent into madness. But consider a slightly milder case of this disorder: the genius has a tendency to break off his work on his intricate designs by starting to work out the implications of his various beliefs, even if they do not bear on what he is doing and even if they are of no interest to him beyond being implications of what he already believes. These obsessive reflections seriously hold up his projects from time to time, although they never take over completely. Alternatively, imagine that the genius has a tendency to go off on tangents. Frequently, he explores thoroughly possible addenda to the device he is designing, though it should be clear to him from the start that they have no good use or do not fit with the overall design of the object. These become little side projects that are abandoned as fruitless after holding up the main project for hours on end. These are, I submit, clear cases of irrationality. Being a genius, the designer's reasoning and representations are beyond reproach even when he goes off on tangents or obsessively works out all the implications of his beliefs. So, what is his shortcoming qua RATIONAL being?

IV

The key to understanding this form of irrationality is to appreciate that it is a shortcoming of a being that uses its cognitive capacities purposefully, that is, of an agent. Imagine a machine that at least closely simulates our powers of representation and reasoning. Like us, it can fall into error, and we may even imagine that it can in some cases detect and correct its mistakes much like we do. Say that this machine replaces fieldworkers who gather and analyze data about various features of the physical environment in remote regions of the world. Now, compare this machine to a fieldworker whom the machine has replaced. The representation and reasoning they use may be very similar. We may even assume that the machine and the fieldworker can be misled in a similar way by an input from the environment, but they both have the ability to catch the mistake and correct it. When the machine fails to correct the mistake, it is malfunctioning, whereas the fieldworker is being sloppy, dense, or irrational. Also, imagine that some input triggers the machine to spend an inordinate amount of time recording data of little interest given the main line of research. It goes off on a tangent so to speak. If a similar thing happens to the fieldworker, we deem her irrational. But such an evaluation does not apply to the machine. It is neither rational, when it functions well, nor irrational, when it functions badly.

The fieldworker's activity of representation and reasoning is embedded in a web of propositional attitudes. She takes various cognitive and conative attitudes towards the representations that she computes. She believes some of them, doubts others, presupposes some for the sake of argument, entertains some as explanations or perhaps as mere theoretical possibilities. She would like to know whether or why some of them are true. In the absence of such propositional attitudes that motivate the next step in the research, we do not have an agent trying to figure out what is the case or how to understand something.[6] I do not know how to render explicit the ascription-conditions for propositional attitudes, but clearly the machine does not meet them. The machine is merely a sophisticated tool used in research. If the machine continues to record and analyze data long after it has been abandoned as a research tool, its operations are not involved in any research. There is no agent trying to figure out one thing or another, even if the machine keeps cranking out representations of its environment.

When engaging in an enquiry, however theoretical it may be, we are exercising our agency. We are not simply crunching out representations or drawing inferences willy-nilly but, rather, engaging in purposeful activity. We are attempting to figure out one thing or another: whether it is the case or how to understand it. Assessments of our cognitive goals aside, there is room for two types of shortcomings in the use of our cognitive capacities for the purposes of

---

[6] This is not to deny that many of the psychological processes needed to sustain an enquiry are subconscious and even sub-personal. Some of them might not even involve full-fledged intentional states.

enquiry: first, mistakes in representation or reasoning and, second, use of our cognitive capacities that does not suit our cognitive purposes. When the genius interrupts his line of enquiry by teasing out the trivial implications of his beliefs or by going off on tangents, he is falling short in the second way. He is using his cognitive capacities in ways that seriously interfere with the pursuit of his cognitive goal. Such a shortcoming need not be a case of irrationality. Just as mistakes in representation and reasoning are not failures of rationality unless they are avoidable given the epistemic position of the agent, this second type of shortcoming is a failure of rationality only if it should be clear to the agent that his cognitive activity is not suitable to his cognitive goals. Since the genius is in a position to appreciate the futility of his little side projects, as well as how badly they sit with his main line of enquiry, he is guilty of irrationality, even if his representation and reasoning are flawless. His irrationality does not have anything to do with the importance of his cognitive goals. Rather, his shortcoming qua RATIONAL being pertains to his ineptitude in using his cognitive powers in ways that are suitable to his cognitive goals. Thus, evaluations of rationality are sensitive not only to the agent's epistemic position but also to his cognitive goals.

V

It may seem as though we have passed from a discussion of theoretical rationality to a discussion of practical rationality. It is common to draw the distinction between theoretical and practical rationality along the following lines: theoretical rationality is displayed in regulating beliefs, while practical rationality is displayed in regulating intentions, plans, or actions. It is a familiar idea that evaluations of practical rationality take into account the goals of the agent. It may seem dubious to suggest that evaluations of theoretical rationality are also sensitive to the agent's goals. One of the sources of theoretical irrationality is wishful thinking: the agent believes what he wants to be true rather than what the evidence available to him suggests is true. This might happen in the context of enquiry, when the enquirer (non-deliberately) gives a faulty assessment of the evidence due to a desire to have results that will lead, say, to a career advancement. Evaluations of theoretical rationality, it is tempting to conclude, are essentially about whether the agent forms epistemically well-grounded beliefs, so they should take into account the epistemic position of the agent and *not* his goals.

The genius's irrationality has nothing to do with forming beliefs for which he does not have sufficient evidence or for which he has sufficient evidence to reject. We can understand his irrationality only against the background of his specific cognitive goals, when by 'specific cognitive goals' I mean *goals of finding out whether something specific is the case or how it is to be understood*. In the genius's case, the relevant cognitive goal is to find a design for a device that makes it perform a specific function (sufficiently or maximally) well. The genius's irrationality has to do with how unsuitable his cognitive activity is to this cognitive goal. However, if we stipulate that his cognitive quirk does not, and he knows that it does not, risk the completion of his project, his job, his friendships, etc., it is hard to see this as a case of practical irrationality. True, he will not be as efficient as he could be in reaching his goals, but we can always stipulate that the delay is of no concern to him. Nevertheless, I would certainly deem the genius irrational if I observed him periodically interrupting his line of enquiry in the way envisioned. Spinning his cognitive wheels in a way that makes no sense, and he should know makes no sense, in light of the matter under investigation detracts from the enquirer's rationality. This, I submit, is better regarded as a defect in theoretical rather than practical rationality, although that requires that we broaden our conception of theoretical rationality.

In any case, it seems overly narrow to conceive of theoretical rationality as being exclusively displayed in forming epistemically well-grounded beliefs. Consider a scientist who makes, during the course of enquiry, a working assumption solely for the purpose of gathering more evidence for or against it. Even if the subjective probability of the proposition is only 50 per cent, the scientist may be displaying great *rationality in assuming it*. For, other things equal, it may be the most promising way of advancing her enquiry at this point. This may be true even if, given her other concerns, it is doubtful whether it is practically rational for her to proceed in this way. Say, she has a senior co-worker who has insisted on a different, less promising, way of proceeding and, predictably, will be irate at being outdone by her. Assume, moreover, that this co-worker is in a good position to damage her research career and is evil enough to be likely to do so out of spite, should she outsmart him in this way. Given this, there is a real issue of whether it is practically rational for her to go ahead and proceed in the way she thinks is most promising. However, this does not seem to be a reason to retract the judgment that she, qua enquirer, would be rational in making the working assumption. Other things being equal, it is an intelligent move in an investigation, and it should be regarded as enhancing her excellence qua RATIONAL enquirer. The way to think about this case, I propose, is that the scientist would be displaying at least theoretical rationality in making the working assumption, even if it is an open question whether she would be practically rational.

It may be objected that the rationality of an agent qua enquirer should not be construed as theoretical rationality, but rather as a restricted form of practical rationality. The agent is being practically rational insofar as his activities are considered in light of his cognitive goals only; all things considered, he may still be practically irrational. However, this way of construing rational-qua-enquirer does not work. Add to the above story that our heroine rationally believes that her co-worker is willing to ruin their research project rather than see the major credit for its success go to her. In that case, it is not obvious that our heroine is, judged against the background of (only) her cognitive goals, practically rational in making the assumption. Nevertheless, she is rational qua enquirer. Rationality-qua-enquirer is not displayed by doing whatever one rationally thinks is required to accomplish one's cognitive goals but, rather, by conducting one's enquiry in an intellectually resourceful and responsible manner. In figuring out whether something is the case or how to understand it, it is not only important to come to a sensible assessment of the evidence while forming beliefs. It is also crucial that the enquirer exercise good judgment in narrowing down his hypotheses, in selecting auxiliary hypotheses, in designing and running (empirical or thought) experiments, in constructing proofs, in designing strategies for gathering more data, and so on. By exercising good judgment in such endeavors, the enquirer is displaying rationality, and the rationality at stake seems to deserve the tag 'theoretical rationality', though I have little interest in quibbling about the use of that term. Of course, ultimately it may not matter how an agent came up with an interesting discovery. Even if he stumbled on it accidentally, relied on a wild guess, or prostituted himself, he is theoretically rational in accepting the resulting discovery if he can, retrospectively, build a good case for its acceptance. But this does not mean that there is no room for evaluations of theoretical rationality in the context of discovery. It only reminds us that sometimes it pays to proceed in a manner that does not demonstrate theoretical rationality.

Our conception of theoretical rationality should be broad enough to allow that it can be displayed in any type of cognitive activity rather than merely in forming beliefs. Moreover, the foregoing discussion suggests that assessments of theoretical rationality need to take into account what it is that the agent is trying to find out or understand, that is, they need to be sensitive to his cognitive goals as well as his epistemic position. An agent's theoretical rationality is reflected in the suitability of his cognitive activity to his cognitive goals as well as in the quality of his representation and reasoning (subject to the epistemic limit proviso).[7]

This way of conceiving of theoretical rationality may be thought to have the undesirable consequence that most of us suffer from a high degree of theoretical

---

[7] I add one more component to this conception of theoretical rationality in n. 12 below.

irrationality just because, during any normal day, we notice a multitude of things and draw all sorts of inferences based on the sounds and sights we take in. It seems odd to think that such cognitive activity, even if it is epistemically well grounded, undermines our theoretical rationality. But much of this activity appears not to be tailored to any cognitive goal and may, indeed, seem badly suited to our cognitive goals.[8] Thus, if evaluations of theoretical rationality took place against the background of the cognitive goals of the agent evaluated as suggested above, these routine cognitive activities would appear to undermine our theoretical rationality. They would, indeed, seem to be on a par with the genius's cognitive quirks with respect to how the subject's theoretical rationality is affected.

I doubt that much of our cognition serves absolutely no purpose. In routine activities like reading, conversing, or paying attention to our environment, there are usually cognitive goals at play: we are attempting to understand something or someone. It need not be an arduous attempt, made in a self-conscious manner. Often, it is only when understanding becomes a challenge that we resort to conscious strategic thinking and come to think of ourselves as trying to find something out. In some cases, we may even resist acknowledging that this is what we are up to. There is room for much self-deception and a lack of self-awareness in this area. Nevertheless, there is undoubtedly some cognition that does not serve any purpose ascribable to the subject. We are probably primed by evolution to notice and draw inferences from certain features of our environment, whether or not it serves any current purpose of ours. Training may have similar results. A house painter, for example, may be apt to notice the flaws in any painted surface and spontaneously draw inferences from her observations. Now, if such purposeless cognitive activity[9] interferes with the agent's cognitive pursuits, the agent's theoretical rationality is diminished much as the genius's theoretical rationality suffers due to his cognitive quirk. But my suggestion that evaluations of theoretical rationality are sensitive to the cognitive goals of the agent should not be construed to imply that any aimless cognitive activity manifests theoretical irrationality on the part of the agent. Such activity may be too insignificant in the agent's overall mental life to detract from his theoretical rationality, much as aimlessly drumming his fingers on the desk may be too insignificant in an agent's life to detract from his practical rationality.

This leaves the question of whether the quality of the representation and reasoning carried on in insignificant and aimless cognitive activity affects the evaluation of the agent's theoretical rationality. Is the painter irrational when

---

[8] Thanks are due to Robert Audi, Don Garrett, and Thomas E. Hill, Jr., for pressing this point.

[9] I have in mind cognitive activity that serves no purpose *ascribable to the agent*. It may still have some biological or psychological function.

she spontaneously forms a poorly grounded belief about the paint used on a wall while driving past it at high speed? Does she display rationality when she spontaneously forms a well-grounded belief at a slower speed? My sense is that the less we can see an individual as engaged in purposeful cognitive activity, the more his cognitive activity resembles that of the machine imagined in the last section and the less it is appropriate to think of that cognitive activity as reflecting on the subject's rationality.[10] Even evaluations of theoretical rationality should, I propose, be seen as applying primarily to agents engaged in purposeful cognitive activity. Theoretical rationality primarily pertains to how well we use our cognitive capacities in enquiry, when *enquiry* is construed broadly as any attempt at discovery or understanding. Using our cognitive capacities well in enquiry does not merely require that we reason and represent well but also that our representation and reasoning is suitable to the cognitive goals that set our line of enquiry.

VI

At this point, my guiding idea should be reformulated as follows: rationality is the excellence of an *agent* qua RATIONAL being, assuming that purposeful activity is the distinguishing mark of agency. I have suggested that theoretical rationality is excellence in the use of one's cognitive capacities for the purposes of enquiry. I now propose that practical rationality be regarded as excellence in the use of one's cognitive capacities for whatever purposes one has.[11] Such excellence consists partly in representing and reasoning as *well* as is feasible, given one's epistemic limitations. The quality of the representation and reasoning is judged by standards that are not agent-relative and have much to do with truth and truth-conduciveness. In the light of the foregoing discussion, I suggest that this excellence also requires that the cognitive activity be *suitable* to the purposes for which the agent wields his cognitive powers. The agent's purposes partly determine what is relevant to his reasoning as well as what successfully concludes it. They help to set the parameters of relevance and success by determining what is appropriate to think through and investigate, but the nature of the subject matter, of course, also affects what is relevant at any given stage of reasoning as well as what makes for a successful conclusion to the reasoning.

---

[10] That a belief is formed during, or even as the culmination of, purposeful cognitive activity should not be taken to imply that the belief is voluntary. We do not believe at will, even if the cognitive activity that led up to the belief was sustained by the desire to know or understand.

[11] I think of this as a first approximation of a defensible conception of practical rationality, but I will not go beyond this approximation here. See, however, n. 15 below.

There is one more component in the excellence under consideration: *appropriate responsiveness* to the output of the cognitive activity.[12] An agent has not displayed excellence in the *use* of his cognitive capacities *for* his purposes (that is, in their service), unless he has both used his cognitive capacities well in figuring out how to attain his ends and put the conclusion to use in advancing these ends.[13]

I am not proposing that practical rationality is a matter of maximally advancing one's ends as neo-Humeans are wont to characterize practical rationality. It need not be irrational to act in such a way as to undermine one's ends overall. For the agent may not be in a position to anticipate this outcome. Such an agent is unfortunate rather than irrational. He is not falling short qua RATIONAL being. However, my conception of practical rationality is very much in the spirit of Hume. First, practical rationality requires only the kind of reasoning familiar from the theoretical domain. There is no special type of reasoning—like submitting one's preference to the test of the categorical imperative—required for using one's cognitive capacities well in the pursuit of one's ends.[14] Second, assessments of an agent's practical rationality are relativized to his purposes such that it is at least conceivable that it would—to echo Hume—be perfectly rational for a scoundrel to engineer a major disaster for others in order to avoid a minor inconvenience to himself.[15]

[12] This is also a component in theoretical rationality. A theoretically rational agent uses his intermediate conclusions to advance his enquiry towards its ultimate cognitive goal and his final conclusion to advance, if feasible, his other cognitive goals (subject to the epistemic proviso). There are some complications, however. In section V, I gave an example in which it is theoretically rational for an agent to use her intermediate conclusion in ways that, other things being equal, would advance the enquiry, though they are not likely to do so in this agent's circumstances, due to factors extraneous to the enquiry.

[13] Given the last condition, 'true irrationality' in Christine Korsgaard's sense is possible on my conception of practical rationality. See Christine Korsgaard, 'Skepticism about Practical Reason', reprinted in her *Creating the Kingdom of Ends* (Cambridge: Cambridge University Press, 1996), 318–25. I believe this opens up a way to understanding the irrationality of the incontinent person as well as that of the seriously depressed, although I will not spell out the account here.

[14] When I speak of requirements of rationality, I am simply speaking of necessary conditions for counting as rational. I reject imperatival and legal models for understanding such talk. There is no mental faculty or more abstract normative authority—called reason or rationality—that dictates how to think, feel, or behave. I conceive of practical rationality as a virtue. In failing to use our cognitive capacities in the service of our ends, we fail to display this virtue rather than violate a command or a law, be it hypothetical or categorical.

[15] Unlike many contemporary neo-Humeans, I think that the relativization has to be to the agent's actual ends, or ends that bear a close relation to the agent's actual ends, rather than to highly idealized ends (e.g. ends that the agent would have under full information). However, some idealization might be warranted. In this context, I would also like to note that my conception of practical rationality is naturally extended to allow for evaluations of an agent's rationality in adopting goals. An agent does not display practical rationality if he shows ineptitude in using his cognitive powers when thinking through and setting (or revising) his goals. Such evaluations are, I believe, holistic and are relativized to the agent's attitudes and goals. I am using 'goal' very broadly. *An agent's goal* is something that he is set to accomplish, promote, respect, or honor. There is room here for self-deception and lack of self-awareness just like in the case of cognitive goals. I use 'goal', 'aim', 'end', and 'purpose' interchangeably.

VII

The relativization of evaluations of rationality, both theoretical and practical, to the agent's goals is controversial. Although I have motivated it by reflections on my guiding idea, it is admittedly not implied by that vague idea. Consider the recognitional view of rationality, sometimes associated with Aristotle[16] or with Plato.[17] This view construes rationality—the excellence of an agent qua RATIONAL being—as a matter both of using one's cognitive capacities well in discovering reasons for belief and action and of basing one's beliefs and actions on these reasons. This view makes perfect sense of why evaluations of rationality apply primarily to agents engaged in purposeful activity. However, it does not relativize these assessments to the purposes of the agent. For an essential ingredient of the recognitional view is that reasons for action and belief are not fixed by the agent's purposes. Rather, whether a consideration is a reason for belief or action is determined by whether and how it bears on the truth of the belief or the value of the action (or its outcome), when both truth and value are objective in the sense of not being fixed by anyone's mental stance on the matter at hand.

It is the commitment to objective values that has deterred many from embracing the recognitional view of practical rationality. Metaphysical and epistemological worries are frequently cited as motivations for rejecting this view.[18] These are not my motivations. By relativizing assessments of rationality to the purposes of the agent evaluated, I am not attempting a naturalistic reduction of rationality. In my characterization of rationality so far, I have relied on the notion of *excellence* in the use of one's cognitive capacities for one purpose or another, and I have not made any promise that this notion can be unpacked in naturalistic terms. I doubt that the limited unpacking already done amounts to a naturalistic reduction of rationality. In any case, my proposal is not motivated by reductive ambitions, even if it might take us a few steps towards an understanding of rationality that can be incorporated into a naturalistic conception of ourselves and our surroundings.

It is not that I am a fan of extravagant ontologies or a foe of naturalism. Rather, the relativization issue is not a metaphysical issue and does not have any obvious metaphysical implications. This can be best appreciated by seeing that even emotivists about evaluative discourse can acknowledge both relativized and non-relativized evaluations. According to them, evaluations that are

---

[16] See e.g. Garrett Cullity and Barys Gaut (eds.), *Ethics and Practical Reason* (Oxford: Oxford University Press, 1997), 13.

[17] See e.g. Onora O'Neill, *Bounds of Justice* (Cambridge: Cambridge University Press, 2000), 13.

[18] See e.g. Cullity and Gaut (eds.), *Ethics and Practical Reason*, 15–18; O'Neill, *Bounds of Justice*, 13–14.

relativized to the ends of the evaluated agent express attitudes, on the part of the evaluating agent, conditioned on the assumption that the evaluated agent has certain ends. In contrast, evaluations that are not thus relativized express attitudes towards the evaluated agent that are in no way conditioned by what sort of ends he has. I am not advocating the emotivist account of what is going on when we make evaluations that are or are not relativized to the ends of the evaluated agent. What I am highlighting is that this contrast between relativized and non-relativized evaluations pertains, first and foremost, to the nature of the mental act of evaluating or the concepts employed in that act. It is a mistake to run that issue together with the *metaphysical* issue concerning whether a value attaches to an object independently of our evaluation of the object.[19] Of course, once we start to ask about the nature of the act of evaluating, metaphysical issues about the mind-independence of values may arise. I would have to be convinced that these issues are more pressing or less tractable if the evaluations are non-relativized rather than relativized.

I reject the recognitional view because it does not relativize evaluations of rationality to the purposes of the agent evaluated irrespective of whether this will lead us into a metaphysical quagmire.[20] Earlier I considered and rejected the proposal that the excellence of a being qua RATIONAL being is in part constituted by not letting an enquiry into less important matters detract from one's enquiry into more important matters. This was not driven by metaphysical worries about objective measures of importance or value, but rather by an intuition about when charges of irrationality are appropriate. Moreover, we were able to understand the irrationality of going off on tangents and of teasing out the trivial consequences of one's beliefs only against the background of the agent's cognitive goals. Typically, our cognitive goals are relatively specific: our goal is to discover or understand some specific phenomenon rather than to discover any old truth or understand whatever there is to be understood. It is only because of this that it is irrational to spend one's energies on discovering or understanding certain facts at the expense of discovering and understanding some other facts. Thus, my motivations for relativizing evaluations of rationality

---

[19] There are, of course, notorious questions about how to construe this metaphysical issue or whether there is a genuine metaphysical issue here. See e.g. Simon Blackburn, *Spreading the Word* (Oxford: Oxford University Press, 1984), 217–20; Ronald Dworkin, 'Objectivity and Truth: You'd Better Believe It', *Philosophy & Public Affairs*, 25 (1996), 87–139; Gideon Rosen, 'Objectivity and Modern Idealism: What Is the Question?', in Michaelis Michael and John O'Leary-Hawthorne (eds.), *Philosophy in Mind* (Dordrecht: Kluwer Academic Publishers, 1994), 277–319; Sigrún Svavarsdóttir, 'Objective Values: Does Metaethics Rest on a Mistake?', in Brian Leiter (ed.), *Objectivity in Law and Morals* (Cambridge: Cambridge University Press, 2001), 144–93.

[20] Thus, I am committed to resist any other view that does not relativize evaluations of rationality to the purposes of the agent evaluated, including Kantian views of rationality.

to the purposes of the evaluated agent rest on intuitions about when charges of irrationality are appropriate as well as an assessment of how these intuitions are best explained. This way we arrived at the simple but compelling thought that ineptitude in using one's cognitive powers in ways suitable to one's goals is a shortcoming of an agent qua RATIONAL being. In its earlier statement, this thought referred specifically to the agent's cognitive goals, but I cannot see that it matters that the goal is cognitive, except insofar as we are distinguishing theoretical from practical rationality. Thus, I am hoping that the foregoing discussion makes my readers more receptive to a controversial idea that I happen to find intuitively compelling, namely, that assessments of rationality are anchored in the purposes of the agent evaluated.

Motivating my proposal by appealing to intuitions may seem dubious. Even intuitions to which I have already appealed may be turned against me. Imagine an agent whose sole aim in life is to have a deductively closed system of beliefs. My proposal has the consequence that it is, both theoretically and practically, rational for such an agent to work out all the implications of his beliefs. This seems to go against the intuition about irrationality on which I have been relying, namely, the intuition that it is irrational to spend one's days teasing out all the implications of one's beliefs. Nevertheless, I accept this consequence of my view. I am not sure that the intuition on which I have been relying is triggered by the purported counterexample when properly understood and, in any case, I would not want to rely on an intuition triggered by this imagined scenario. It is difficult to get an imaginative fix on an agent whose only aim is to have a deductively closed system of beliefs. You have to imagine an agent who does not aim to understand anything but the implications of his current beliefs—an agent who has such a cognitive aim, but not the practical aim of staying alive and well. Otherwise it is doubtful that we have an agent whose cognitive as well as other ends are, on balance, served by his working out all the implications of his beliefs. Well, perhaps we can imagine such a guy. Conjure up the image of an independently rich guy sitting in his study teasing out all the implications of his beliefs as a servant brings him sustenance. He passes his days in euphoria, going through one trivial implication after another until sleep overtakes him. Do we have an irrational agent or simply a weirdo? I would not let my understanding of rationality hinge on the intuition triggered by this case or similarly far-fetched cases.

I would be satisfied if my conception of rationality matched and made sense of intuitions about relatively realistic cases. However, the prospects for this are grim, especially when it comes to intuitions about practical rationality. Our intuitions conflict. For example, many find it counterintuitive to think that an agent with awfully silly endeavors could be practically rational.[21] Imagine a person who sets out to discover how many men named John live in Durham, North Carolina. Admittedly, I would suspect this person of irrationality, *both* theoretical and practical. For it is difficult to believe that his life is so impoverished that spending his intellectual resources in this way does not detract from cognitive goals and other endeavors closer to his heart. But if I am wrong on this score, I don't see that his shortcoming is that of irrationality, especially if he pursues the matter in the most ingenious way. The man is just silly and shallow—an awfully uninteresting person, indeed. My intuition here is strong and plays a crucial role in motivating me to advance a neo-Humean conception of rationality.

Alas, the intuition is not widely enough shared to provide solid grounds for defending such a conception of rationality. As often in philosophy, we face conflicting intuitions and a dispute about who bears the burden of argument. Neo-Humeans tend to assume that what they have to say about the nature of rationality has to be accepted by everyone as at least a partial account of rationality, so the burden of proof falls on those who claim there is more to rationality. However, anti-Humeans have, recently, gone on the offensive and posed challenges to neo-Humeans.[22] They have questioned whether neo-Humeans can adequately account for the justificatory or critical force of verdicts of rationality. This is, I believe, a serious issue that neo-Humeans have to address, though not necessarily on the terms set by their opponents.[23] I aim

---

[21] Perhaps the most difficult cases for me involve self-destructive agents. Consider a severely depressed agent whose only aim is to find a way to end his life, even if he has been informed that with proper medical treatment he will get out of the depressive state and enjoy life again. Is he displaying rationality when he uses his cognitive capacities, in the most ingenious way, to fool the person who stands a suicide guard over him and to find the means to end his own life? If he fails to do this, is he failing to display the virtue of rationality? My intuitions are shaky about this case and I am wary of resting my conception of rationality on the intuitions that this example triggers (in me or others). This case involves a person suffering from mental illness. Although we often continue to evaluate the mentally ill in terms of rationality or irrationality, it is far from clear that it is appropriate to apply such evaluations to them. Attempts to understand insanity in terms of irrationality seem misguided. I would like to come back to this issue, once I have provided a deeper and more theoretical understanding of why the virtue of rationality is best regarded as excellence in the use of one's cognitive capacities in the service of one's ends—the sort of understanding for which I call below. Thanks are due to Walter Sinnott-Armstrong for pressing the case of the suicidal depressive on me.

[22] See Christine M. Korsgaard, 'The Normativity of Instrumental Reason,' in Garrett Cullity and Berys Gaut (eds.), *Ethics and Practical Reason*, 215–54; Derek Parfit, 'Reasons and Motivation,' *The Aristotelian Society Supplementary Volume*, 71 (1997), 99–130; and Warren Quinn, 'Rationality and the Human Good,' reprinted in his *Morality and Action* (Cambridge: Cambridge University Press, 1993), 210–27.

[23] For example, Kantian formulations of the challenge tend to presuppose that neo-Humeans accept that there is a hypothetical imperative of reason. But I reject imperatival and legal models of practical rationality. See n. 14. Also, the claim is usually that neo-Humeans cannot do justice to the *normative* force of verdicts of rationality. The notion of *normativity* is much thrown around, but it is not entirely clear what it designates. It seems, however, to relate to the notion of *obligation* or at least of (deontic) *ought*. Since I am proposing that we think of rationality as a virtue, I question whether there is anything like requirements of rationality expressed by a sentence containing a deontic *ought*. See also n. 14. The challenge is, therefore, better formulated as questioning whether neo-Humeans can account for the justificatory and critical force of verdicts of rationality.

to build a defense of my view of rationality that meets such challenges. However, here is not the space to do so. A brief explanation of how I conceive of that project will have to do for now.

VIII

There are two main questions that need to be addressed: First, are there genuine evaluations that pertain to how well people use, given their epistemic position, their cognitive capacities in the service of their ends? Second, assuming that these are genuine evaluations, why is rationality best understood as the virtue epitomized in this type of evaluation? Both questions need some clarification. It is far from obvious what would constitute adequate answers to them. The first question, I submit, requires that we be given a good sense of why it matters that people use their cognitive capacities well in the service of their ends—matters in such a way that this can be considered a virtue. The second question, I submit, requires that we be given a good sense of why an excellence in the use of one's cognitive capacities in the service of one's ends is *the* virtue of agents qua RATIONAL beings. Moreover, it must be elucidated why the verdict that someone uses his cognitive capacities well in this way has a justificatory force, while the opposite verdict has a critical force—the sort of justificatory and critical force that verdicts of rationality and irrationality are commonly understood as having.

It is far from trivial to meet these requirements. This can best be appreciated by imagining an evil or a silly person who uses his cognitive capacities superbly in advancing his evil or silly ends.[24] Can we really think of him as justified in his evil or foolish ways just because they result from an excellent use of his cognitive capacities in the service of his ends? Don't his ends have to be worthy as well? Can we really think of the excellence of this person's use of his cognitive capacities as mattering in the way that virtues matter? Can we think of it as *the* virtue of agents qua RATIONAL beings? Does that virtue not also consist in having worthy ends—or at least ends that are such that there is a reliable connection between using one's cognitive capacities well in the service of them and ending up having true beliefs and doing valuable things? Isn't that required for verdicts of rationality to have the justificatory or critical force that they are commonly understood as having?

These challenges assume that the justificatory force of verdicts of rationality and the status of rationality as a virtue cannot be elucidated unless rationality is shown to serve reliably truth and value. This is an assumption that I want to

---

[24] Compare Warren Quinn's challenge to neo-Humeans in 'Rationality and the Human Good'.

challenge, even if I believe that, as a matter of fact, rationality tends to serve truth and value. Understanding why rationality is a virtue and, in particular, why verdicts of rationality have justificatory force requires that we probe deeper into the nature of the type of agents—RATIONAL agents—that are subject to evaluation of rationality. What sort of agents can be *justified in* or *criticized for* forming a belief or an intention to act? It seems that the ability to use one's cognitive capacities purposefully does not suffice for being such an agent. What is required is the ability to reflectively assess and revise one's beliefs, intentions, and possibly some other mental attitudes. Such reflections can only take place against the background of other beliefs and concerns. There is no way of stepping outside of one's mental stance to figure out what to believe or do. However, an agent may use his cognitive capacities better or worse in the course of reassessing and regulating his beliefs, intentions, and other mental attitudes. Evaluative notions such as responsibility, conscientiousness, and integrity find their natural niche in assessing how such an agent regulates his cognitive and practical endeavors. So does, I want to argue, the notion that an agent can be more or less justified in forming a belief or an intention.

Such deepened understanding of RATIONAL agency is the key for understanding why evaluations of rationality have a credible justificatory or critical force, even if they are relativized to the agent's mental states in such a way that there is no guarantee that rationality will serve truth and value. It will also cast light on why rationality, as understood here, matters in such a way that full justice can be done to my guiding idea: namely, that rationality is *the* virtue of agents qua RATIONAL beings. At the same time, it will require that my conception of practical rationality be further developed. An agent can display practical rationality not only in acting one way rather than another but also in forming and revising intentions, plans, and other commitments. Moreover, evaluations of practical rationality need to take into account not only the agent's goals but also his various attitudes regardless of whether they are reflected in his current aims. Alas, I have issued a lot of promissory notes. Let me stop before I sink further into debt.

4

Intrinsic Value and Reasons for Action

Robert Audi

The concept of the good—or at least *some* concept of the good—has been a central topic in ethical theory since Plato. Moral philosophers have generally recognized a distinction between what is good only as a means and what is good in itself. The latter, often called the *intrinsically good*, has proved difficult to explicate and, by contrast with the former, seems to many philosophers to be mysterious. G. E. Moore sought to clarify the notion of the intrinsically good, and his theory of value was probably the most influential axiology developed in the twentieth century. The theory is closely tied to his metaphysics, his epistemology, and his normative ethics; but much of what he says about the good can be maintained without commitment to all of his major claims in those three domains. My project here is to set out a theory of intrinsic value that incorporates the best elements of Moore's account of the notion but avoids commitment to his overall view in metaethics.

1. Some major elements in Moore's theory of value

Since my aim is to produce a sustainable account of intrinsic value, I must be brief in introducing the elements in Moore's account that form a good basis for critical discussion and for comparison with my view. I begin with his famous claim

that 'good' is a simple notion, just as 'yellow' is a simple notion; that, just as you cannot, by any manner of means, explain to any one who does not know it, what yellow is, so

This paper has benefited from comments by Stephen Barker, Panayot Butchvarov, Roger Crisp, Jonathan Dancy, James Dreier, Brad Hooker, Judith Thomson, Derek Parfit, Robert Stecker, and Mark Timmons, and from discussions at the Universities of Georgia, Memphis, Missouri, Notre Dame, and Oxford. In *Southern Journal of Philosophy*, 61 (2003 supplement) where this paper first appeared, Barker published a commentary immediately following my paper. My reply is in 'Intrinsic Value, Inherent Value, and Experience,' *Southern Journal of Philosophy*, 61 (2003): 323–7.

you cannot explain what good is. Definitions of the kind that I was asking for, definitions which describe the real nature of the object or notion denoted by a word, and which do not merely tell us what the word is used to mean, are only possible when the object or notion in question is something complex.[1]

Moore also says that he means by 'good' a property (17). His terminology and his uses of inverted commas vary considerably. Tracking them would be a major task, and rather than undertake that I shall simply be guided by the context in interpreting him. For him, as for most writers on intrinsic value, the phrases 'intrinsically good' and 'intrinsically valuable' are sometimes used interchangeably, though with the understanding that the *theory* of intrinsic value extends to the notion of what is intrinsically bad. (This is sometimes called *disvaluable*.)

Moore is famous for his 'principle of organic unities': '*The [intrinsic] value of a whole must not be assumed to be the same as the sum of the [intrinsic] values of its parts*' (28; cf. 29, 152). He illustrates this with an aesthetic case:

to be conscious of a beautiful object is a thing of great intrinsic value; whereas the same object, if no one be conscious of it, has certainly comparatively little value, and is commonly held to have none at all. But the consciousness of a beautiful object is certainly a whole of some sort in which we can distinguish as parts the object . . . and the being conscious . . . Now this latter factor occurs as part of a different whole, whenever we are conscious of anything; and it would seem that some of these wholes have at all events very little value, and may even be indifferent or positively bad. . . . Since, therefore, mere consciousness does not always confer value upon the whole of which it forms a part, even though its object may have no great demerit, we cannot attribute the great superiority of the consciousness of a beautiful thing over the beautiful thing itself to the mere addition of the value of consciousness to that of the beautiful thing. (28)

I particularly want to bring out here two points whose significance Moore himself (among many others) seems to have missed. First, he is attributing intrinsic value to two radically different kinds of things: consciousness and, on the other hand, external objects, where consciousness is conceived as internal to the mind, or at least as having an element that is. Secondly, he is exhibiting an awareness that the value, even of a beautiful object, is comparatively little in abstraction from the consciousness of it and, thus abstracted, is 'commonly held' to be nil.[2]

---

[1] G. E. Moore, *Principia Ethica* (Cambridge: Cambridge University Press, 1903), 7 (references to this book will hereinafter be included parenthetically in the text).

[2] Cf. Sidgwick, *The Methods of Ethics*, 7th edn. (London: Macmillan, 1907), 114 and Moore, *Principia Ethica*, 221–5. Moore says in one place that although 'the mere existence of what is beautiful does appear to have *some* intrinsic value . . . Prof. Sidgwick was so far right in the view there discussed, that such mere existence of what is beautiful has value, so small as to be negligible, in comparison to that which attaches to the *consciousness* of beauty' (189).

This duality regarding what sorts of things are intrinsically good significantly contrasts with the view Moore held by the time he published *Ethics* nine years later. He says there that 'It may, in fact, be held, with great plausibility, that no whole can ever have any intrinsic value *unless* it contains some pleasure.'[3] Pleasure, by contrast with paintings, is or at least entails a form of consciousness. He rejects, however, the ostensibly implied view that 'intrinsic value is always in proportion to quantity of pleasure' (*Ethics*, 152; cf. 153). For, on the principle of organic unities, the addition of pleasure to a whole can reduce its intrinsic value; and (in a quite different formulation) he reaffirms this principle in the context (151–2). He also holds that

Whatever single kind of thing is proposed as a measure of intrinsic value, instead of pleasure—whether knowledge, or virtue, or wisdom, or love—it is... not such a measure; because it is quite plain that, however valuable any of these things may be, we may always add to the value of a whole which contains any one of them... *by adding something else instead.* (152)

His positive view concerning value and consciousness is that 'it does seem as if nothing can be of intrinsic value unless it contains *both* some feeling and *also* some other form of consciousness' (153). (A similar view is found in Ross's *The Right and the Good.*[4])

There is one other element in Moore's conception of intrinsic value that I want to bring out before I present my own account. In responding to Frankena (in 1942), Moore says that

if what Mr. Frankena means to assert is that the propositional function '*x* is intrinsically good' may be *identical* with the function 'the fact that an action which you can do would produce *x* is *some* reason for supposing that you ought to do that action,' then *one* condition necessary for the possibility of this being true is fulfilled... there is a two-way necessary connection between these functions... But nevertheless I think there is a *good* reason, if not a conclusive one, for doubting whether they are identical.... Is it not possible to *think* that a thing is intrinsically good without thinking that the fact that an action within our power would produce it would be a reason for supposing that we ought to do that action? It certainly seems as if we can.[5]

---

[3] See G. E. Moore, *Ethics* (Oxford: Oxford University Press, 1912), 148.

[4] See W. D. Ross, *The Right and the Good* (Oxford: Oxford University Press, 1930), 86. In n. 14 of ch. 11 of *Moral Knowledge and Ethical Character* (Oxford: Oxford University Press, 1997), I comment on Ross's view of the element of consciousness in the intrinsically good.

[5] G. E. Moore, 'A Reply to my Critics,' in Paul Arthur Schilpp (ed.), *The Philosophy of G. E. Moore* (New York: Tudor Publishing Co., 1942), 151–2. Note that in treating reasons for action as entailing the production of intrinsic goodness, Moore either presupposes that reducing such evils as pain is producing such a good or simply neglects to take into account that it is with intrinsic *value* rather than with positive intrinsic value alone that reasons for action are essentially connected.

The view Moore takes Frankena to attribute to him—roughly, an identification of the intrinsic goodness of something with the existence of a reason for favorable action towards it—is important and represents one way (though not Moore's way) of explicating intrinsic goodness. A theory of intrinsic value should help us appraise this view, and I shall return to the question.

2. Intrinsic, instrumental, and inherent value

I have emphasized that Moore attributes intrinsic value both to consciousness of a beautiful object and to that object itself. He also attributes it to such things as knowledge, virtue, wisdom, and love.[6] Aware that it is 'commonly held' that a beautiful thing by itself has no intrinsic value, and wanting to do justice to the role of pleasure as an intrinsic good, he expresses sympathy for the view that pleasure is intrinsically good, and (as noted) he maintains that nothing can be of intrinsic value unless it contains *both* some feeling and *also* some other form of consciousness, though (in *Principia*) without suggesting that pleasure must be an element in the consciousness in question. It apparently did not occur to him that a beautiful painting 'contains' neither form of consciousness. And consider the other elements in question. Knowledge, virtue, wisdom, and love need not contain any feeling, at least if this means that they can exist over an interval of time only if their possessor has some feeling during at least part of that time. Moreover, when they are not being manifested, they do not even entail the occurrence of any form of consciousness. Granted, all of them may have conceptual connections to consciousness. But nothing about them will sustain Moore's suggested view.

I believe that Moore has not done adequate justice to the data he himself recognizes and that a more fine-grained theory is required to account for them. I propose (as I have in earlier work[7]) that we take the bearers of intrinsic value to be concrete *experiences* on the part of individuals (in this paper I consider only experiences of persons, but I acknowledge the existence of valuable experiences on the part of non-persons). I cannot give a full-scale analysis of the notion of an experience (and will return to the notion), but what I want to say here may be clear enough on the basis of the rough idea that an experience (1) is an occurrent state of consciousness, such as paying careful attention to a painting, or a certain kind of unified set of events in consciousness, such as daydreaming about a vacation trip; and (2) has an object, at least in the sense of a content, hence is not

---

[6] See e.g. Moore's at least implicit ascription of intrinsic value to knowledge, virtue, wisdom, and love in *Ethics*, 152.   [7] In ch. 11 of *Moral Knowledge* I have discussed bearers of intrinsic value in some detail.

merely a matter of one's being awake. An experience cannot be what we might call a period of *empty consciousness*: something like an utterly blank moment in which one has a mere receptivity to stimuli but is aware of nothing.

I am taking the notion of experience central here to be internal in a sense implying that an experience *need* not have an external object, as it does in the case of something that is actually seen and is thus, in an external sense, visually experienced and also experienceable by others. The experience *as of* seeing the same object when one is only hallucinating would be internal and in a sense non-relational, since its occurrence is not even partly constituted by a relation to anything other than the person having it.[8] But suppose one is actually experiencing a symphony. Call this second case experience *in the relational sense*. If one has the latter, one has the former as what might be called its psychological base, but not conversely. It is apparently experiences in the internal sense that are the basic bearers of intrinsic value. This does not imply that enjoying a symphony cannot have intrinsic value. It surely does; the proposal is only that it has that value in virtue of its internal, experiential qualities, hence that what might be called *basic* intrinsic value is wholly experiential. Thus, silently enjoying reciting a poem to oneself would be intrinsically good; being pained at the thought of having cancer would be intrinsically bad. Hallucinatory experiences might also have intrinsic value on this view, and that possibility calls for comment. Before I address difficulties for the view I am proposing, however, let me develop it further.

How can the experientialist account of intrinsic value do justice to the value of a beautiful painting, which is not an experience? Isn't it good 'in itself,' hence intrinsically good? The phrase 'in itself' has doubtless been misleading. I find it too crude to serve centrally in understanding intrinsic value. It plainly applies to the goodness of an intrinsically good experience: such an experience is not only non-instrumentally good, it need have no relational kind of goodness. But 'good in itself' also applies to things whose goodness is quite different, in ways I will bring out, from intrinsic goodness. Granted, since the non-instrumental goodness of a beautiful painting resides in its beauty and that, in turn, is consequential (supervenient, in one sense of that term) upon its intrinsic—in the broad sense of 'non-relational'—properties, it is very natural to think of the painting as good *in itself*. Moore and many others have apparently so conceived such objects and partly for that reason considered them intrinsically

---

[8] I have in mind 'concrete' objects; on some views, an experience of, for example, thinking about a problem or even hallucinating a painting requires being in a relation to propositions or properties. It might also be noted that on a content externalist view, certain experiences are not possible apart from the existence of external objects; but supposing this is so, those objects need not be, as it were, constituents in the experience, rather than suitable factors in the life of, the subject.

good. But here we do well to recall Aristotle. Among the pertinent points he made are these: that one good is more 'final' than another if we seek the latter for the sake of the former, and that *the* good is that which makes life 'choiceworthy.'[9] Surely we (properly) value (e.g. go to see, preserve, celebrate, etc.) beautiful paintings in order to *view* them, and indeed not *merely* to view them but to do so in a way that is aesthetically rewarding. Viewing them in that way yields having an aesthetically valuable *experience* (by which I mean one that is good from the aesthetic point of view, not one that is a good *object* of aesthetic appreciation, though that status is not ruled out for special cases). I take experiences having such value to be intrinsically good. I also take them to be 'more final' in Aristotle's sense than their objects.

A related point emerges when we ask how one should conceive beautiful paintings in relation to Aristotle's thesis about *the* good. Do they contribute to the ultimate choiceworthiness of a life simply by their physical presence in our environment or through our *viewing* them—hence visually experiencing them—in a way that is aesthetically good? Plainly they would not so contribute if we never viewed them or, on viewing them, never had a good experience in doing this or in experiencing anything else in which they figure.

Are beautiful paintings, then, just instrumentally good after all, say means to aesthetic enjoyment? One could call them *constitutive means*; for they are constituents in, and not mere instruments for attaining, such enjoyment. But the term 'means,' used by itself, is highly misleading. They are not means in the ordinary, instrumental sense implying a non-constitutive, contingent role in bringing about the intrinsic good in question. They are, in Moorean terms, part of it. We cannot have the pleasures of reciting Shakespeare's sonnets without reciting them. We *can* produce heat in our homes by various alternative means.

A useful term to employ in reference to objects that are good in themselves is 'inherent value'. C. I. Lewis called inherent values those

which are resident in objects in such wise that they are realizable in experience through presentation of the object... The value in question is one which is found or findable in the object itself... in the sense of being one which is disclosed or disclosable by observation of this object and not by examining any other object.[10]

---

[9] Aristotle says, 'We call that which is pursued as an end in itself more final than an end which is pursued for the sake of something else' (*Nicomachean Ethics*, trans. Martin Ostwald (Indianapolis: Hackett, 1962)). Cf. Terence Irwin's translation, 2nd edn. (Indianapolis: Hackett, 1999), which uses 'complete' in place of 'final'. I take Aristotle to be referring not to mere pursuit but to a kind that is 'proper.' The idea of the 'self-sufficiency' of happiness (the good), in virtue of which it makes life choiceworthy, is explicit in 1097b.

[10] C. I. Lewis, *Analysis of Knowledge and Valuation* (La Salle, Ill.: Open Court, 1946), 391 (Lewis makes no reference to Moore in the context).

By contrast, he saw 'intrinsic value [as] attaching exclusively to realizations of some possible value-quality in experience itself' (389; cf. 390–1). He called this realization the only 'ultimately good thing' (390) and went on to advance the experientialist view that 'What is *ultimately* desirable is not merely that this object and this property of it called its beauty should exist, but that this beauty of it should illuminate the experience of some beholder' (391).

Lewis does not give a detailed account of intrinsic value or, especially, inherent value. I make no claim to be giving an interpretation of his view; but I find the term 'inherent value' useful, and I want to clarify the notion I have in mind.

First, I seek a wider notion than the one sketched by Lewis. We should allow that an experience of silently reciting a poem can be intrinsically good; but this is not a case of observation. I suggest that we conceive an inherently good thing more broadly, as roughly one such that an appropriate experience of it is intrinsically good. There are many kinds of appropriateness. A mere visual experience of seeing a beautiful painting need not be intrinsically good; some aesthetic appreciation is normally required. A mere walk on a beautiful beach may be dull; a zesty one graced by mild temperature and a fresh breeze may be delightful. And an aesthetic appreciation of a silent poetic recitation can be intrinsically good even if there is no external object thereof.

More must be said to explicate appropriateness (more, unfortunately, than can be said here), but a necessary condition is that an appropriate experience of an inherently good thing be an experience of a suitable subset of its intrinsic properties (though not necessarily of all or only the intrinsic properties of it). This conception suggests that inherent value has at least a great deal in common with what are usually called secondary qualities. But if we take it to be such a quality, we must note that there is no implication that inherent value properties are not 'in' the object. Indeed, they are non-relational, and in that sense intrinsic, properties; but their constitutive manifestations, like those of colors, entail relations to living things.

I also want to allow, as Lewis might not have, that what is intrinsically good can *also* be inherently good. How can this be if the bearers of intrinsic value are experiences? Surely there can be intrinsically good *second-order* experiences. Suppose I view with pleasure my own enjoyable silent recitation of a poem. May I not be taking pleasure in the contemplation of the enjoyable experience, happily noting that I seem to be getting intonations that are difficult to capture? Granted, this could be argued to be not an experience of reflecting on another experience, but simply a complicated first-order experience. It is, however, a reflective experience in which one thinks about a present experience, whereas the recitation (for most poems) involves no such thoughts. This difference in content would seem to warrant countenancing two different experiences; and the content of the former apparently warrants considering that experience second-order.

Perhaps, moreover, we may go further and allow that I can experience, for instance, *your* pleasure in singing a song you audibly delight in singing. If I can, then the intrinsically valuable first-order experiences of *others* can also have inherent value for me: my experience of your pleasure can be intrinsically good. To be sure, I must experience your pleasure through its expression in your behavior; but there is a sense in which I see your pleasure *in* that conduct as well. We may thus take 'inherently good' to apply to certain intrinsic goods constituted by various kinds of first-order experiences. The case also illustrates a kind of relativity possessed by inherent, as opposed to intrinsic, goodness. The latter is experientially realized in the life in which it occurs; the former, though good 'in itself,' is realizable in intrinsically good experiences only on the part of beings who can appropriately experience it. Not everyone can enjoy atonal music or abstract art.

The general idea suggested by these reflections is that something is inherently good provided that an appropriate experience of it is intrinsically good, and it is inherently bad provided an appropriate experience of it is intrinsically bad, where the range of appropriate experiences is limited to those that are responses to certain of its intrinsic properties. (These will include at least some of the properties of the thing in question on the basis of which it is plausibly considered good or bad in itself.) Which properties are crucial is, in a certain way, relative to the kind of value in question. If the value is aesthetic, then the appropriate experience must include some sense of the object's aesthetic properties (or at least those they are grounded in). If the value is moral, the experience must similarly include a sense of morally relevant properties, such as harming or helping. If the value is philosophical, the experience must include considering conceptual or other 'intellectual' properties. And so forth. In the light of the kinds of properties in question, an experience may be aesthetically good or bad, morally good or bad, and so on for other kinds of value. An experience of certain harmonious sounds, for instance, can be aesthetically good; an experience of being tempted to cheat can be morally bad, say shameful.

There is another part of my characterization of inherent value that needs comment. Suppose *A*, a bully, maliciously gives *B*, who is timid and much smaller, an unprovoked sharp slap in the face. I want to call this deed inherently (morally) bad. One appropriate experience in response to it is indignation. Is the experience of indignation in such a case intrinsically bad? It is likely to be both unpleasant and morally distressing. Equally important, perhaps, one might quite reasonably prefer that it not have been called for. On the other hand, it is a response that we are glad an observer has in such a case. Our positive attitude toward it is a clue to its status. Perhaps we should say that the response may be, overall, both inherently good and intrinsically bad. As an experience, it may be intrinsically bad overall (though it need not be, depending on the mix of distress and, say, felt righteousness); but in the circumstances, it is good *that* we have it: our having it is a state of affairs that is inherently good and can be viewed, and in that sense experienced, with moral satisfaction.

Similarly, suppose that *A* sadistically teases *B* and greatly enjoys this. *A*'s experience is intrinsically good, at least hedonically; *B*'s experience, let us assume, is one of suffering and is intrinsically bad. Still, the overall concrete event, *A*'s enjoying sadistically teasing *B* and thereby causing *B*'s suffering, seems inherently bad. We properly tend to feel *at least* displeasure, and perhaps a kind of moral repugnance, in the contemplation of it; and its inherent badness can provide sufficient reason to intervene. To say that it *provides* a reason is not to say it *constitutes* a reason; I take providing a reason to entail the existence of a reason, usually either by having the reason as its content, as with desires and intentions, or by virtue of something quite evident in the context, as where it is obvious that intervening would prevent the bad thing from coming to be. Here what constitutes the reason is (generically) the fact that the action would prevent the suffering in question.

3. Intrinsic value, inherent value, and organic unity

This case of taking pleasure in someone else's suffering can be used to help in motivating another principle concerning value, inherent as well as intrinsic. Why is displeasure in experiencing a sadist's action and its effect appropriate? And why is it so even if the sadist's pleasure is very great and the suffering in which it is taken is only slight? It seems to me very plausible to say that this pleasure *ill-befits* its object; there is a basic inappropriateness in taking pleasure in someone else's suffering—the more so if one is causing it. It is thus appropriate to be displeased upon experiencing someone's taking pleasure in someone else's suffering. On my view, even if the pleasurable experience of the sadist is intrinsically good, it may be inherently bad. I think that (depending on the details) it almost certainly will be inherently bad, even if the pleasure is quantitatively greater than the suffering the sadist causes. For the pleasure has an inappropriate kind of object; and accordingly, an appropriate second-order experience of that pleasure is *intrinsically* bad in the relevant way.

Why is it that suffering is an inappropriate kind of object of pleasure? There is much room for theory here. One answer available to those who countenance intrinsic value and connect it with objective reasons for action in the way Moore and many others do is as follows. Consider the point that there is a basic reason (though not necessarily an undefeated reason) for action to realize or continue the pleasurable thing, whereas there is a basic reason (though not necessarily an undefeated one) to avoid or extinguish a painful or unpleasant thing. Taking pleasure in causing or even observing someone else's suffering, then, provides a reason for producing or sustaining something that there is reason to avoid. The kind of experience in question has properties with opposing valences: one kind, we might say, calls for realization, the other for avoidance. There is no contradiction here, but there is a kind of axiological incoherence, at least on the assumption of the objectivity of the kinds of reasons in question.[11] This in part accounts for the intuition that such pleasure ill befits its object. If we extend this idea, it can be applied to taking pleasure in *thinking* about causing someone suffering. Envisaging or imagining suffering is still a case of having before the mind something of negative valence and taking a positive (non-instrumental) attitude toward it. It mirrors, in a sense, the enjoyment of actual sadistic conduct.[12]

I am suggesting that sadistic pleasure is (perhaps with special exceptions) inherently bad in part on the basis of its intentional object, the kind such pleasure has even if the sadist only mistakenly thinks the other person is suffering or, somewhat similarly, is taking pleasure in the mere *thought* of someone's suffering. I am not assuming, but am allowing, that, overall, the pleasure is also intrinsically bad. It may seem that it *must* be so at least where the suffering caused is greater than the pleasure taken in causing it. But perhaps it need not be so in special circumstances, such as causing suffering in administering deserved punishment, as where the jailer—within limits—takes pleasure in causing the pain that an unrepentant violent criminal feels in being locked up. In any event, the *intrinsic* value of the pleasure cannot be decided on the basis of how much suffering the pleasurable action causes; for in that case we have an experience with an external effect: the having of that object is a relational property of the experience, whereas I am assuming, as Moore and others have, that the bearers of intrinsic goodness have it in virtue of at least one of their

---

[11] That pleasure and pain (whether actual or in prospect) provide, as Moore thought, objective reasons for action is of course controversial; I assume it in this paper, but have argued for it in detail in *The Architecture of Reason* (Oxford: Oxford University Press, 2001), esp. chs. 4–6. Cf. *Principia*, where Moore says, 'when I talk of a thing as "my own good" all that I can mean is that something which will be exclusively mine, as my own pleasure is mine (whatever be the various senses of this relation denoted by "possession") is also *good absolutely*; or rather that my possession of it is good absolutely ... everyone else has as much reason for aiming at it as I have myself' (99).

[12] The attitude must be non-instrumental to rule out cases in which one takes pleasure in someone's suffering because it is a means to, for example, the person's recovery from depression or a cleansing penance for a wrong.

non-relational properties. The complex consisting of an experience and its external effects can have inherent but not intrinsic value.[13]

The sorts of cases we are considering make it natural to posit Moore's principle of organic unities. I prefer, however, a broader formulation that specifies parts *or aspects* of the bearer of value. I also think that the resulting principle should be applied to inherent as well as intrinsic value. Recall the sadist's taking pleasure in someone's suffering. Even if the pleasure is much greater than the suffering, the inherent value of the complex whole can be negative, illustrating that the inherent value of the whole is not the 'sum' of the inherent values of the 'parts' (I assume that these are the only parts, or the only relevant ones, and that the relevant notion of a sum is not strictly quantitative).[14]

As to the case of intrinsic value, we can speak of one aspect of the experience of pleasure in someone's suffering as the pleasant quality of the experience and of another as its content, in the sense of its being directed at the suffering. We can now say that the pleasant quality of the experience is inappropriate to this content and that even if the former is intense, the *overall* intrinsic value of the experience is either negative or at any rate much less positive than that of an experience differing from it only in the pleasure's being taken in something neutral. The same point applies even if we suppose the person only mistakenly thinks the other is suffering and we hold all else fixed. It is important to see, however, that even if inherent badness is the only kind of badness possessed by these experiences, it may have sufficient magnitude to warrant the kinds of negative appraisals we require, for instance judging that such experiences are non-instrumentally bad and that one should avoid bringing them about.

Aesthetic cases more readily illustrate the organicity of inherent and intrinsic value. Consider paintings and poems. Both can have parts and aspects that have no inherent value, such as a blank white space in a painting, a certain rhythmic shift in a musical composition, and ellipsis marks in a poem. But the overall inherent value of these artworks may be very positively affected by such elements, so that the value of the whole is greater than the sum of the values of

---

[13] If one wonders how a relational experience, such as pleasure in a symphony, can have intrinsic value at all, given that the symphony is not intrinsic to its internal side, two points should be stressed: first, the symphony *is* intrinsic to the experience qua *relational*; but, second, the internal side of that experience is also intrinsic to it, and it is in virtue of this (which includes intentional content) that the overall experience has intrinsic value.

[14] The non-additivity claim in the principle of organic unities does not entail that there *cannot* be a case in which intrinsic or inherent value is additive. Consider two qualitatively identical experiences. Might we say that—provided one has a determinate value—the pair has twice that value? This would be important for the theory of rational action as well as for the theory of value. Extensive discussion of the principle and a defense of it are provided by Noah Lemos in *Intrinsic Value: Concept and Warrant* (Cambridge: Cambridge University Press, 1994) and 'Organic Unities,' *Journal of Ethics*, 2 (1998). For criticism of the principle, see Michael A. Zimmerman, *The Nature of Intrinsic Value* (Lanham, Md.: Rowman & Littlefield, 2001).

the parts or aspects. This can hold even if all of the parts and aspects are inherently good. Similar points apply to intrinsically valuable experiences. Consider a pause in musical work: as experienced in itself, it may be aesthetically empty but, as part of the overall musical experience, valuationally important.

4. Some problems of specificatory incompleteness

An apparent difficulty for my view may seem to arise in the light of some important points made by Aristotle in the *Nicomachean Ethics*:

Good is spoken of in as many ways as being . . . as God and mind; in quality, as the virtues; in quantity, as the measured amount; in relation, as the useful . . . Hence it is clear that the good cannot be some common [nature of good things] that is universal and single; for if it were, it would be spoken of in only one of the categories, not in them all. (1096a 24 ff.)

Following Aristotle, one might point out, as Peter Geach and Judith Jarvis Thomson have, that, contrary to the impression Moore sometimes invites, a thing cannot be just good.[15] It must be a good *F*, for some appropriate *F*, or good in a way, or good as a thing of a certain sort, and so on. Is Moore committed to denying this? I do not see that he is; in any case, he *need* not be if, like many others (including me), he takes goodness to be a consequential property, as he seems to.[16] By this I mean roughly that things are good in virtue of other properties they have, in a sense of 'in virtue of' that implies (but is not equivalent to) the impossibility of two things differing in their goodness though they are alike in *all* their other properties. For intrinsic and inherent value, the relevant base properties are, in my view, intrinsic and, in some intuitive sense to which I shall return, 'descriptive.'

If this view is correct, then we might expect the context of a predication of goodness, especially inherent on intrinsic goodness, to indicate the relevant kind of thing.[17] Call this a *value-anchoring kind*, since specifying it anchors the

---

[15] See Peter Geach, 'Good and Evil,' *Analysis*, 17 (1956): 33–42; and Judith Jarvis Thomson, 'The Right and the Good,' *Journal of Philosophy*, 94 (1997): 273–98.

[16] Moore's term for 'consequential upon,' at least in what I believe is his last published essay on intrinsic value, is 'depends on.' He says, for example, that whether and to what degree anything possesses intrinsic value 'depends *solely* on the intrinsic nature of the thing . . . anything *exactly like* it, must, in all circumstances, possess it in exactly the same degree.' See 'The Conception of Intrinsic Value,' in Moore's *Philosophical Studies* (Patterson: Littlefield, Adams, 1959), 265 (originally published by Routledge & Kegan Paul in 1922).

[17] Indeed, if the consequentiality of goodness is a priori and necessary, a thing absolutely cannot be just good, rather than good by virtue of being something else, whereas it is not a priori that a thing can't be (say)

use of 'good' in question. The ascription 'She is good' implies goodness as a person in one context, goodness as an athlete in another; 'Beautiful paintings are among the good things in life' implies that viewing them is (intrinsically) good; and so forth. When we know what kind of thing is being called good and what kind of goodness is attributed to it, we can begin to figure out what sorts of experiences of it are intrinsically good and what sorts of qualities it must have to yield those experiences.

If, however, the bearers of intrinsic value are experiences, don't we need to make sense of the locutions 'a good experience' and 'a bad experience' even apart from any context? Not entirely apart from any context, for there are at least two commonly accepted constraints on a theory of intrinsic goodness—and perhaps on any normative discourse embodying notions of intrinsic goodness—that can help us here. First, it must be clear how what is properly thought good in itself (whether intrinsically or inherently) can contribute to making life choiceworthy. Second, and related to this, it must be clear that what is intrinsically good can provide reasons for action. This is not to say that the goodness itself *constitutes* a reason; what constitutes a value-based reason for action is typically, and perhaps will always be, something connecting the action with that in virtue of which the relevant experience is good (or bad), say the fact that doing the thing in question will be enjoyable.[18] I take a choiceworthy life to be (roughly) one constituted by a favorable balance of good experiences relative to bad ones.

Moreover, I take it to be a non-contingent and probably a priori truth that the fact that an experience would be intrinsically good provides a reason—some reason, at least—to seek it (in a very wide sense that can include trying to bring it about for someone else) and that the fact that an experience would be intrinsically bad provides a reason for avoiding it. More specifically, the kinds of qualities of experiences in virtue of which they are good or bad experiences—most

---

yellow but not in virtue of anything else true of it (this does not hold for all descriptive properties, such as being colored, since it is a priori that a thing cannot have this property except in virtue of having a specific color property). I am not sure whether Moore noticed this contrast.

[18] I am again allowing that an intrinsic good might 'provide' a reason without *constituting* one. Suppose, for example, that we adopt T. M. Scanlon's 'buck-passing' view of goodness and value (hence presumably of basic reasons for action as well), on which reasons are constituted by the specific things in virtue of which something is good—say, being enjoyable—not by its goodness as such. See *What We Owe to Each Other* (Cambridge, Mass.: Harvard University Press, 1998), esp. 95–100. We can still speak, however, of intrinsically good experiences as providing the reasons, though in *virtue* of their grounds, such as pleasurable qualities of experience. We could also distinguish between elements' directly and indirectly constituting reasons and between specific and general reasons. I might do a thing because it is good even if I think it is good only *because* of some particular property of it. Suppose, moreover, that I do it only because, entirely on your testimonial authority, I believe it will be good. It would appear that even if I would pass the buck to you given an enquiry into the status or basis of my reason, my generic reason—to do something good—is where the buck stops for me. To be sure, it stops there *on* your authority, but that does not make my reason *doing what you suggest*.

obviously being enjoyable or painful—constitute grounds for desire and thereby for action. Is there, then, reason for the sadist who would enjoy torturing a terrorist to death to do so? If we keep in mind that there can be a reason that is defeated by the presence of better reasons for something else, I believe we should answer affirmatively. How such a question is to be decided will be addressed in section 6.

Countenancing things that are inherently good but not intrinsically good can be seen to cohere with this partial account of intrinsic goodness. There is, for instance, non-instrumental reason to preserve a beautiful painting because it is a potential constituent in an intrinsically good aesthetic experience of it. The account is also sufficiently pluralistic to accommodate the variety of inherent and intrinsic goods we should countenance. For each inherent good, we can imagine intrinsically good experiences in which it is a constituent; and each such experience grounds reasons for positive action regarding the inherently good thing.

To be sure, if, in requiring a specification of the kind of object said to be good—the specification of a value-anchoring kind—as a condition of the intelligibility of predicating intrinsic value, one seeks to *reduce* the predication to a 'descriptive' statement, then my view may not be accommodating. A good knife may be simply one that cuts certain things easily and retains its edge through multiple uses, but it is not at all clear that a good person is simply (say) one who performs certain tasks efficiently and tries to help, and never to harm, others (this gains some plausibility, however, if we take 'help' and 'harm' to be richly normative terms, as where helping people is understood to imply contributing to their moral well-being). Perhaps 'good knife' admits of a descriptive, if vague, analysis; but 'good person' surely does not. If we distinguish between *reductive* and *identificational* uses of phrases in which 'good' is anchored by a specification of the relevant kind, then, for ascriptions of intrinsic and inherent goodness, my account welcomes the latter uses but makes no commitment to the former.

If predications of goodness are intelligible only relative to some value-anchoring kind, are they also implicitly comparative, and might they be analyzable in terms of comparative, perhaps even 'descriptive,' statements? Granted, *knowledge* of intrinsic goodness may require comparing the thing in question with other things of the relevant kind, or at least a readiness to make such comparisons. But it does not follow, and I think is not true, that the attribution of intrinsic goodness is equivalent to a comparison of the thing with others or, especially, to a ranking of it in relation to them on the basis of some descriptively specifiable property such as efficiency in producing a certain effect. One can know an experience of a beautiful painting to be intrinsically good without being committed to this experience being, say, at least as enjoyable as most of one's pleasurable experiences of viewing paintings.

There is another kind of incompleteness we must consider: 'evaluative incompleteness.'[19] Consider someone's experiencing pleasure. How should we evaluate such an experience? If, as hedonists and others hold, pleasure is intrinsically good, it would seem to follow that we must call this experience intrinsically good; but, as we saw, the pleasure may have an object which pleasure ill befits.

It is useful here to view intrinsic goodness on the model of prima facie duty as understood by Ross. Consider promising. If all I know is that you promised to do something, I am not entitled to infer that you ought (in the sense of final obligation) to do it. But surely I can know that you have a prima facie obligation, in a sense that implies final duty if no set of other duties overrides this one.[20] In this sense, we might say, promising is *intrinsically obligating*. Similarly, suppose I can tell that you are taking pleasure in something, but I do not know what it is. May I not infer that there is something *intrinsically good* (good-making) in your experience, indeed something such that, if nothing in or regarding your experience defeats this good, the experience is, in an overall way, intrinsically good? I think so; and if this is so, then just as promising is intrinsically, though not necessarily *finally*, morally obligating, pleasure is intrinsically normative—since it is *good-making*—and, where its value is not overbalanced by some other element(s) in or regarding the experience to which it belongs, renders that experience intrinsically good overall. Moreover, pleasure, like moral obligation, is 'practical' in implying a reason for action.

We now face another question. Why should we not say that pleasure is only prima facie good? Let me make two points about this.

First, we *may* say that pleasure is prima facie good, so long as we take prima facie goodness to be a kind of intrinsic goodness: the pleasure cannot fail to be good qua pleasure, even though the whole of which it is an aspect can fail to be intrinsically good, just as an action cannot fail to be obligatory qua promised even if other facts about it prevent it from being obligatory on the whole. This kind of defeasibility does not imply a relational status; that pleasure does not necessarily make the experience it characterizes intrinsically good *overall* does

---

[19] See Michael Zimmerman, 'Evaluatively Incomplete States of Affairs,' *Philosophical Studies*, 43 (1983): 211–24, and *The Nature of Intrinsic Value*. He says in the latter, regarding the state of affairs, John's being pleased at time t, 'Is there *any* reason to think that contemplation of a state of this form as such requires that you favor it? ... If it occurs in virtue of a state of the form [John's being pleased at Mary's pain] ... What reason is there to think that *anything* good has happened?' (145) Here intrinsic goodness is 'defeated.'

[20] I have argued for this in 'Moderate Intuitionism and the Epistemology of Moral Judgment,' *Ethical Theory and Moral Practice*, 1 (1998): 14–34. For a treatment of Ross's analogy between goodness and prima facie duty, see Lemos, 'Organic Unities' (I take Lemos's defense of intrinsic value here to be at least largely compatible with my response to the analogy).

not imply that the pleasure itself is good only in relation to something else, *or* only when certain conditions are met.

One way to see this point about pleasure is to note that we recognize, as a basic reason for performing an action—even if a defeated reason—that one will enjoy it. Another way is to note why it is that we do not look favorably on pleasure on the part of a malicious person who in no way merits it (here I vary a well-known example Kant used in the *Groundwork*). The best explanation of this is that we take the pleasure to be a good the person should not have. The explanation of this, in turn, is not, or not only, that the pleasure itself is inherently bad; we might think the person should not have it even if we believe that the pleasure is not the kind that ill befits its object. Virtually regardless of the object, we take the pleasure to be a good that the person should not have.[21] More specifically, the state of affairs, that malicious person's having it, is (as indicated earlier) virtually always inherently bad. Pleasure can ill befit its possessor, just as it can ill befit its content.[22]

The second point is that the experientialist theory of value I am proposing is not as such committed to taking any particular kind of experience to be intrinsically good *overall*. It may be combined with the view that the overall intrinsic goodness of an experience cannot be determined until its relevant content, particularly its phenomenal and intentional properties, is taken into account. Overall intrinsic value would then be what Ross calls a 'toti-resultant attribute.'[23]

A complication here is that individuation of experiences is no easy matter. If I read a beautiful poem while hearing crude, ugly music, am I having a single mixed experience or two experiences, a good literary one and a bad auditory

---

[21] I say 'virtually' rather than always to allow for the possibility that such people of bad character might take pleasure in the thought of doing things to make amends for their past wrongs and to improve their character. But if we are happy to see them have this kind of pleasure, it seems in part because we take it to show at least that they have enough decency to look with pleasure on what morality calls for. Cf. Moore's view that 'When I talk of a thing as "my own good" all that I can mean is that something which will be exclusively mine . . . is also *good absolutely*. The *good* of it can in no sense be "private" . . . The only reason I can have for aiming at "my own good" is that it is *good absolutely* that what I so call should belong to me . . . which, if I have it, others cannot have' (*Principia*, 99). On the surface, this precludes Moore's holding that an experience of pleasure might be intrinsically good, yet I should not have it. But perhaps he could here invoke the principle of organic unity and claim that enjoying causing someone pain would not normally constitute my own good. In any case, my theory allows us to say both that sadistic pleasure may be intrinsically good, qua pleasure, but not good, considered overall, *and* that it may in any case be inherently bad. The latter point alone might imply that there is adequate reason to oppose it.

[22] In 'Organic Unities' Lemos uses this kind of example to show that evaluative incompleteness does not undermine the view that intrinsic value (construed as encompassing inherent value) is organic. He notes that (on highly plausible assumptions) S's being wicked, deserving no pleasure, and having none is, in itself, better than S's being wicked, deserving no pleasure, and *having* it, even apart from the content of the pleasure. See pp. 330–1.   [23] Ross, *The Right and the Good*, 28.

one? There is no simple way to determine plausible criteria here, but that is not crippling. We can say that there is one experience with good and bad qualities and seek to determine its overall value, or we can countenance two simultaneous experiences, one good and one bad. On the latter alternative, we can ask whether the person's experience is *overall* (intrinsically) good or bad. This is not to posit additivity of intrinsic value and abandon organicity but to recognize a kind of *combinability* of the separate intrinsic values of experiences over moments of life. Such combination is something we must reckon with in any case to assess how good a life is.[24]

One further point is appropriate here. My positive intuitive notion of a good experience has been partially explicated by appeal to the concept of the kind of experience that makes life choiceworthy. Is my account circular because I define 'intrinsically good' in terms of, in effect, 'intrinsically good life'? I am not giving a definition or analysis of 'good life' in any sense, as opposed to an explication (and I am willing to leave open whether Moore was right in thinking that there is a significant sense of 'indefinable' in which 'good' is indefinable). But one point to note is that if only experiences are intrinsically good, then one's life, not being an experience, cannot be intrinsically good, as opposed to inherently good. Still, this is only because a succession of experiences is not necessarily an experience. It is, however, in a broad sense *experiential*. We need a term for a good life or indeed for any desirable whole made up of intrinsically good experiences, or of a kind and proportion of them such that it is overall desirable to realize that whole. 'Choiceworthy' might do for lives, and perhaps also for sequences of experiences, say those constituting an evening. But it must be understood in terms of the things we intuitively take to be good, such as enjoyable social and aesthetic experiences. Another possibility is the term 'compositely good' (or 'compositionally good'); not all goods are such, and basic ones cannot be.[25]

It may help to draw an analogy to epistemology. The general idea is to explicate intrinsic goodness intuitively, in terms of experiences, as we do grounds of justification, and then to provide a way to use the notion to guide choice as we use the notion of justification to guide the formation and criticism of belief. Certain social, hedonic, and aesthetic qualities of experiences are the sorts of things for which we (rationally) choose to have experiences; the choiceworthy experiences are the kinds of thing for which we ultimately choose lives themselves.

---

[24] For a defense of the additivity of intrinsic value (once we have 'basic' intrinsic values to work with), see Zimmerman, *The Nature of Intrinsic Value*, esp. ch. 5.

[25] For support of the idea that we must rely on intuitive starting points in the theory of value and discussion of how overall value is to be understood in the light of those he chooses for his base clauses in a recursive value theory, see Thomas Hurka, 'Two Kinds of Organic Unity,' *Journal of Ethics*, 2 (1998).

5. The ontology of intrinsic value

Nothing I have said entails that intrinsic or inherent goodness is a non-natural property. If, however, they are consequential in the way I have suggested, then they are indeed properties, and thus a kind of realism is implied. This realism is of a special sort, however; for experiences of the kind that have intrinsic value are *mind-dependent*, or at least *life-dependent*. Hence there cannot be anything of intrinsic value in a world in which there are no persons—or minds or at least living things capable of experience.

By contrast, an *inherently* valuable thing can exist in an otherwise empty world. But there is a sense in which such a thing is axiologically unfulfilled. It is, to be sure, good 'in itself,' as non-relationally and non-instrumentally good.[26] Inherent goodness is a significant status, but inherently good things do not *directly* provide reasons for action nor, simply as unexperienced inherent goods, contribute to the experiential goodness of any life. This is not to deny that a life in which one's friends flourish is better than a life experientially just like it in which one has the same evidence that they do, but is wrong. The former life is even better in itself—inherently. We could also call the former more choiceworthy if we are thinking of choosing in the light of knowing the important facts about each, including the error in one of them. Its inherent superiority makes it preferable in the contemplation of it; its entailing the realization of additional intrinsic value—which it does since the friends' flour-ishing entails that realization—provides an other-regarding reason to choose it over the alternative.[27] But for the person in question, neither life is better in the living of it. We can and indeed should insist that the point of view of the subject living a life is not the *only* one from which to make assessments of its goodness; but this does not require treating all non-instrumental goodness as intrinsic or taking the inherent to be as basic as the intrinsic.

What about Moore's idea that (the property of being) *good* is simple? Butchvarov has suggested that it is a generic property, presumably a determinable

---

[26] Arguably, we may say non-relationally *hence* non-instrumentally good. But suppose one makes a device for capturing emissions that do not and may never exist. Could we not say it is a good pollution control device, where the goodness is plainly instrumental? We might reasonably rule that this is *potential* instrumental good-ness and that actual instrumental goodness requires the existence (past, present, or future) of something to which the instrumentally good thing is a means. I cannot here explore the merits of the main alternatives on this matter; the contrast between inherent and instrumental value that I make use of is that the former, but not the latter, is strictly (presumably even conceptually) necessary for that to which it is a means.

[27] Suppose we know that creating something of a kind that has inherently good instances *could* not lead to anyone's having a valuable experience of it. Perhaps a painting could be created such that the attempted viewing of it immediately destroys it (nor does it have any other way of figuring in a valuable experience). Does it (as opposed to, for instance, the intrigue of producing it) provide any reason to create it? (If the impossibility is *logical*, of course, the thing in question is not inherently good.)

such as shape.[28] There are indefinitely many shapes, as there are colors. Are these determinable properties simple? There is a sense in which they may be: one does not define them (or the determinates under them) by genus and difference. Something at least highly analogous seems to hold for the property of being a good experience.

Shapes and colors, however, are apparently natural properties; why not, then, conceive value properties as natural? Moore said one thing on this score that impressed C. D. Broad and needs examination.[29] It is that there is a sense in which what we intuitively call natural properties are *descriptive*, and goodness is not. Insofar as 'fully' describing anything makes sense, can we not fully describe something that is intrinsically good without saying whether it is intrinsically good? This would seem so if, from our description, as with a description of a painting, it does not 'analytically' follow (as Moore could plausibly claim it does not) that it is good or that it is not good. For in that case we cannot be plausibly thought to have 'implicitly' described it as good or as not good. That will remain, in *one* sense, an 'open question.'

To look at the matter from the other direction, if I tell you that a painting (for instance) is good, have I even partially described it? One plausible reaction is that I have not; but another, perhaps as natural, is 'You've described it as good, but now tell me more about it.' Still another is 'I know what sorts of things characterize a good painting; which do you have in mind?'

Pushing this line further, we might get something it is natural to call *normative disjunctivism*, the view that an attribution of a normative property is equivalent to an ascription of a disjunction of relevant grounding properties. If we suppose that for each normative property, there are certain natural properties on which, as a matter of conceptual truth, it is consequential, this view gains some support. The supposition also provides for a contrast with natural properties, since, so far as the notion of a natural property is clear, the counterpart point apparently does not hold for them. But must there be a definite list of base properties for each normative one? And, if not, do we, for any context of normative attribution, have a way to determine what base properties are implicitly ascribed? We need at least a theory of normative properties and a theory of kinds of description, and apart from such theories it is not clear how

---

[28] For a detailed account of goodness along these lines see Panayot Butchvarov, *Skepticism in Ethics* (Bloomington: Indiana University Press, 1986), esp. 63–6.

[29] Explicating Moore, Broad said, 'a description of a thing can be complete even if it omits those characteristics of it which, though determined solely by its intrinsic nature, are not themselves intrinsic. E.g., a pleasant experience, which is also good, could not be completely described unless its pleasantness was mentioned. But it could be completely described without its goodness being mentioned. I find it most difficult to follow or accept this.' But he does admit that goodness is a 'derivative characteristic' ('Moore's Ethical Doctrines,' in Schilpp (ed.), *The Philosophy of Moore*, 60).

much weight to give to Moore's initially plausible claim that goodness is a non-natural property.

There is something further we should note, something perhaps more controversial. It is not clear that the properties of being intrinsically or inherently valuable or, for that matter, any broadly normative properties, have causal power. Their non-normative base properties do. If this is correct—if, for instance, injustice's causing a revolt is a matter of the elements underlying the injustice doing the causal work, then the point may help to explain why normative properties are not plausibly considered natural or, perhaps, even descriptive.[30] (One might also take it to imply that they are not really properties at all.) But, one might reply, does shape, as such, have causal power, as opposed to the circularity, say, of a wheel's having it? One answer is that a circular thing may have causal power qua circular, where *being circular* is a shape property. Does injustice, for instance, have causal power qua normative property, say as a moral evil? The reality of moral intrinsic value, like that of other kinds of intrinsic value, does not self-evidently entail that *as* intrinsically valuable, such things have causal power.

If intrinsic value properties (of which the most generic are being intrinsically good, being intrinsically bad, and being intrinsically neutral) are natural properties, they are then certainly real. But surely they can be real without being natural, and they can perhaps be natural without being causal. I leave open whether they are causal, but I am taking them to be real properties. Are they, however, as Moore and others have thought, *essential* to their possessors?[31]

If intrinsic value properties belong to *experiences*, and if the (intrinsic) value properties of experiences are (necessarily) consequential on their phenomenal properties, then there is reason to take the former to be essential. For the phenomenal properties of an experience are plausibly considered essential to it. What about thought properties, such as silently reciting a certain Shakespearian sonnet? If these are not phenomenal, they in any event seem essential to the experiences that have them. But we again find difficulty regarding criteria of individuation. An experience of a painting in which I am conscious of a yellow patch in that painting is not of the same experience-type as one in which I am conscious of red in the same spot. Asked which color I like better, I might respond by saying I can answer only on the basis of experiences of each. Suppose, however, that a painting is designed to have that spot go from yellow

---

[30] In 'Ethical Naturalism and the Explanatory Power of Moral Properties' (in *Moral Knowledge*) I have explored in detail the question whether moral properties are causal.

[31] For discussion of the apparent essentiality of intrinsic value see Zimmerman, *The Nature of Intrinsic Value*, e.g. 47–9; and Lemos, *Intrinsic Value*, esp. ch. 3.

to red with each viewing. Then one might be inclined to speak of a single, changing experience of the painting rather than of two experiences differing in respect of the difference between yellow and red.

We might, then, speak of a *qualitative, fine-grained mode of individuation* and of a *coarse-grained, temporal unification mode*, the kind illustrated by the second case. In the second case, pragmatic factors may also enter in. If, for instance, we are concerned with viewing paintings, then even two viewings in rapid succession with only a movement of the head between them will yield two experiences; if we are concerned with how a person likes the experience of entering a newly decorated room, then a view of paintings, furniture, and rugs may count as a single experience.

In replying to his critics Moore said something quite pertinent to this question: that there is a sense in which pleasure is not intrinsic to an experience. For you and I can have the same experience of the taste of caviar and one of us like it, the other not. He does not, however, take up criteria of individuation at this point. Presumably pleasure is not intrinsic to any experience *non-hedonically*, say gustatorily, characterized, since any such experience could be enjoyed or not; but on a qualitative standard of individuation, pleasure is surely an intrinsic experiential property.[32] Indeed, he goes on to say that if we speak of an experience of being pleased by the taste of caviar, then the pleasure in question *is* intrinsic. Calling an experience one of being pleased is giving it a hedonic characterization. (Perhaps he is thinking of experience-*types*. Doubtless pleasure is not intrinsic to an experience-type unless it is essential to it, and pleasure is not intrinsic or essential to the type, tasting caviar. But Broad, to whom Moore was responding here, was presumably thinking of experience-tokens, as I am when I speak of experiences as the bearers of intrinsic value.)

A further point is that, plainly, to call an experience one of the taste of caviar is not to give a phenomenally 'complete' description (whether we speak of types or of tokens). Perhaps we can say that if a description of an experience (token) is phenomenally complete, it will include any hedonic properties the experience has, and if one of them is pleasure, then the token necessarily has that property, presumably in virtue of (another set of) its intrinsic properties. In that case, if a pleasurable experience is necessarily good, then its goodness is also essential to it.

Moore must have seen something we need not deny: we *can* specify a type of experience in a coarse way by specifying what its object is; and when we do this,

---

[32] This would be denied by a proponent of the conative (intrinsic desire) theory of pleasure suggested by Richard B. Brandt. I have noted serious difficulties for that theory in 'Prospects for a Naturalization of Practical Reason: Humean Instrumentalism and the Normative Authority of Desire,' *International Journal of Philosophical Studies*, 10 (2002).

we do not foreclose whether it is pleasant or not, since an experience even of, say, a backrub may not be pleasant. But this is quite compatible with saying that when an experience is pleasant, its pleasantness is an intrinsic property of it. For calling the experience one of a backrub is a coarse specification in terms of a single object (note that one can have an experience that is of both the taste of caviar and the sound of crude music, but we may refer only to the former if that is the *focal* object or is salient), whereas calling an experience pleasant is (in one way) a more fine-grained—and is a phenomenally more specific—characterization.

Inherent value properties might seem to admit of the same treatment as their intrinsic value counterparts. But there is at least one important difference. An inherently valuable thing can retain its identity across changes that alter its inherent value. A beautiful painting can be damaged without ceasing to be the painting it is; this is clear, at least, where it is fully restorable. If, however, we specify inherent value *given the exact (non-relational) condition of the thing in question*, then there is the same kind of reason for saying that the inherent value properties of a thing are essential to it as for saying that intrinsic value proper-ties of a thing are. I do not, however, claim that it is clear that we *must* consider either kind of property to be essential.

6. The epistemology of intrinsic value

I will be brief in discussing the question of how we know propositions about intrinsic value. This is in part because I have addressed the topic in some detail elsewhere[33] and in part because my most important points are neutral with respect to the various plausible positions on the epistemology of value.

In *Principia* Moore made the sweeping claim that propositions about the good are all synthetic, and he clearly took some of them to be a priori as well.[34] Here again the concept of goodness as a determinable is a useful focus. There is some reason to think that the domain of determinables and their determinates is one where synthetic a priori truths occur. But do they? I doubt that anyone has shown that the proposition that nothing is red and green all over at once is either analytic or empirical, and the proposition that if something is square, then it is not round seems quite similar on this score.[35] Do we, however, know a priori that, for instance, pleasure is (intrinsically) good and that burning

---

[33] In e.g. ch. 11 of *Moral Knowledge* and in 'Moderate Intuitionism.'

[34] He said, for example, that 'propositions about the good are all of them synthetic and never analytic' (7).

[35] This position is defended in ch. 4 of my *Epistemology*, 2nd edn. (London: Routledge, 2003).

people to death is morally bad? We need a lot of experience to be in a position to know these things; the background knowledge needed, involving such notions as that of the intrinsically good and the morally bad, requires considerable conceptual sophistication. But arguably the required experience is only that needed to acquire the concepts and is not evidential. Could we know general propositions about value, say that pain is intrinsically bad, in the way we know empirical truths, such as laws of nature? I doubt this, largely on account of the different kinds of grounds appropriate to each; but I will not pursue the matter here.

There is another way to approach the epistemological issue. Suppose it is not only necessary but a priori that, as Moore held, between 'the propositional function "*x* is intrinsically good"... and the function "the fact that an action which you can do would produce *x* is *some* reason for supposing that you ought to do that action"... there is a two-way necessary connection.' Then, if we know a priori that producing pleasure is a basic reason for action, we may conclude by a priori reasoning that it is intrinsically good. This does not presuppose that the notion of a reason for action is more basic than that of the intrinsically good, though it is compatible with that view.[36] Indeed, we can treat both goodness and reasonhood as common consequences of the same supervenience bases, including pleasure and pain. For Moore, however, reasonhood implies intrinsic goodness; and unless he countenances moral goodness, he could not (as I would) take the fact that an act would be, say, a breaking of a promise or a deprivation of liberty as a basic reason for action.

Suppose, on the other hand, that basic axiological knowledge is empirical. If value properties are causal, or indeed natural in any sense, this would seem possible. Might one not still have a kind of intuitive knowledge of such propositions as that enjoying viewing a beautiful painting is intrinsically good? And might one not still be able to have non-inferential knowledge of some propositions attributing intrinsic value to experiences? I cannot see why these possibilities must be ruled out. It is not as if only a priori knowledge could be intuitive and non-inferential.

Moreover, even apart from whether principles of practical reason can be known non-inferentially, the most important point here is that much the same ones may be retained as on a rationalist epistemology. I refer to principles indicating that there is reason to avoid pain, to seek pleasure, to weigh future

[36] This view is suggested by some (but only some) of what Thomas Nagel says in *The View from Nowhere* (Oxford: Oxford University Press, 1986). See e.g. ch. 8, sections 5 and 6. A position further in the direction of taking rationality to be more basic than value is Elizabeth Anderson's view that 'to be intrinsically valuable is to be the immediate object of such a rational attitude' (she refers to 'love, respect, consideration, affection, honor and so forth'). See *Value in Ethics and Economics* (Cambridge, Mass.: Harvard University Press, 1993), 20.

goods on a par with present ones other things equal, to take account of probabilities in deliberation, and so forth. Thus, although I favor a moderate rationalist conception of such principles, I do not think that the kind of theory of intrinsic value I am developing requires it in order to sustain highly similar principles for guiding and appraising conduct. Those principles could also be retained if, instead of distinguishing intrinsic from inherent value, we took inherent value to be a kind of intrinsic value. Neither my preferred epistemology nor my proposed taxonomy interferes with the selection and defense of plausible normative principles.

7. The intrinsically valuable as a basis of reasons for action

Suppose that there is a close connection between intrinsic value and reasons for action. More must be said to indicate how my account of intrinsic value may contribute to the general theory of practical reason. Let me first bring out the advantage of conceiving the bearers of intrinsic value as experiences rather than concrete objects or even such dispositional elements as knowledge and virtue.

I assume that reasons for action are always expressible in (though not only in) the kind of infinitive clause that indicates the content of an intention or follows 'in order to' in an explanation of action, as in 'I agreed to read the book in order to satisfy a long-standing curiosity.'[37] The contents of these clauses are apparently types of events, especially act-types, all of which are things that can be realized (and in that sense brought about). More important, if their being realized (tokened) in a certain way has intrinsic value, then—as indicated earlier—there is some reason for the agent to act to realize them, though the ascription of intrinsic value does not specify just what it is that has that value. Now experiences, like actions, admit of a type–token distinction, and to bring either one about is to token it. Might we not say, then, that experiences of performing actions are among the bearers of intrinsic value? Surely the experience of conversing, of singing, of swimming, and of many other actions can be intrinsically good. These often prominently include the experience of *producing* something inherently good, such as a fine poem or a beautiful sculpture.

To see how this idea is best understood, consider what it is to do something 'for its own sake.' This is to do it for qualities of performing it that attract us on their own account. These are always experienceable qualities; and there is much plausibility in taking the experience we have in acting, particularly in respect of

[37] I argue for this view in ch. 5 of *The Architecture of Reason*, where I also suggest some contrasts between the propositional and infinitival forms of expression of reasons for action.

these qualities, to be the bearer of any intrinsic good we seek in performing the action. If I want to satisfy my curiosity for its own sake, I want to experience the acquisition of the relevant knowledge, not merely to acquire it. To have a machine implant the relevant knowledge in me by brain manipulation while I sleep would not fulfill the particular desire I have. It is the experience of gaining the knowledge that I specially want, and if that experience is rewarding in a certain non-instrumental way, it will be intrinsically good.

In part, the general idea is this. If there is anything intrinsically good (or intrinsically bad), it provides a basic (if defeasible) reason for action to bring it about (or continue its existence, which is roughly equivalent to bringing about a later stage of the thing in question). Intrinsically good things should thus be the *kinds* of things that can be realized in the way the act-types (or at least experience-types), which are (or are specified by) the contents of reasons for action, can be realized. Experiences can be realized in that way; paintings, as opposed to the actions of producing and viewing them, cannot. If intrinsic goodness belongs to certain kinds of experiences, it can accordingly figure in the content of reasons for action, and intrinsically good experiences will figure centrally in the content of the most basic kind of reasons for action: to enjoy a symphony, for instance, or to swim in cool waters, to talk with a loved one, or reduce the pain of a headache.

The suggested view of reasons is connected with the idea that the intrinsically good is that in virtue of which a life is choiceworthy. Surely a life is choiceworthy on the basis of the experiences that—as I would put it—constitute that life. Knowledge and virtue are, to be sure, good 'in themselves'—where that means *inherently good*. But would they make a life good apart from experience? In principle, a person could be created with a great deal of both, but in a deep sleep; if such a person ceased to exist before experiencing anything, would the person's life be good? Inherent goods provide non-instrumental reasons for action because of their constitutive place in intrinsically good experiences. This gives them incalculable normative importance. But their existence in itself, as opposed to the experiences we bring about in which they essentially figure, does not make anyone's life, as lived, better.

Might the *only* reasons for action be grounded in considerations of intrinsic value, for instance of pleasure and pain? Suppose this is so. It would not follow that the *notion* of intrinsic value, as opposed to that of something which *has* it, must come into the concept of a reason for action. Still, not only instrumental reasons, but also non-instrumental reasons deriving from inherently good things, might ultimately depend on a relation to what *is* intrinsically good or intrinsically bad. We can say this without treating the concept of value as a constituent in that of a reason for action. I do not want to presuppose, however, that all reasons for action are grounded in considerations of value. I leave open, for instance, that a deontological reason such as that a deed would be dishonest can provide a reason independently of intrinsic value (at least of non-moral intrinsic value).

I am supposing, however, that some experiences are *moral* and have moral intrinsic value. Moral reasons, then, need not derive from non-moral grounds even if they do ultimately depend on considerations of intrinsic value (including disvalue), and they can be a kind of basic reason for action. I have mentioned indignation; an experience of this emotion can be intrinsically good qua moral, as well as inherently good on the basis of its overall moral character, yet intrinsically bad hedonically. The *experience* of being done an injustice can be not only painful, and in that way intrinsically bad, but also (intrinsically) morally bad; and in my view even the felt attraction to doing an injustice is an intrinsically morally bad experience.[38]

To be sure, to say that some basic reasons for action derive from considerations of moral value leaves open whether all moral reasons for action so derive. I have said nothing implying that the good is more fundamental than the right, as it in some sense would be if all moral reasons derive from considerations of intrinsic moral value. But my view certainly makes that position intelligible and indicates some of the questions that must be pursued in appraising it.

One further matter needs attention to fill out my sketch of the connection between intrinsic value and reasons for action. Is there, in the domain of such reasons, an analogue of the organicity of intrinsic value? Recall the case of *Schadenfreude*. If I enjoy teasing someone, I thereby have a (normative) reason to do it; but if I am pained by (the experience of) causing someone else to suffer and believe that the person in question will suffer from my teasing, I thereby have a (twofold) reason not to do it. Now suppose that my pleasure will (quantitatively and qualitatively) outweigh her suffering. Do I thereby have better reason to tease her than not to? Not if, as is quite rational, I believe that pleasure taken in something that one knows causes pain as this does is unbefitting to its object in a way that renders the pleasure inherently bad. Experiencing such pleasure even in prospect is intrinsically aversive, say repugnant; this kind of experience provides reason to avoid realizing that prospect. Indeed, I do not have to believe anything this theoretical in order to have non-instrumental reason to avoid the teasing. As I have described the case, then, I apparently have better reason not to tease. Suppose this is so. Is it something I know by summation of the values in question? I think not.

---

[38] It is of course not self-evident that experience (or anything else) can have moral intrinsic value; that it can is argued in my 'The Axiology of Moral Experience,' *Journal of Ethics*, 2 (1998).

Indeed, summation, so far as it is possible in a rough-and-ready way, would not work to give me a decision even apart from considerations of fittingness. We must use practical judgment to decide how to weight the good against the bad or, more generally, sets of positive against sets of negative intrinsic values. This is something Ross insisted on in connection with conflicts of prima facie duties. It applies to what we have overall reason to do, as well as to ascertaining what is intrinsically good overall.

If basic moral reasons for action depend entirely on things of intrinsic value, then the kind of organic composition of prima facie duties Ross saw as yielding final duty is to be expected. It might in fact be expected even if values play a lesser role in grounding duties, say because some duties are purely deontological. For instance, if there are duties of beneficence and also of self-improvement, each set concerns promotion of good things and elimination of bad ones in the lives of others or in one's own life. The best overall result will often be determinable only by taking into account the organicity of the values in question. Reading all afternoon might best promote my knowledge; helping a friend might best reduce his suffering; and there may be many other considerations pertinent to my decision regarding the same period of time.

Conclusion

The theory of intrinsic value sketched here is experientialist, pluralistic, internalist but not subjectivistic, realistic about values, and, in the way the most plausible kinds of intuitionism are, moderately rationalist about knowledge of certain propositions about value. It takes what is intrinsically good to provide basic reasons for action, but does not imply that every basic reason for action is grounded in intrinsic value. The theory is consonant with the idea that goodness—whether intrinsic or inherent—is unanalyzable, but it is not committed to that view. It is also consonant with the idea that value properties are not natural properties—so far as that idea is clear—but is not committed to that either. It is committed to the view that value properties are consequential on non-value properties. If these are properly characterized as natural or, as seems plausible, 'descriptive,' value properties can be consequential on them whether or not they themselves are natural. Although a property cannot be identical with the set of properties on which it is consequential, it may or may not be of the same ontological kind.

How Moorean does all this make the position? This depends in part on how much significance attaches to distinguishing between intrinsic and inherent value and attributing, to many things Moore considered intrinsically valuable, inherent value instead. It also depends on how much significance attaches to avoiding Moore's commitment to non-natural properties. Another difference is that moral value is specifically posited by the theory I have introduced, but not by Moore's;[39] nor does Moore's view provide for basic deontological reasons for action. I have also broadened the principle of organic unities both in considering aspects of the valuable as well as parts of it and in applying the principle to the inherently as well as the intrinsically valuable.

Still another difference between my view and Moore's concerns the connection between the right and the good. He holds a kind of maximizing consequentialism. No such position follows from the theory of value I have sketched here (and I do not endorse it). It may indeed not follow from Moore's theory of value either, but the idea that the right is, in a quasi-quantitative way, derivable from the good is a major strain in his ethical thought.[40]

There is a great deal more that must be said to appraise the theory I have presented. The sketches of the relevant notion of experience and of criteria for individuating experiences need extension; the revised principle of organic unities and its application need further explication; and the nature of value properties and of their grounding in what seem to be natural properties is an unending philosophical problem. But I believe that at least if a cognitivist view is sound, then the kind of experientialist, pluralistic axiological intuitionism presented here is a major option for ethical theory.

[39] I do not take this to be obvious. But given Moore's presentation of his utilitarian view of goodness and such remarks as that 'so far as definition goes, to call a thing a virtue is merely to declare that it is a means to good' (*Principia*, 173), this is a plausible reading.

[40] In e.g. *Ethics*, Moore says that 'the total consequences of right actions must always be as good, intrinsically, as any which it was *possible* for the agent to produce under the circumstances' (98).

5

Personal Good

Connie S. Rosati

When we survey the variety of lives people lead, we discover a great many ways of living in which a person's life can go well. We find a correspondingly diverse array of goods, things the presence of which can help to make a life go well. A person can engage in many avocations, such as gardening, running, woodworking, or music-making. She can undertake various jobs or careers, becoming a doctor or a lawyer, a preacher or a parent, a sales agent or a soldier. She can live a life centered on spiritual, intellectual, material, artistic, or social values, a life alone, in a convent, or in love. But while there are many goods and many ways of living good lives, it isn't true of any arbitrary individual that the presence of just any of these goods or the choice of just any good way of living would make *her* life go well. Perhaps she cannot care about or take an interest in certain activities or pursuits; perhaps she lacks the talent or aptitude for others. What is the exact nature of the relation between a person and certain good things or good ways of living that constitutes their being good *for her*?[1]

Any attempt to answer this question and explain what it is for something to be good for a person must come to grips with our dual nature.[2] We are

I want to thank Sarah Buss, Richard Dees, David Sobel, Mark Timmons, and members of the philosophy department at the University of California, San Diego, for their helpful comments on earlier versions of this paper.

[1] My discussion assumes that a person's intrinsic, nonmoral good is comprised of things that are themselves good, or at least not bad. I proceed in this way in order to bracket certain difficult questions that could not be explored adequately in the space of this essay, among them, the question of whether bad or even evil things can be noninstrumental parts of an individual's welfare. I suspect that if they cannot be parts of our welfare, it is not because a correct analysis of personal good precludes them. Rather they are wholly or largely precluded because of our nature as rational agents and our nature as a particular type of biological creature. Again, I won't be able to explore these suspicions here, though I will very briefly address the problem of evil activity as an apparent counterexample to my analysis. My discussion also makes the simplifying assumption that a good life is a life in which a person largely obtains things good for her. In fact, though, any more global assessment of a person's life will have to attend, among other things, to how 'narrative relations' among life events can affect the value of that life. See Velleman (1991). Velleman has suggested in conversation that the impact of narrative structure on the value of lives is just an instance of the phenomenon of organic unities.

[2] Amartya Sen makes a seemingly similar point. See Sen (1985: 185–7, 1987: 41). But he argues for a duality in the sense that a person's success isn't to be judged purely in terms of his well-being, but also in terms of his agency, since persons may value goals and commitments not a part of their well-being. Sen's point thus

humans—a certain type of biological creature. As such, we have determinate properties which, as Peter Railton has stressed, are not a matter of how we conceive ourselves (1986a: 14–16). Yet we are also agents—creatures with a capacity for autonomy that enables us, at least to some degree, to engage in self-transformation and, thus, to be as we conceive ourselves. Whether something is good for us will surely depend on both our humanity and our agency, on our determinate features and our capacity to determine our futures.

Any attempt to specify what it is for something to be good for a person must also come to grips with the paradoxical experience of our good. We commonly encounter our good as a discovery, indeed, a revelation. We uncover our untapped talent for comedy; we marvel at our sudden interest in the history of polar exploration; we unexpectedly find a new love in an old friend. Yet as we plan and live out our lives, our good often seems to be up to us—it seems for us to decide what to pursue and so for us to decide where our interest shall lie.[3] We decide to be parents rather than priests, soldiers rather than salesmen, understanding full well that we thereby shape our current and future interests. This duality in how we experience our good no doubt reflects our dual nature.

My aim in this essay is to sketch an analysis of personal good that squares with our humanity and our agency and with our experience of our good as both discovered and invented.[4] I mean for this sketch to be preliminary, and so while I attempt to make an intuitive case for the view and to show how it can begin to address certain theoretical challenges to accounts of welfare, I will not attempt to deal fully with the many questions it will no doubt raise.

I will generally use the expression 'personal good' in place of more common terms, such as 'flourishing', 'welfare', 'well-being', and 'self-interest'. I do so because it encapsulates three points that these other terms may not so readily call to mind.[5] First, an account of personal good is an account of goodness for

---

bears on the relative significance of a person's well-being and his other values, whereas my point concerns how the duality of our nature affects the proper characterization of well-being itself. For discussion related to Sen's, see Sobel (1998).

[3] R. M. Hare (1963) attempted to accommodate both freedom and reason in his universal prescriptivism. But Hare's notion of freedom differs from the notion of autonomy that I employ, and he means something different when he talks about being constrained by reasons than I mean when I talk about discovering one's good. See Rosati (2003: n. 46).

[4] This essay offers a first stab at an analysis of good for a person. A fuller treatment of the nature of a person's good would offer not only a characterization of the *good for* relation but of what it is for things to be better or worse for a person and of what makes for a good life for a person. I will have little to say in this essay about alternative theories of personal good. See Rosati (1995a, 1995b, 2000, and manuscript a) for critical discussion of certain important views.

[5] Stephen Darwall has also used the expression 'personal good'. See Darwall (1983: chs. 8–9), where he appears to endorse a view like Rawls's. For his more recent ideas, see Darwall (2002). Darwall has indicated that he finds no great difference among the expressions 'a person's interest', 'welfare', 'benefit', 'well-being', 'good', 'happiness', or what 'would make her life go best'. Joseph Raz has distinguished between the notions

persons—beings who, as just noted, are not only humans but also autonomous agents. Second, an adequate theory of goodness for a person must allow that what is good for one person may not be good for another.[6] Finally, because we are persons, our good is personal in the more mundane sense that, at least under favorable conditions, individual choice and effort figure crucially in how some things come to be a part of our good.

An account of personal good has implications, of course, for what things comprise an individual's good, but it does not itself concern substantive welfare. Instead, like G. E. Moore's account of the nonrelational property *good*, an analysis of the relational property *good for a person* concerns a particular normative feature of things in the world, most notably, of choices, activities, pursuits, commitments, relationships, and, derivatively, states of affairs. The goodness at issue is nonmoral, nonaesthetic, and nonperfectionist, although an individual's good may include as components moral, aesthetic, and perfectionist values.[7] As is well known, Moore himself was skeptical of the idea that things could be 'good for' someone; I briefly address this skepticism later.

According to the analysis offered here, goodness for a person must be understood on the model of a healthy love relationship. Such relationships have characteristic features that explain both their importance in our lives and their reason-giving force. Achieving our good at a time is a matter of bringing ourselves into relations with various persons and pursuits, activities and undertakings, that exhibit these same features. Faring well is, we might say, a form of successful loving.

1. 'Fit'

The property of being good for a person is instantiated when a particular relation holds between a person and some activity, pursuit, individual, or undertaking. We would therefore expect theories of welfare to specify the nature of this relation. Yet some of the more prominent theories of welfare in fact say little, if anything, about it, and this suggests that they must be offering analyses or accounts of some property other than personal good. It may be true, for example, that what is good for a person, P, is something she would want herself

---

of well-being and self-interest, treating 'well-being' as 'the general term for evaluating success in life' and treating self-interest as a largely biological notion. But he treats the notions of well-being and welfare as the same. See Raz (1986: 294–5).

  [6] For a clear discussion of the notion of relational value, see Railton (1986a: 10–11).
  [7] I here follow Wayne Sumner's way of expressing the point. See Sumner (1996).

to want were she fully informed and rational—were she 'P+'.[8] Presumably P+ would see what relations obtain between P and X, and so what P+ would want for P in light of what she sees may reliably indicate P's good—at least if her desire springs in part from concern for P.[9] Even so, the fact that P+ would want X for P does not tell us the nature of the relation between X and P. Likewise, what is good for P may be what anyone (including P) *ought* to want for P out of concern for her or *for her sake*.[10] But surely whether one ought to want X for P for her sake *depends* on the relation between X and P. And so to say that what is good for P is what one ought to want for her sake is not yet to tell us what that relation is.[11]

As a starting point in our effort to understand personal good, we might say that it consists in a relation of 'fit' or 'suitability' between persons and things: those activities and pursuits, commitments and relationships, that are intrinsically, nonmorally good for a person are all and only those that fit or suit her. Taking this metaphor as our lead, we might describe the central problem for theorizing about personal good as the problem of characterizing the relation of fit or suitability between a person P and any X that constitutes X's being (intrinsically, nonmorally) good for P. The notion of goodness for a person is itself a normative notion. Accordingly, any characterization of the relation of fit or suitability must be normative: when that relation obtains, the fact of its obtaining must give rise to normative reasons.

Now whether activities, pursuits, commitments, or relationships fit or suit a particular individual depends on a variety of factors, among them, her physical makeup, personality, capacities, and circumstances, including her culture. And those goods that do fit or suit her may come to do so in various ways. Some goods come ready to wear—they fit right off the rack. The clearest cases concern those instrumental goods that we need, physiologically, in order to develop properly and exist in good health, such as appropriate nutrition and medical care, and those 'primary goods' that a person will want no matter what

---

[8] See Railton (1986*b*). See also Railton (1986*a*). Railton defends a view like this, though it is not altogether clear whether he means it as an account of welfare, as some of his writings suggest, or of what is good from a person's point of view. See Darwall (2002: 109 n. 6, 111 n. 21).

[9] Darwall (2002: 31) has observed that 'if any informed-desire standard can serve as a plausible criterion of welfare, . . . it will be something like the following. Something is for someone's good if it is what that person would want for herself, as she actually is, insofar as she is fully knowledgeable and experienced *and* unreservedly concerned for herself.' Darwall does not himself embrace such an analysis. I believe that it would fail, in any case, since it still tells us nothing about the good for relation. My point here is that a fully informed person who cares for someone and, thus, is disposed to want what will benefit her, may well respond to the appropriate relation when she sees it.   [10] Darwall (2002) has recently defended this analysis.

[11] I develop this objection to Darwall's analysis of personal good in Rosati (forthcoming) and Rosati (manuscript *a*).

her conception of the good.[12] But 'ready-made' goods may include things intrinsically good for persons as well, as when an individual has a natural gift and affinity for an activity. Other goods come to fit us only with effort, with some alteration or tailoring, deliberate or accidental, undertaken by ourselves or (as is typical in childrearing) by others on our behalf. The needed adjustments may sometimes include that we alter ourselves; some things come to be a part of our good not because they fit us just as we are but because we bring ourselves (or circumstances bring us) to fit them. We may need to revise our relationships, change jobs, or adjust our routines and pastimes. But we may also need to develop our interests and capacities or to modify our temperaments and motivational tendencies. These considerations suggest that we can realize our good in two chief ways: we can find or produce those things that already fit us, or we can bring ourselves to fit those things we can find, including those we can dream up.

2. The *good for* relation

So what relation must an individual stand in to goods that come to fit her in these different ways such that some and not others suit her—are good *for her*— at least at a particular time? I see no way to make progress in identifying this relation without assuming that some of our judgments about a person's good are roughly correct and then investigating the relationship that seems to hold between a person and those things judged to be a part of her good.[13] I shall proceed accordingly, though my path will be a bit circuitous. I first look outward in an effort to identify important aspects of a person's achievement of her good. I then explore how a person must sometimes work to bring herself into the *good for* relation with things. Finally, I turn inward to our experience of our activities and undertakings in order to uncover the nature of that relation itself.

An example

Let's begin with an example of a life in which an individual attains things we would judge to be good for him and, indeed, attains them despite difficult

---

[12] For discussion of the place of biological wants and needs, see Raz (1986). Rawls first presented the notion of primary goods in (1971: § 15). I suggest here that primary goods are instrumental goods, but careful examination may show some, in fact, to be intrinsic.

[13] To proceed in this way is not to privilege our intuitions about personal good. We seek a plausible interpretation of our experience and a corresponding metaphysical picture of personal good, and the results of our enquiry might well upset some of our antecedent assessments of how an individual is faring.

circumstances. As he tells the tale in his *Autobiography*, Malcolm X was born to a dark-skinned Baptist minister and a light-skinned mother (Haley and Malcolm X 1965). Perhaps because of the difference in skin tone, Malcolm speculates, his parents fought bitterly, his father sometimes beating his mother. As a young boy, his family's home in Michigan was burned by members of a white racist group, and when Malcolm was 6, his father was killed, presumably by members of this same group. The effects of his father's death, compounded by the effects of the depression, were devastating. Ultimately, the pressures of poverty, of caring for eight children, and of fending off insensitive state welfare workers drove Malcolm's mother into a mental illness from which she never recovered. Malcolm and his siblings were dispersed to various foster homes. His misbehavior led to his placement briefly in a detention center at 13. Malcolm describes as the 'first major turning point' of his life an encounter with a teacher the year before he was to enter high school. When Malcolm, who was among the top students in the class, expressed interest in becoming a lawyer, the teacher responded that this 'was no realistic goal for a nigger' and suggested that he become a carpenter instead (ibid.: 38).

Malcolm found himself withdrawing from white people, he tells us. He moved to Boston to live with a half-sister from his father's first marriage, and his years there marked a steady decline. He obtained his first job, shining shoes at the Roseland State Ballroom, and moved on to positions as a busboy and then a dishwasher and a sandwich man on a train. As his own drug use progressively escalated, he turned to drug dealing, pimping, and finally to burglary. He hit bottom when he was ultimately busted for the last in a string of robberies, receiving a ten-year prison sentence. He was then not quite 21.

During his imprisonment, Malcolm's siblings began to write to him about the teachings of the black Muslim leader Elijah Muhammad. He went from a state of nonbelief—his fellow prisoners had nicknamed him 'Satan'—to a state of devout faith: 'I had sunk to the very bottom of the American white man's society when—soon now, in prison—I found Allah and the religion of Islam and it completely transformed my life' (ibid.: 153). He began the transformation by following his brother's instructions to stop eating pork and smoking cigarettes, which he initially thought his brother offered as part of a ploy to procure his release. Over many years, he developed through deliberate exercises (such as copying the dictionary) his reading and writing ability. He expanded his knowledge through voracious reading of books in the prison library. He engaged in a lengthy correspondence with Elijah Muhammad. And he learned how to pray. 'I still marvel at how swiftly my previous life's thinking pattern slid away from me, like snow off a roof. It is as though someone else I knew had lived by hustling and crime. I would be startled to catch myself thinking in a remote way of my earlier self as another person' (ibid.: 173). Malcolm went on to become, as we all know, a prominent Muslim leader; he married, and had a loving relationship with his wife and children. He had begun to moderate his views about the evil of whites as a result of a trip to Mecca shortly before his assassination.

Now we can well imagine many ways in which Malcolm's life might have gone better for him. It would have been better for Malcolm had his father not died, had his mother not become ill, had he been able to pursue his dream of becoming a lawyer, and, most fundamentally, had he not lived in a racist society.[14] Still, it is a remarkable fact that, against many odds, Malcolm X ultimately achieved a good life. Indeed, he salvaged what could have been a lost life.

So how was Malcolm able to succeed under such adverse circumstances? How is it that despite horrible experiences as a child, despite meager options and misguided choices as a teen and a young adult, Malcolm managed to achieve a good life rather than a life ruined for good? The short answer, in my view, is that he was an autonomous agent—the sort of being whose good is achieved, in intriguing ways, largely through autonomous activity. As I will suggest, Malcolm X's life illustrates the fact that we cannot be passive in the realization of our good and not simply because we must search out our good or because our good includes activities of various kinds. Rather, we cannot be passive because our activity is essential to *making* certain things a part of our good. Like a successful relationship, achieving and maintaining our good requires effort. Some goods do, as already noted, come to a person naturally. But many of the more fundamental parts of a person's good—including many of her deepest commitments, longer-term projects, and central avocations—require that she *work herself into a relationship* with a particular good.

In speaking of working one's way into a relationship with something, I mean to point to a familiar experience. We have all, at one time or another, undertaken a new activity or pursuit—say, climbing or dancing, practicing law or accounting—that we did not initially find intrinsically motivating. Perhaps we struggled with it, perhaps we even disliked it, perhaps we pursued it solely for instrumental reasons. Over time, however, engaging in it came to seem quite natural to us, even if not effortless. Our question, again, concerns, the relation that holds in these and other cases.

---

[14] Dworkin (1990: 73) has argued that the circumstances that make a life better and are too often unavailable include that a society be just. Obviously, we don't know for certain that Malcolm's life would have been better had it been different in the enumerated ways. But our ordinary value judgments favor the prediction that it would have been better.

Making something our good

It may help us to get a grip on that relation if we first look at how a person can get herself into it. How can she bring it about that something she may not, heretofore, have valued is now a part of her good? We can gain some hints of what the process might involve from Pascal's advice to the person who finds himself unable to believe in God even though he accepts the conclusion of the wager argument. The would-be-believer regards belief in God as unsupported by the evidence and as foreign to himself, though he recognizes the apparent value of believing. Pascal instructs him as follows:

Endeavour then to convince yourself, not by increase of proofs of God, but by the abatement of your passions. You would like to attain faith, and do not know the way; you would like to cure yourself of unbelief, and ask the remedy for it. Learn of those who have been bound like you, and who now stake all their possessions... Follow the way by which they began; *by acting as if they believe, taking the holy water, having masses said, etc.* Even this *will naturally make you believe....* (1910: 233, emphasis added)

Pascal's advice is akin to Aristotle's familiar ideas about the role of habit in the acquisition of moral virtue, though as I will explain in a moment, his discussion contains an additional point of importance to personal good. Pascal prescribes that the would-be-believer 'go through the motions', imitating the person who already believes. We might likewise suggest that to make one's own what was formerly alien a person must imitate the person who already values that thing.[15] She must act toward it as does the person who already regards it as a part of his good, treating that person's relation to that thing as an ideal.[16] Of course, learning to value in this way requires work and practice. We become better friends, spouses, parents, and colleagues, better practitioners of our hobbies and crafts, with effort and experience.

But just what is one trying to achieve in imitating the believer or the valuer? As Pascal describes it, these outer imitations have an internal aim: the alteration of a person's motives and, often concomitantly, the alteration of her self-conception. The would-be believer enacts the role of the believer in order to induce genuine belief—to *become a believer*—not merely to put on a good performance. Pascal might also have said that he seeks to induce genuine love of God: he tries to bring it about that his believer-like actions come from the inside out, from the natural motive to such action. The would-be valuer is similarly trying to induce

---

[15] If, as Elizabeth Anderson has argued, there are different modes of valuing appropriate to different types of goods, then this will partly involve coming to feel as natural the mode of valuing appropriate to a given thing. See Anderson (1993).

[16] Velleman (2002) describes a process akin to the one described by Pascal and like the one discussed in this essay.

an attitude toward a thing that will govern her actions, feelings, and intentions, so that her valuing actions likewise come from the inside out. Having induced that attitude, she comes to occupy a perspective from which she sees herself as having various noninstrumental reasons for action.

We see this basic process at work in the life of Malcolm X. Malcolm came to engage, initially for instrumental reasons, in the activities of the person for whom practicing Islam is a central good. Over time, he underwent motivational change and acquired a radically new self-conception, with the result that he acted and valued from the inside out, living the life of a genuine believer, a genuine valuer of his wife and children, a genuine honorer of his commitments, a genuine contributor to his community.

To emphasize, as I have thus far, Malcolm's own role in bringing about the goodness for him of the life he had is not to overlook the constraints within which he operated. After all, he didn't choose his upbringing or circumstances. He didn't choose to be in jail or select the religion adopted by his siblings. Moreover, given the facts about Malcolm, it is surely no accident that his decision to become a follower of Islam and to structure the life he did from within that religion worked out so well for him. He clearly had the intellectual aptitude, personality, and capacity for self-discipline to have become a lawyer, had circumstances permitted, and to become, as circumstances did permit, a spokesperson and leader in his church and community.[17]

Still, it would be a mistake to say that the life of a devotee of Islam was good for Malcolm *just as he was* when he first learned of the religion. Of course, it was true even at that time that it was *possible* for him to achieve a good life as a member of Islam. It was true of him, even at that time, that were he to choose this life and were he to pull it off, then it would be good for him. What wasn't true of him at that time was that *being* a devotee of Islam was good for him, that the tenets of Islam gave him noninstrumental reasons for action. The problem is not the epistemic difficulty that he didn't realize that it was good for him or that it gave him noninstrumental reasons for action. Rather, he did not stand in a relation to the practice of Islam such that it was true of Malcolm that it was good for him. He had to make it true through successful transformation of himself. Of course, to say that being a devotee of Islam did not give him noninstrumental reasons to act is not to say that he had no reason to act as he did. It is only to say that, with some qualifications, neither the reasons he had for undertaking his religious practice nor the reasons he had for acting as one would from within that practice concerned what was good for him at that time.

---

[17] In addition, Malcolm's father evidently advocated black-race purity and the return of black Americans to Africa, and so he must have had early exposure to ideas not unlike the teachings he ultimately embraced.

One might suggest that, nevertheless, undertaking to *become* a devotee of Islam was good for Malcolm even before *being* a devotee of Islam was good for him. I think we can acknowledge at least two senses in which this claim is true. First, perhaps any self-discipline intrinsically benefits a person, even when it will not produce a successful conversion; in that sense, the undertaking was good for him. Second, in Malcolm's case, where the conversion succeeded, the undertaking put him on the track to a transformation that enabled him to achieve a life good for him; it made (instrumental) sense for him to try to realize that life insofar as his concern was to achieve a good life. Yet to concede these two points is not to allow that in advance of his self-transformation, it was true of Malcolm that being a devotee of Islam or even becoming one was intrinsically good for him. We can say in advance only that it would be good for him if he chose it and made it good for himself, and so when we say, in advance of an agent's efforts, 'you should do X, it will be good for you', or 'if you did X, it would be good for you', the implicit suggestion of a benefit yet to be brought into existence must often be taken seriously.

There is the promise of a benefit, as it were, but a promise premised on a gamble. This is the extra element, I suggested earlier, that we find in Pascal's advice to the would-be believer and his appeal to habituation. As Pascal describes it, the would-be believer does not seek to believe because theoretical reason convinces him of God's existence. Rather, he draws a practical conclusion in favor of making the wager. He does not—indeed, cannot, as Pascal describes the balance of arguments—know in advance that God exists or that he will benefit from belief in God. Instead, he gambles on the benefits of belief and his efforts at habituation are in the service of making the wager. The person who seeks her good often finds herself in the position of making a gamble. She need not be convinced antecedently that something is good for her, and indeed, often cannot know in advance that it either is or will be good for her. But she might nevertheless see how it could be rationally supportable for her, yielding a life that would make sense to her while she was living it and affording her reasons for action. She may, as a result, draw the practical conclusion that it makes sense for her to regard it as her good 'in prospect'.[18]

---

[18] Let me here emphasize two qualifications to my description of the process of making something a part of one's good. First, we ought not to think of it as implying rigidly ordered and temporally distinct steps. It isn't, for example, that a person must first grasp how a certain good could be rationally supportable for herself, then engage in activities in order to induce motivational change. In the case of Malcolm X, for instance, he began to follow some of the instructions urged on him by his siblings before coming to believe in the truth of Islam and coming to accord it a central place in his life. A person may come to see how something might be rationally supportable for herself, for instance, only after she has come to engage in certain activities and begun to induce various other cognitive and motivational changes. Second, we shouldn't over-intellectualize the work done by an agent in seeing how a certain good might be rationally supportable for herself. She needn't have an argumentative scheme before her. Nor need she recognize something as

When a person, P, undertakes an activity, adopts an aim, or begins a relationship, claiming that she does so in order to achieve her good, she becomes subject to various agent-relative, hypothetical requirements. That is, having undertaken to X, certain hypothetical requirements come to apply to her, such as the requirement to undertake A, if A is a necessary means to X. Someone can, of course, be under a hypothetical requirement while lacking any reason to act at all.[19] The requirement on her is simply this: having undertaken to X and believing A is a necessary means to X, P must not continue to pursue X *and* refuse to undertake A. P might satisfy this requirement either by giving up X or by undertaking A. The requirement is hypothetical in that it is conditional on a hypothesis P accepts in adopting X as an end, namely, that in achieving X she will achieve something that is good for her.[20] The person who self-interestedly undertakes a pursuit thus makes a certain gamble—in choosing a particular career, for instance, she may gamble on a successful transformation of herself. No evidence she has at the outset can force her to—or assure her of—the conclusion that what she has undertaken will in fact be good for her.[21] If her hypothesis is correct, then she will have had reason to undertake or achieve X. But its being correct is contingent upon the success of that very undertaking. She will be justified in going after X *as a part of her good* only if the outcome of that very endeavor is success in making X good for her—success in entering into the *good for* relation with X.[22] Malcolm's undertakings, then, were not good for him at the time of his undertaking them, but in acting successfully on his choices, he brought it about that certain things were good for him and that he therefore had reason for—was justified in—having acted as he did.[23]

rationally supportable or good for her under that description. She must, however, have some sense of considerations in light of which a good makes sense for her.

[19] I have benefited here from Darwall's recent defense of his 'rational care' theory of welfare, adapting a line of argument he makes in discussing the normativity of welfare. See Darwall (1983: 15–17, 43–50). See also Broome (1999).

[20] Darwall (2002) argues that what is good for a person is what one ought to want for her for her sake, that is, insofar as one cares for her. One who cares for another, he maintains, is under certain hypothetical requirements, requirements conditional on a hypothesis the person accepts in caring for another, namely that the object of his concern is worthy of care. I here make a structurally similar point about those things one undertakes or seeks out as a part of one's good.

[21] The point I make here is akin to the point Velleman (1989b) has made in his discussion of epistemic freedom.

[22] The idea conveyed in this sentence may seem to resemble Bernard Williams's claims about 'moral luck', but our ideas differ in a critical respect. On Williams's view, the success of certain choices, which depends on matters outside of one's control, determines whether one was justified in what one did. The underlying picture seems to be that one fails or succeeds, in large measure due to luck, in achieving something the actual value of which is fixed quite apart from one's efforts. If I am right, in the case of personal good, whether something of value exists to be realized at all often depends on one's successful efforts. See Williams (1979).

[23] Of course, a person's choice can be justified even if her endeavor fails, at least in the sense that the choice was, in light of the information available to her at the time, a rational or reasonable one to make. It involved, we might say, a reasonable risk.

One might be tempted to say more. Given the truth of determinism, there will be a fact of the matter about what Malcolm would choose and about his prospects for success. His gamble, one might argue, is thus purely a function of his epistemic position and has no metaphysical import. It is, of course, true, that in knowing he would succeed, were he to undertake certain pursuits, he no longer makes a gamble. Still, what he would have known about had the facts become available to him is not a benefit independent of his efforts, but, rather, one conditional on his efforts, and conditional in a particular way; he will stand in a certain normative relation to some things only as a result of his efforts. Because his standing in the *good for* relation to a thing is conditional on his efforts, it remains true that it is up to him whether it will be a part of his good, and nothing forces it upon him as his good. We can thus acknowledge the deterministic truths behind the claim that any gamble in Malcolm's efforts was epistemic, while insisting that being a devotee of Islam became good for him only by his having chosen it and having succeeded in his efforts at self-transformation and that undertaking to become a devotee was good for him only in those senses already allowed.

An analysis of good for a person

So what relation did Malcolm have to Islam and to his other pursuits and commitments after his transformation, when they were good for him, that he didn't have before? Thus far, I have assumed an intuitive grasp of that relation. We must now examine it directly. Our ordinary judgments that something is good for us or good for another rest on our experience. If we are to understand the feature that we seem to detect, we must attend, then, both to our observations of others and to the phenomenology, to the experience of our own involvement in various activities and pursuits. Of course, I can speak directly only of my own experiences, but I hope that the two I will recount prove sufficiently familiar to yield some useful insights.

Here is the first experience. About two years ago I took up running. While I prefer swimming, running (I have read) better helps to maintain bone density. I have managed to keep up this exercise regimen with moderate success, but I still don't enjoy it. I like how I feel after running but not the running itself. It's a big, sweaty bore. And so these two years later, I still have to drag myself to the gym. I do think that running is good for me but not intrinsically, not in the way it was, say, for Florence Griffith Joyner, and not simply because, as a runner, FloJo was spectacular whereas I am spectacularly bad. For a person's good surely can include things for which she has no real talent and, conversely, exclude some things for which she has great talent.

Here is the second. A number of years ago, I took a brief hiatus from philosophy to study law. During the academic year, my law courses were all consuming. But in between semesters, I would sometimes steal away to a café and try to do a bit of philosophy. I would sit, sipping tea and contemplating some deeply perplexing problem, and I would experience a sense of calm. Kinesthetically, a warmth spread throughout my body; my muscles and mind were relaxed. Psychologically, I felt at home with myself and my activity; I understood and felt comfortable with who I was and what I was doing. It was not always like this. I can remember as an undergraduate finding philosophy awfully dull reading. I found the issues interesting and challenging, to be sure; I saw philosophy as genuinely valuable. But in contemplating whether to go to graduate school, I wondered whether I would ever develop the requisite internal motivation and, more deeply, whether I would ever come to think of myself as a philosopher.

Now I am inclined to say that doing philosophy—or more precisely, engaging in the kind of intellectual exploration characteristic of, if not peculiar to, philosophy—is good for me. Not instrumentally, as running is, but in something like the way that running was good for Joyner and practicing Islam was good for Malcolm X. Assuming that this is correct, the question is how to understand it. I doubt that we should simply say that in those moments of doing philosophy, I was happy or contented. While true, this oversimplifies the experience and disguises more subtle elements of it. For it was nothing like the happiness I feel on encountering an old friend, or the satisfaction I feel when successfully completing a task, or the pleasure I feel watching trashy television.

I said earlier that one must work oneself into a relationship with many of those things that comprise one's good, that like a successful relationship, achieving and maintaining one's good requires effort. I want to take this comparison to interpersonal relationships quite seriously. Ordinary talk suggests that we should. People often speak of their work, for instance, as they would of a lover. They are passionate about it, they tell us; they find it exciting or stimulating or fascinating. They talk of finding their niche much as they talk of finding their 'soul mate'. Of course, interpersonal relationships can be good or bad, healthy or unhealthy. I propose to explore common characteristics of healthy love relationships. The good for relation is especially salient in such relationships and so exploring them will prove useful to understanding personal good.

Consider, then, typical features of such relationships. First, they tend to support their participants' sense of their own value. Having a sense of one's own value should not be confused with having those feelings of self-esteem that come from worthwhile activities or accomplishments.[24] In fact, to have a sense

---

[24] I say more about this distinction in Rosati (manuscript *b*).

of one's own value is not really to have a feeling at all. Rather, it is to have internalized a piece of knowledge that informs how one thinks and feels more generally. Partners in a relationship obviously will not feel good about themselves in all ways at every moment; their self-esteem will be affected by events both external and internal to the relationship. But healthy relationships tend to support the partners' stable sense of themselves as basically lovable, that is, as worthy of love. Second, such relationships tend to be enlivening rather than enervating. Relationships require work; they can be frustrating and tiring. But healthy relationships tend to increase or at least support people's receptivity and to expand, deepen, or support their interests, whereas unhealthy ones can lead them to be withdrawn, angry, depressed, and apathetic. Third, they provide an important component of an individual's identity and a sense of direction in life; in these ways, they contribute to an individual's self-understanding. Partners think of the 'we' as a part of who they each are, and the relationship serves as one organizing principle in their lives. Finally, healthy relationships tend to be self-perpetuating (which is not to say eternal), sources of internal motivation. People who are in a healthy love relationship have an appreciation of the relationship and their partner and tend to behave in ways that both manifest and maintain their investment in it.

When love relationships deteriorate or fall apart, especially when one party is betrayed, the wronged or abandoned parties often feel uncertain of who they are and what their lives are about. They may find themselves feeling aimless and uprooted, insecure and depressed, and in doubt about whether they are lovable. In these ways, the breakup of an important relationship tends to be especially devastating.

Healthy love relationships obviously differ in many ways from the other things that are good for us, but I believe that those things that are intrinsically, nonmorally good for a person all exhibit essentially the same features sketched above. They tend to support or not undermine an individual's sense of her own value, to enliven rather than enervate, to provide identity and direction, and to furnish self-supporting sources of internal motivation. When a person is engaged with an activity, a pursuit, or another person in a way that exhibits these features, the item in question is indeed good for that person.

Must each intrinsically good thing for a person exhibit every feature listed above? Perhaps, instead, goodness for a person is, as Richard Boyd has suggested of other normative properties, a homeostatic cluster property (1988: 196). Though far more discussion of this question is needed than I can supply here, I think it is reasonable to assume that all of these features must be present at least to some degree. For one thing, a fuller characterization of these features would arguably show them to be connected in quite fundamental ways.

It would hardly be surprising, for instance, that those things that sustain a sense of our value can provide self-supporting sources of internal motivation, or that those things that provide a sense of identity and direction tend to be motivating and to sustain a sense of our value. And many apparent counterexamples that the assumption may invite can be adequately addressed, or could be, given further refinements. I cannot defend this last claim fully here, of course, but let me quickly address a few seeming difficulties, since doing so may help to clarify the claims I have been making.

One might be tempted to suggest that, on my account, well-being could be supplied by a drug.[25] Even if this were true, it does not strike me as a problem. Remember, first, that this possibility would be realized only by a drug that exhibited all of the features I have described; on my view, being good for someone is not to be confused with a bare subjective state like pleasure or 'desirable consciousness'. I don't know whether imbibing any currently existing drug works like this, but if it did—if, for instance, this were the way that anti-depressants work—then it seems to me that taking that drug could be good for a person. But second, I have addressed only the question of what makes something good for someone. That leaves entirely unsettled questions about what is better or worse for a person or about what makes for a good life for a person. A drug could be good for a person, but if it blocked achievement of other goods or diminished a person's life considered as a whole, she would have reason not to take it anyway. In such cases, a person would confront, with respect to the drug, issues she confronts with respect to many other things in her life.

Similar responses might be offered to the worry that, although I have talked about the relation we stand in to *goods* of various kinds, it seems an individual could stand in the good for relation to quite wicked things. I have been told that John Lee Malvo, the younger of the Washington, DC snipers, reportedly spoke with enthusiasm and pride about the details of the killings. He expressed no regrets and in fact indicated that he found the killings personally fulfilling.[26] Again, being good for a person is not, on my view, a bare subjective state, and so Malvo's feelings, even assuming we can trust his report, are not dispositive. Still, quite complex questions exist about whether distasteful, even evil, things are precluded from being good for a person conceptually or only contingently.[27] Whatever we might finally say about these difficult questions, even if Malvo's activity did satisfy the analysis offered here, which I doubt, an

---

[25] Thanks to Sarah Buss for raising the question about drug use.

[26] I am grateful to Mark Timmons for asking about this example.

[27] While I cannot address these questions here, we should remember that people do seem to flourish in cultures whose practices we would regard as unethical.

overwhelming case would exist for saying that a good life for him would not include being a killer.

Finally, one might be tempted to suggest that on my account, we cannot say that chocolate, for example, is good for a person, because as wonderful as chocolate is, chocolate consumption does not have the features I have described.[28] This does not seem to me to be a problem either, because I am inclined to deny that chocolate is, in the usual case, good for a person. This example simply illustrates the broader point that many of the things we may ordinarily consider good for a person are only instrumentally good for her. My analysis concerns what it is for something to be *intrinsically*, nonmorally good for a person.

I have assumed that when something is good for a person all of the afore-mentioned features are exhibited. But my claim is not quite that goodness for a person is identical with these features. It is that being good for a person is the second-order relational property of being productive of this set of features. P stands in the good for relation to X when X is productive of this set of features for P. Since the features are ones exhibited in a healthy love relationship—a relationship of reciprocal love—we might say that the things that are good for a person are those she can successfully love. When I say she can *successfully* love them, I mean that her love of them is, in the way already described, rewarded; her activities, pursuits, and so on 'love her back', so that her relation to them exhibits the features described. Unfortunately, the word 'love' may conjure up ideas of romance and sexual passion that form no necessary part of the relation I have in mind, so we might say instead that goodness for a person is a relation of rewarded appreciation.

I believe that my analysis captures our experience better than alternative views.[29] This matters because the goodness of something for a person at least seems to be detectable in experience—in our observations of others lives as well as our own—and so our experience should provide clues as to the nature of the property.[30] I believe that it is precisely when a person stands in the relation

---

[28] Thanks to David Sobel for raising this problem.

[29] Even sophisticated forms of analytical hedonism, I believe, must oversimplify, either ignoring some of the features I have described or adopting an implausibly broad notion of pleasure in an effort to encompass all of them. And some important theories of personal good, such as Darwall's recent analysis of welfare as what one ought to want for a person for her sake, do not address our experience at all or do so only at the level of normative theory. See Darwall (2002: ch. 4). In my view, the nature of personal good is to be found in those features of our experience that explain *why* one ought to want them for someone for her sake. Full information informed-desire theories take account of our experiences in the sense that, through the require-ment of full information, an individual considers what her experience of different choices would be like. See Railton (1986*b*). But that is not the kind of experience I have been discussing.

[30] The claim that goodness for a person is a property detectable in experience should not, of course, be confused with the claim that goodness for a person just is an experience or subjective state.

described above to her principal activities and undertakings, and to the central people in her life, that we are inclined to describe her as thriving. It is precisely when she stands in this relation to a particular aim, activity, or person that we are inclined to say that it 'fits' or 'suits' her. When we judge X good for P we are, accordingly, doing one of three things. First, we may be acknowledging or remarking on the actual existence of this relation between X and P. Consider how we respond when a friend has finally found the 'right' person and we see him happy, open, and planning his future, or how parents respond when an adult child settles into a career she finds exhilarating. Second, we may be expressing our belief that P *could* stand in this relation to X, as when we remark that X would be good for her. We sometimes think it would be a good for a friend if he devoted himself to an undertaking for which he has some talent— he would feel better about himself, would stop floundering, would be less insecure. Finally, we may be noticing and reporting that such a relationship is developing. A parent watches her child's face light up as he progressively masters more difficult pieces of music; we watch a friend become increasingly invested in and excited about a project he started as a lark.

3. Theoretical challenges

Thus far, I have offered intuitive support for my analysis. I now want to explore more theoretical considerations that lend it support. I believe that the account of personal good sketched here is well positioned not only to account for the dualities with which we began but to address certain longstanding problems that any plausible account of personal good must be able to address.

The dualities

I suggested at the outset that an account of personal good must square with our nature as both humans and agents and with our experience of our good as both discovered and invented. I believe that my analysis succeeds in both respects.

Return for a moment to interpersonal relationships. Whether such relationships will be healthy, whether they succeed in exhibiting the features described earlier, depends on a number of factors. In general, they require for success a basic compatibility of the parties—attraction and affection, some mutuality of interests and fundamental values, and complementary toleration for differences and idiosyncrasies. Whether these general requirements are met clearly depends on facts about the individuals involved, and, to that extent, on matters partly beyond their control.

But whether they are met also depends very much on what those individuals *do*. A person can, for example, behave in ways that communicate attraction and affection, and behaving in these ways can induce, strengthen, or perpetuate the relevant feelings. He can treat the other party in a manner consonant with his or her value as a person, that is, in a manner that expresses recognition of the other's value. He can change his own bad habits and behaviors, cultivate interests that spark another person's interest, and so on. Perhaps a person cannot choose his basic attractions, but he can choose to behave in ways that help to begin, nurture, and maintain a healthy relationship.

In the same way, whether any pursuit, undertaking, or relationship fits or suits a particular individual, whether it can 'love her back' so that her engagement rewards her in the way described, depends on facts about what she is like and about the culture in which she operates. Indeed, it depends on such a complex array of facts that we can likely have, at best, only more or less useful generalizations, and those generalizations rest on facts about our human nature. We tend, for instance, to have some preference for undertakings and pursuits that we can understand and appreciate, or can begin to understand and appreciate, and for which we have some facility. Usually, an activity can reward us only when we can meet the basic physical and intellectual demands of the activity. But the success involved in the *good for* relation, while generally requiring some facility at an activity, shouldn't be confused with success at that activity. Someone who is tone deaf, for example, may stick with those singing lessons if, given other facts about him, his efforts are nevertheless rewarded.

At the same time, whether a pursuit, undertaking, or relationship fits or suits a person also depends very much on what he does, as the life of Malcolm X illustrates. Now I have not offered any particular theory of autonomy, but it seems plausible to think that a great many of the actions we undertake in pursuing our goals, developing our skills, and changing ourselves count as autonomous, even if done with no grand view of our lives in mind. It seems plausible at least to the extent that these actions do not display those features that lead us to doubt that an action is autonomous. Personal good, as I conceive it, captures the way in which our good depends on our nature as autonomous agents by recognizing our active role in determining our futures and making our good. But it also squares with our agency in a deeper way, which I explore momentarily.

Having shown how the analysis of personal good agrees with our dual nature, it is easy enough to see how we might explain the duality of our experience of our good. A person will experience her good as a discovery in a number of typical instances. The most obvious will be in cases of ready-made goods. But in addition, in the process of living her life, a person will ordinarily learn a great deal about herself, her capacities, likes, and dislikes. To learn that she has a capacity for an activity and enjoys it, even if the capacity requires development and the enjoyment only comes over time, is to learn something about her good. She learns not, as noted earlier, that the activity was good for her all along, but that her good could, and now does, include that activity.

Although we often experience our good as a discovery, it is not surprising, on my analysis, that our good often seems to be up to us, for it is. Insofar as something becomes good for us as a result of our efforts, it is for us to decide where our interest shall lie. A person's actions do not, of course, create the property of being good for a person, but they do often determine whether it is instantiated and, thereby, whether it is true that something is good for her. Facts about our nature as humans and individuals will partly determine the success of our experiments—our success in bringing ourselves into the *good for* relation with things. But whether a good for us exists to be realized often depends on our undertaking the experiment. Our good is invented as well as discovered.

Two Moorean challenges

Moore famously argued that proposed analyses of good, whether naturalistic or metaphysical, leave an 'open question' and, therefore, fail, because 'good' expresses a simple, nonnatural, unanalyzable property. Though Moore targeted analyses of good, his argument presents a more general challenge that would apply as well to proposed analyses of good for a person. Moore did not himself raise the open question against analyses of welfare perhaps chiefly because he recognized no such species of value. On the contrary, he challenged as nonsensical the idea that something could be 'good for' me or 'my own good'. I believe that my analysis of personal good may be able to go some way to meeting each of Moore's challenges.

The open question argument

Commentators disagree, of course, about whether the open question argument has any force, and those who think it does disagree about what problem it exposes and about whether and how the problem can be met. I limit my remarks here to suggesting how my analysis might begin to address two related diagnoses of the force of Moore's argument.

Noncognitivists (and some others) have argued that the open question argument exposes the inherent or automatic recommending and expressive force of 'good', an apparent conceptual connection with the guidance of action (Darwall, Gibbard, and Railton 1992). I am persuaded by the noncognitivists' claims and believe that extant forms of naturalism fail to capture the recommending force of ethical judgments. But I believe, and have argued elsewhere, that this failing rests on a deeper one, namely, that existing natural-istic accounts of personal good do not bear the right relationship to our agency (Rosati 2003). Moore's argument exposes the challenge of providing an account that can capture how something's being good for us engages those capacities and motives in virtue of which we are autonomous agents. Although I will not be able to make the case fully here, let me say a bit about why my analysis may be able to meet this challenge. As a consequence, to call something good for someone will serve to recommend it and to guide attitude and action.

Suppose, as some have suggested, that autonomous action would not be possible if persons lacked certain cognitive capacities and motives that specially equip them to function as autonomous agents. These might be, as has variously been suggested, intrinsic desires for self-awareness and self-understanding (Velleman 1989*a*) or an inclination toward autonomy (Velleman 1996), a disposition toward coherence (Smith 1997), or standing desires for desires con-sonant with reality and for one's own long-term happiness (Brandt 1979).[31] Without these 'autonomy-making' capacities and motives, individuals would not be able to evaluate and act, in any reliable way, contrary to the press of their presently strongest lower-order motives.

I have taken no position on the nature of the autonomy-making motives and capacities, but it is plausible to believe that whatever they might turn out to be, a person can function effectively as an autonomous agent only if she is able to trust and value herself. Indeed, when self-trust and a sense of one's own worth are seriously undermined, autonomous functioning tends to be impaired. Without self-trust a person will not be disposed to treat her choices and assess-ments as authoritative and to govern herself in accordance with them, and without self-regard she won't care to do so. Those things that engender our trust in ourselves, that enable us to understand and feel at home with ourselves and to appreciate our own value, will naturally engage our autonomy-making motives. To enter into the *good for* relation with things is, at one and the same time, to enhance our well-being and our autonomous functioning. It is because personal good, as characterized here, is a feature of things that engages our autonomy-making motives that the judgment that something is good for a person, or will or would be good for her, has recommending force and guides

---

[31] See also Rawls (1980). Velleman seems to mean for his apparently different characterizations to come to the same thing. See Velleman (1997: 41 n. 20). Smith (1997: 318) more precisely claims that freedom is a matter of 'orthonomy' rather than autonomy. Brandt's discussion of standing motives is not offered as part of a full account of autonomy but, rather, to explain how we might act now against a presently strongest desire. His view, however, exhibits the basic structure of interest here. For discussion of these ideas in relation to personal good, see Rosati (2000, 2003).

attitude and action. The fundamental point, of course, is not that one's good makes one more autonomous—that our faring well and functioning well are importantly related—although that is true.[32] Rather, the point is that as autonomous agents we have motives that are naturally engaged by those things that support our sense of our own value, and no error lies in this. There is no antecedent reason to think that the motives that help to make us autonomous will turn out to be irrational; we have no reason to believe that reflection would undermine them. And our sense of ourselves as valuable is not mistaken—we are valuable.

Good v. good for

In his discussion of egoism as a doctrine of ends, Moore expressed incomprehension of the idea that something could be 'good for' an individual.[33] He writes, 'In what sense can a thing be good *for me*? It is obvious, if we reflect, that the only thing which can belong to me, which can be *mine*, is something which is good, and not the fact that it is good. When, therefore I talk of anything I get as "my own good", I must mean either that the thing I get is good, or that my possessing it is good' (1993/1903: 98). Perhaps the chief difficulty Moore alleges for the idea of relational good is that it would be a strange kind of value—one that could give the individual but no one else a reason for action. 'The only reason I can have for aiming at "my own good" is that it is *good absolutely* that what I so call should belong to me... But if it is *good absolutely* that I should have it, then everyone else has as much reason for aiming at my having it, as I have myself' (1993/1903: 99). Something can be normative— can be valuable or good at all, Moore appears to have thought—only if it gives everyone a reason for action: normativity is essentially agent-neutral. There may be grounds for rejecting this idea, since it amounts to rejecting any agent-relative values or reasons for action (Smith 2003). But I think that an individual's good does afford more than agent-relative reasons, and it would be hard to sustain the apparent moral importance of personal good were this not so.[34]

The appropriate answer to Moore, I believe, lies in certain Kantian ideas about the structure of value, which a number of philosophers have recently explored and which I mean to exploit as well. According to what I will call the

---

[32] See Rosati (manuscript *b*).

[33] See Moore (1993/1903: 96–105). Donald Regan, who agrees with Moore, has argued that the notion of relational value is incoherent. See Regan (1983), but compare Regan (2002), where he suggests that Mooreans can accept a picture that comes close to what 'good for' theorists have in mind. For critical examination of the idea of good as a distinct property, see Geach (1956) and Thomson (2001).

[34] Welfare theorists certainly seem to suppose that individual welfare has more than agent-relative importance. See e.g. Sumner (1996). For a skeptical take on the need for a theory of welfare, see Scanlon (1998: ch. 3).

'Kantian structure', the normativity of welfare, or of states of affairs involving persons, depends on the value of persons; a person's good matters because *she* matters.[35] The importance of her good thus depends on her agent-neutral value. If persons indeed have agent-neutral value, then they are worthy of our concern and anyone has reason to value them. Valuing persons, insofar as they are beings whose lives can go better or worse, will involve acting in ways that advance, or at least in ways that do not impede, the realization of their good, and anyone has reason to so act. If the normativity of personal good derives in this way from the value of persons, then personal good, contrary to what Moore thought, gives agent-neutral and not merely agent-relative reasons for action.

The Kantian structure is obviously controversial, and I cannot attempt to defend it here. I merely mean to note how it permits my analysis to address the difficulty. Of course, once we accept this view of the structure of value, then the basic strategy is available no matter what the correct analysis of welfare might be, and so proponents of any theory of personal good could appeal to it in order to defend the agent-neutral normativity of welfare as they conceive it.[36] Nevertheless, I believe that the analysis of personal good offered here fits especially well with this structure.[37]

If a person's welfare matters because she matters, it makes sense that her good would consist in those things that support her as the valuable being she is, that respond to her value by both supporting her sense of herself as valuable and enhancing her functioning. What is good for a person responds to the goodness of a person. Notice that on this picture, value exhibits something like the recursive structure we find in Moore's theory of organic unities. A person is valuable and her welfare consists in those things that sustain a sense of her own value. The acts of another in furtherance of her welfare amount not only to an acknowledgment or appreciation of her value but, given the nature of personal good, of her appreciation of her own value.[38]

---

[35] Velleman (1999) has suggested this in his discussion of the right to die. Most recently, Darwall (2002) has argued that the normativity of welfare is agent-neutral and depends on the agent-neutral value of persons.   [36] See Rosati (manuscript *a*).

[37] In making this claim, I avail myself of a move that Darwall (2002) has made in defending his account of welfare. He suggests that his analysis fits well with the agent-neutral normativity of welfare. I have argued elsewhere that Darwall's theory does not fare better than alternative theories of welfare in accounting for the agent-neutral normativity of welfare, both because appeal to the Kantian structure is available no matter what the analysis of welfare and because his theory does not actually provide an analysis of welfare but, rather, identifies a property necessarily coextensive with goodness for a person. See Rosati (manuscript *a*, forthcoming). I accept Darwall's suggestion, however, that some analyses of welfare may seem a more intuitive fit with the Kantian structure.

[38] For helpful discussion of Moore's theory of organic unities and their recursive structure, see Hurka (1998).

Conclusion

I have suggested that when something is good for a person she stands in a certain relation to it, that goodness for a person is a form of successful loving or rewarded appreciation. This proposal fits well, I have argued, with our dual nature and accounts well for our experience. Much more work will certainly be needed to address the many questions the account raises. But if the sketch offered herein is roughly correct, we can easily understand the reason-giving force of considerations of our welfare, as well as our efforts as parents, teachers, and advisers, to raise children who can fare well because they can function well. We see to our own good by bringing ourselves into the requisite relation, as circumstances and our own capacities permit, to a variety of persons, activities, and pursuits. We see to the good of children by raising them to be autonomous beings—that is, beings who live good lives, at least in large part, because they can, through their own successful functioning, make their own good.

References

ANDERSON, E. (1993). *Value in Ethics and Economics*. Cambridge, Mass.: Harvard University Press.

ARISTOTLE (1990). *The Nichomachean Ethics*, trans. David Ross. Oxford: Oxford University Press.

BOYD, R. N. (1988). 'How to be a Moral Realist', in G. Sayre-McCord (ed.), *Essays on Moral Realism*. Ithaca, NY: Cornell University Press: 181–228.

BRANDT, R. B. (1979). *A Theory of the Good and the Right*. Oxford: Clarendon Press.

BROOME, J. (1999). 'Normative Requirements', *Ratio*, 12: 398–419.

DARWALL, S. L. (1983). *Impartial Reason*. Ithaca, NY: Cornell University Press.

—— (2002). *Welfare and Rational Care*. Princeton: Princeton University Press.

—— GIBBARD, ALLAN, and RAILTON, PETER (1992). 'Toward *Fin de Siècle* Ethics: Some Trends', *Philosophical Review*, 101: 115–89.

DWORKIN, R. (1990). 'Foundations of Liberal Equality', in Grethe Peterson (ed.), *Tanner Lectures on Human Value*, vol. xi. Salt Lake City: University of Utah.

GEACH, P. (1956). 'Good and Evil', *Analysis*, 17: 33–42.

GIBBARD, A. (1990). *Wise Choices, Apt Feelings: A Theory of Normative Judgment*. Cambridge, Mass.: Harvard University Press.

HALEY, A., and X MALCOLM (1965). *The Autobiography of Malcolm X*. New York: Ballantine Books.

HARE, R. M. (1963). *Freedom and Reason*. Oxford: Oxford University Press.

HURKA, T. (1998). 'Two Kinds of Organic Unity', *Journal of Ethics*, 2: 299–320.

MOORE, G. E. (1993/1903). *Principia Ethica*, rev. edn. Cambridge: Cambridge University Press.

OVERVOLD, M. (1980). 'Self-Interest and the Concept of Self-Sacrifice', *Canadian Journal of Philosophy*, 10: 105–18.

PASCAL, B. (1910). *Thoughts*, trans. W. F. Trotter. New York: P. F. Collier & Son.

RAILTON, P. (1986*a*). 'Facts and Values', *Philosophical Topics*, 14: 5–31.

—— (1986*b*). 'Moral Realism', *Philosophical Review*, 95: 163–207.

RAWLS, J. (1971). *A Theory of Justice*. Cambridge, Mass.: Harvard University Press.

—— (1980). 'Kantian Constructivism in Moral Theory: The Dewey Lectures 1980', *Journal of Philosophy*, 9: 515–72.

RAZ, J. (1986). *The Morality of Freedom*. Oxford: Clarendon Press.

REGAN, D. H. (1983). 'Against Evaluator Relativity: A Response to Sen', *Philosophy & Public Affairs*, 12: 89–132.

—— (2002). 'The Value of Rational Nature', *Ethics*, 112: 267–91.

ROSATI, C. S. (1995*a*). 'Persons, Perspectives, and Full-Information Accounts of the Good', *Ethics*, 105: 296–325.

—— (1995*b*). 'Naturalism, Normativity, and the Open Question Argument', *Nous*, 29: 46–70.

—— (2000). 'Brandt's Notion of Therapeutic Agency', *Ethics*, 110: 780–811.

—— (2003). 'Agency and the Open Question Argument', *Ethics*, 113: 490–527.

—— (forthcoming). 'Darwall on Welfare and Rational Care', *Philosophical Studies*.

—— (manuscript *a*). 'Darwall's Rational Care Theory of Welfare'.

—— (manuscript *b*). 'Autonomy and Personal Good: Lessons from Frankenstein's Monster'.

SCANLON, T. (1998). *What We Owe to Each Other*. Cambridge, Mass.: Harvard University Press.

SEN, A. (1985). 'Well-Being, Agency and Freedom', *Journal of Philosophy*, 82: 169–221.

—— (1987). *On Ethics and Economics*. Oxford: Blackwell.

SMITH, M. (1997). 'A Theory of Freedom and Responsibility', in Garrett Cullity and Berys Gaut (eds.), *Ethics and Practical Reason*. Oxford: Clarendon Press: 293–320.

—— (2003). 'Neutral and Relative Value after Moore', *Ethics*, 113: 576–98.

SOBEL, D. (1998). 'Well-Being as the Object of Moral Consideration', *Economics and Philosophy*, 14: 249–81.

SUMNER, W. (1996). *Welfare, Happiness, and Ethics*. Oxford: Clarendon Press.

THOMSON, J. (2001). *Goodness and Advice*. Princeton: Princeton University Press.

VELLEMAN, J. D. (1989*a*). *Practical Reflection*. Princeton: Princeton University Press.

—— (1989*b*). 'Epistemic Freedom', *Pacific Philosophical Quarterly*, 70: 73–97.

—— (1991). 'Well-Being and Time', *Pacific Philosophical Quarterly*, 72: 48–77.

—— (1996). 'The Possibility of Practical Reason', *Ethics*, 106: 694–726.

—— (1997). 'Deciding How to Decide', in Garrett Cullity and Berys Gaut (eds.), *Ethics and Practical Reason*. Oxford: Clarendon Press.

—— (1999). 'A Right of Self-Termination?' *Ethics*, 109: 606–20.

—— (2002). 'Motivation by Ideal', *Philosophical Explorations*, 5: 89–104.

WILLIAMS, B. (1979). 'Moral Luck', in *Mortal Questions*. New York: Cambridge University Press, ch. 3.

6

Moore on the Right, the Good, and Uncertainty

Michael Smith

In *Principia Ethica* G. E. Moore famously argues that there is an analytic connection between facts about which actions are right and wrong and facts about the goodness and badness—that is, the value—of actions' outcomes.

> All moral laws, I wish to shew, are merely statements that certain kinds of actions will have good effects. The very opposite of this view has been generally prevalent in Ethics. 'The right' and 'the useful' have been supposed to be at least *capable* of conflicting with one another, and, at all events, to be essentially distinct. It has been characteristic of a certain school of moralists, as of moral common sense, to declare that the end will never justify the means. What I wish first to point out is that 'right' does and can mean nothing but 'cause of a good result,' and is thus identical with 'useful'; whence it follows that the end always will justify the means, and that no action which is not justified by its results can be right. That there may be a true proposition, meant to be conveyed by the assertion 'The end will not justify the means,' I fully admit: but that, in another sense, and a sense far more fundamental for ethical theory, it is utterly false, must first be shewn. (Moore 1903: 146–7)

Though Moore here claims that it is analytic that right acts maximize value, he later came to amend this under the influence of Russell (Russell 1910, Moore 1942). He subsequently suggested that it is a priori, but not analytic, that right acts maximize value. But though even this weaker claim can be and has been challenged (Rawls 1971, Scanlon 1998), I will take the stronger claim that it is analytic for granted in what follows. For what interests me is not the status of the claim that right acts maximize value, but rather what those who accept it, whether as analytic or a priori, should say when they are reminded that we cannot be certain about the consequences of our actions. This is the question that Moore goes on to address in the relevant section of *Principia Ethica*. Before proceeding, however, let me anticipate a couple of misgivings.

First, as we will see, Moore moves seamlessly between talk of defining rightness in terms of the maximization of value and talk of defining duty in such terms. But, it might be objected, to say that an act is right is to say that it is permissible, and hence that it is not the case that one has a duty not to do it. It is not to say that it is one's duty to do it. I will, however, overlook this difference in what follows. If it is one's duty to maximize value then acts that are permissible, but not one's duty, are presumably those that produce at least as much value as some other act that maximizes value. Right acts maximize value just the same as duties. As between the options that one faces, one's duties are simply those acts that are uniquely right.

Second, far from being analytic, or even a priori, some might think that Moore's consequentialist account of right action isn't so much as true. As such, they might say that they have no interest in what one who accepts it should say in the light of uncertainty. But this would be a serious mistake. For the kind of consequentialism that is true, even if what Moore says is analytic, is a kind of consequentialism that deontologists can and should happily accept (Dreier 1993, Louise 2004). While Moore's own view was that value is a simple property, and hence would presumably have favoured a formalization of his definition of right action along the following lines:

$$(x)(x\text{'s } \phi\text{-ing at time } t \text{ is right iff } x\text{'s } \phi\text{-ing at } t \text{ maximizes value})$$

we can allow that values might be relativized to persons and times in a way congenial to deontology (Smith 2003). A formalization of the following kind might therefore be more accurate:

$$(x)(x\text{'s } \phi\text{-ing at time } t \text{ is right iff } x\text{'s } \phi\text{-ing at } t \text{ maximizes value}_{x,t})$$

My keeping my promise now might maximize value$_{me,now}$, and so be the right thing for me to do, even though my now breaking my promise would maximize value$_{me,later}$ and perhaps even maximize value$_{me,over\ time}$. Moore's puzzle about the impact of uncertainty on the definition of right action is thus a puzzle for everyone.

The paper is in four main sections. In the first I spell out Moore's view of the way in which uncertainty affects the proposed definition of rightness in terms of the maximization of value. In the second section I compare Moore's view with an alternative put forward more recently by Frank Jackson (1991). In the third and fourth sections I offer my own account and say why it should be preferred to both Moore's and Jackson's views. To anticipate, it turns out that Moore and Jackson are both right about something and wrong about something. The correct view combines elements from both.

1. Why Moore thinks that uncertainty is a problem

Why is uncertainty an issue, given the proposed definition of 'rightness' in terms of 'maximization of value'? Moore explains the problem this way.

> In order to shew that any action is a duty, it is necessary to know both what are the other conditions, which will, conjointly with it, determine its effects; to know exactly what will be the effects of these conditions; and to know all the events which will be in any way affected by our action throughout an infinite future. We must have all this causal knowledge, and further we must know accurately the degree of value both of the action itself and of all these effects; and must be able to determine how, in conjunction with the other things in the Universe, they will affect its value as an organic whole. And not only this: we must also possess all this knowledge with regard to the effects of every possible alternative; and must then be able to see by comparison that the total value due to the existence of the action in question will be greater than that which would be produced by any of these alternatives. But it is obvious that our causal knowledge alone is far too incomplete for us ever to assure ourselves of this result. Accordingly it follows that we never have any reason to suppose that an action is our duty: we can never be sure that any action will produce the greatest value possible. (Moore 1903: 149)

The problem is thus supposed to be that, since we can never be certain of all of the effects of the actions we perform, still less all of the effects of the actions which we don't perform but which were options for us, it follows that 'we never have any reason to suppose that an action is our duty.' But if this is the problem, then it seems to be rather overblown. If we cannot be certain of the effects of our actions then, let's agree, there can be no *conclusive* reason to suppose that any particular action is our duty. But that doesn't entail that there are no reasons at all to suppose that any particular action is our duty—or rather, that would follow only if reasons for belief had to be conclusive reasons, and there seems to be no good reason to suppose that this is so.

As subsequently becomes clear, however, the claim that there is no reason at all to suppose that any particular action is our duty is not crucial to the problem Moore wishes to raise. He goes on as follows.

> Ethics, therefore, is quite unable to give us a list of duties: but there still remains a humbler task which may be possible for Practical Ethics. Although we cannot hope to discover which, in a given situation, is the best of all possible alternative actions, there may be some possibility of shewing which among the alternatives, *likely to occur to any one*, will produce the greatest sum of good. This second task is certainly all that Ethics can ever have accomplished: and it is certainly all that it has ever collected materials for proving; since no one has ever attempted to exhaust the possible alternative actions in any particular case. Ethical philosophers have in fact confined their attention to a very

limited class of actions, which have been selected because they are those which most commonly occur to mankind as possible alternatives. With regard to these they may possibly have shewn that one alternative is better, i.e. produces a greater total of value, than others. But it seems desirable to insist, that though they have represented this result as a determination of *duties*, it can never really have been so. For the term duty is certainly so used that, if we are subsequently persuaded that any possible action would have produced more good than the one we adopted, we admit that we failed to do our duty. It will, however, be a useful task if Ethics can determine which among alternatives *likely to occur* will produce the greatest total value. For, though this alternative cannot be proved to be the best possible, yet it may be better than any course of action which we should otherwise adopt. (Moore 1903: 149–50)

The real problem that concerns Moore is that there is no plausible task for Practical Ethics in the absence of certainty about which actions are right. There is no way of getting from the abstract knowledge of what it is about an act that is right that makes it right to a decision about what to do in concrete situations in which we have only limited knowledge of consequences.

There are two parts to Moore's response to this problem. In the first he details a 'humbler' task for Practical Ethics. Even though we can never be certain which acts maximize value, there is, he tells us, still something 'useful' we can establish, namely, 'which among the alternatives, *likely to occur to any one*, will produce the greatest sum of good.' In other words, in the absence of certainty about which actions maximize value, we can still say which acts are *likely* to maximize value, given our limited knowledge. And then in the second part he argues that, since what we would conclude if it were to emerge that an act that we classified as 'right' on the basis of our limited knowledge didn't in fact maximize value is that our classification of the act as 'right' was in error, it follows that acceptance of this humbler task for Practical Ethics gives us no reason to question our original definition. When we call an act 'right' what we mean to be saying of it, even when we engage in the humbler task, is that that act maximizes value, not merely that (say) to the best of our knowledge at the time of speaking it maximizes value.

Moore appears to be on strong ground in giving this two-part response. For a similar set of worries arises in the case of less controversial definitions, and the solution, in such cases, is the very solution Moore proposes. Consider the definition of 'bachelor' as 'unmarried male.' The worry in this case is that, since we have only limited knowledge of the things that people have done in the past, we can never be certain whether any particular person is an unmarried male. There is, however, still something 'useful' we can do in our search for bachelors in the absence of such certainty, for we can classify people on the basis of the evidence available to us. In compiling a list of bachelors we thus decide whom to put on the list on the basis of the *likelihood* that they are unmarried males. But if it subsequently comes to light that someone we classified as a bachelor was married at the time that we made our list, then we conclude that it is our list that is in error. To say of someone that he is a 'bachelor,' even when we engage in the humbler task of classifying people on the basis of the evidence available to us, is thus to say of him that he is an unmarried male, not merely that (say) to the best of our knowledge at the time of speaking he is an unmarried male.

For all the appearance that Moore is on strong ground, however, both parts of his response have been challenged. In the following section I will compare Moore's definition of right action, and his resultant account of the 'useful' task to be undertaken in Practical Ethics, with a competing definition of right action and account of the task of Practical Ethics proposed by Frank Jackson. Though Jackson does not explicitly mention Moore, the arguments he gives look like they could well have been formulated with the aim of refuting both parts of the Moorean view.

2. Jackson versus Moore

As we have seen, Moore's view has two parts. The first is the claim that right acts are those that maximize value. The second is his account of the 'humbler' task of Practical Ethics, given that we cannot be certain which acts maximize value. We decide what to do by figuring out which acts are *likely* to maximize value. Let's begin by focusing on the second component.

Frank Jackson provides what seems to me to be a quite decisive refutation of Moore's account of the task of Practical Ethics. The refutation takes the form of a counter-example. He asks us to consider Jill, a physician, who has to decide on the correct treatment for her patient, John, who has a minor but not trivial skin complaint.

Jill has only two drugs, drug X and drug Y, at her disposal which have any chance of effecting a cure. Drug X has a 90% chance of curing the patient but also has a 10% chance of killing him; drug Y has a 50% chance of curing the patient but has no bad side effects. Jill's choice is between prescribing X or prescribing Y. It is clear that she should prescribe Y, and yet that course of action is not the course of action most likely to have the best results. (Jackson 1991: 467)

What Jackson's counter-example suggests is that, at least when we do Practical Ethics, we have no special interest in which actions are most likely to maximize value. Though Jill's prescribing drug X has a 90 per cent chance of maximizing value—that is, of bringing about a complete cure—and prescribing drug Y only has a 50 per cent chance of having this result, our intuitive response is that Jill should prescribe drug Y, not drug X. Jill should prescribe drug Y, notwithstanding the fact that it *is not* most likely to maximize value.

Jackson makes explicit his alternative conception of the task of Practical Ethics in his discussion of another variation on the example of Jill, the physician, and her patient, John. This time

Jill . . . has three drugs to choose from: drug A, drug B, and drug C. Careful considera-tion of the literature has led her to the following opinions. Drug A is very likely to relieve the condition but will not completely cure it. One of drugs B and C will com-pletely cure the skin condition; the other though will kill the patient, and there is no way she can tell which of the two is the perfect cure and which the killer drug. What should Jill do?

The possible outcomes we need to consider are: a complete cure for John, a partial cure, and death. It is clear how to rank them: a complete cure is best, followed by a partial cure, and worst is John's death . . . But how do we move from that ranking to a resolution concerning what Jill ought to do? The obvious answer is to take a leaf out of decision theory's book and take the results of multiplying the value of each possible outcome given that the action is performed, summing these for each action, and then designating the action with the greatest sum as what ought to be done. In our example there will be three sums to consider, namely:

Pr(partial cure/drug A taken) $\times$ V(partial cure) + Pr(no change/drug A taken) $\times$ V(no change)

Pr(complete cure/drug B taken) $\times$ V(complete cure) + Pr(death/drug B taken) $\times$ V(death)

and

Pr(complete cure/drug C taken) $\times$ V(complete cure) + Pr(death/drug C taken) $\times$ V(death)

Obviously, in the situation as described, the first will take the highest value, and so we get the answer that Jill should prescribe drug A. (Jackson 1991: 462–3)

What this example shows is that there is a clear alternative to Moore's suggestion that when we engage in Practical Ethics, we should try to figure out which action is most likely to maximize value. For, much as decision theory tells us that the right action to choose is the one that maximizes *expected utility*, so we might suppose that when we engage in Practical Ethics the right action to choose is the one that maximizes *expected value*. This allows us to make good sense of our reaction to the two drugs example. For though prescribing drug X is more likely than prescribing drug Y to maximize value—90 per cent versus 50 per cent—the 10 per cent chance that prescribing drug X will have a very

very bad outcome—it will kill John—as opposed to the 50 per cent chance that prescribing drug Y will merely leave him with his minor but not trivial skin complaint, means that the expected value of prescribing drug X is much lower than the expected value of prescribing drug Y. This well explains why we think that Jill should prescribe drug Y rather than drug X.

So far I have portrayed Jackson as offering an alternative task for Practical Ethics. But in fact Jackson thinks that—with a qualification to be mentioned presently—the two- and three-drugs examples show not just that the second component of Moore's view is mistaken, but that the first component, his definition of right action, is mistaken as well. Here is the relevant passage.

The other possible account of how to recover what a person ought to do from consequentialism's value function that we need to consider holds that a person's beliefs . . . do not come into the picture. What is crucial is simply which action in fact has, or would have, the best consequences. Many consequentialists write as if this was their view . . .

There are two problems with this proposal. First, it gives the intuitively wrong answer in the [three] drugs case. In the [three] drugs case, either it is prescribing drug B or it is prescribing drug C which is the course of action which would in fact have the best consequences—and Jill knows this, although she does not know which of the two it is—but neither prescribing drug B nor prescribing drug C is the right course of action for Jill. As we observed earlier, it is prescribing drug A which is the intuitively correct course of action for Jill despite the fact that she *knows* that it will *not* have the best consequences. We would be horrified if she prescribed drug B, and horrified if she prescribed drug C.

The second problem arises from the fact that we are dealing with an ethical theory when we deal with consequentialism, a theory about action, about what to do. In consequence we have to see consequentialism as containing as a constitutive part prescriptions for action. Now, the fact that an action has in fact the best consequences may be a matter which is obscure to the agent. In the drugs example, Jill has some idea but not enough of an idea about which course of action would have the best results . . . We need, if you like, a story from the inside of an agent to be part of any theory which is properly a theory in ethics, and having the best consequences is a story from the outside. It is fine for a theory in physics to tell us about its central notions in a way which leaves it obscure how to move from those notions to action, for that passage can be left to something which is not physics; but the passage to action is the very business of ethics. (Jackson 1991: 465–7)

The two related problems with Moore's proposed definition of right action are first, that it gives the wrong answer in the three-drugs example, and second, that since it defines a concept that is not and cannot be action-guiding, it cannot be a definition of our ordinary concept of right action.

However, as subsequently becomes clear, the second objection is much more important than the first—here we come to the qualification I mentioned earlier.

... I need to note an annoying complication. I have been arguing for an interpretation of consequentialism which makes what an agent ought to do the act which has the greatest expected moral utility, and so is a function of the consequentialist value function and the agent's probability function at the time. But an agent's probability function at the time of action may differ from her function at other times, and from the probability function of other persons at the same or other times. What happens if we substitute one of these other functions in place of the agent's probability function at the time of action? The answer is that we get an annoying profusion of 'oughts' . . .

I think that we have no alternative but to recognize a whole range of oughts—what she ought to do by the lights of her beliefs at the time of action, what she ought to do by the lights of what she later establishes . . ., what she ought to do by the lights of one or another onlooker who has different information on the subject, and, what is more, what she ought to do by God's lights, that is, by the lights of one who *knows* what will and would happen for each and every course of action. . . . I hereby stipulate that what I mean from here-on by 'ought,' and what I meant, and hope and expect you implicitly took me to mean when we were discussing the examples, was the ought most immediately relevant to action, the ought which I urged to be the primary business of ethical theory to deliver. When we act we must perforce use what is available to us at the time, not what may be available to us in the future or what is available to someone else, and least of all what is available to a God-like being who knows everything about what would, will and did happen.(Jackson 1991: 471–2)

Jackson's concession here is both subtle and important.

Though our concept of right action is the concept of an action that maximizes expected value, Jackson suggests that this concept is, as such, incomplete. In order to classify actions we need to know whose expectations are at issue. There are therefore as many concepts of right action as there are creatures with expectations: the agent at the time of acting, an observer, the agent in retrospect, and even, at the limit, God with his perfect knowledge of everything. The latter is, in effect, Moore's view. But though it follows that Moore is right when he says that 'the term duty is . . . so used that, if we are subsequently persuaded that any possible action would have produced more good than the one we adopted, we admit that we failed to do our duty'—there is indeed a concept of right action relative to which this is so—we must not conclude, on this basis, that our primary or most central concept of right action is the concept of an action that (say) maximizes value.

In support of Jackson's 'profusion of "oughts" ', it is perhaps worth emphasizing that, in the sorts of situations Moore imagines in which we evaluate actions with hindsight, expectations still matter. An action performed by an agent at t_1, but evaluated subsequently at t_2, is still appropriately judged to be right just in case that action maximizes *expected* value, it is just that the expectations in question are those the evaluator has subsequently at t_2. Imagine the original three-drugs example evaluated in retrospect when (say) it is believed that the original assignment of probabilities was mistaken. Instead of drug A being very likely to relieve John's skin condition but not completely cure it, and one of drugs B and C being almost certain to effect a complete cure, while the other will kill the patient, the new view is that it is drug B that is very likely to relieve the skin condition, but not completely cure it, and one of drugs A and C which is almost certain to completely cure the condition, while the other will kill the patient, with there being no way to tell which will do what. In this case the subsequent evaluator should surely suppose that the right thing for Jill to have done was to give John drug B, not drug A. In other words, by the subsequent evaluator's lights, it is still virtually certain that the right thing for Jill to do is not what will maximize value. It is just that it is her subsequent expectations, not Jill's original expectations, that are crucial for evaluating rightness.

But notwithstanding the 'profusion of "oughts",' Jackson argues that one 'ought' stands out from the others as the 'ought' that is 'most immediately relevant to action.' What I take it he means by this is that only one of the 'oughts' grounds genuine *criticism* of the agent. Only one links up, in the right kind of way, with a story about what the agent can appropriately be held responsible for doing, and this should therefore be identified as our primary concept of right action. Imagine again the revised three-drugs example. The subsequent evaluator might well think that Jill ought to have given John drug B, not drug A, as this is what maximizes expected value where the expectations in question are the subsequent evaluator's own. But if the information about the drugs wasn't available to Jill, then there is no sense in which she failed to live up to her responsibilities as an agent in giving him drug A. Indeed, if Jill had given John drug B, then there is surely a sense in which the subsequent evaluator would still be totally horrified. Jill would have done what the evaluator thinks is the right thing to do, but her right conduct could at best have been a complete fluke, relative to her own reasons for acting. But if this is right—if Jill can only be held responsible for doing the best she can, given the information available to her—then, Jackson argues, the 'ought' that it is 'the primary business of ethical theory to deliver' is the 'ought' defined in terms of maximization of expected value where the expectations are those of the agent at the time of acting.

Let me sum up. Contrary to Moore, Jackson argues that the task of Practical Ethics is to establish which acts maximize expected value, not which acts are most likely to maximize value. Moreover and much more importantly, again contrary to Moore, Jackson argues that though there are alternative concepts of right action—there are as many concepts of right action as there are expectations relative to which we could assess the maximization of expected value—right action in the sense of action which maximizes expected value, where the expectations are the agent's own at the time of acting, is the primary ethical concept, the one that hooks up in the right kind of way with what we can hold an agent responsible for doing. Moore is thus doubly wrong when he says ' "right" does and can mean nothing but "cause of a good result." ' 'Right' can mean 'maximizes expected value' and this meaning is primary.

3. The definition of 'right'

Moore and Jackson give us competing definitions of right. But who is right and who is wrong?

According to Jackson, the primary meaning of 'right' is the meaning that is 'most immediately relevant to action.' As I have said, I take it that his idea is that right acts, in this primary sense, are those we can legitimately expect agents to do and criticize them for failing to do. As Jackson sees things it follows that the primary definition of right action must be given in terms of the maximization of expected value, not, as Moore thinks, in terms of the maximization of value *tout court*, and it must be given in terms of the maximization of expected value where the expectations are the agent's at the time of action, not those of the agent at some other time or someone else. Unfortunately, however, there is a gap between Jackson's premise and conclusion. We can no more legitimately expect agents to maximize expected value than we can expect them to maximize value.

A striking feature of Jackson's definition of 'right' is an asymmetry in the treatment of evaluative and non-evaluative facts as determinants of right action. Suppose I observe an agent behaving and wonder whether she is failing to live up to her responsibilities as an agent, so leaving herself open to criticism. What exactly does this involve? Jackson rightly points out that, on the non-evaluative facts side of things, all we can reasonably expect is that an agent does the very best she can, given the information available to her: the full exercise of such rational capacities as she has. Putting to one side cases of impaired rationality, this means that she must form her beliefs about the means to her desired ends in a responsible manner, given the evidence available to her, and she must subsequently act on such beliefs in an appropriate manner as well. When she believes that there are alternative ways of realizing her desired ends, she must prefer the more certain option, and when she is equally certain that acting in different ways will realize different desired ends, she must prefer the option that realizes the desired end that she desires more. But since no mere exercise of such rational capacities as an agent has will ensure that the non-evaluative facts manifest themselves to her, it follows that the mere fact that she lacks knowledge does not, as such, render her liable to criticism.

Yet while this well explains why Jackson insists that right action is action that maximizes *expected* value, it doesn't explain why he thinks that right action maximizes expected *value*. Indeed, anyone impressed by Jackson's argument on the non-evaluative facts side of things should surely suppose that an equally impressive argument could be made for the conclusion that right action consists not in the maximization of expected *value*, but rather in the maximization of expected *value-as-the-agent-sees-things*. For no mere exercise of such capacities as an agent has looks like it will ensure that what is really valuable will manifest itself to her either.

There are, after all, cultural circumstances in which it would be wildly optimistic to suppose that agents could, merely through the exercise of their own rational capacities, come to judge to be valuable what's really valuable. Cultures that are dominated by oppressive religions, and the like, would seem to make it very difficult, perhaps even impossible, for ordinary people even to contemplate alternatives to what is portrayed within their culture to be valuable. More generally, to the extent that we think that our own values are an improvement on those of our parents, the wrong thing for us to think is that we have been more responsible than our parents in the formation of our evaluative beliefs. Indeed, this would be a remarkably arrogant thing to think. The right thing to think is rather that the evidence available to us, as opposed to our parents, is different, and, as a result, we are simply better placed to form evaluative beliefs.

If this is right, however, then it seems that the most that we could ever expect of a normal agent—that is to say, again putting to one side cases of impaired rationality—is that they form their evaluative commitments in a way that is sensitive to such evidence as is available to them and that they form their desires in a way that is sensitive to their evaluative commitments. Probabilities or confidence levels come into the picture twice over. They come in once because we have different levels of confidence that various means are means to our desired ends. And then they come in again because we have different levels of confidence about what we judge to be intrinsically valuable. When an agent is equally confident about the intrinsic value of two things, but she judges one more valuable than the other, then she must desire more strongly the one that she judges more valuable, and when she judges two things to be equally intrinsically valuable, but is more confident of the value of the one than the other, then she must desire more that about which she is more confident. The upshot is that whether we would criticize an agent for failing to maximize expected *value* turns very much on that agent's epistemic circumstances: whether or not they had available to them evidence of what is really valuable.

The situation can be diagramed as follows (Smith 2004).

facts about → *available*   → *means-ends*
means to   *evidence*   *beliefs*
desired ends   *about means to*
                 desired ends

                                  $+ →$ *attempt* → desired
                                                                        end

                                  desires for
                                  ends
                                  ↑

facts about → *available*   → *judgements*
what is   *evidence about*   *about what*
of value   *what is of value*   *is of value*

What we hold agents responsible for is, at most, the elements in bold italics, for these are the elements whose relations are governed by the agent's exercise of such rational capacities as she has. Has the agent attended to all of the available evidence as regards both what is of intrinsic value and means to her desired ends in the formation of her evaluative judgements and means-end beliefs? Do the agent's desires for ends reflect her judgements about what is intrinsically valuable? Is what the agent attempts to do an appropriate reflection of his desires for ends and means-end beliefs? But if this is right then, contrary to Jackson, we simply do not hold agents responsible for failing to maximize expected *value*. At most we hold them responsible for failing to maximize expected *value-as-they-see-things*. Maximizing expected value-as-they-see-things is the right thing for them to do, in the sense that is 'most immediately relevant to action.' This is what we can legitimately expect them to do and criticize them for failing to do.

Once this becomes clear it seems to me that we see much better the attractions of Moore's definition of right action. Unlike Jackson, Moore adopts a completely symmetrical approach to both evaluative and non-evaluative facts as determinants of right action. Even though we can only hold agents responsible for failing to maximize expected value-as-they-see-things, that just goes to show that our concept of a right action isn't tied so closely as Jackson thinks to what we can legitimately hold agents responsible for doing. If people live in an oppressive culture in which they are epistemically cut off from what's really valuable then the very best that they can do is to maximize expected value-as-they-see-things. But since, in so doing, they fail to maximize expected value, even Jackson must conclude that they fail to do the right thing, albeit through no fault of their own. The concept of a right action, in the sense relevant to ethics, must therefore be the concept of a certain sort of ideal, one that abstracts away from the possibility of this kind of error for which we cannot hold an agent responsible.

But once we have distinguished the concept of right action from the concept of what we can legitimately hold agents responsible for doing in this way, there would seem to be no stable stopping point short of the Moorean definition. People who maximize *expected* value, but fail to maximize value *tout court*, also fail to act in accordance with an ideal. Moreover the explanation is much the same as the explanation in the case where people maximize expected value-as-they-see-things, but fail to maximize expected value. In each case they are epistemically cut from a relevant domain of facts, in this case, facts about what the means to their desired ends really are. It is therefore this latter concept, the concept of an action that maximizes value *tout court*, a concept that incorporates two ideals—one on the evaluative side of things and the other on the non-evaluative side of things—that properly captures the concept of right action. We should therefore accept Moore's definition of right action, not Jackson's.

4. The task of Practical Ethics

So far, so good; but what about the task of Practical Ethics? How do we get from abstract knowledge of what it is about an action that makes it right—that it maximizes value—to a decision about what to do in a concrete situation? Isn't Jackson right that the Moorean view will either force us to conceive of the task of Practical Ethics in the completely wrong way, ensuring that we get the wrong answer to which action we should choose—this is what Moore himself does— or else make that transition altogether opaque? The answer is that it doesn't, and that it is instructive to see why not.

The fundamental problem with Moore's conception of the task of Practical Ethics is not his conception of right action, but rather his conception of moral motivation. Suppose that right actions are those that maximize value. Does this imply that, as a right-minded agent, I will be moved, at bottom, by an intrinsic desire to maximize value? Though Moore is not explicit on the issue, this does seem to be his view, for having this intrinsic desire is precisely what's required for agents to take an interest in which action is most likely to maximize value when they decide what to do. Imagine again the two-drugs example.

If what Jill cares about, fundamentally, is that she maximizes value, then of course she will prescribe drug X rather than drug Y. For prescribing drug X has a much better chance of achieving what really matters to her. In so far as we have the reaction that we do to the two-drugs example, we implicitly assume that this is not what we fundamentally care about. But in that case what do we fundamentally care about? And how does what we fundamentally care about lead us to make a more sensible decision, a decision that squares with our account of right action?

Consider again the relations charted in the diagram above. If I believe that experiencing pleasure is intrinsically valuable then, insofar as my desires are formed correctly in response to my evaluative beliefs, I will have an intrinsic desire that I experience pleasure. And if I believe that being autonomous is intrinsically valuable, then, insofar as my desires are formed correctly in response to my evaluative beliefs, I will have an intrinsic desire that I be autonomous. Being right-minded thus requires not that I have an intrinsic desire to maximize value but rather, since it requires that my desires are appropriately sensitive to my evaluative judgements, that I have intrinsic desires for the things I judge to be valuable themselves. This suggests a completely straightforward explanation of why, if I am right-minded, I will decide to perform the action that maximizes expected value-as-I-see-things.

Suppose, to begin, that I believe that experiencing pleasure is more valuable than being autonomous. If we abstract away from the levels of confidence associated with each of these beliefs—let's assume I am equally confident—then, insofar as my desires are formed correctly in response to my evaluative beliefs, my intrinsic desire that I experience pleasure will be stronger than my intrinsic desire that I be autonomous. And if we suppose that I am more confident of the value of pleasure than the value of being autonomous, but we abstract away from the degree of value I assign to each—let's assume that I assign them equal value—then, insofar as my desires are formed correctly in response to my evaluative beliefs, my intrinsic desire that I experience pleasure will again be stronger than my intrinsic desire that I be autonomous.

Putting these two conclusions together, suppose that I am very confident that being autonomous is valuable, but not very valuable, and that I am fairly confident—not as confident, but still quite confident—that experiencing pleasure is valuable too, but more valuable than being autonomous. Insofar as my desires are formed correctly in response to my evaluative beliefs the relative strengths of my intrinsic desires to experience pleasure and be autonomous will then depend entirely on the levels of confidence and associated degrees of value. The strength of my intrinsic desires will track the product of the levels of confidence and associated degrees of value: the greater that product, the greater the strength of my intrinsic desire. My intrinsic desire to be autonomous might therefore even be stronger than my intrinsic desire that I experience pleasure if the difference in the relative levels of confidence is greater than the difference in the associated degrees of value.

Finally, let's suppose that we plug these intrinsic desires into a standard expected utility calculation, a calculation that takes account of the different levels of confidence I have about the various means to my intrinsically desired ends. It then emerges that, in so far as I am right-minded, I will decide and choose to act not just so as to maximize expected utility, but so as to maximize expected value-as-I-see-things.

This, it seems to me, is the right thing to say about the task of Practical Ethics. We must decide to do what maximizes expected value-as-we-see-things, and, when we offer advice to others, we must in effect tell them what we would decide to do if we found ourselves in their circumstances. The ambiguity of what it means to find ourselves in another's circumstances—whether we imagine ourselves with our own values and the other person's expectations, or both our own values and our own expectations—supports and explains a profusion of 'oughts' of the kind noticed by Jackson.

Importantly, however, note that even if I manage always to act so as to maximize expected value-as-I-see-things, and so act responsibly and avoid all criticism, and even if others manage always to do exactly what I would do if I found myself in their circumstances, we can still quite happily admit that such actions may yet fail to meet an ideal. For it is a simple fact of life that we act in an environment in which we are epistemically cut off from all sorts of facts about both what is really valuable and what the means to ends really are. We can therefore quite happily admit that the right action for anyone to perform in their circumstances, the one against which their own perfectly responsible behaviour in those circumstances may well and quite appropriately be judged to be a failure, is the act that maximizes value.

Conclusion

At one point Jackson says, in defence of his own definition of right action:

We need, if you like, a story from the inside of an agent to be part of any theory which is properly a theory in ethics, and having the best consequences is a story from the outside. It is fine for a theory in physics to tell us about its central notions in a way which leaves it obscure how to move from those notions to action, for that passage can be left to something which is not physics; but the passage to action is the very business of ethics. (Jackson 1991: 467)

One way of putting the argument of this paper is that Jackson gets things exactly the wrong way around. We already have a story from the inside of an agent, a story that is not ethics. This is the story of rational decision-making as outlined in the diagram above, the story that is formalized—or anyway partially formalized—in decision theory. The passage to action is thus not the business of ethics itself; or, at any rate, it is not the business of that part of ethics itself whose concern is to provide a definition of right action. The business of that part of ethics is to come up with a definition of right action which dovetails in the right kind of way with the theory of rational decision-making. My suggestion is that that definition will be an idealization of the story of rational decision-making and that this is what Moore's definition of right action provides.

References

DREIER, JAMES (1993). 'Structures of Normative Theories', *The Monist*, 76: 22–40.

JACKSON, FRANK (1991). 'Decision Theoretic Consequentialism and the Nearest and Dearest Objection', *Ethics*, 101: 461–82.

LOUISE, JENNIE (2004). 'Relativity of Value and the Consequentialist Umbrella', *Philosophical Quarterly*, 54: 518–36.

MOORE, G. E. (1903). *Principia Ethica* (Cambridge: Cambridge University Press).

—— (1942). 'A Reply to my Critics', in P. A. Schilpp (ed.), *The Philosophy of G. E. Moore* (Evanston, Ill.: Northwestern University): 543–667.

RAWLS, JOHN A. (1971). *Theory of Justice* (Cambridge, Mass.: Harvard University Press).

RUSSELL, B. (1910). 'The Elements in Ethics', repr. in *Philosophical Essays* (London: Routledge, 1944): 13–59.

SCANLON, T. M. (1998). *What We Owe to Each Other* (Cambridge, Mass.: Harvard University Press).

SMITH, MICHAEL (2003). 'Neutral and Relative Value after Moore', *Ethics*, 113: 576–98.

—— (2004). 'The Structure of Orthonomy', in J. Hyman and H. Steward (eds.), *Action and Agency*, Royal Institute of Philosophy Supplement, 55 (Cambridge: Cambridge Univerisity Press): 165–93.

7

Scanlon versus Moore on Goodness

Philip Stratton-Lake and Brad Hooker

G. E. Moore's *Principia Ethica* started twentieth-century moral philosophy with the open question argument. At the end of the century, T. M. Scanlon, in his *What We Owe to Each Other*, says that he is led by Moore's open question argument, not to Moore's own view of the relation of goodness to reasons, but to the buck-passing account of goodness. The buck-passing account of goodness is the view that goodness is not a property that itself provides practical reasons (i.e. reasons to desire, to admire, to pursue, etc.) but rather is the purely formal (higher-order) property of having some other properties that provide reasons. According to the buck-passing account, the power to provide practical reasons is passed from goodness itself to the properties on which goodness is based. In this paper we will explore the question of whether there is a good argument from the open question argument to the buck-passing account of goodness. We will argue that the case for the buck-passing account of goodness is stronger than some of Scanlon's critics make out. We will not, however, offer a full defence of the buck-passing account of goodness. Such a defence would have to respond to the various objections to the buck-passing view itself, and that is beyond the scope of this paper.

1. The open question argument

Moore presents the open question argument as an argument for the view that naturalists commit a fallacy. Unfortunately, Moore was rather vague about what this fallacy is supposed to be (see Frankena 1939). Moore most often portrays the naturalistic fallacy as the mistake of thinking that 'good' is definable. But what is most important to Moore (1993: 19) is to insist not that 'good' cannot be defined, but that it cannot be defined in *naturalistic* terms, and we

For helpful comments on earlier drafts of this paper, we gratefully thank Roger Crisp, Jonathan Dancy, Rahul Kumar, Rob Lawlor, Mike Ridge, Bart Streumer, Mark Timmons, and Andrew Williams.

will interpret his naturalistic fallacy in this way. Moore also thought that the fallacy is committed if one identifies goodness with some metaphysical property, such as the property of being commanded by God. But Moore focuses on naturalistic definitions, and we will follow him in this respect.

What is a natural property? Moore himself seemed unclear what the answer is (Moore 1993: 12–13; T. Baldwin in Moore 1993: pp. xxi–xxii). One answer he offers is that a natural property is one that can exist by itself in time (Moore 1993: 93). Another answer is that a natural property is one with which it is the business of the natural sciences or psychology to deal (Moore 1993: 13). There are problems with both these answers, and there are other possible answers. How exactly to characterize natural properties remains controversial.

This is not the place to explore the natural/non-natural distinction. To give some content to the discussion, however, we will adopt a version of the epistemological account of this distinction. This epistemological account is intimated by Moore's definition in terms of the natural sciences and more recently developed by Copp (2003: 181; cf. Sturgeon 2003: 534–8). According to this account, a natural property is one that can be known by empirical means, and so is an appropriate object of study by the empirical sciences. And, on this account, a non-natural property is one that cannot be known by empirical means, and so is not an appropriate object of study by the empirical sciences. If the naturalism/non-naturalism distinction is understood in this way, the naturalistic fallacy is committed whenever goodness is defined wholly in terms of empirical properties.

Moore's open question provides the argument for the view that goodness cannot be defined naturalistically, according to Moore. Moore works with two versions of his question, which we will call the 'property' version and 'object' version.

According to the property version, the open question is 'Is it good that A is *n*?', where *n* is the natural property with which good is to be identified. This is the version of the question that Moore uses when he considers the attempt to define 'good' as 'that which we desire to desire'. He argues that 'good' cannot be defined in this way, because when we

ask ourselves 'Is it good to desire to desire A?' it is apparent, on a little reflection, that this question is itself as intelligible, as the original question 'Is A good?'—that we are, in fact, now asking for exactly the same information about the desire to desire A, for which we formerly asked with regard to A itself. (Moore 1993: 67)

The object version of the question does not ask whether it is good that A is *n*, but asks whether an A that is *n* is good. Here the question is not whether it is good that something possesses the natural property in terms of which 'good' is to be defined, but whether the thing that has this property is good. This is the more familiar version of the open question, and is the one with which we will work.

Moore claims that all questions of the form 'Is an A that is *n* good?' have an open feel that they would not have if goodness were the same thing as *n*ness. It is because such questions have this open feel that goodness cannot be a natural property.

There are many explanations of the openness of questions of the form: 'Is an A which is *n* good?' One of these explanations is Moore's own. A second is favored by non-cognitivists. A third comes from Scanlon.

Moore thought that such questions have an open feel because the answer is unobvious and debatable. He took it that the answer would not be unobvious and debatable if 'good' were definable as '*n*'.

In contrast, non-cognitivists hold that the openness of the open question is explained by the possibility of motivational indifference to anything characterized in purely naturalistic terms. The non-cognitivist background to this explanation starts with the claim that judging that something is good is *per se* to be motivated to act in certain ways towards that thing. But judging that something has some naturalistic property does not necessarily imply the presence of such a motivational attitude towards that thing.

Scanlon offers a normative explanation of the openness of the open question. Judgements about what is good entail practical conclusions about what would be reasons for acting or responding in a certain way. Natural facts may provide the ground for such practical conclusions, but judging that these facts obtain need not involve explicitly drawing these conclusions. Scanlon (1998: 96) writes,

> Questions such as 'This is C, but is it valuable?' (where C is the term for some natural or 'metaphysical' property) therefore, have an open feel, because they explicitly ask whether a certain practical conclusion is to be drawn.

Judging that some natural fact obtains does not entail judging that we have reason to respond to that thing is some positive way. We do not judge that we have such reason until we judge that that thing is good.[1] So such judgements are always normatively open.

Scanlon (1998: 96) says that he was led to the buck-passing account of value by this account of the open feel of the open question. The normative account

---

[1] For Scanlon's normative explanation of openness to work, he must assume not only that when we judge that A is good we judge that we have reason to care about A, but also that we do not judge that we have such reason *until* we judge that A is good. Otherwise it is not clear why the question whether we have reason to care about A is normatively open until, and just until, we judge that A is good.

of the open question argument involves three things: the natural properties in virtue of which A is good, the fact that A is good, and the fact that we have reason to respond in certain positive ways towards the good, that is, towards A. What led Scanlon to the buck-passing account of value is that he thinks that it offers the best account of the relation of these three things.

2. Two preliminary points

Before we evaluate Scanlon's arguments for the view that the buck-passing account of value provides the best account of the relation between natural properties, reasons, and goodness, it will be useful to make two preliminary points.

First, the question Scanlon's buck-passing account of goodness is supposed to answer need not be restricted to the relation between the natural, goodness, and normative reasons. The question is how the properties on which goodness supervenes (the base properties) relate to goodness and normative reasons. Whether the base properties must be natural properties will depend on whether thick evaluative properties, such as the property of being kind, or generous, can be divided into distinct natural and evaluative elements.

If thick evaluative properties can be divided in this way, then the normative buck will be passed down to their naturalistic components. If, say, kindness can be understood as a disposition to act in certain (naturalistically specifiable) ways towards others, plus the fact that this disposition is good, then the base property will not be kindness as such. Rather the base property will be the naturalistic *component* of kindness, i.e. the disposition to act in certain ways towards others. The evaluative component of kindness, the goodness of this disposition, will not be a part of the base property, but will *supervene on* this naturalistic base.

If, on the other hand, thick evaluative properties like kindness do not involve distinct naturalist and (thin) evaluative components, then someone's kindness itself could be located wholly within the base level. On this supposition, the normative buck could not be passed down to a distinct naturalistic component of kindness, as there is no distinct naturalistic component to play this reason-giving role. So if thick evaluative properties cannot be divided into distinct naturalistic and (thin) evaluative components, the base properties need not be naturalistic. They might be non-natural, thick evaluative properties.

Second, Scanlon distinguishes valuing something from claiming that the thing has value:

To value something is to take oneself to have reasons for holding certain positive attitudes towards it and for acting in certain ways in regard to it. Exactly what these reasons are, and what actions and attitudes they support, will be different in different cases.

They generally include, as a common core, reasons for admiring the thing and for respecting it, although 'respecting' can involve quite different things in different cases. (95)

According to Scanlon, '[t]o claim that something is valuable (or that it is "of value") is to claim that others also have reason to value it, as you do' (95).

The distinction between valuing something and thinking it valuable is a useful one. As Scanlon points out, 'it is natural to say, and would be odd to deny, that I value my children; but it would be odd for me to put this by saying that they are valuable (except in the sense that everyone is)' (ibid.). This point is brought out more strongly in comparative evaluative judgements. We value our children more than any other people's children, but we do not think our children more valuable than any other children.

But given how Scanlon defines valuing something, judging that something has value cannot be understood as judging that others also have reason to value it, as you do. For then, judging that something is of value would turn out to be judging that others have reason to judge that they have reason for holding certain positive attitudes towards it and for acting in certain ways in regard to it. This is, at best, awkward.

What Scanlon should have said is that for you to judge that something A is good is for you to judge that you *and others* have reason for holding certain positive attitudes (e.g. desiring or admiring A) and for acting in certain ways (e.g. pursuing, promoting, or publicly applauding A). For you to judge that A is good is *not* for you to judge that they have reason *to judge* that they have reason for holding certain positive attitudes towards A and for acting in certain ways towards it. Put more succinctly, the idea is that for A to be good is for more or less *everyone* to have reason to *care* about A.

Bearing the above points in mind, we need to clarify the relation between A's base properties (be they natural or not), the property that A has of being good (being of value), and the reasons we have to care about A.

Scanlon claims that these things can be related either according to the Moorean view or according to the buck-passing account.

Moorean view:	The base properties of A make A good, and the goodness of A gives us a reason to care about A. Reasons supervene on goodness, and goodness supervenes on the base properties.
Buck-passing account:	The base properties of A make A good and provide reasons to care about A. The goodness of A does not provide an additional reason to care about A, but rather is the purely formal (higher-order) property of having some other properties that provide reasons.

Moore's own view, at least in its classic early formulation, combined three theses: (1) the thesis that good is non-natural, (2) the thesis that 'good' is unanalyzable, and (3) the buck-stopping thesis that we refer to here as the 'Moorean view'.[2] This third thesis is the one that Scanlon primarily has in mind when he contrasts his own, buck-passing account with Moore's account. But a related contrast between Moore's account and Scanlon's concerns analyzability. The buck-passing account, unlike Moore's own, does provide an analysis of good, namely that 'good A' means 'an A that has other properties that provide reasons to care about it'.

3. Scanlon's two arguments

Now let us consider the content of Scanlon's two arguments for the buck-passing account over the Moorean view. The first is that, at least in some cases,

natural properties provide a *complete* explanation of the [practical] reasons we have.... It is not clear what further work could be done by special reason-providing properties of goodness and value, and even less clear how these properties could provide reasons for action. (1998: 96)

The second is that

many different things can be said to be good or to be valuable, and the grounds for these judgements vary widely. There does not seem to be a single, reason-giving property that is common to all these cases. (1998: 97)

Scanlon's first argument is poorly stated. As we understand him, the point he is making here is not that natural properties provide a complete *explanation* of the reasons we have. His idea is that the fact that A has such-and-such natural properties *provides* the reasons we have. So he thinks those natural properties provide a complete *list* of the reasons we have when the base properties (the properties on which goodness supervenes) are natural properties. We take his point to be that thinking of the goodness of A as adding to the reasons provided by the base properties of A commits a kind of category mistake. If the reason why the holiday resort is good is because it is pleasant, then the reason to choose the holiday resort is just that it is pleasant, not because it is pleasant and because it is *good*.

---

[2] For example, Moore states, that '[t]he only reason I can have for aiming at "my own good", is that it is good *absolutely* that I should *have* something, which, if I have it, others cannot have' (1993: 150).

But let us ask whether this is an argument not against the Moorean view that goodness is the only reason, but against the view that goodness is an *additional* reason? That is, contrast:

Moorean view: The base properties of A make A good, and the goodness of
                   A gives us a reason to care about A. Reasons supervene on
                   goodness, and goodness supervenes on the base properties.

with

Alternative view: The base properties of A make A good and provide
                   reasons to care about A, and the goodness of A gives us
                   an additional reason to care about A. Goodness super-
                   venes on the base properties, and reasons supervene
                   both on the base properties and on goodness.

Scanlon's first argument (as we understand it) certainly seems to work against what we're here calling the alternative view. If the properties on which goodness supervenes provide practical reasons, then unnecessary philosophical problems are created if goodness is taken to supply an additional practical reason. The alternative view seems to multiply reasons pointlessly. The buck-passing account has what is needed from the alternative view but without the unnecessary proliferation.

But does Scanlon's first argument work against the Moorean view? If Scanlon's argument is effective against the alternative view, it is even more effective against the Moorean view. The strong intuition Scanlon points to is that we seem to have exhausted the list of reasons to care about something once we have listed the features that make it good. We do not need to add the fact that it is good to complete the list. This intuition clearly assumes that the good-making features are reason-giving, which the Moorean view simply denies. So the intuition Scanlon mentions in his first argument is even more incompatible with the Moorean view than it is with what we are calling the alternative view.

Scanlon's attack on the Moorean view may seem to put too much weight on explanations in terms of natural properties. Scanlon offers the following examples of 'complete explanations' of practical reasons: 'the fact that a resort is pleasant is a reason to recommend it to a friend, and the fact that a discovery casts light on the causes of cancer is a reason to applaud it and to support further research of that kind' (1998: 97). Is Scanlon wrong to focus on natural properties in these examples?

It may be objected that natural facts never provide reasons by themselves, because, when fully stated, the reason-giving fact will always involve an evaluative component. So, for example, it may not be the mere fact that something is pleasant that gives us a reason to choose it, but the fact that it is pleasant and the fact that this pleasure is *innocent*. Similarly, it may not be the natural fact that some discovery has been made that gives us reason to applaud it. The reason to applaud it is the fact that it is a *significant* discovery. But the fact that it is a *significant* discovery may not be itself a natural fact.

We take no stand in this paper on the issue of whether reasons always, sometimes, or never are constituted by purely natural facts. But as we noted earlier, it is not essential to Scanlon's argument that the base properties be natural properties. The issue is whether it is the base properties (whatever their nature is) or the goodness of A that provides us with reason to care about A.

Let us now move to Scanlon's second argument for the buck-passing theory over the Moorean theory. The crucial part of Scanlon's second argument is his claim that 'there does not seem to be a single, reason-giving property' that is common to all things that are good (1998: 97). As a first step in assessing that claim, let us distinguish two different ways that there may conceivably be a single, reason-giving property common to all goods.

One of these possibilities is that there may be a single, reason-giving property at the supervening level. In fact, this possibility is just what Mooreans hold to be the case—i.e. that the goodness shared by all good things is the reason-giving property. This Moorean position was the target of Scanlon's earlier argument that a complete list of reasons mentions the base properties but not goodness.

The other way that there may conceivably be a single, reason-giving property common to all goods is that there is a reason at the level supervened upon, the base level. To embrace this possibility would be to accept a monism about grounds of goodness and of reasons. Such a view might hold, for example, that all good things contribute to well-being.

Scanlon argues at length that well-being is not such a master value. Admittedly, showing that well-being is not the master value does not show that there is no master value. Still, well-being does seem to be the leading candidate for being a master value. If Scanlon successfully argues against this candidate, no other seems likely to do better. So let us grant to Scanlon that pluralism about goodness is correct.

Scanlon's buck-passing account of goodness in effect claims that, whatever the practical reason-giving properties are, what they all have in common is only that they generate practical reasons. This relation to practical reasons can be expressed by saying that all things with those properties are good. The Moorean account, in contrast, claims that they all have an extra property, goodness, and that this property is not merely a relation between other properties and reasons.

Thus the Moorean view holds that there are three different kinds of thing to explain the relations among: base properties, goodness, and reasons. And the Moorean view holds that none of these are to be defined in terms of the others. The buck-passing account holds that there are really only two things to explain the relation between: base properties and reasons. And the buck-passing view then defines goodness in terms of the base properties and reasons. This contrast between the Moorean view and the buck-passing account reveals the buck-passing account's greater parsimony. This greater parsimony counts in favour of the buck-passing account.

But does Scanlon's argument about the plurality of good do any real work against the Moorean?

Suppose a pluralist view about the grounds of practical reasons—that is, about what the reason-giving properties are. Suppose a, b, c, d, and e are the reason-giving properties. On the buck-passing view, that things which are either a, b, c, d, or e are good is nothing more than the fact that a, b, c, d, or e provide reasons to care about those things.

For the sake of contrast, now suppose a monist view, e.g. that e is the only reason-giving property. The buck-passing account, as such, is perfectly compatible with this monistic view. A buck-passing form of this monistic view would hold that the fact that only something that is e is good is nothing more than the fact the only e is a reason-giving property.

Since the buck-passing account can take either pluralistic or monistic forms, the buck-passing account is neutral as between pluralism and monism. Similarly, the Moorean view that goodness 'stops the buck' is neutral between monism and pluralism. Thus Scanlon's argument from value pluralism cannot establish that the buck-passing account is superior to the Moorean view.

4. Neglected alternatives

Consider the objection that, even if Scanlon succeeds in showing that the buck-passing account is better than the Moorean view, this hardly shows the buck-passing account to be superior to other possible accounts. Scanlon argues for the buck-passing account merely by trying to eliminate the Moorean view. Some critics reply that there are other views Scanlon should have considered.

According to Dancy (2000: 163), Scanlon's argument works by eliminating two alternatives—the teleological account of goodness and the Moorean buck-stopping account. According to the teleological account of goodness, to be good is to be *to be promoted*. In contrast to Dancy's understanding, we think that Scanlon's argument does not work by eliminating the teleological account of goodness.[3]

We take the teleological account to be just one specific form that the generic buck-stopping theory might take. In other words, some versions of the buck-stopping theory of goodness are not teleological. Indeed, we formulated the Moorean view above so as to allow for such versions. A *non*-teleological buck-*stopping* theory of goodness denies that the only appropriate response to the good is promotion, but holds that the goodness of something provides a reason to desire, admire, applaud, *or* (sometimes) promote that thing.

Furthermore, the teleological account of goodness does not dictate a buck-stopping view of the relation between goodness and reasons. A *teleological* buck-*passing* theory holds that the appropriate response to the good is always promotion, but also holds that the reasons to promote do not come from the goodness but from whatever base properties ground the goodness.

Since a buck-stopping theory of goodness can be non-teleological, rejecting the teleological account does not establish the buck-passing view. Since accepting a teleological account of goodness does not require rejecting the buck-passing view, a defence of the buck-passing view need not eliminate the teleological account. So Scanlon's argument cannot work by eliminating the teleological account.

Scanlon has separate arguments against the teleological conception of goodness. His main point is not that this conception implies that goodness is reason-giving (as we have just explained, there is no such implication), but that the teleological account artificially restricts the range of responses to the good to just one—promotion (Scanlon 1998: 87–94). The argument for the buck-passing account of goodness does not proceed by denying that promotion is the only appropriate response to goodness. It instead proceeds by denying that goodness is a property that warrants a positive response from us in addition to the positive responses warranted by the base properties. The buck-passing account is not itself inconsistent with the view that the only response the base properties warrant is promotion.

On the question, then, of whether goodness is reason-giving, Scanlon thinks there is only one competing theory—the Moorean account, where the relevant feature of this account is its being a buck-stopping account. If Scanlon is right about this, then if he can show that his own account is better than Moore's, he will have shown that the buck-passing account is the best account of the

---

[3] It should be noted here that Scanlon occasionally seems to think of the buck-passing view as an alternative to the teleological view (1998: 93). But this is confused. The teleological view is, primarily, about what the appropriate response to the good is, whereas the buck-passing view is about what gives us reason to respond in the appropriate way, whatever this is.

relation of goodness, the ground of goodness, and reasons. But Dancy maintains that there are at least two theories that Scanlon ignores, and thus that Scanlon's argument from elimination does not work.

The first theory that Dancy (2000: 164) accuses Scanlon of ignoring is a Rossian view according to which the sort of things that can ground reasons need not be the same as the sort of things that can ground goodness. Ross maintained that actions can be right but not good, and that motives can be good but not right (1930: 4 ff.). But if an act is right (which for Ross meant 'obligatory'), then I have reason to do it. The reason I have to do this act is provided by whatever grounds the obligation to do it. This ground cannot be the same as the ground of its goodness, for, on Ross's view, obligatory acts are never good. In this respect, then, Ross's view differs from Scanlon's view that reasons and goodness always share the same ground.

The difference between Ross's view and Scanlon's should not be exaggerated. When Ross says that acts are never good, he means that they are never *intrinsically* good. But, in chapter 3 of *The Right and the Good*, Ross distinguishes four senses of 'good': intrinsic, instrumental, attributive and contributive (1930: 72–3). Although Ross denies that acts are ever intrinsically good, he does not deny that they can be good in some other sense. So although he holds that the reason we have to do some act cannot be provided by the ground of the act's intrinsic goodness since an act cannot have intrinsic goodness, he can allow that a reason to do the act may be provided by the ground of whatever non-intrinsic goodness the act has. The buck-passing view is an account not merely of intrinsic goodness, but of all forms of goodness. So the buck-passing view is compatible with the view that we could have reason to do acts that are not intrinsically good.

Nonetheless, there still seems to be a divergence between Ross's view and the buck-passing view. Ross's view allows that we *might* have reason to care about some act that is *in no way* good, i.e. is neither intrinsically, instrumentally, attributively, or contributively good. Since the act is in no way good, the reason we have to care about it cannot be provided by whatever makes it good (contra Scanlon), or by its goodness (contra Moore). Since Ross's view is different from Moore's view, the argument Scanlon provides against Moore's view does not dispose of Ross's view.

The second view that Scanlon fails to consider is Dancy's own. This view shares elements with both Moore's and Scanlon's accounts. It accords with Moore's account insofar as it denies that the property of being good can be identified with the second-order property of having other reason-giving properties. It accords with Scanlon's view in that it denies that goodness is a property that adds to the reasons provided by its ground (Dancy 2000: 164).

Dancy is right that the view we have just attributed to him and the view he attributed to Ross need to be considered. Scanlon's argument by elimination needs to eliminate these views, if the buck-passing view is to be the only alternative not eliminated. Nevertheless, these views are indeed inferior to the buck-passing view, as we shall now explain.

Consider first Ross's view, as sketched by Dancy. The buck-passing account of goodness can allow that an agent can have reason to do some act which is in no way good. It would allow this if the features that gave the agent a reason to care about his doing act A did not give anyone else reason to care about his doing act A. The buck-passing view does not entail that if the agent has a reason to care about A, then A is good (in some way). Rather, the buck-passing account of goodness entails the following bi-conditional:

A is good if and only if A has properties that both give an agent reason to care about A and give others reason to care about A.

Consider cases where you are the only person who has reason to care about whether you do A. In such cases the fact that your doing A is in no way good does not conflict with the above bi-conditional, and so is compatible with a buck-passing account of goodness.

Ross's view would conflict with the buck-passing view only if Ross held that there could be cases in which both (1) your doing A has features that give you *and others* reason to care about your doing A, and yet (2) your doing A is in no way good. Ross might allow for the possibility of (1) and (2) because the reason you and others have to care about doing A stems from what makes A obligatory, and obligatory acts need not be good in any way. We do not think this is a plausible view. If you are obligated to do A, then the features that give you reason to do A will also give others reason to approve of your doing A. And if others have reason to approve of your doing A, then your doing A must be good in some way.[4]

This is because the attitude of approval is only ever appropriate when it is directed at things that are good. Ross thought that this is because it is the fact that A is good that makes approval an appropriate response to A (1939: 261). This makes Ross look like a buck-stopper. However, one need not agree with Ross about that. One might just as plausibly maintain that approval is appropriate only towards things that are good because what makes the attitude of approval appropriate is what makes its object good.[5] In any case, if others

---

[4] Ross would certainly not deny that if others have reason to approve of something, then that thing is good (1939: 261).

[5] Our view is that we do not approve of certain things because they are good. Rather, we approve of different things for different reasons. We approve of good things because of their good-making features. We admire good acts because they are heroic, or brave, or selfless, etc., not because they are good (though we cannot approve of them unless we think they are good).

have reason to approve of your doing A then your doing A must be good in some way.

Turn now to the view we attributed to Dancy himself. This view agrees with Scanlon that, say, the pleasantness of a resort could be a reason to choose it, and agrees that the fact that it is a good resort does not give us an additional reason to choose it, but denies that the fact that it is good is the fact that it has other features that provide reasons to choose it. Dancy thinks that the second-order property of having other properties that provide reasons to choose something is distinct from the property that thing has of being good, though if something is good it will have this distinct second-order property. On this view, then, we always have reasons to choose things that are good (though not because they are good).

We think there is reason to prefer the buck-passing account of goodness to Dancy's view. Dancy maintains both that we always have reason to care about the good and that goodness never adds to the reasons provided by its ground. But unlike the buck-passing view, his account leaves unexplained why goodness *cannot* provide us with an additional reason. In this respect, then, the buck-passing account is a better option for those who agree with Scanlon that goodness is never reason-giving. For the buck-passing account of goodness explains *why* the fact that something is good never gives us a reason to care about it. On the buck-passing account, the fact that something is good is the fact that it has other properties that provide reasons to care about it, and the fact that it has such properties *cannot* provide an *extra* reason to care about it.

Roger Crisp picks out a different neglected position in Scanlon's argument. Crisp starts from Moore's famous example about choosing between two uninhabited worlds, one beautiful, the other an ugly pile of filth. Moore held that the beautiful world is better than the ugly one, and that this fact gives us reason to bring it into existence. But, Crisp argues, we need not embrace the buck-passing account of the relation between value and reasons if we reject Moore's view. We might opt for what Crisp calls a 'welfarist buck-keeping non-welfarist buck-denying' account. Crisp refers to this account as W. He frames W as follows:

[V]alues are properties that make their bearers good, or better, whilst reasons are facts that speak in favour of acting in a certain way: According to view W, the beautiful universe is indeed valuable; it is better that it exist than not. But since it matters to no one whether it exists or not, there is no reason to bring it about. (Crisp 2000: 240)

Since W works with a welfarist view about reasons, W holds we have no reason to bring about such a world if no one benefits from it. But since we are here working with a non-welfarist account of value, such a world could, nonetheless, be good.

W does not seem as plausible as the buck-passing view. If W is true, then the beautiful world can be good and the ugly not, without there being any reason to prefer the good world to the bad one. But it seems that, if the beautiful world is good and the ugly one not good, then there is a reason to prefer the good world. So W seems false.

Crisp might reply by saying that no one would judge a beautiful world good unless they cared about such things or were too depressed to care about what they judged valuable. No doubt this is right, but it is not at all clear why it should be right if W is true. If, as W allows, one's value judgements are independent from one's concerns and the reasons that go with these, it is not at all clear why we have to care about something to think that it is good.

Crisp might now issue a different and more general objection. On Scanlon's account, the goodness of A is nothing more or other than there being practical reasons to care about A. But there is a difficulty with taking reasons for action as being built into (or analytically entailed by) the very concept of goodness. Crisp's W, for example, holds precisely that the grounds of and criteria for goodness simply do part company with the grounds of and criteria for practical reasons. And, in making that claim, W is hardly alone!

Consider philosophers who hold both (i) that some form of consequentialism, or the Categorical Imperative, or some form of contractualism, or Rossian pro tanto duties determine what is morally right, and (ii) that reasons for action are always determined exclusively by the agent's desires (or alternatively by the agent's long-term self-interest). All such philosophers presumably agree with Crisp's W in finding it intelligible that your doing A would be good yet you have no reason to do A, nor anyone else reason to care about your doing A. Since the buck-passing account claims that A is good if and only if there are reasons to pursue, desire, admire, or approve of A, the buck-passing account rules out many (seemingly intelligible) combinations of theories about goodness and reasons.

We admit that such combinations of views are intelligible (as well as popular). But are they as plausible, on balance, as the buck-passing view? In the spirit of the normative explanation of the open question argument, we want to note that any combination of theories that introduces a gap between goodness and reasons invites a 'so what?' objection to judgements that something is good. In other words, if you can judge that A is good without judging that you have any reason to care about A, your response to instances of good might rightly be 'so what?' On the contrary, if there can't be a 'so what?' objection to a judgement that something is good, this seems to imply that judgements that A is good do indeed entail the normative judgement that there is reason to care about A.

As an illustration, consider Bernard Williams's example of Owen Wingrave. Wingrave comes from a family with a strong military tradition, but the thought of a life in the army leaves him cold. Now Wingrave could acknowledge all of the facts that his parents might cite in trying to persuade him to pursue a life in the army. He might accept that in pursuing such a life he would be carrying on the family tradition, that he would acquire various skills he would otherwise not acquire, that he would be more self-disciplined and organized, and so on. He could accept all this and still perfectly coherently respond 'so what?' What is not, in our view, coherent is for him to accept that these considerations make an army life a *good* life for him while responding 'so what?' This is incoherent because to accept that these considerations make an army life a good life is, at the same time, to accept that they count in favour of living this sort of life. To accept that they count in favour of living this sort of life is, of course, to accept that they provide reasons to live such a life.

That the buck-passing account of goodness rules out the possibility of simultaneously accepting that A is good and responding 'so what?' provides strong prima facie evidence in favour of the buck-passing view. Any view that denies that judgements that A is good entail judgements that we have reason to care about A invites a 'so-what?' objection to the judgement that A is good. That is the fate awaiting any combination of a theory of goodness and a theory of practical reasons that with one hand specifies the ground of and criteria for goodness and with the other hand specifies a quite different ground of and criteria for practical reasons.

5. Multiplying gaps

Let us now move on to other arguments. Moorean realism takes goodness to be a real, simple, non-natural property that supervenes on other properties. A difficulty with Moorean realism, according to Blackburn (1971; 1984: ch. 6; 1985; 1998: 315–17), is that it really has no explanation of why goodness supervenes on other properties. If goodness is a simple property, then it is not clear why it must supervene on other properties.

But on Scanlon's view, goodness is not a simple indefinable property, but is the property of having other properties that give us reason to care. As Stratton-Lake (2002: 15–16) points out, given this account of goodness, there is no mystery why it must supervene on other properties. It must supervene on other properties, because it is the property those properties have of providing reasons. For Scanlon, reasons just are such properties of things as that they produce pleasure or might lead to an improvement in our understanding of cancer. The reasons to care about things are properties that can be described without use of the concept of 'practical reasons'. Goodness, in turn, is the non-natural property those properties have of providing reasons (Parfit 1997: 124; Scanlon 1998: 57, 60, 61, 97; McNaughton and Rawling 2003: 30–3).

It may be argued that the buck-passing account of goodness does not solve the problem, but merely moves it back. Goodness is defined in terms of reasons, but the property of being a reason supervenes on other properties. Blackburn could, therefore, insist that the puzzle remains: why must the property of being a reason supervene on other properties?

We do not see the difficulty here. It is a conceptual truth that if you have a reason to care about A, then there must be something that provides that reason. This something is what the reason supervenes on. If the reason you have to go for a walk is that it will be pleasant, then this reason supervenes on the pleasantness of the walk. If the reason you have to cycle to work is that it will keep you fit, then this reason supervenes on the fact that cycling will keep you fit. Reasons supervene on other properties because there must be something that provides the reason. There is nothing mysterious about this, nothing here that stands in need of further explanation.

One might ask why reasons supervene on one property rather than another. The question might be why, for example, the fact that you have promised to feed the neighbours' cat while they are away gives you a reason to do so, whereas the fact that grass is green does not. This is not, however, a metaethical question, but a normative one. The answer will depend on normative principles about what people should do and why.

Here is a related argument in favour of Scanlon's account over the Moorean one. Scanlon holds that the openness of the open question argument does not stem from the supposed fact that if goodness were the same as some natural property this would be obvious to us. He thinks the openness of the open question argument stems from the fact that judgements about whether A is good express practical conclusions about reasons we have to care about A. The open feel is dispelled once we judge that A is good because in judging that A is good we judge that we have reason to care about A.

In contrast, the Moorean account does not hold that we judge we have reason to care about A insofar as we judge that A is good. According to the Moorean account, the goodness of something and the practical reasons that the goodness supplies are different things. So Mooreans must hold that to judge that we have reason to care about A is to make a *further* judgement over and above the judgement that it is good. They must hold that, in this respect, judging that A is good is just like judging that it has some natural, reason-giving property. We may think that certain natural properties as well as goodness are reason-giving; but, just as we do not explicitly judge that we have reason to care about A simply insofar as we judge that A has some natural property, so, on the Moorean account, to judge that something is good is not yet to conclude that we have reason to care about it.

In short, according to Scanlon, (*a*) there is openness between judging that A has some natural property and judging that A is good, (*b*) there is openness between judging that A has some natural property and judging that there is reason to care about A, *but* (*c*) there is *no* open feel between judging that A is good and judging that there is reason to care about A. According to the Moorean view, again (*a*) there is openness between judging that A has some natural property and judging that A is good, and again (*b*) there is openness between judging that A has some natural property and judging that there is reason to care about A, *and* (*c**) there *is* an open feel between judging that A is good and judging that there is reason to care about A. If we think (*c*) rather than (*c**) is correct, then we have to line up with Scanlon.

6. The open question again

If the buck-passing account of goodness is right, then to be good is to have properties that provide reasons to care. So, if the buck-passing account is right, then not only does goodness entail reasons to care shared by the agent and others, but also, conversely, reasons to care shared by the agent and others entail goodness. The buck-passing account's commitment to the entailment of goodness from reasons to care makes the buck-passing account vulnerable to a series of objections. These objections insist that we can coherently judge that we and others have reason to care about something yet deny that this thing is good.

There are various forms this sort of objection can take, and we cannot address them all here.[6] But one way of capturing the general idea behind such objections can be expressed as an open question objection to Scanlon's buck-passing account of goodness. It may be insisted that the buck-passing analysis is false because the question 'Is something that has properties that provide reasons for the agent and others to care about it good?' has an open feel. The Moorean argument that led Scanlon to the buck-passing account of goodness may, therefore, provide a strong reason to reject it.

---

[6] A particularly forceful form of this objection is put forward by Rabinowicz and Rønnow-Rasmussen (2004). They consider the possibility of an evil demon who demands of us, under threat of severe punishment, that we admire him precisely on account of his determination to punish us if we don't. Here we clearly have reason to admire the demon, and to admire him on account of his maliciousness. Nonetheless, his maliciousness is in no way good. Whether the buck-passing account of goodness can rebut this objection is not something we have space to consider here—but see Stratton-Lake (2005).

Is it an open question whether something that has properties that provide reasons for the agent and others to care about it is good? If there is openness to the question, it cannot be *normative* openness. For once we accept that something has properties that provide reasons to care about it, the question of whether there is reason to care about it is clearly closed. So if Scanlon's normative explanation of the open feel of the open question is the best account of that question, then his account of goodness cannot be vulnerable to the open question argument. Hence, if his account of goodness is vulnerable to an open question, the question must be open in the sense that his definition either is non-obvious and debatable or leaves open the possibility of motivational indifference.

If it is open whether something that has properties that provide reasons to care about it is good, and if this openness is merely a consequence of Scanlon's definition of goodness being non-obvious and debatable, then it is not clear that the openness raises difficulties for Scanlon. For, insofar as this definition of goodness is interesting and informative, one would hope that it *is*, prima facie, non-obvious and debatable. We accept that, if Scanlon's account of 'good' is an accurate account of what we *mean* when we judge that something is good, the question 'Is something that has properties that provide reasons to care about it good?' is ultimately closed. But it strikes us as unsurprising that this question should initially feel open in the sense that the answer is not obvious.

Is this question motivationally open? The motivational explanation of openness is premised on the view that to judge that something is good is *per se* to have a directed (motivational) attitude towards that thing. This is because judgements about goodness are essentially practical judgements, and on this view, practicality is understood motivationally. But judgements about what we have reason to do and feel are also essentially practical judgements. So if the essentially practical nature of evaluative judgements is to be understood motivationally, then the practical nature of judgements about what we have reason to do and feel is presumably to be understood motivationally. This would mean that to judge that we have reason to respond in certain positive ways towards something would *per se* involve having a positive attitude towards that thing. But then the question 'Is something that has properties that provide reasons to care about it good?' would not be motivationally open. Our view is, then, that someone who thinks that Moore's open question argument is best understood in motivational terms would not expect there to be an open feel to the question whether something that has properties providing reasons to care about it is good.

We do not, therefore, think that Scanlon should be troubled by an open question objection to the buck-passing account of goodness. The only sense in which it is likely to be open is in the sense that the definition is non-obvious and thus debatable. But this feeling of openness is to be expected from an interesting and informative account of goodness. If this feeling persists after reflection, this would cast doubt on the analysis of goodness in terms of reasons. But if the analysis survives such reflection—which it will have to do if it is a plausible analysis—this feeling of openness would dissolve.

References

BLACKBURN, S. (1971). 'Moral Realism', in J. Casey (ed.), *Morality and Moral Reasoning*. London: Methuen.

—— (1984). *Spreading the Word*. Oxford: Oxford University Press.

—— (1985). 'Supervenience Revisited', in I. Hacking (ed.), *Exercises in Analysis*. Cambridge: Cambridge University Press. Reprinted in Blackburn's *Essays in Quasi-Realism*. New York: Oxford University Press, 1993: 130–48.

—— (1998). *Ruling Passions*. Oxford: Oxford University Press.

COPP, D. (2003). 'Why Naturalism?' *Ethical Theory and Moral Practice*, 6: 179–200.

CRISP, R. (2000). 'Contractualism and the Good' (review article of T. M. Scanlon, *What We Owe to Each Other*), *Philosophical Books*, 41: 235–47.

DANCY, J. (2000). 'Should We Pass the Buck?', in A. O'Hear (ed.), *The Good, the True and the Beautiful*. Cambridge: Cambridge University Press: 159–73.

FRANKENA, W. (1939). 'The Naturalistic Fallacy', *Mind*, 48: 464–77.

MCNAUGHTON, D., and RAWLING, P. (2003). 'Naturalism and Normativity', *Proceedings of the Aristotelian Society Supplementary Volume*, 77: 23–45.

MOORE, G. E. (1993). *Principia Ethica*, 2nd edn by Thomas Baldwin. Cambridge: Cambridge University Press. Original edition published in 1903.

PARFIT, D. (1997). 'Reason and Motivation', *Proceedings of the Aristotelian Society Supplementary Volume*, 71: 99–130.

RABINOWICZ, W., and RØNNOW-RASMUSSEN, T. (2004). 'The Strike of the Demon: On Fitting Pro-attitudes and Value', *Ethics*, 114: 391–423.

ROSS, W. D. (1930). *The Right and the Good*. Oxford: Clarendon Press. Reprinted with an introduction and bibliography by Philip Stratton-Lake. Oxford University Press, 2002.

—— (1939). *Foundations of Ethics*. Oxford: Clarendon Press.

SCANLON, T. (1998). *What We Owe to Each Other*. Cambridge, Mass.: Harvard University Press.

STRATTON-LAKE, P. (2002). 'Introduction', in P. Stratton-Lake (ed.), *Ethical Intuitionism*. Oxford: Clarendon Press: 1–28.

—— (2005). 'How to Deal with Evil Demons: Comment on Rabinowicz and Rønnow-Rasmussen', *Ethics*, 115: 788–98.

STURGEON, N. (2003). 'Moore on Ethical Naturalism', *Ethics*, 113: 528–56.

8

Opening Questions, Following Rules

Paul Bloomfield

There are two types of assessment of G. E. Moore's intellectual character by Ludwig Wittgenstein recorded in Norman Malcolm's *Memoir* of Wittgenstein. First is that Moore was 'deep', honest and serious; at one point Wittgenstein 'observed that if one were trying to find exactly the right words to express a fine distinction of thought, Moore was absolutely the best person to consult' (1958: 67). The second is that

> Wittgenstein once remarked that what Moore primarily did, as a philosopher, was to 'destroy premature solutions' of philosophical problems. . . . But he added that he did not believe Moore would *recognize* a *correct* solution if he were presented with one. (66)

Malcolm writes that Wittgenstein thought Bertrand Russell 'was extremely "*bright*" is how he put it: Moore, in comparison, was less so' (68). If we put all this together we get the idea that Moore was 'deep but not too bright' and from anyone but Wittgenstein, this would certainly be 'Damning With Faint Praise'. Regardless of any possible insult to Moore, however, Wittgenstein may have been right.

At least in regard to the open question argument, it seems clear that Moore himself was not at all clear about what he was on to. Perhaps everyone agrees that he was on to something and that it was something both deep and important. Exactly what it is, however, is still a bit of a mystery. The problem arises when we note that we have defined 'good' in such a way that we call all tokens of type X we've encountered in the past 'good' and here in the present we are encountering another token X. Why is it not a foregone conclusion that we think this new X is good? Why does there always seem to be an open question with regard to the goodness of each instance of X we encounter? Why do all putative definitions of 'good' leave this lingering doubt? If we believed some particular definition of 'good' was the true one, then it would be 'true by

I'd like to thank Donald Baxter, Terry Horgan, Len Krimmerman, Michael P. Lynch, Mark Timmons, and David Schmidtz for their helpful comments and discussion.

definition' that an item which satisfied the criteria of the definition is 'good'. But instead of an 'open and shut case', at each new possible predication of the word 'good', we are presented with an open question about whether the item in question is, in fact, 'good'.

Such considerations very well might lead us to conclude that 'good' is indefinable, as they obviously led Moore. Even if we agree with Moore about this, one might nevertheless have a lingering doubt about whether indefinability can really explain what is going on in the open question argument. Have we ever really gotten a satisfactory account of what keeps the open question open?

The canonical interpretation of the open question argument is that there is a peculiar form of normativity accompanying the use of the word 'good' and this normativity keeps us from definitively closing our open questions; there is something peculiar about the way the predication of 'goodness' guides action. Goodness comes with some special 'normative force' which necessarily incites (defeasible) motivation. Because such force cannot be captured by a definition, all putative definitions of 'goodness' strike us as incomplete and we get the open question. This interpretation has had a large influence on the course of metaethics in the twentieth century. Darwall, Gibbard, and Railton wrote in their 1992 *Philosophical Review* 'Fin de Siecle' piece that non-cognitivism is the 'real historical beneficiary of the open question argument' (1992: 119). Indeed, it seems fair to say that the non-realist family of theory that includes non-cognitivism, emotivism, prescriptivism, quasi-realism, norm-expressivism, etc. was the dominant metaethical family of the last century. Given the traditional interpretation presented briefly above, it is a short step to inferring that it is, in fact, the pro-attitude attending predications of 'good' which keeps the definition of 'good' open: we can always imagine ourselves not being motivated by some item, or a token of a type of item, which we called 'good' in the past. The normative force of 'goodness' must be all in the head, for if it were 'out there' in the world, it would be ontologically 'queer'. If goodness has to be accompanied by a motivationally charged, psychological state of mind, then 'goodness' cannot be defined in terms of some mind-independent, external entities, as moral realists, like Moore, thought. In this way, moral non-realism found perhaps its strongest support in Moore's open question argument.

If, however, there were good reason for thinking that the sort of normativity which keeps the open question open is not something special (queer) about 'good' (or 'right' or their cognates), if what we have is actually not a *sui generis* form of moral normativity, but rather just a sort of normativity which we find in another area of philosophy, then the consequences for metaethics are apparent: the dominant metaethical theory loses perhaps its strongest motivation for acceptance.[1] This is the idea to be explored below. In particular, the conclusion is that the normativity which keeps Moore's ethical open question open is the same sort of normativity which is driving Wittgenstein's rule following considerations.[2] The main thesis of this essay is that there is no peculiar or queer *sui generis* form of normativity which infects the meaning of the word 'good'; whatever it is that keeps the definition of 'good' open also keeps the definitions of other words, like 'plus', 'mass', and 'triangle' open. In general, we simply cannot be sure that our words are being used now in a way that is consistent with the way we used them up until now.

Regardless of whether or not this is a genuine problem or a pseudo-problem, the point is that there is only one problem here, not one for ethics and a different one for everything else. The questions 'how ought I to use this word?', 'what ought I to believe in this situation?', and 'what ought I to do now?' stem from semantics, epistemology, and morality respectively but the underlying problem of normativity is the same in all: how can features of the world establish conditions under which it makes sense for us to say that there are ways we ought to conduct ourselves (with regard to our actions, our speech, or our beliefs) and other ways which ought not to be followed? Even if normativity is a mystery, even if it is somehow in the end rightly called 'queer', still, there is no need to multiply mysteries beyond what is required and, a fortiori, there is no reason to think that the normativity attaching to how we ought to behave morally is different than that attaching to how we ought to speak semantically or what we ought to believe epistemologically. If this is true, then the metaethical situation is far different than what is required for metaethical expressivism (et al.) to be supported in the way that it is typically taken to be supported. If one were to reason from the open question argument to expressivism when engaging metaethics, then, assuming the argument below is sound,

---

[1] A comment late in production has shown me that just a few sentences here can ward off what amounts to a very serious objection. Some may read this paper and think I am defending the idea that there is no distinctive moral normativity but that I am trying to reduce moral normativity to semantic normativity, or perhaps eliminate the former, supplanting it with the latter. This is mistaken. I do think there are general features of semantic, epistemic, and moral normativity such that each of these are a form of normativity, a satisfactory general account of which is still in the offing. (For my own attempt to begin such a theory, see Bloomfield 2001: 143–52.) The limited conclusion of this paper, which concerns Moore's open question argument and the meaning of the word 'good', is only that the meanings of moral terms do not carry with them any queer sort of normativity beyond the semantic normativity carried by the meanings of other words.

[2] This is a possibility which Darwall, Gibbard, and Railton (1992) acknowledge but do not pursue in footnote 5 of their paper.

One who supports the traditional interpretation of the open question argument might reason as follows: if the open question argument supports non-realism in other areas of philosophy beyond metaethics, then so be it and non-realism should thereby spread into those areas. This may be the case, but then it must be acknowledged that moral realists have no special burden to carry in defending their metaethical theory. What we have then is a general metaphysical debate about realism and we have left metaethics *per se* behind.

consistency would demand the same reasoning applies when engaging in semantics and epistemology. Since expressivism is not a going general theory of semantics or epistemology, one should seriously doubt the reasoning that leads to it in metaethics.

Obviously, these issues are very complicated. The crux of the matter can be driven in upon first by clearing away surrounding red herrings that might otherwise create a variety of possible conflations; after this the workings of Moore's open question argument and Wittgenstein's rule following considerations may be more directly inspected. So, first, this means distinguishing the open question argument from the misbegotten naturalistic fallacy as well as from the 'paradox of analysis'; it also means distinguishing the rule following considerations from the argument against private language as well as from concerns about family resemblance. Finally, and prior to all this, a large caveat is required. The aim of this essay is admittedly polemical and as such Moore and Wittgenstein are treated as historical stalking horses and not philosophical saints: the goal is not to present new scholarship that sheds light on a solution to the open question argument or the rule following considerations as traditionally construed, nor is it to shed light on the philosophical methods of either Moore or Wittgenstein. Undoubtedly, below certain points of philosophical development are emphasized and others are completely ignored. The choices are driven by the interests of philosophy (particularly of metaethics) and not of scholarship or hagiography. The suggestion is that, given the improved perspective of hindsight on these particular issues, the best way to understand what both Moore and Wittgenstein were up to is to see them as pursuing the same set of issues, clustered around the idea of semantic normativity, though both pursued them through different questions and with obviously different methodologies and philosophical temperaments.

We can begin with 'naturalistic fallacy' and dispatch with it quickly enough. All that is truly required for this is to cite Frankena's 'The Naturalistic Fallacy' (1939/1986), but perhaps just a few more words here can sufficiently sum up the situation. In his *Principia*, Moore, of course, recognized that the 'naturalistic fallacy' never really had anything special to do with naturalism, as he applied it to metaphysical, as well as to natural, definitions of 'good'. We learn from C. Lewy (1964) that as early as 1921, Moore saw that there was no real fallacy involved, insofar as fallacies require inferences and Moore thought that those who committed the 'naturalistic fallacy' were merely confused. About what were they confused? It seems that each of them thought that one of a variety of possible definitions of 'good' were complete and correct. How do we know they were all confused? Because the open question argument shows us that any such definition is not actually complete. The 'naturalistic fallacy' is best thought of as a substantial philosophical thesis, the content of which is that the open question argument shows us that all definitions of 'good' are at best incomplete. Since all the work here is being done by the open question argument, our attention can be focused upon it and we may leave the naturalistic fallacy (almost) behind us.

The 'almost' is because it will help us to keep it in view while attending to the paradox of analysis. In *Principia's* discussion of the naturalistic fallacy, Moore uses language which is very similar to the language found in discussions of the paradox of analysis. For example ' "That we should desire to desire A is good" is *not* merely equivalent to "that A should be good is good" ' (§ 13). In fact, Lewy (1964) gives one interpretation of the naturalistic fallacy that takes it to be 'a particular instance' of the paradox of analysis. As Lewy notes, this is a mistake. The paradox of analysis asks us how any definition or analysis can be both complete and informative; quoting Alonzo Church, 'This would seem to reduce [a successful] analysis to something trivial and uninformative' (1946: 132). The important point for our work here is that the paradox of analysis obviously assumes that the definition under consideration is complete and this is explicitly what the open question argument is supposed to show is impossible for any definition of 'good'. Insofar as 'good' is concerned, the paradox of analysis assumes and the open question argument denies the possibility of a complete definition of 'good' and as such we can leave the paradox of analysis behind.

The relationship between Wittgenstein's rule following considerations and his argument against private language is more complicated. The traditional view is that the former are a step toward establishing the latter, since the former immediately precedes the latter, which begins at § 243 within *Philosophical Investigations*. Others (e.g. Kripke 1982) think the rule following considerations are what constitute the argument against private language, the conclusion of which is thus given in § 202;[3] on this view, what the tradition takes as the private language argument is actually an application of that argument to sensations which give the prima facie appearance of being a counterexample to the private language argument. Our concern here, however, is not with private

---

[3] In § 202, Wittgenstein says, 'Hence it is not possible to obey a rule "privately": otherwise thinking one was obeying a rule would be the same thing as obeying it.' Note however, contra Kripke, that in § 199 (on the same page as § 202) he says, 'To obey a rule, to make a report, to give an order, to play a game of chess are *customs* (uses, institutions)' where institutions are surely public; at § 206 he says, 'Following a rule is analogous to obeying an order. We are trained to do so; we react to an order in a particular way. But what if one person reacts in one way and another in another to the order and the training? Which one is right?'; here the concern is interpersonal. And in § 204, the concern is with rules which no one ever follows. In general, Wittgenstein does not seem to be particularly, much less primarily, concerned with *private* rules at this point in his dialectic.

language at all. This can be seen because the rule following considerations present a set of problems for public languages just as much as for private language: the question 'what is it for us to all be now following the same rule?' arises through the rule following considerations with as much force, and perhaps more, than the question 'what is it for me to be following now the same rule I followed yesterday?' The intrapersonal diachronic difference between me today and me yesterday is identical from a formal point of view to a synchronic interpersonal difference. Problems regarding the meanings of words are not purely private problems, but are public language problems as well. So, even if we agree with Kripke in thinking that the conclusion to the private language argument comes at § 202, we can still see this as a special application of a more general problem about following rules. For our present purposes, we are trying to isolate whatever it is that is generating the problems we find in understanding how we follow rules. Since there is no a priori reason to think that issues concerning privacy are at the bottom of the rule following considerations, we can set aside problems concerning private language in our consideration of the rule following considerations.

It might appear that Wittgenstein's notion of family resemblance is driving at least part of the rule following considerations.[4] If one thought that rules needed necessary and sufficient conditions to be fulfilled in order for the rule to apply, then pointing out the fact that we apply some rules which do not admit of necessary and sufficient conditions might show us a way into problems concerning our following rules. Admittedly, the application of family resemblance concepts is a bit mysterious; we find ourselves saying odd things like 'I can't quite put my finger on it, but something about you reminds me of your parents.' But again, we do not want to supplant a general problem with a particular instance of it (indeed this is contrary to the spirit of the essay) and that is the mistake we would make were we to think that family resemblance drives the rule following considerations. The reason for this is that the rule following considerations may apply to rules driven by family resemblance

---

[4] Wittgenstein did, at least at one point, think that some of the problems in understanding 'good' were due to something like family resemblance. Quoting from lecture notes written by Moore in 1931 of lectures given by Wittgenstein: 'And of the word "good" he [Wittgenstein] said similarly [as he said of "beautiful"] that each different way in which one person, A, can convince another, B, that so-and-so is 'good' fixes the meaning in which 'good' is used in that discussion— 'fixes the grammar of that discussion'; but that there will be 'gradual transitions', from one of these meanings to another, "which take the place of something in common" ' (Wittgenstein 1993: 104). 'Good' may be a vague predicate, but I think it is a mistake to think that the mysteries surrounding 'good' are to be located by attending to its vagueness *per se*; we will not find a solution to those mysteries by adopting any particular theory of vagueness or by solving the Sorites paradox. Maybe I am wrong and the troubles surrounding 'good' are due to a family resemblance problem; even so, remember that the thesis of the paper is to argue that 'good' presents no *sui generis* problems. If I am wrong and the mystery of 'good' is to be located in its character as a family resemblance notion, this still does not demonstrate that 'good' presents any *sui generis* problems.

concepts, like 'game', but they also apply to rules which can be made as precise as anyone could like: Kripke's contribution to the dialectic is that he brought the generality of the problem to the forefront. It arises for 'plus' just as much as it does for 'game'. The problem is located in how it is that we succeed in following rules, and whether or not the rules are precise or driven by family resemblance, the same problem arises. Granted, there may be extra complications with family resemblance concepts but these are not needed to generate the rule following considerations *per se*, and as such we can leave behind these complications and focus on the rule following considerations directly.

Having cleared the board of some possible red herrings, let us now turn forthrightly to the open question argument and the rule following considerations respectively. The open question argument comes in § 13 of *Principia Ethica* as the argument which, all by itself, is supposed to show that the meaning of 'good' is simple and indefinable. Moore gives us an argument by cases beginning with the idea that the only options to the simplicity and indefinability of 'good' are either that it means something complex or that it has no meaning at all. The open question argument is used to show that both of these alternatives fail.

In the case in which 'good' denotes something complex, the argument goes as follows. We are explicitly asked to apply such a complex definition of 'good' to a particular case, A, asking 'Is A good?', and we may say that 'A is good' if and only if it is one of the kind of thing which falls under the extension of the complex definition of 'good' under consideration. So, working with Moore's own example, let's use the complex notion that good things are the things which we 'desire to desire' and then we can answer the question 'Is A good?' by noting that it is if and only if A is one of the things which we desire to desire. So far, so good. We can pursue the matter further, however, by asking a second question 'Is it good to desire to desire A?' and when we do so, we find out that the fact that A is one of the things which we desire to desire does not settle this second question. In fact, the information we are asking about in the second question is the same as the information we were asking about in the first question 'Is A good?': having the definition and applying it to a particular case does not automatically close the question about whether or not that particular case falls under the extension of the original predicate. As Moore says,

> It may indeed be true that what we desire to desire is always also good; perhaps even the converse may be true: but it is very doubtful whether this is the case, and the mere fact that we understand very well what is meant by doubting it, shews clearly that we have two different notions before our mind. (§ 13, 1902/1988:16)

The empirical fact that every individual thing which in the past we have desired to desire has been good is insufficient to show us that 'good' denotes only those things which we desire to desire. At the most, what can be shown is that the extension of 'good' is the same as the extension of what we 'desire to desire', but even this would not allow us to define 'good' in terms of being something which we desire to desire. It does not show us that it is impossible for there to be something which we desire to desire but which in fact is not good at all, nor that it is impossible for there to be something which deserves to be called 'good' even though it is not something which we desire to desire. Either of these two possibilities represent an 'open question' by showing us that it is not 'true by definition' nor by 'the meanings of the words' that what it is to be good is identical to what it is to be what we desire to desire.

This is supposed to show us that any complex definition of 'good' will not work, though it is not clear what role complexity plays in the argument. Leaving this issue aside for the moment, the other alternative is that 'good' fails to denote anything at all, that it is meaningless, and Moore tries to use the open question argument, once again, to show us that this alternative fails. The argument now goes like this: if we think that it is true by definition that 'pleasure is good', then we have only one notion before our mind and if this is the case then it cannot make sense to go on and ask 'Is pleasure after all good?' (1902/1988: 16). Moore takes it as obvious, and perhaps it is, that we all understand the question 'Is this good?' and that this is a distinct question from 'Is this pleasurable or desirable or approved?' So, once again, given an identification of what is 'good' with what is, say, 'pleasurable', we are still left with the open question embodied by meaningfully asking a question of the following form: 'We know it is pleasurable, but is it good?' So because the question 'Is this thing, A, good?' is meaningful and distinct from asking about A if it is anything else other than 'good', we can conclude that 'good' is not meaningless.

Does this actually show that 'good' is not meaningless or that it fails to denote anything? This seems dubious at best because the argument as it stands seems to rest on the assumption that if what is 'good' is in fact identical to ('='), e.g., what is 'pleasurable', then either 'good' is meaningless or it fails to denote anything, and this seems like a false assumption. From the premise identifying what is 'good' with what is 'pleasurable', one cannot conclude that 'good' is meaningless or fails to denote; and yet this is the inference which Moore seems to make in this second application of the open question argument. Contra Moore, it seems that if the premise is true then 'good' does not *fail* to denote anything, rather it denotes all the pleasurable things in the world.[5]

---

[5] To say 'good' is to mean 'pleasure' but this may not be the same as intending to use 'good' to mean 'pleasure'. As Church (1946) notes in regard to the paradox of analysis, Frege's distinction between meaning (sense) and denotation (reference) is surely lurking in the background here. 'Good' may be the sense while 'pleasure' is denoted.

Settling this particular question is not necessary either, since the idea that 'good' is meaningless is not plausible in the first place. All parties to present debate in metaethics seem to agree that 'good' is not meaningless. (Even if expressivism is right and 'good' can no more be defined than 'hooray', we would not thereby conclude that 'good' is meaningless.) If we can assume that 'good' is meaningful, we can nevertheless learn something from the second application of the open question argument: no possible definition of 'good' could be the true or correct one if the only reason for accepting it is through an appeal to the meaning of the word. This may sound trivial, but in fact it is not. It may make more sense to say it this way: we cannot understand the meaning of 'good' through any possible definition. What we learn, finally, from the open question argument is that any definition of 'good' is open to question because it can never be a foregone conclusion that the definition, as it stands, works for every present or future application of the word 'good': for any new case, we can always question whether or not the item is good even after we note that it fulfills the criteria given in the definition we have supposedly accepted. Our past experience with using the word in a particular way does not tell us that we ought to continue to apply the word to things in the world in that same way in the present or in the future.

The open question argument may therefore be summed up as follows. Any putative definition of the word 'good' shows itself to be incomplete through its failure in the *practical* application of 'good' to a particular case, P; such that, when we encounter P we cannot automatically conclude 'P is good' even though it may be apparent that P fulfills the criteria laid out in the putative definition. The doubt always remains that 'P is good' is false even though it satisfies the semantic rule constituted by that definition. This doubt, this open question, cannot be closed by appeal to past things which have satisfied the definition nor by the meaning of 'good' as given by the definition. The semantic rule for 'good' must be seen as, in this sense, open-ended. According to Moore, the way we tell whether or not 'P is good' is through 'intuition'; no definition of 'good' can be *proved* true.[6] Therefore, regardless of the particulars of the definition, we can conclude that it is incomplete, that it has left something out, that the meaning of 'good' is not fully captured by the terms specified in the definition.

---

[6] Moore writes, 'Again, I would wish it observed that, when I call such propositions "Intuitions," I mean *merely* to assert that they are incapable of proof; I imply nothing whatever as to the manner or origins of our cognition of them. Still less do I imply (as most Intuitionists have done) that any proposition whatever is true, because we cognise it in a particular way or by the exercise of any particular faculty: I hold, on the contrary, that in every way in which it is possible to cognise a true proposition, it is also possible to cognise a false proposition' (1902/1988: preface, p. x). This is a form of the argument for moral realism from error which merits separate attention.

What is it that is left out? What is it that keeps the open question open? Moore wants to answer the question by pointing to the simplicity of goodness. But while simplicity might rule out the possibility of analysis, it is far from obvious why we cannot trust ourselves to some degree to be able to sometimes recognize goodness when we see it, especially since we all seem to be able to use the word 'good' in a variety of ways that indicate that we know what it means. The problem is not in affirming or denying the possibility of giving a full analysis of goodness or a definition of 'good'. The problem is, as just mentioned, a practical one regarding how it is that we can properly use a word without being able to ever be sure that we are using it correctly. The problem is not over whether or not the rule governing the use of the word 'good' ought to engage in the face of something either simple or complex. The problem is in understanding how the meaning of a word can be governed by a rule. Simplicity and complexity are beside the point. While Moore is to be credited for pointing out the open question and for explicating some of its implications, he does not satisfactorily explain why the open question stays open.

Turning now to Wittgenstein, the rule following considerations are not so neatly compacted in a page or two as the open question argument is in *Principia*; arguably they run all the way through *Philosophical Investigations* insofar as the idea of a 'language game' (first mentioned in § 7) is perhaps the central theme of the book and rules constitute the formal aspects of all games, including logic. If people don't follow the rules then there will come a point at which they have stopped playing the game. The giving of definitions and the meanings of words can rightly be considered the central examples of rules in the book. In § 81 and § 82, we find the following:

All this [concerning the idea of Ramsey's that logic is a 'normative science'], however, can only appear in the right light when one has attained greater clarity about the concepts of understanding, meaning, and thinking. For it will then also become clear that what can lead us to think that if anyone utters a sentence and *means* or *understands* it he is operating a calculus according to definite rules.

82. What do I call 'the rule by which he proceeds'?—The hypothesis that satisfactorily describes his use of words, which we observe;—But what if observation does not enable us to see any clear rule, and the question brings none to light?—For he did indeed give me a definition when I asked him what he understood by 'N', but he was prepared to withdraw and alter it.—So how am I to determine the rule according to which he is playing? He does not know it himself. . .

In § 84, Wittgenstein asks what a game looks like whose rules 'never let a doubt creep in', and in § 85 he says, 'A rule stands there like a sign-post'; but it does not tell us to follow in the direction of the finger rather than in the direction of the wrist. Even chalk marks on the ground can be interpreted in different ways

(§ 85). Doubt always remains about whether or not we are following the rule that we are intending to follow.

In terms of structure, a plausible reading may take the 'rule following considerations' to begin at § 143 where we are asked to consider writing down a 'series of signs according to a certain formation rule'. At § 147, Wittgenstein notes that one can 'know the application of the rule of the [algebraic] series quite apart from remembering actual applications to particular numbers'. At § 151, we are introduced to the idea that any finite amount of data underdetermines a rule. From § 156 to § 171, we get a digression on reading, and at § 179 we return to our case at § 151. This is followed by the example of trying to teach someone '+2' in such a way that the pupil will not 'change' to '+4' (a different rule) after reaching an arbitrary point, like 1,000. The notion of 'queerness' makes its appearance at § 194 and the problem is summed up in full force for the first time at § 201:

This was our paradox: no course of action could be determined by a rule, because every course of action can be made out to accord with the rule. The answer was: if everything can be made out to accord with the rule, then it can also be made out to conflict with it. And so there would be neither accord nor conflict there.

It can be seen that there is a misunderstanding here from the fact that in the course of our argument we give one interpretation after another; as if each one contented us at least for a moment, until we thought of yet another standing behind it. What this shews is that there is a way of grasping a rule which is *not* an *interpretation*, but which is exhibited in what we call 'obeying the rule' and 'going against it' in actual cases.

Immediately after this, Wittgenstein becomes occupied with the idea of 'obeying a rule' and keeps almost exclusively to this thought until § 243 when he famously turns his attention to the particular problem of reidentifying 'private' sensations (again, according to a rule). After this, in the *Investigations*, what we have learned about rules is somewhat in the background but must be seen as constituting the bedrock of subsequent discussions of 'meaning as use', the point or purpose of a game, the notion of 'intention', etc. One cannot hope to capture the breadth or depth of Wittgenstein's dialectic, but the present discussion can carry on by attending to three points: overcoming the underdetermination of a rule by data, the supposed 'queerness' of thinking that 'future development must in some way already be present in the act of grasping the use and yet isn't present', and, finally, the idea of 'obeying a rule'.

At § 151, we find a series of numbers: 1, 5, 11, 19, 29; and it is pointed out to us that different mathematical functions can be used to describe the series: it can be $a_n = n^2 + n - 1$ or one could spot the series 4, 6, 8, 10 being added to each successor. There is no fact of the matter about which function is *the* function defining the series; the options are logically equivalent. If we are looking for a determinate answer about what is really going on in that series of numbers, the situation only worsens when we note that the options may capture equally well all past data but nevertheless diverge in the very next case or at any point in the future. When our pupil works in a way that seems to be in accord with the rule '+2' until 1,000 is reached and then carries on 1,004, 1,008, 1,012, we think that something has gone wrong and cannot help but to wonder at what rule our pupil was following all along. The problem is not that we cannot know the rule which our pupil was following; rather the problem is that there may not have been any fact at all about what rule our pupil was following. The reason for this is that we do not know how to capture in a single application the entire meaning of a rule, and multiplying applications does not help because the same incompleteness is present in each new application.

'The steps are *really* already taken even before I take them in writing or orally or in thought.' And it seemed as if they were in some unique way predetermined, anticipated— as only the act of meaning can anticipate reality. (§ 188)

We do overcome this underdetermination of data: the fact that we are not (yet) extinct shows that we are doing something right. We can learn rules which help us to survive on our own and communicate with each other. We do succeed in playing games, we do seem to be able to follow rules regarding, say, which side of the street to drive on, and the exceptions are aberrations which do not last long, on pain of death. (We are perhaps touching on the essence of natural selection.) It would be wrong to say that all of human life or all of life in general is a game; this would be demeaning. Life is the 'real thing'; games are not. Nevertheless, the formal relationship which human life bears to rules is the same as the one which human games bear to rules.

We do overcome this underdetermination of data, but Wittgenstein is not as clear as one could hope about how this is done. We 'grasp the whole use of the word in a flash' (§ 191), in a way which determines our future usage while not being determined by past usage.[7] This may sound mysterious and Wittgenstein is sensitive to this. He writes, 'When does one have the thought: the possible movements of a machine are already there in it in some mysterious way?—Well, when one is doing philosophy' (§ 194). Is this sort of grasping rightly considered a 'mystery' something to be thought of as 'queer'? Wittgenstein says it is only philosophers who will see it as queer. Philosophers will say, 'I don't mean that what I do now (in grasping a sense) determines the future use causally and as a matter of experience, but in that

---

[7] § 138 is the earliest use of the idea that we 'grasp' the meaning of a word 'in a flash'.

queer way, the use itself is in some sense present' (§ 195).[8] And Wittgenstein thinks that the philosophers are right except for their invocation of queerness. We think on one hand that 'there is no doubt that we understand the word, and on the other hand its meaning lies in its use' (§ 197). And here there is no special queerness, as long as we remember that to 'understand a language means to be master of a technique' (§ 199). We can grasp meanings and understand rules, we do it all the time, it is how we survive, and though we may not as yet have a full explanation for the phenomenon, we need not think that grasping the meaning of a word 'in a flash' or following a rule is 'a queer process': amoeba behave in a manner closely akin to the way in which we obey rules each time an amoeba encounters acidic water and swims in the opposite direction. At some point, justifications for behavior end, our 'spade is turned', and at that point we are left with nothing to say but, 'This is simply what we do' (§ 217).[9]

We are still left, however, with the question of how rules are followed. Wittgenstein's answer to this is that what we grasp when we grasp a rule or understand the meaning of a word is not an interpretation of the rule but is rather the grasp of a practice or a technique. We make a hypothesis about how to proceed and then employ the hypothesis, all the while keeping an open mind about the possible need to amend the hypothesis in the future.[10] Wittgenstein thinks that we can understand how we follow rules by considering the 'analogy' of it to how we 'obey a rule'. We hold on to the idea that some actions 'obey' the rule and others 'go against it', and so we may conclude that 'to think one is obeying a rule is not to obey a rule' (§ 202). Thus, it is the normativity behind the determinations of what obeys the rule and what goes against it that is the crux of the project of figuring out the meanings of words. Importantly, this is a problem of practical rationality, much like a chess problem is a problem of practical rationality. The distinction between theory and technique dissolves. Once we grasp the rule, we do not 'choose' our move; rather, we obey *'blindly'* (§ 219). We carry on with our hypotheses until our experience trips us up.

---

[8] '... When we do philosophy, we are like savages, primitive people, who hear the expressions of civilized men, put a false interpretation on them, and then draw the queerest conclusions from it' (§ 194).

[9] I have changed here from Wittgenstein's first person singular to first person plural. The original § 217 is 'This is simply what I do.' The quotation marks do not here indicate an quotation from the text, but are to indicate what we might say in the described circumstance.

Those with more realist tendencies than Wittgenstein might think that the bedrock is found in some very unmysterious 'fact of the matter' ('if we eat those berries we die') upon which our practices are founded or without which our practices cannot continue. The bedrock may be the world when the game is to dig a ditch; the bedrock may be our conventions when the game is proper table etiquette.

[10] '82. What do I call "the rule by which he proceeds"?—The hypothesis that satisfactorily describes his use of words . . .'

When we do get tripped up we give explanations to 'remove or avert' the misunderstanding (§ 87).

Must I *know* whether I understand a word? Don't I also sometimes imagine myself to understand a word (as I may imagine I understand a calculation) and then realize that I did not understand it? ('I thought I knew what "relative" and "absolute" motion meant, but I see that I don't know.'). (footnote, following § 138)

The oblique reference to Einstein is helpful. The word 'mass' used to denote a quantity which is invariant with regard to speed. After Einstein, the word denoted a quantity which does vary with speed. We do not need to take sides in the debate about Kuhnian incommensurability in order to consider the rule constituting the meaning of 'mass' and wonder whether it always meant what Einstein taught us it meant or whether he changed the rule so that the word started to mean something different than it used to before him. The important point for us is that we can conceive of Einstein as questioning the rule constituting the meaning of the word 'mass'; Einstein opened up the question about the meaning of the word 'mass' when everyone else had long thought that this particular question was permanently closed. He forced us to question whether or not we were going to continue to apply the word 'mass' as we thought we were up until that point. Our pre-Einsteinian hypothesis regarding the meaning of 'mass' was shown to require adjustment in order to comport with new possibilities. We learned that if we continued to apply the word under exactly the same conditions in which we applied it in the past, we would sometimes 'go against' the rule governing the meaning of the word. We need not bother here with the distinction between retrospectively identifying unnoticed mistakes and the deliberate changing of our ways to better 'obey' the rule. We need not ask whether it was the same rule all along and Einstein helped us to get clear about it or if he changed the rule.

What is crucial is that we see the question which Einstein opened with regard to the definition of 'mass' as being the same as the open question which Moore pointed out with regard to 'good'.[11] The meaning of 'mass' may have seemed more closed than the meaning of 'good' ever could be, but if we remember the stricture to 'question our assumptions', then we will learn that the meanings of perhaps all our words, and most certainly our more theoretically laden words, like 'mass' and 'good', always have an open question attached to them. Their meanings can never be assumed to be certain in such a way that their future applications are necessarily or logically determined by present

---

[11] Interestingly, Moore and Einstein were working on *Principia* and the Special Theory of Relativity, respectively, at approximately the same time.

usage. In Riemannian space, 'triangles' can be composed of three right angles. Why should the meanings of our words be held sacred? We will continue to carry on as we have, humanely plodding along, one step at a time, adjusting or adapting as we need to, and, crucially, there is nothing 'queer' at all about it.

The proper question to be asking is not 'how can the meaning of "good" guide (or goad) behavior?', nor even 'how can the meaning of "justified" guide my behavior?' but rather 'how can the meaning of *any* word, like "plus" or "mass" or "triangle", guide behavior?' given that speaking and writing are quite literally forms of behavior. To move to full generality, the question we really ought to be asking is 'how can anything in the world guide behavior?' In what sense is it possible for behavior to be guided? Guided by what? With what authority? To what end?

Luckily, once again, these questions do not need determinate answers to pursue the matter at hand. The goal here is not to figure out the 'mystery' of normativity, but to show that the open question argument does not support moral non-realism as most moral philosophers think, because what keeps the open question open is no special *sui generis* type of normativity that attaches to the words 'good' or 'right' or their moral cognates. The way to do this is to show how the rule following considerations provide a broader explanation of the open question argument allowing us to see the latter as a problem which does not uniquely concern the word 'good' or morality but rather as an instance of the general phenomenon or the problem of normativity. As Moore says in the preface of *Principia*, the first question he is concerned with is 'What kind of things ought to exist for their own sakes?'; the second is 'What kind of actions ought we to perform?' What we have formulated here is the problem of normativity in its fullest human generality. Moore pursues these problems through investigating the nature of intrinsic value or the properties of the goodness of objects and the rightness of actions. This would have to include not only 'good people' but 'good knives' and 'good chess players', as well as proper or fitting or appropriate speech as a form of 'right' action. With each fresh circumstance in our lives, day by day, often moment by moment, we are confronted with the question 'what ought to be done here?' and we cannot assume that we can immediately gain our answer by looking to the past or unthinkingly applying old rules. In almost all cases, we must inspect the circumstance anew to make sure that we are responding to it appropriately; in all other cases we are, one might say, on 'autopilot'. How to sort out all these issues is the grand problem of normativity and incorporates the programs of both *Principia Ethica* and *Philosophical Investigations*.

Proving this in any systematic way may in fact be impossible. What can be done is to show how, at a number of points, Wittgenstein's concerns mirror those found that naturally arise when considering the open question argument: similarities between Moore's 'intuitions' and Wittgenstein's 'grasping in a flash'; that the 'queerness' of 'good' stands or falls with the 'queerness' of 'mass'; and finally that the only normativity needed to keep the open question open is of the same sort which keeps all linguistic and epistemic behavior infused with an 'open question'. There is nothing which marks off behavior with regards to morality as 'special' which does not also mark off behavior with regards to meaning and belief formation generally: all this is equally normative. Wittgenstein's concerns *are* Moore's, only writ larger, deeper, and broader.

Both Moore and Wittgenstein focus on both the unprovable aspects of our intuitions about 'good' and our grasping of rules, respectively. Moore says we have intuitions about what counts as 'good' and, as noted above, what he means by this is that our intuitions about what is 'good' are unprovable. For Moore, the unprovability of the contents of intuitions does not prevent us from having moral knowledge; such knowledge is simply not open to discursive proof. For Wittgenstein, whatever it is that takes place in the grasping of a meaning 'in a flash', it may be seen as a way to sum up the shift from the *Tractatus* to the *Investigations*: life and language cannot be pictured by truth tables; in the end there are no proofs to be had. If the rule following considerations have shown us anything, it must be that we cannot ever prove that we understand the meaning of a word: no amount of using it properly proves anything, given the fact that our next application of it may seem to others as our pupil saying, '. . . 996, 998, 1,000, 1,004, 1,008 . . .' seems to us.

We cannot know with any certainty that we understand; again, at bottom our justifications run out and we say, 'Well, that's just how we've been doing it . . .' We may seem to be on firmer ground with respect to knowing the meaning of other words than we are with 'good' but what Einstein shows with regard to 'mass' or Riemann shows with regard to 'triangle', this terra firma may be quite illusory. This lack of firm ground is a problem running all through philosophy. In philosophy of math, there is still no real consensus on what a number is. In philosophy of mind, we cannot rule out the possibility that eliminative materialists about the mind are wrong and that, in fact, we have no 'beliefs' or 'attitudes'. In epistemology, we cannot simply stipulate that epistemic skeptics are wrong for we must keep an open mind about what we say we 'know', or what we are 'justified' in believing. In metaphysics, we need only to gesture towards Berkeley on the meaning of 'substance' or Hume on the meaning of 'causality'. In more modern times, we learn that these problems go beyond the meanings of terms which we typically think of as being 'theory laden': Peter van Inwagen (1990), not to mention many quantum physicists, tells us that the words 'river' and 'mountain' apply to things which are radically different than we typically think, and Derek Parfit's (1984) thought experiments about 'identity' tell us that it may not be predicated of particular cases in obvious ways.

Are these words 'action-guiding' in any important sense? Well, of course they are. The answers to questions of identity may determine our actions in any number of circumstances, e.g. in cases of proposed euthanasia. Whether or not 'allowing' is as much of a 'cause' as 'making' has been at the center of many important life and death debates. We need not come down on one side of any of these debates to see that the meanings of the words under contention, the rules according to which we may think, speak, write, and act, either already have open questions attached to them or the philosophers who initiate the debates are the ones who are doing the opening. The meaning of 'good' presents us with undoubtedly difficult problems, and problems whose solutions do not admit of proof; but so far there are no reasons to think of these problems as being particular to ethics or moral philosophy.

Under these circumstances, it is hard to see as mere coincidence Wittgenstein's (or his translator, Anscombe's) use of the word 'queer' in the context of the rule following considerations when this very word has subsequently played a large role in the development of perhaps the most significant attack on the property of 'moral goodness', as found, most famously, in John Mackie's *Ethics: Inventing Right and Wrong* (1977). Things which we call 'good' are supposed to have some special power over us; such items are said to necessarily affect our motivations when we recognize them. The implausibility of thinking that ontologically real, 'mind-independent' properties could have such power over us has become one of the leading reasons for rejecting moral realism, and, as noted above, the ability to explain why we are motivated by the items we call 'good' has been perhaps the strongest argument in favor of non-realistic metaethical theories like norm-expressivism and quasi-realism. But what is so queer? Thinking or calling something 'good' means that we will react to it in a way different than if we thought it 'bad' or thought it was neither 'good' nor 'bad'. So we can conclude that how we think about things affects how we behave toward them. There are rules according to which we act when we recognize something as 'repulsive' and other rules when we find something 'attractive'. Well, of course. And perhaps there is a mystery here, but there is no special mystery about 'good' or 'bad' or their moral cognates: from this point of view, all meaning has behavioral implications coming along with it. The behavior of a physicist may be guided differently by thinking that 'mass' does or does not vary with speed. Where is the special queerness about moral terms? Well, thinking something is 'good' is often said to require us to be motivated toward it in a particular way; we must feel positively about it. This is the position often termed 'internalism'. It would be decisive perhaps to secure a *sui generis* queerness for the meaning of 'good' if there were no open question about the possibility of being repulsed or at least feeling negatively about something which is recognized as 'good'. Internalism is not itself a 'foregone conclusion' but a substantive thesis for which a philosopher must argue. There is an open question whether internalism is true for at least the following reason.

Moore pointed out that an item's fulfilling the criteria of a definition of 'good' does not all by itself allow us to conclude that this item is 'good'; we must have an intuition of its goodness. But there is the further open question being pressed by someone not moved by internalism: why is it impossible to feel anything but positive towards the things which we recognize as 'good'? This question remains open because we can imagine people receiving training which makes them respond negatively to what they recognize as 'good'. This could be the opposite of the sort of training which occurs at the end of Burgess's *A Clockwork Orange*: there the subject is made to feel ill by images of violence and other things which are recognizably 'bad' but which the subject felt positively towards prior to the training. Surely, it would be possible, though inhumanly malevolent and evil, to train people to be repulsed by things which they recognize as 'good'. In any case, it seems that we could train people to have the same positively 'queer' motivations toward any old thing which we typically think we have towards those items we call 'good'. We can be just as motivated and 'queerly' committed to solving an outstanding mathematical problem, writing a string quartet, or making the longest chain of paper clips in the world, as we are to being a friend, promoting world peace, or working towards the elimination of hunger. If it is my goal to make the longest chain of paper clips in the world, then I will necessarily, automatically be motivated by recognizing any paper clips in the room, just as I may necessarily, automatically be motivated by helping my friends when I recognize that they are in need. There is nothing special about the motivations which most frequently come when people recognize things as being 'good'. We can be motivated positively or negatively by these things, just as we can be towards anything in the world. In any case, our motivations are affected by how we think of things, how we think of things affects how we behave toward those things, and if this is queer here then there is equal queerness everywhere. But 'ubiquitous queerness' is either an oxymoron or a contradiction in terms. As such, whatever it is, it ceases to be queer. Wittgenstein is right: queerness is a philosopher's invention.

It is a philosophical platitude nowadays that there are normative aspects to both semantics and meaning as well as to epistemology and justification. Why should we think that the normativity of morality is something special or even primary? One can create a modus ponens or a modus tollens from how one answers this question. If one thinks that moral normativity is primary or special, then one may be led to conclude that metaethics should 'turn imperialistic' and that we should see semantics or epistemology become subfields of metaethics. In his Hempel Lecture (1992), Allan Gibbard suggests that semantic normativity is a special case of moral normativity and in her book on virtue epistemology, *Virtues of Mind* (1996), Linda Zagzebski suggests that epistemology should be enveloped as a subfield of metaethics. This does not put the cart before the horse, because there is no a priori reason to think that epistemology or language precedes morality any more than there is to think that morality precedes epistemology or language.

If one answers the above question about the 'specialness' or 'primacy' of moral normativity in the negative, then there is no reason to think that the normativity which attaches to morality is *sui generis*, in a way that requires moral non-realism to explain. There are skeptics about epistemology, meaning, and morality; but there are very few *expressivists* in the field of epistemology, and there are also few, if any, who think that *all* language deserves an expressivist's interpretation. Being a global non-cognitivist or expressivist would be a difficult trick to pull off, and one would have to wonder at the motivation behind it.

We are human beings, members of *Homo sapiens*. We are agents who form beliefs according to rules, communicate with our conspecifics according to rules, and use rules generally to 'guide' almost all our behavior. We are concerned with how we ought to act, what we ought to believe, and what we ought to say to each other. These are aspects of our existence which might be thought to be central to, if not essential to, the 'human condition' and there is no way around these practical problems. Still, obviously, we carry on. Most of us, most of the time, are guided by what we ought to do, or at least we try to be guided by what we ought to do, or at least we ought to be guided by what we ought to do. The regulation of conduct falling under the provenance of morality is no more nor less normative than the regulation of conduct falling under the provenance of communication or epistemology. At the very least, the burden of proof should be on those who claim a special normativity for morality which is somehow missing from communication or epistemology.

Of course, it would be wonderful to have a full explanation of normativity in general. The question has received some attention, but few truly ingenious ideas have been found and there is little if any consensus about the nature of normativity. At least nowadays, philosophers all explicitly recognize the problem. In large part, we are capable of seeing the problem now, in its full scope, due to the work of Moore and Wittgenstein; we might indeed think that they established the philosophical problematic for the twentieth century by helping us to formulate our questions and we are just beginning now to wrestle our way towards answers. Moore's open question argument started us off by forcing us to confront the problems involved in following the semantic rules of moral terms, but it was Wittgenstein's rule following considerations which showed us that the problem lies not in moral terms *per se*, or even in semantic rules *per se*, but in the very idea of 'rule-guided behavior'. Perhaps we will be realists about normativity, or instead, in the end, we may adopt one form of non-realism or another. But when we do so, our stance will not be one which is a metaethical stance; rather it will be a stance toward normativity in general. It will only be subsequent to this that we will be forced to deal with the repercussions of our general theory of normativity as they ramify through epistemology, the philosophy of language, and moral philosophy.

References

BLOOMFIELD, PAUL (2001). *Moral Reality*. New York: Oxford University Press.

CHURCH, ALONZO (1946). 'A Review of 4 Articles on "The Paradox of Analysis" ', *Journal of Symbolic Logic*, 11: 132–3.

DARWALL, S., GIBBARD, A., and RAILTON, P. (1992). 'Toward a *Fin de Siecle* Ethics', *Philosophical Review*, 101/1: 115–89.

FRANKENA, WILLIAM (1939/1986). 'The Naturalistic Fallacy'. Reprinted in P. Foot (ed.), *Theories of Ethics*. Oxford: Oxford University Press: 50–63.

GIBBARD, ALLAN (1992). 'Normative and Explanatory Meaning', Hempel Lecture I (draft).

KRIPKE, SAUL (1982). *Wittgenstein: On Rules and Private Language*. Cambridge, Mass.: Harvard University Press.

LEWY, CASIMIR (1964). 'G. E. Moore on the Naturalistic Fallacy', *Proceedings of the British Academy*, 50: 251–62.

MACKIE, JOHN (1977). *Ethics: Inventing Right and Wrong*. London: Penguin Books.

MALCOLM, NORMAN (1958). *Ludwig Wittgenstein*. London: Oxford University Press.

MOORE, G. E. (1902/1988). *Principia Ethica*. Buffalo, NY: Prometheus Books.

—— (1942). 'A Reply to my Critics', in P. A. Schilpp (ed.), *The Philosophy of G. E. Moore*. LaSalle, Ill.: Open Court.

PARFIT, DEREK (1984). *Reasons and Persons*. Oxford: Clarendon Press.

VAN INWAGEN, PETER (1990). *Material Beings*. Ithaca, NY: Cornell University Press.

WITTGENSTEIN, LUDWIG (1929). 'Lecture on Ethics'. Delivered in November 1929 to the Heretics Society, Cambridge University.

—— (1958). *Philosophical Investigations*, trans G. E. M. Anscombe. New York: Macmillan Publishing.

—— (1993). *Philosophical Occasions, 1912–1951*, ed. J. C. Klagge and A. Nordmann. Indianapolis: Hackett Publishing.

WRIGHT, CRISPIN (1984). 'Kripke's Account of the Argument against Private Language', *Journal of Philosophy*: 759–78.

ZAGZEBSKI, LINDA (1996). *Virtues of the Mind*. Cambridge: Cambridge University Press.

9

Was Moore a Moorean?

Jamie Dreier

Mooreanism in metaethics consists of two theses: that Good[1] is unanalyzable and that it is a non-natural property. It is an important position in twentieth-century metaethics, not, primarily, because it was thought to be correct or even especially plausible, but as a kind of backdrop against which some of the main debates took place. Some metaethicists today are self-avowed Mooreans, but not many. More commonly, philosophers interested in the nature of Good will either deny the first thesis or else accept the first thesis but maintain that the denial of the second thesis is compatible with the first. The latter seems to be the most popular approach these days. So, for instance, Expressivists agree that Good is unanalyzable, but deny that it is a non-natural property because, they think, 'Good' is not the name of a property at all. And Cornell naturalists also agree that Good is unanalyzable, but argue that this unanalyzability is a feature of a word or concept and that an unanalyzable word may still be the name of a complex natural property. By and large, *Principia Ethica* (Moore 1903, hereafter *PE*) set the stage for twentieth-century metaethics by challenging philosophers to show how the second, more metaphysical thesis could be avoided in the face of the very compelling first (and more conceptual) thesis. Mooreanism itself threatens naturalistically inclined metaethicists: it is the position they will be forced to adopt if they can neither see how to reject the first thesis nor show how the first thesis can be made compatible with the rejection of the second.

Thanks to Jordan Bleicher for research assistance and helpful discussion at the inception of this paper; to audiences at Macquarie University, Charles Sturt University, and the Australian National University for comments.

[1] I will follow Moore in using the word 'Good' as a (purported) name for a property, instead of calling it 'goodness' as most philosophers now would. Although Moore says that he is talking about the property, and not about the word 'good' or the concept of good, it is not always clear that that is what he is in fact talking about. However, I will take him at his word. Moore very often does not capitalize the word, though sometimes he does. I will capitalize it for the sake of clarity.

There aren't many Mooreans around these days. G. E. Moore himself was presumably one. But was he, really? I want to raise a doubt about Moore's own position with respect to the second thesis of Mooreanism. Moore does say that Good is a 'non-natural' property. But *we* properly attribute this view to him only if in so saying he meant by 'non-natural' something that we mean when we use the term. Philippa Foot once pointed out that we cannot attribute to someone the belief that he is sitting on a pile of hay just because he says, 'I am sitting on a pile of hay.' For suppose he goes on to explain: 'yes, it has four legs and a stiff back and was produced for the purposes of providing people with a place to sit.' Then we should conclude that by 'pile of hay' he means what we call a chair. Similarly, we should be careful in attributing to Moore the thesis that Good is a non-natural property, at least until we are confident that we have some clear idea of what he meant by a 'non-natural property'. Attention to Moore's writings should shake our confidence. For nowhere in his work is there a clear and coherent explanation of which properties are non-natural that is also consonant with his claim that Good is non-natural.

I will proceed as follows. In the first section, I investigate the *locus classicus* of Mooreanism, namely, *PE* chapter I. Moore's official explanation of what makes a property non-natural is, to say the least, unhelpful. I then turn to another chapter of *PE*, the one on 'metaphysical ethics', because 'metaphysical' is supposed to contrast with 'natural'. Some of Moore's remarks in that chapter are very suggestive, but they are ultimately unsatisfying. In the third section, I look at some of Moore's later work, especially 'The Conception of Intrinsic Value' (1965), where he has another try at what appears to be the natural property/non-natural property distinction put in other terms. A passage identified by Broad as the key passage is indeed a crucial one, although not exactly for the reason that Broad thought it was. In the last section I explain why I think Moore was *almost* an Expressivist, and more important, what distinguishes his view from Expressivism. Roughly, my suggestion is that Moore differs from Expressivists in the way he takes certain phenomena to be explained. It's that special kind of explanation that distinguishes Moore as a Moorean after all.

1. Natural properties in *Principia Ethica* IB

I'll begin by looking at what Moore said in *PE* about non-natural properties. First I'll look at chapter I ('The Subject Matter of Ethics') where the main argument that Good is a simple, unanalyzable, non-natural property takes place. The good news is that in that chapter Moore offers an explicit criterion for the naturalness of a property. The bad news is that the criterion makes no sense. Then I'll turn to chapter IV ('Metaphysical Ethics'), where Moore discusses theories according to which Good is not a natural property. We might expect to find Moore's own view counted among the 'metaphysical' theories, but we don't. After a detour through the (alleged) distinction between being and existence, I'll conclude that there is no coherent conception of 'non-natural' properties in *PE*.

Simple vs. non-natural

I am no historian, but I do know that to figure out what a philosopher meant by something, it's a good idea to look at the arguments he gave for what he said, and also, of course, to see what use he made of his idea. Moore does not seem to have made much use of the idea that Good is non-natural. However, he is widely supposed to have given some argument for it, namely, the open question argument. But the open question argument does not appear to be an argument to the conclusion that Good is non-natural. It appears to be an argument to the conclusion that Good is simple, unanalyzable—the first Moorean thesis.

Now, it *might* be thought that there really is no more to Moore's claim that Good is non-natural than that it is unanalyzable. The 'non-natural' in the description 'simple, non-natural, unanalyzable property' is a redundancy, according to this interpretation. But this cannot be right. Recall this passage from *PE*:

> There is, therefore, no intrinsic difficulty in the contention that 'good' denotes a simple and indefinable quality. There are many other instances of such qualities. Consider yellow, for example. We may try to define it, by describing its physical equivalent; we may state what kind of light-vibrations must stimulate the normal eye, in order that we may perceive it. But a moment's reflection is sufficient to shew that those light-vibrations are not themselves what we mean by yellow. *They* are not what we perceive. Indeed we should never have been able to discover their existence, unless we had first been struck by the patent difference of quality between the different colours. The most we can be entitled to say of those vibrations is that they are what corresponds in space to the yellow which we actually perceive. (1903: 10 § 10)

If it were not obvious (as Moore thinks) that yellow is a simple property, we could determine that it was simple by an open question argument. I can wonder whether something is yellow even when I know that it reflects 'light-vibrations' of such and such a kind; but I cannot wonder whether it reflects those light-vibrations when I know that it does; so yellow cannot be the same thing as reflecting those light-vibrations. The case of yellow is supposed to soften us up, in case we were inclined to be skeptical about the possibility of simple properties. However, Moore did *not* think that yellow is a non-natural property. So he is not thinking of 'non-natural' as just being, or following from, simple. And this makes sense, after all. Since there are natural properties, there must be simple ones. So showing that a property is simple could not be taken to show that it is non-natural.

The official *PE* Account of 'natural property'

In section 26 of *PE*, Moore gives a general explanation of what he counts as 'nature', and what he means by a 'natural object'. Natural objects are those which exist in time, he says, meaning to include experiences (which he thinks do not exist in space but clearly do exist in time) and exclude numbers (on which more below). Nature is the totality of what exists in time. However,

There is, indeed, no difficulty about the 'objects' themselves, in the sense in which I have just used the term. It is easy to say which of them are natural, and which (if any) are not natural. But when we begin to consider the properties of objects, then I fear the problem is more difficult. Which among the properties of natural objects are natural properties and which are not? For I do not deny that good is a property of certain natural objects: certain of them, I think, *are* good; and yet I have said that 'good' itself is not a natural property. Well, my test for these too also concerns their existence in time. Can we imagine 'good' as existing *by itself* in time, and not merely as a property of some natural object? For myself, I cannot so imagine it, whereas with the greater number of properties of objects—those which I call the natural properties—their existence does seem to me to be independent of the existence of those objects. They are, in fact, rather parts of which the object is made up than mere predicates which attach to it. If they were all taken away, no object would be left, not even a bare substance: for they are in themselves substantial and give to the object all the substance that it has. But this is not so with good. If indeed good were a feeling, as some would have us believe, then it would exist in time. But that is why to call it so is to commit the naturalistic fallacy. It will always remain pertinent to ask, whether the feeling itself is good; and if so, then good cannot itself be identical with any feeling. (1903: 41 § 26)

Moore's test is a thought experiment that we can all try. Let's try it out on Good. *If* you find that you cannot conceive of Good existing by itself in time, and not merely as a property of some object, then you will agree that Good is not a natural property. And, I'll wager, you will all agree that Good does not pass this test; you cannot imagine it existing by itself in time. The only problem is that you may have quite a lot of difficulty imagining *any* property existing by itself in time and not merely as a property of some object. I have this problem myself. I can't help thinking that maybe I am not understanding what it is that Moore wants me to try to imagine.

There is some faint plausibility to the idea that we could imagine yellow, say, existing by itself in time. I am supposing that Moore wants us to focus on a trope, as we would now say; for example, the yellowness of a certain yellow flower. Maybe we are to imagine this yellowness just floating there—the idea that the yellowness is a *part* of the yellow object suggests this, as if the yellowness were the two-dimensional part, the surface. Or maybe we are to imagine a shaped yellow patch—though in that case, as I put it into words it sounds as if there *is* a yellow object: the patch. Maybe we are to imagine an entirely yellow visual field? In any case, whatever faint plausibility there is to the idea that yellow might pass the test, I can't see any at all in the thought that, say, having a one-kilogram mass might pass it. I don't know how to begin to try to imagine the property of being one kilogram in mass, existing by itself in time, and not as the property of any object.[2]

Broad, in his contribution to the Library of Living Philosophers volume on Moore, wrote:

Now it seems to me that *every* characteristic of a natural object answers to Moore's criterion of non-naturalness, and that *no* characteristic could possibly be natural in his sense. I do not believe for a moment that a penny is a whole of which brownness and roundness are parts, nor do I believe that the brownness or roundness of a penny could exist in time all by itself. Hence, if I accepted Moore's account, I should have to reckon brownness, roundness, pleasantness, etc., as *non-natural* characteristics. Yet he certainly counts them as *natural* characteristics.[3]

It is hard to disagree. It turns out that it was impossible for Moore himself to disagree with Broad. In his 'Reply', Moore confessed: 'This suggestion which I made in *Principia* seems to me now to be utterly silly and preposterous' (Schilpp 1968: 581–2). And then, 'I agree, then, that in *Principia* I did not give any tenable explanation of what I meant by saying that "good" was not a natural property.'

This is surprising, I think. There is no viable explanation of what a natural property is in *PE*. So we don't know what Moore meant by the hard-to-believe feature of his view, because he gave no tenable explanation of what he meant by saying that 'good' was a non-natural property. Now, an obvious strategy would be to look to Moore's other work to see if he had something illuminating to say about which properties are natural. I will do that in a few minutes. For a little

---

[2] In some other contexts, when Moore wants an example of a natural property, he chooses experiential properties: *having an experience of a scarlet patch* is an important example in his 1968: 587. Possibly, then, he was thinking of an example like that when he described the test for natural properties in *PE*. I don't see how it would work, if we really do try to imagine the property *having an experience of a scarlet patch* without anybody doing the having, so to speak. So maybe Moore was thinking of the experience itself as existing in time all by itself, and not as the experience of some person. It is not clear to me that this makes any sense, but in any case it is not what Moore needs. The experience is an object, not a property.

[3] Broad 1968: 59. In that essay, Broad was grappling with more or less the same problems of interpretation of Moore as I am. It will be obvious in what follows that I found Broad's paper very helpful.

while longer, though, I want to stay in the confines of *PE*. Let's see what Moore says about *non*-natural properties there.

2. Metaphysical ethics

Chapter IV of *PE* is about what Moore calls 'metaphysical' conceptions of Good. What does he mean by 'metaphysical'?

What, then, is to be understood by 'metaphysical'? I use the term, as I explained in Chapter II., in opposition to 'natural'. I call those philosophers preeminently 'metaphysical' who have recognised most clearly that not everything which *is* is a 'natural object.' 'Metaphysicians' have, therefore, the great merit of insisting that our knowledge is not confined to the things which we can touch and see and feel. They have always been much occupied, not only with that other class of natural objects which consists in mental facts, but also with the class of objects or properties of objects, which certainly do not exist in time. . . . To this class, as I have said, belongs what we mean by the adjective 'good'. It is not *goodness*, but only the things or qualities which are good, which can exist in time—can have duration, and begin and cease to exist—can be objects of *perception*. (1903: 110–11 § 66)

So it looks like a metaphysical conception of Good is one according to which Good is a non-natural property. That is, of course, what Moore believes; he was, I dare say, one of those philosophers 'who have recognised most clearly that not everything which *is* is a "natural object".' So one might expect that the chapter on metaphysical theories would include Moore's own view. But instead that chapter is purely critical. The chapter is obviously aimed at *refuting* metaphysical conceptions. How can this be? What did Moore believe that the Metaphysicians did not?

It turns out that the answer is evident in a short bit I left out in the passage quoted above. Here it is (in boldface):

'Metaphysicians'. . . have always been much occupied . . . with the class of objects or properties of objects, which certainly do not exist in time, **are not therefore parts of Nature, and which, in fact, do not *exist* at all.** (Moore 1903: 110 § 66)

Good is a non-natural property, according to Moore; the Metaphysicians were correct about that. Where they went wrong was in thinking that Good *exists*. What is this supposed to mean? Well, Moore holds the same ontological views about numbers.

It is quite certain that two natural objects may exist; but it is equally certain that *two* itself does not exist and never can. Two and two *are* four. But that does not mean that either two or four exists. Yet it certainly means *something*. Two *is* somehow, although it does not exist... (1903: 111 § 66)

Likewise, Good does not exist. Everyone knows that Moore held Good to be a simple, non-natural property. Nobody mentions that he also held that Good doesn't exist. How is it that this last feature of his metaethics, every bit as radical as the familiar ones, has received so little subsequent attention? My provocative question has a mundane answer. Moore's claim that Good does not exist has no significance except as a historical curiosity.

The distinction between being and existence is very mysterious to me. No doubt it was commonplace in Cambridge in the early twentieth century, so much so that Moore didn't think he needed to explain it. But there is not much point in looking to this distinction to try to work out what Moore really thought about Good, since he later gave up on the distinction. In the middle of a series of lectures given in 1911, Moore announced:

I used to hold very strongly, what many other people are also inclined to hold, that the words 'being' and 'existence' do stand for two entirely different properties; and that though everything which exists must also 'be', yet many things which 'are' nevertheless do emphatically *not* exist. I did, in fact, actually hold this view when I began these lectures; and I have based the whole scheme of the lectures upon the distinction.... But nevertheless I am inclined to think that I was wrong, and that there is no such distinction between 'being' and 'existence' as I thought there was. There is, of course, a distinction of usage, but... (Moore 1953: 300)

but, he goes on to say, it has no real importance. We do not feel right saying that numbers exist, though we are happy to say that there *are* such things, but Moore has decided by early 1911 that this is a superficial fact of language.

I might say a few words about a kind of move I have now made twice. The official *PE* criterion for naturalness (of properties), and now the being/ existence distinction are both bits of metaphysics that Moore came to reject, and I have felt warranted in rejecting them as elements of an explanation of what he meant (by distinguishing natural from non-natural properties). This move looks shaky. It is entirely possible that Moore meant something at a certain time and then later came to reject it. Could that be what's happening here? I don't *think* it is. In neither case did Moore have a definite substantial view that he later decided there were reasons for discarding. Rather, in each case, when he reflects on what he once said or thought, he cannot see any sense in it at all. The being/existence distinction looks to him like no distinction at all, and the independence in time criterion for natural properties, he says, strikes him as silly and preposterous. What seems to have happened is something like this: Moore did have some distinction in mind between natural and non-natural (properties), but he had only an intuitive grasp of it. When he tried to make it explicit, he was proposing suggestions for capturing what seemed to him an entirely intuitive idea. These suggestions he later decided were wrong, and indeed empty.

This suggestion, that the distinctions were misguided and not what Moore really meant, seems more clearly true about 'natural' properties than about being/existence. In the latter case, it is more plausible that he did think there was an ontological chasm between the existent and the non-existent, among things that *are*, and that this was what he really did have in mind when he wanted to distinguish himself from 'metaphysicians'. But there is a separate reason for eliminating this hypothesis. That reason becomes clear when we look at what Moore was actually doing in the chapter on Metaphysical theories.

What's wrong with Metaphysical theories?

Moore has an objection to Metaphysical ethics that doesn't depend on the being/ existence distinction, namely that these theories commit the naturalistic fallacy.

It was for this reason that I described 'Metaphysical Ethics' in Chapter II. as based upon the naturalistic fallacy. To hold that from any proposition asserting 'Reality is of this nature' we can infer, or obtain confirmation for, any proposition asserting 'This is good in itself' is to commit the naturalistic fallacy. . . . Such an assertion involves the naturalistic fallacy. It rests upon the failure to perceive that any truth which asserts 'This is good in itself' is quite unique in kind—that it cannot be reduced to any assertion about reality, and therefore must remain unaffected by any conclusions we may reach about the nature of reality. This confusion as to the unique nature of ethical truths is, I have said, involved in all those ethical theories which I have called metaphysical. (1903: 114 § 67)

Metaphysicians identify Good with some metaphysical *non-natural* property, and yet they are guilty of the naturalistic fallacy, because they reduce statements of what is Good to assertions 'about reality'. At this point, one might conclude that Moore is being willfully opaque. The one fallacy a Metaphysician could not be guilty of is the naturalistic fallacy. And what does Moore mean by an assertion 'about reality'? Maybe this: reality is the totality of what *exists*. Statements of value are not about reality, but about, well, whatever is left over when reality is removed. But this can't be right; it can't be what Moore meant. If it were, then Moore would have had a very different criticism of Metaphysical theories of Good from the one he actually had. He would have said that Metaphysicians were right, except that they say that Good exists. There would be a good chance of converting a Metaphysician's theory to a correct theory by changing all occurrences of the verb 'to exist' to occurrences of the verb 'to be'. But Moore says nothing like this. His actual criticism of

Metaphysicians is that they, like Naturalists, want to *reduce* statements of value to other statements (statements 'about reality'). That is, in a way, the same fallacy as the Naturalists commit, only the type of the reduction statement is different. 'Naturalistic fallacy' is a bad name for this fallacy, but it is still the same fallacy in each case.[4]

That Moore's point about the 'naturalistic fallacy' is really a point about reducibility rather than having anything to do with the natural suggests that the distinction he had in mind when he insisted that Good was in some special class of its own was not a distinction that had especially to do with any division between the natural and the non-natural as most philosophers would think of that division. Again, what he meant to be saying about Good by calling it non-natural cannot be merely that it is unanalyzable, since yellow is also unanalyzable. Still, what he had in mind clearly did have something to do with Good's unanalyzability. In the next section we turn to a later paper of Moore's, 'The Conception of Intrinsic Value'. In that paper together with his reflections on it Moore confirms that what he meant in *PE* by calling Good non-natural does indeed have to do with its peculiar logical relation to the other, natural properties that good things have. Before turning to 'The Conception of Intrinsic Value', let me make one quick observation about this claim of Moore's, which I just quoted above in its context.

[A]ny truth which asserts 'This is good in itself' is quite unique in kind—that it cannot be reduced to any assertion about reality, and therefore must remain unaffected by any conclusions we may reach about the nature of reality. (Moore 1903: 114 § 67)

When Moore says that statements of value are not about reality, he sounds an awful lot like an Expressivist. Of course, he wasn't an Expressivist. But he was awfully close. Toward the end of this paper, I'll be arguing that Moore *was* awfully close to being an Expressivist, and I will try to say what distinguished Moore's actual view from Expressivism.

3. Natural properties in 'The Conception of Intrinsic Value'

In 'The Conception of Intrinsic Value', Moore explains what he means by saying that some value is intrinsic.

To say that a kind of value is 'intrinsic' means merely that the question of whether a thing possesses it, and in what degree it possesses it, depends solely on the intrinsic nature of the thing in question. (1965: 260; italics in original)

---

[4] Support for this interpretation comes from some contemporary sympathizers of Moore's. Frankena (1939) (not really a sympathizer) suggested 'definist fallacy'; Wood (1937) suggested 'valuational fallacy'; J. Laird says: 'The essential point is the irreducibility of values to non-values' (1926: 94 n.).

But although the intrinsic value of something does depend solely on the intrinsic nature of the thing, Moore insists, rather perversely, that value is not an intrinsic property. It is a property. And it is intrinsic. But it is not an intrinsic property. This is a puzzle. It is not, as Moore appears to have thought, a metaphysical puzzle (how could this strange thing be, that a property which is intrinsic turns out not to be an intrinsic property?), but for us rather a terminological puzzle (what on earth was Moore talking about?). Broad suggested that what Moore meant by a 'natural property' in *PE* is what he here, in 'The Conception of Intrinsic Value', means by an 'intrinsic property'. I think this is a very good suggestion. Moore had identified, inarticulately, something he found odd about Good, something that led him to say that it is non-natural. In 'The Conception of Intrinsic Value', he again finds himself confronted with the same oddness, and this time it leads him to say that even intrinsic goodness is not an intrinsic property.

In his 'Reply', Moore agrees with Broad that the natural/non-natural distinction of *PE* is the very same distinction as the intrinsic property/non-intrinsic property distinction of 'Conception'. He apologizes for the outlandish terminology that forced him to say that some properties that are intrinsic are not intrinsic properties. Moore writes:

[I] will now drop the awkward terminology of *Philosophical Studies*, and speak instead of a distinction between intrinsic properties which are 'natural' and intrinsic properties which are *not* 'natural;' since I think that the feature, additional to that of being 'intrinsic,' which a property must possess in order to be what I called in *Philosophical Studies* an 'intrinsic property,' is the very one which would have led me, in *Principia*, to call it a *natural* intrinsic property. The question is: What is this feature? What is the difference between a 'natural' intrinsic property and one which is *not* natural? Mr. Broad says truly enough that in *Philosophical Studies* I give no clear account of this distinction.[5]

Moore did give *some* account of the distinction in 'The Conception', only not a clear one. In fairness to Moore, he confessed right away that he could not give a clear account. Here is what he wrote in 'The Conception of Intrinsic Value':

[T]here must be some characteristic belonging to intrinsic properties which predicates of value never possess. And it seems to me quite obvious that there is; only I can't see *what* it is. . . . I can only vaguely express the kind of difference I feel there to be by saying that intrinsic properties seem to *describe* the intrinsic nature of what possesses them in a sense in which predicates of value never do. If you could enumerate *all* the intrinsic properties a given thing possessed, you would have given a *complete* description of it, and would not need to mention any predicates of value it possessed; whereas no

---

[5] Moore 1968: 584–5. Here and hereafter, Moore's references to *Philosophical Studies* are always to 'The Conception of Intrinsic Value', which appears in the collection of his papers, *Philosophical Studies*.

description of a given thing could be *complete* which omitted any intrinsic property. (1965: 272 ff.)

Like Broad, I think this passage contains the crux of the matter. First let's see what Broad made of the distinction. Next, we'll take a look at what Moore said about it upon reflection. Unfortunately, what he said renders the distinction more confusing. I'll try to untangle things a little, and then return to the crucial passage with my own suggestion about what was going on, and how in light of everything I understand the non-naturalism of Moore's metaethics.

What Broad said

Broad says,

> I am inclined to think that the fact which Moore has in mind here is that goodness, in the primary sense, is always dependent on the presence of certain non-ethical characteristics which I should call 'good-making'.... We might, therefore, distinguish the characteristics of a thing into the following two classes, viz., *ultimate* and *derivative*. Goodness would certainly fall into the class of derivative characteristics. (1968: 60)

This is the distinction we would now recognize as the distinction between supervening ('derivative') properties and the base of properties on which they supervene, the 'ultimate' properties, or as Hare puts it, the *subjacent* properties.[6] Broad's suggestion is that when Moore says that a 'complete description' of something might still leave out certain properties, he must be thinking of the supervening properties. The point would then be that goodness is a supervening property. Broad gives an example of supervening properties:

> Now there is a sense in which one might say that a thing could not be completely described if any of its ultimate characteristics were omitted, but that it could be completely described without mentioning all its derivative characteristics. In describing a circle, e.g., it is not necessary to mention explicitly any of the innumerable properties of circles which follow of necessity from their definition together with the axioms of Euclidean geometry. (1968: 60–1)

But Broad then points out that in the first place, the way in which goodness supervenes on the nature of an object seems to be importantly different from the way in which the derived properties of circles supervene on the ultimate

---

[6] It is not *quite* the same distinction. First, subjacent properties need not be ultimate, since they may themselves supervene on further properties. Ultimate properties, presumably, supervene on no *other* properties. Second, supervenience may obtain in a trivial way, as for example the property of being self-identical supervenes on shape merely because it supervenes on anything and nothing. 'Derivative' suggests that the properties from which the derivative ones derive figure in the derivation. Broad's idea of being derivative is, quite reasonably, a vague one; supervenience is a sharper tool with which to cut the same material.

ones; and in the second place, properties that supervene on natural properties certainly do not seem *generally* to be non-natural in any recognizable intuitive sense.

In the first place, the way in which ethical properties of a thing depend on its non-ethical properties seems to be quite unlike the way in which the remaining properties of a circle depend on its defining properties. In the latter case the dependence is equivalent to the fact that the possession of the remaining properties can be *inferred deductively* from the axioms of Euclid and the presence of the defining properties. But the connexion between the non-ethical bad-making characteristic of being an emotion of delight at another's pain and the ethical characteristic of being morally evil is certainly not of this nature.

   Moreover, it is surely quite as evident that pleasantness and unpleasantness are derivative characteristics of an experience as that goodness and badness are. (Broad 1968: 61)

The first point is somewhat suggestive. The supervenient properties of a circle follow deductively from the subjacent properties, whereas, at least according to Broad, and surely according to Moore, goodness does not follow deductively from any of the 'good-making' properties, the natural properties on which goodness supervenes. This failure to follow deductively leaves ethical properties in a peculiar realm, for the explanation for supervenience present in the relatively straightforward case of geometric properties is not available for ethical ones. Though Broad doesn't say so, it's somewhat plausible that it is precisely this peculiar feature of ethical properties that Moore had in mind—maybe only in the back of his mind—when he called them non-natural, and again when he said that they are not intrinsic.

What Moore said in reply to Broad

Now, a couple of things that Moore says in reply to Broad tend to strengthen this interpretation. First, he says that his original criterion for being an intrinsic property was not quite correct, since some intrinsic properties—the ones that 'follow from' other natural intrinsic properties—could in fact be left out of a 'complete description' of an object. In the 'Reply', he changes the criterion:

No description of a thing could be *complete* which omitted any of those among its natural intrinsic properties, which are *such that no other natural intrinsic properties which the thing possesses entail them.* (1968; italics in original)

So by this criterion, the supervening properties of a circle would count as natural intrinsic properties, even though a complete description of a circle could omit them. Here, apparently, Moore intends to be allowing the derivative properties of circles into the class of natural intrinsic properties while still keeping ethical properties out of the class. And this does tend to strengthen the hypothesis that what's 'non-natural' about ethical properties is precisely that they supervene on the natural intrinsic base without 'following from' it.

Second, here is Moore's confirmation that he always did believe that goodness supervenes on natural properties:

It is true, indeed, that I should never have thought of suggesting that goodness was 'non-natural,' unless I had supposed that it was 'derivative' in the sense that, whenever a thing is good (in the sense in question) its goodness (in Mr. Broad's words) 'depends on the presence of certain non-ethical characteristics' possessed by the thing in question: I have always supposed that it did so 'depend' . . . (Moore 1968: 588)

So far so good. But then Moore throws a wrench into the works:

I have always supposed that it did so 'depend,' in the sense that, if a thing is good (in my sense), then that it is so *follows* from the fact that it possesses certain natural intrinsic properties, which are such that from the fact that it is good it does *not* follow conversely that it has those properties. (1968: 588)

This passage is a hermeneutic disaster. I was strongly tempted to pretend it didn't exist. For here Moore declares that the fact that a thing is good *follows* from the fact that it possesses certain natural properties. And this, I had always thought, was precisely the claim that he had so famously refuted with the open question argument.

I still think so. And I think that what he says in the disastrous passage is something he simply did not mean. One way of avoiding the awful implication is to suppose that when Moore says that goodness 'follows' from the natural properties, he is talking about something other than logical implication. Unfortunately, in the very same essay, Moore advises us that he has always been using 'follows from' in the logical sense:

This partially explains how I have been using 'follows' as applied to *propositions*: I have been so using it that it can only be said with truth that a proposition *q* follows from another *p*, when it can also be said with truth that '*p*, but not *q*' is self-contradictory. (1968: 607)

My hypothesis is that he has not, in fact, been using 'follows' in the way that he claims he has. Moore identifies looser senses of 'follows', and as an example he says that

Before aeroplanes were invented you could have said with perfect truth, on hearing that a man was in New York the day before yesterday, 'Then it follows that he wasn't in London yesterday.' And this is a way in which 'follows' is used in ordinary speech. (1968: 607)

The way in which the fact that something is good follows from the fact that it has such-and-such natural properties is not just like the way it follows from the fact that a man was in New York the day before yesterday that he wasn't in London yesterday, since the latter is a kind of natural necessity and the former is metaphysical. Still, we may, and I think we must if we are to avoid attributing to Moore a completely incoherent view, suppose that in the infamous Admission of Supervenience passage Moore was using 'follows from' in one of the non-logical, more ordinary senses. Back in 'The Conception of Intrinsic Value' Moore mulls over the kinds of necessary implication, and in connection with just the same point about supervenience:

You cannot say that an intrinsic property is a property such that, if one thing possesses it and another does not, the intrinsic nature of the two things *must* be different. For this is the very thing which we are maintaining to be true of predicates of intrinsic value, while at the same time we say that they are *not* intrinsic properties. Such a definition of 'intrinsic property' would therefore only be possible if, we could say that the necessity there is that, if *x* and *y* possess different intrinsic properties, their nature must be different, is a necessity of a *different kind* from the necessity there is that, if *x* and *y* are of different intrinsic values, their nature must be different, although both necessities are unconditional. And it seems to me possible that this is the true explanation. But, if so, it obviously adds to the difficulty of explaining the meaning of the unconditional 'must,' since, in this case, there would be two different meanings of 'must,' both unconditional, and yet neither, apparently, identical with the logical 'must.' (1965: 272)

Broad called 'The Conception of Intrinsic Value' a 'very difficult paper', no doubt on the basis of passages like this one. I do think, however, that Moore's struggle with the perplexing idea that the goodness of a thing follows with *some* kind of necessity from its natural intrinsic qualities even though it never does follow deductively *that* the thing is good, just from propositions about its natural intrinsic qualities, justifies discarding his self-interpretive dictum about what he always means by 'follows from'.

4. What disinguishes a Moorean?

To summarize, then: there is something very odd about ethical properties, namely, that although they supervene on the straightforwardly natural properties they do not follow deductively from them. This odd feature somehow led Moore to say that ethical properties are not natural, and also, later, that they are not intrinsic properties.

Just why might it have led him to say these things? Well, we might think of the supervenient properties of something that do not strictly *reduce* to the intrinsic properties as somehow 'floating' on top of the proper intrinsic properties, 'emerging' from them, so to speak, and so not quite 'inhering' in them. All very metaphorical, but perhaps enough to lead Moore to think of them as lacking a certain sense of 'intrinsicness'. But why non-natural? Because they, the ethical properties, do not *reduce* to the paradigm of natural properties? But then we immediately run into the old problem: yellow is just as Good an example of a supervening property as Good is—it supervenes, though perhaps not quite in the same way as Good, on the scientific properties of its objects— and yet yellow is used by Moore as an example of a *natural* irreducible property. So, suggestive as all of this talk of supervenience may be, I am afraid it is not after all the source of Moore's idea that Good is non-natural. Still, I do think we had the right passage in our sights just a moment ago.

I can only vaguely express the kind of difference I feel there to be by saying that intrinsic properties seem to *describe* the intrinsic nature of what possesses them in a sense in which predicates of value never do. If you could enumerate *all* the intrinsic properties a given thing possessed, you would have given a *complete* description of it, and would not need to mention any predicates of value it possessed; whereas no description of a given thing could be *complete* which omitted any intrinsic property.

I think this is the crux of the matter, for Moore. We don't describe anything by calling it good.

What do you call a metaethicist who maintains the following theses?

Ethical terms do not reduce to non-ethical ones.
'Good' is not the name of any natural property.
Ethical statements are not about reality.
Ethical statements do not describe anything.

Without further information, we would probably conclude that he is an Expressivist. So, was Moore an Expressivist? I would hate to think so. What Moore says about predicates of value failing to describe their object sounds like something Allan Gibbard (an Expressivist) or Mark Timmons (whose view is a close relative of Expressivism) might say (Gibbard 1990, Timmons 1999). My hypothesis is that Moore was a *proto-Expressivist*. I am not saying this merely to be perverse. I think it explains the data. And not just these that I have been pre- senting; I think there are other surprising things Moore says that are also very close to what Expressivists say. For instance, his views about the connection between ethical judgment and the will are much more like R. M. Hare's or Gibbard's than has generally been recognized.[7] But it would be alarming, and

---

[7] I hope to explore this parallel in another paper.

to my mind disappointing, to discover that Moore *was* an Expressivist. Disappointing because it has been important historically, and it still is dialectically important today, to have Mooreanism as a contrastive position to Expressivism.

So, why was Moore a Moorean after all? What did he believe that Expressivists do not believe? Moore actually says that some *properties* describe an object, and that Good does not. That's a funny thing to say. We would say (I take it) that some words, or a person, describe an object. But Moore says that it's properties. Did he mean this literally? Moore is not always careful about distinguishing use and mention, so it's possible that when he said that properties describe an object he meant that the predicates that denote those properties describe the object. Still, I think it is significant that he insists that properties describe objects. The point is that description inheres in properties, not in predicates.

This much seems clear: the metaethics of *PE* takes as its centerpiece the divide between the ethical and the non-ethical. I'd like to suggest that Moore *mis*described this distinction as the distinction between the natural and the non-natural. Even supposing that he had *something* coherent in mind when he wrote of natural and non-natural properties (and I am not at all sure that he had), his assertion that Metaphysical ethics is also guilty of the naturalistic fallacy shows that it's unlikely that *natural* is what he really thought Good lacked. Instead, I am suggesting, the distinction he was after was the one between the descriptive and the evaluative. Combine what he says in his Library of Living Philosophers essay with what he said in 'The Conception of Intrinsic Value', and it looks like Moore came close to the same conclusion about what he must have meant in *PE*.

But if the controversial thesis of *Principia Ethica* is that the evaluative is not reducible to the descriptive, what made him a Moorean rather than an Expressivist? It must be that according to Mooreans, the gap between the descriptive and the ethical is a gap between *properties*. All of us (almost) think that there is a logical gap between description and evaluation. Hare famously argued that the gap is accounted for by proper attention to forms of expression: moral judgments do not describe because they prescribe, they don't fail to describe because they are about special non-descriptive properties. Allan Gibbard puts the responsibility on normative concepts. But Mooreans think the logical gap between description and evaluation (or prescription, or judgments of what to do) is explained by a matching gap between kinds of properties.

In some of his recent work, Allan Gibbard has suggested that one way of individuating properties is by what they explain. I am suggesting that a way of distinguishing what Moore believed from what Gibbard believes is according to what explains the gap between description and evaluation. Expressivists say the explanation is to be found in the different roles that concepts play in planning; Prescriptivists say it is to be found in the different speech acts that declarative sentences can perform. Mooreans say it is to be found in the different sorts of properties that there are.

I don't see how Mooreans could be right about this. But at least, if I am right, I now know what makes them Mooreans. I know what it is they believe that I cannot believe.

References

BROAD, C. D. (1968). 'Moore's Ethical Doctrines'. In Schilpp 1968.

FRANKENA, WILLIAM K. (1939). 'The Naturalistic Fallacy'. *Mind*, 48: 464–77.

GIBBARD, A. (1990). *Wise Choices, Apt Feelings.* Cambridge, Mass: Harvard University Press.

LAIRD, J. (1926). *A Study in Moral Theory.* London: G. Allen & Unwin.

MOORE, G. E. (1903). *Principia Ethica.* Cambridge: Cambridge University Press.

—— (1953). *Some Main Problems of Philosophy.* London: G. Allen & Unwin.

—— (1965). 'The Conception of Intrinsic Value'. In *Philosophical Studies.* Totowa, NJ: Littlefield, Adams & Co.

—— (1968). 'A Reply to my Critics'. In Schilpp 1968.

SCHILPP, P. A. (ed.) (1968). *The Philosophy of G. E. Moore.* 2 vols. La Salle, Ill.: Open Court.

TIMMONS, M. (1999). *Morality without Foundations.* Oxford: Oxford University Press.

WOOD, L. (1937). 'Cognition and Moral Value'. *Journal of Philosophy*, 34/9: 234–9.

10

Ethics as Philosophy

A Defense of Ethical Nonnaturalism

Russ Shafer-Landau

It is early days in the *Principia Ethica* when Moore presents us with his famous argument from elimination on behalf of ethical nonnaturalism. Moore thought that there were three options when it came to a diagnosis of ethical concepts. Ethical notions are either meaningless, susceptible of a naturalistic analysis, or nonnatural. Neither of the first two options appealed. Ethical nonnaturalism won by default.

It took only a long generation before nonnaturalism's star began to fade. The ascendancy of noncognitivist views, and the resurgence of naturalistic ones, were prompted by the perception that nonnaturalism suffered from fatal flaws. By century's end, this perception had become so widespread as to be rightly considered a bit of conventional philosophical wisdom. I think that this critical, and often dismissive, attitude is mistaken—as mistaken as Moore's contention that he had identified a line of argument that proved, once and for all, the falsity of ethical naturalism.

It is a commonplace that philosophical preferences are cyclical, and that the runt of the litter in one era may elbow out its competition in later times. Ethical nonnaturalism, for decades consigned to second-class status, is due a reappraisal.

The nonnaturalism I favor is a brand of moral realism. As I understand it, moral realism is the view that says that most moral judgments are beliefs, some of which are true, and, when true, are so by virtue of correctly representing the existence of truth-makers for their respective contents. Further, and crucially, true moral judgments are made true in some way other than by virtue of the attitudes taken towards their content by any actual or idealized human agent.

My thanks to Paul Bloomfield, whose sense and gentle suasion I too frequently ignored in preparing the final version of this paper. Thanks also to Terence Cuneo, who gave me a number of incisive criticisms and suggestions for improvement.

Not all nonnaturalisms are realistic—Kantian views, for instance, reject the assimilation of moral to natural properties, and yet also reject realism. I will proceed on the assumption (unargued here) that realism is the best path for nonnaturalists.[1] After describing nonnaturalism, and identifying the most serious worries that face it, I will undertake a partial defense against a number of those problems. My preferred strategy for doing so invokes a parallel between philosophy in general, and ethics in particular. My contention is that once we pay special attention to this relationship, a number of the traditional concerns about nonnaturalism begin to seem less pressing than they have for a long while.

1. The nature of nonnaturalism

Ethical nonnaturalism is, first and foremost, a metaphysical doctrine. It claims that there are instantiated moral properties that are not natural properties.

There are instantiated moral properties: this element distinguishes nonnaturalism from all forms of moral nihilism.[2] Moral nihilism is the view that either there are no moral properties, or there are, but none that are ever instantiated. On this view, there is no moral reality at all. Nonnaturalism asserts the existence of moral properties—there really is such a thing as being (e.g.) morally forbidden, or morally good—and asserts, too, that these properties are sometimes exemplified.

Nonnaturalism *per se* is, in two respects, neutral as to the exact nature of moral properties. It is first of all ecumenical regarding the conditions under which these properties are instantiated. Many substantive normative ethical theories are compatible with a nonnaturalistic metaphysics. And, second, nonnaturalism is compatible with any number of specific views about what a property is. Nonnaturalists can await a verdict from the metaphysicians on this question, and incorporate their best answer into a comprehensive metaethic.

Ethical nonnaturalism is true only if moral properties are not natural properties. There is no agreement on what makes a property a natural one. The criteria that immediately come to mind—a property is natural in virtue of its

---

[1] I argue against alternatives to realism in Part I of *Moral Realism: A Defence* (Oxford: Clarendon Press, 2003). Many of the ideas that appear in this essay receive much fuller development in that book. I have also appropriated a couple of sentences from my *Whatever Happened to Good and Evil?* (New York: Oxford University Press, 2004). My thanks to the Press for permission to rely on this material here.

[2] The following, in my book, all qualify as versions of nihilism: emotivism (e.g. Ayer 1936; Stevenson 1937, 1948), prescriptivism (Hare 1952, 1963), expressivism (Blackburn 1993, 1998; Gibbard 1990), assertoric nondescriptivism (Timmons 1999, Skorupski 1999), and error theories (Mackie 1977; Garner 1994; Joyce 2001).

being instantiated nonconventionally, materially, or tangibly, or being describable without reliance on evaluative vocabulary—will not do. If nonnaturalists are right, then morality is not conventional. That doesn't make them naturalists. Some paradigmatically natural properties are realized nonmaterially (e.g. being a vacuum). Not every realization of a natural property is tangible—one can't literally touch a muon or a gluon. And, as Nicholas Sturgeon rightly points out in a recent essay (2003), one can't always tell a natural property by the vocabulary in which it is described. If naturalists are correct, then moral worth, virtue, and rightness are natural properties, though all are surely also evaluative notions. The debate between naturalists and nonnaturalists cannot be solved just by noting salient features of the terms we use to describe it.

I suggest that we take a different tack, that of offering a disciplinary conception. The natural is whatever is the object of study by the natural sciences. The obvious problem of having just pushed the definitional problem back a step is usually solved by defining the natural sciences ostensively: something is natural just in case it figures ineliminably in true propositions that emerge from (on some accounts, the perfected versions of) physics, chemistry, molecular biology, astronomy, etc. Leave astrology off that list. Film studies, too.

It would be nice to have an account of what makes a natural science natural. This for two reasons. First, we'll want to know how to fill in that 'etc.', especially for contentious cases. And ethics is likely to be among the most contentious. But, second, we presumably don't want to limit the natural domain to the things studied by (even perfected versions of) the sciences we now recognize— we want to allow for the emergence of natural sciences that we haven't yet dreamed of.

I don't think that ethics is a natural science. Its fundamental principles are not inductive generalizations. It is not primarily concerned with causal efficacy. Its central principles are not descriptive of historical contingencies. The phenomena it does describe are supervenient as a matter of conceptual requirement. It allows for a much greater degree of indeterminacy and vagueness than is found in typical natural sciences. It has only a very little concern for mathematical quantification and precision. Unlike any of the recognized sciences, its truths are normative truths that direct and guide, rather than (in the first instance) predict the course of future events or explain what has already occurred. Moral truths provide justifying reasons that are often ignored. Physics and geology and hydrology don't do that.

Of course, ethical naturalism may be correct even if ethics is not a science. Ethical naturalism is true so long as moral properties are the proper object of natural scientific study. They might be, even if ethics isn't the science that does the studying.

But if ethics isn't the relevant science, then what is? Sociology and psychology, if we admit them into the pantheon, might do yeoman's work—they will be required to aid us, for instance, in determining how many people are made happy by various actions, or what it was that actually motivated agents to do what they did. All quite helpful information. But neither sociology nor psychology, nor any other science that I know of, will do much to fix the content of our fundamental moral principles. That is the job of ethics proper.

Suppose my truncated case against the scientific status of ethics is way off base. So let us grant, provisionally, that ethics is a science. Still, is it a natural science? We might, for instance, also allow mathematics to qualify as a science. But not many think of it as a natural science. What explains this, it seems to me, is the nature of mathematical investigation. Mathematics is done in a largely a priori fashion. And this leads us to the following thought: a science is a natural science just in case its fundamental principles are discoverable a posteriori, through reliance primarily on empirical evidence.

Any definition of naturalism is bound to be to some extent stipulative. Yet this characterization is true to all instances of avowed ethical naturalism that I know of, and does seem to capture what many have thought to be essential to the classification. But notice, now, that the difference between naturalists and nonnaturalists, usually taken to be a metaphysical one, turns out on this accounting to be epistemological. Ethical nonnaturalists are those who claim that moral properties are not natural ones. This means, on the present understanding, that fundamental moral truths are discoverable a priori. If I am right, prospects for nonnaturalism depend crucially on the possibility of gaining such knowledge.

It isn't my intention here to offer a direct defense of a priori moral knowledge.[3] Instead, I will present some ancillary arguments that constitute an invitation to see ethical enquiry as importantly dissimilar from empirical, natural scientific investigation. The rationale and the structure of these supporting arguments is best appreciated by noting the classical objections to nonnaturalism.

2. Objections to nonnaturalism

Many have opposed ethical nonnaturalism just because they have thought a priori moral knowledge an impossibility. Scientific confirmation is our model of epistemic success; if morality fails to conform to the model, the only alternative

---

[3] I offer a somewhat programmatic defense in *Moral Realism*, ch. 11. See also Audi 1997, 1999, 2004, and the fine collection edited by Stratton-Lake (2002).

(it has seemed) is moral skepticism. Before I sketch my preferred path to resisting this conclusion, we must consider other potent objections to nonnaturalism.

The first of these is motivational: moral judgments are thought to bear a necessary connection with motivation. But if nonnaturalists are right, then moral judgments represent efforts to report on the instantiations of nonnatural properties. How could such (putative) reports necessarily engage the will?

The second worry focuses on practical reasons. Many believe that our moral obligations constitute or entail categorical reasons, i.e. reasons that apply independently of our inclinations. But how could the instantiations of nonnatural properties supply such reasons? Our reasons stem, ultimately, from what each of us most cares about. But the link between our existing concerns, and nonnatural properties, will be tenuous, at best.

A third concern is metaphysical: if moral properties are not natural properties, then what can they be? Everything *else* we know of in the universe is (potentially) scientifically explicable. Nonnaturalism insists on a class of *sui generis* properties, and this (it is said) amounts to ontological profligacy.

Next comes the epistemological concern. If scientific methods don't answer moral questions, then how are they to be answered? For nonnaturalists, this problem has always taken a quite specific form. Nonnaturalists, by definition, deny the identity of moral and natural properties. They are also agreed that, for any moral and natural property, there are no relations of necessary coextension that link them.[4] There is no way to fill in the following blank: necessarily, something is good [right/virtuous/praiseworthy, etc.] if and only if it is _____ [fill in a term designating a natural property]. In the absence of the relevant biconditionals, it is easy to see how we might be epistemically confounded. If we don't know the natural conditions under which moral properties are invariably instantiated, then it is hard to know when they are instantiated at all. That is precisely the epistemic problem facing nonnaturalism.

The epistemological problem is very closely related to the last significant problem for nonnaturalism—that of explaining persistent moral disagreement. When we compare the plausibility of two hypotheses introduced to account for such disagreement—(i) some parties are misapprehending the relations linking nonnatural and natural properties, or (ii) the interlocutors are giving

---

[4] I don't believe that this is a defining feature of nonnaturalism, but it is a claim that all nonnaturalists I am familiar with have endorsed. Of course, if necessary coextension entailed identity, then such aversion is readily explicable. But that entailment fails, or so I believe. Being self-identical and being either red or not red are necessarily coextensive properties. They aren't identical. Being a plane figure with a side and being one with an angle are also necessarily coextensive. But being an angle is not the same thing as being a side. (For the contrary view, see Jackson 1998: 126–7.)

voice to parochial commitments they've been raised and socialized to accept—the simpler explanation has always seemed to be the latter. Rather than attributing some cognitive failing(s) to people involved in moral disagreements, we do better to see such cases as exemplifying what Mackie has called 'patterns of objectification' (1977: 42 ff.). The reason, of course, is that citing cognitive failings in this context is plausible only in the presence of a successful moral epistemology that provides epistemic standards for measuring such failings. And that is just what we don't have. Why invoke *sui generis* properties when familiar kinds of projection can do the trick?

These longstanding worries are legitimate and serious. There is obviously no practicable way to reply to all of them here. Since that is so, I will simply summarize my preferred direction of argument for some cases, and then devote the rest of the paper to the general strategy that I think, with development, can lead to satisfying solutions for the remainder of the worries.

I'll take a pass here on the first two problems. My explanation for this in the case of the motivational problem is that it is, as traditionally conceived, a difficulty equally for any cognitivist. Cognitivists see moral judgments as truth-evaluable beliefs, as intended efforts to report on the nature of a moral reality. If, as Hume claims, beliefs of any stripe are unable to motivate all by themselves, then every cognitivist view (ideal-observer theories, varieties of relativism and subjectivism, sensibility theories, Kantian views, and the miscellany of moral realisms) will fall to the ax. I don't think any argument can be that powerful. In any event, nothing about nonnaturalism *per se* makes it any more vulnerable to this worry than any of its competitors in the cognitivist camp.

There are two ways to defend against the motivational argument. The first is to argue that beliefs—especially evaluative ones—are capable of motivating all by themselves, or, by themselves, are able to generate derived desires that together yield motivation. The second is to deny that moral judgments necessarily motivate, and to provide an explanation for why such judgments, when sincerely held, nevertheless do manage to motivate as often as they do. I think that both strategies can be successfully brought off, though obviously not here.

I have a different basis for avoiding any discussion of the worries regarding practical reason. Here, some of realism's cognitivist competitors *are* at an advantage. Specifically, all of those who make our moral duties some function of our attitudes can readily explain why we have reason to do what morality requires of us. It takes a lot more work to show that realists—naturalists *or* non-naturalists—can do as good a job of explaining morality's normativity.

The typical realist response to these charges is to deny that moral obligations do in fact entail reasons for action. Sometimes we may lack any reason to do as morality demands. The standards that specify the content of our moral obligations do not have their source in human attitudes; reasons do; therefore there can be the relevant disconnect. My way out of this problem begins by insisting that moral duties *do* entail excellent practical reasons, but proceeds to deny that such reasons must be reachable from sound deliberation that starts from our existing commitments. I don't see any short way of substantiating these points, however, and I don't expect anyone just to take my word that successful solutions to these problems are possible.[5] Instead, I suggest that we bracket these concerns at this point. Even if my promissory notes can be adequately cashed, that still leaves plenty of other problems for the nonnaturalist realist to deal with.

3. Ethics as philosophy

Ethics is a branch of philosophy. Few would dispute that. Yet this fact has significant, wide-ranging implications, many of which have gone little noticed in debates about the status of ethical judgments. My central claim is that there are very close parallels between ethical investigation and that pursued in philosophy quite generally. These parallels provide excellent reason for rejecting some of the main lines of criticism just rehearsed. They also generate positive reasons to favor nonnaturalism over its competitors.

I locate the central claim within a central argument. Here it is:

1. Ethics is a species of enquiry; philosophy is its genus.
2. A species inherits the essential traits of its genus.
3. There are (among others) two essential traits of philosophy: the realistic status of its truths, and its status as something other than a natural science.
4. Therefore nonnaturalistic ethical realism is true.

In what follows, I will try to make the first premise plausible. I'll just assume the truth of premise (2). As for (3), I will say something (but not nearly enough) to defend the claim that philosophy is something other than a natural science. I will say a good deal more about why we should construe philosophical truths realistically.

To see ethics as philosophy is to appreciate a certain kind and degree of methodological similarity. Let me start with an admission: I don't have a nice, precise characterization to offer of the philosophical method. In large part,

---

[5] I address the motivational problems in Part III, and the worries to do with practical reason in Part IV, of *Moral Realism*.

I think philosophy is distinguished from other disciplines as much by the questions it asks as by the methods it uses to pursue their answers. We know philosophy when we see it, and can distinguish it, in practice, fairly easily from any of the disciplines whose lines sometimes blur into its territory (religious studies, anthropology, economics, psychology, sociology, etc.).

To get an approximation of what it is to pursue a philosophical question, consider what would have to happen in order to answer the question of whether there are universals. First, we'd have to remove ambiguities and fix our subject, so as to avoid talking past one another. Then we would have to gather and bring forward any empirical evidence that was thought to be relevant to determining an answer to our question. We would have a careful look at arguments already on offer, from both those whose views are largely in sync with our own, and the best of our critics. We would test our claims for logical consistency, and decide, in the face of contradiction, which of our competing views is least well supported. And we would have to investigate to see whether ours, among competitors, best exemplifies a host of theoretical virtues—economy, stability across cases, avoidance of ad hoc assumptions, preservation of existing beliefs, explanatory breadth, etc.

Every single stage of this process is fraught with controversy, since all but the second (that of obtaining relevant facts) primarily involves philosophical exploration. 'Universal' is not univocal. The appraisal of a sympathetic argument, as well as a critic's challenges, is no less a philosophical task. The consistency of one's views isn't always transparent. The comparative assessment of whether one view best exemplifies a theoretical virtue is often a very tangled affair, and in any event is not to be resolved by appealing exclusively to the evidence of the senses.

So far as I can tell, things are just the same when it comes to ethical investigation. When there is a disagreement, for instance, about the morality of abortion, we must first ensure that we are not talking past one another. We have to settle on the meaning of the relevant terms (e.g. what it is to be human, or a person), so that we are on the same page. We must gain the relevant nonmoral facts. We have to advance a view that is internally consistent, or amend it so as to make it so. We try out the best of our arguments against the competition, and vice versa, and make changes accordingly. We see whether our view best comports with a battery of theoretical virtues. And, finally, the ultimate resolution of the issue is not to be decided solely or even primarily by direct appeal to empirical evidence. We rely on such evidence to tell us what is the case. To know what ought to be the case, we need to push further. That is not, in the first instance, an empirical matter.

Philosophy is not primarily an empirical discipline, but an a priori one. Its truths are ordinarily discoverable, when they are, not exclusively by appeal to what our senses can tell us. We don't bump into such things as universals, free will, or modalities; we can't see them, or hear or touch them. We may have reason to deny the existence of such things, but not because we aren't sure what they taste like. Dismissing such things from our ontology, or ratifying their inclusion in it, is something that no scientist is able to do. Such things are dealt with in an a priori way.

At this point I'd like to invoke another of my promissory notes. Substantiating the claim that fundamental philosophical truths are a priori is work for a paper unto itself (at the least). This isn't that paper. Yet this claim about philosophy, while contentious, isn't on the face of it that implausible. Of course there are those who deny the very possibility or existence of a priori knowledge. But for all others, basic philosophical principles should be quite attractive candidates. Philosophy must run a close second to mathematics as an exemplar of an a priori discipline (if indeed there are any such exemplars). Part of this is explicable by reference to the metaphysically or conceptually necessary status of the principles that are the object of philosophical investigation. And part of this is explicable by reflection on cases. Consider for a moment Leibniz's law of the indiscernibility of identicals, or the modal principle that anything that is necessary is possibly necessary. These certainly don't seem to be inductive generalizations, or conclusions of inferences to the best explanation. The role of sensory evidence in establishing such claims is peripheral, at best. I might be mistaken about this, and nothing to come will absolutely protect against this possibility. But the view that makes the justification of such principles a matter of empirical confirmation is (much) more contentious than the one I am prepared to rely on.

As ethics is a branch of philosophy, we have excellent reason to think that fundamental ethical principles share the same status as fundamental philosophical principles. When we want to know whether something is right or wrong, admirable or vicious, we will certainly want to know what's going on in the world. The evidence of our senses may tell us that happiness has been maximized, or that the words of a promise have been uttered, but that's only the beginning, not the end, of our ethical investigations. When trying to verify the basic standards that govern the application of moral predicates, we will only secondarily (if at all) advert to what the physicists and botanists and hydrologists say. The conditions under which actions are right, and motives and characters good, aren't confirmed by the folks with lab coats. They are confirmed, if at all, by those who think philosophically. And much of that thinking, especially when focused on non-derivative, core principles, is undertaken without clear reliance on what we can see, or hear, or touch.

Since doing ethics is doing a kind of philosophy, we shouldn't be surprised at the similarities just mentioned. But these similarities can insulate nonnaturalism from some of the standard critical charges, enumerated above in section 2. In what follows, I will rely on the parallels between the species (ethics) and its genus (philosophy) in a way that aids nonnaturalist realists in answering three of the most pressing objections against their views.

The first objection says that the intractability of ethical disagreement sustains an antirealist diagnosis of ethical thought and talk. The second criticism claims that this disagreement in any event undermines any justified belief we may have for our moral views, provided that they are meant to tell us about how the world really is. The third asserts that the causal inefficacy of moral facts provides excellent reason to deny their existence. Note that success in refuting such criticisms is still short of a complete defense against the metaphysical and epistemological objections I outlined above. But the criticisms I discuss are some of the most important elements of these families of objections, and I think that they can be met. That is work enough for a day, if it can be accomplished.

4. Moral disagreement as a metaphysical objection

Nonnaturalism stands for the idea that there are nonscientific moral properties. But if there are such things, why is there so much disagreement about them? Many believe that objective properties of any kind must be such as to garner consensus about (the conditions of) their instantiation, at least among people who are well situated to appreciate such things. But it doesn't take an expert to realize that such consensus is extremely elusive in ethics. So persistent moral disagreement presents us with a choice. Perhaps there are no moral properties at all. Or there are, but ones that are not objective—rather, they are constituted by partial or parochial human attitudes. As such, the conditions of their instantiation, and the instantiations themselves, would presumably be empirically verifiable, at least in principle. Either way, the nonnaturalist loses.

There are really two ways to run this skeptical argument, though they usually remain entangled in the literature. One is as an argument that seeks to draw an inference to the best explanation, the explananda being the scope of actual ethical disagreement we see in our world. The second is as an a priori argument that has us anticipating persistent disagreement amongst even hypothetical, idealized moral deliberators. In both cases, the presence of intractable disagreement is said to be sufficient to draw an antirealist conclusion: there are no real, objective moral standards that could serve as guideposts to our moral investigations. In ethics, we make it all up.

The first version of the argument, as an inference to the best explanation, is inconclusive at best. Certainly there is intractable moral disagreement—plenty of it. But just as surely, such disagreement might be well explained as a product of insufficient nonmoral information, or adequate information insufficiently 'processed.' Such processing failures cover a wide range of cases, from errors of instrumental reasoning, to a failure of nerve, sympathy, empathy, or imagination. One explanation (not the only one) of these errors is that there's typically much more personally at stake in ethical matters than in scientific ones, and these stakes tend to introduce biasing factors that skew correct perception. It may be that for any given real-world ethical disagreement, we could cite at least one of these failings as an explanation for its continued existence.

I think that one's expectations of (lack of) consensus are largely an expression of one's antecedent metaethical commitments, rather than anything that could serve as an independent argument in this context. Imagine away all of the failings mentioned in the previous paragraph: will there or won't there be any disagreement left to threaten moral realism? I'm not sure. If not, then the realist can rest easy. But suppose disagreement persists, even in the counterfactual situation in which we rid our agents of the flaws that impede correct moral reasoning. Even here, however, realists can sustain their view with a minimum of damage. They will have to say that impeccable reasoning may nevertheless fail to land on the truth. There can be a gap between epistemic accessibility and truth. If we are to posit an absence of consensus amongst even perfected enquirers, then the idealized picture of moral enquirers will fail to guard against their fallibility.

At this point we can introduce the ethics–philosophy parallel and use it to defend nonnaturalism from the argument from disagreement. The breadth and depth of philosophical disagreement is just as great as that found within ethics (perhaps greater). There's still no consensus on the merits of compatibilism, the analysis of knowledge, or the relation of the mental and the physical. Nor is there broad agreement about which methods are needed to unequivocally confirm the right answers for us.

If the intractability of disagreement in an area is best explained by antirealist assumptions about its status, then we must be global philosophical antirealists. The judgments we render, and the arguments we offer on their behalf, must all be seen either as incapable of truth, as expressions of conative commitments only, or as claims whose truth is contingent on personal or interpersonal endorsement. But that's not a very plausible take on the status of our philosophical views. There is a truth—a real, objective truth—about whether the mental is identical to the physical, or about whether certain kinds of freedom are compatible with determinism. Once we are sure of our terms and concepts, the judgments that affirm or deny the existence of such things are literally either true or false, in as robust a sense as we can imagine. We don't have the final say about the truth of such judgments, and the content of these judgments is indeed something other than whatever conative or practical commitments contingently accompany them.

I invite you to reflect on the status of the philosophical judgments you hold most dear, and have worked most carefully to defend. Do you imagine that your views, and their supporting arguments, are either untrue, or possessed of only the sort of minimal truth that is attainable by having been sincerely endorsed from within a parochial perspective? No matter how skeptical you might be about some alleged philosophical entities (universals, free will, or moral facts), you presumably take your confident opinions about such matters as having registered a real truth, one that is a function neither of your attitudes towards it, nor of the language you have used to comprehend it. That truth, you believe, is independent of the circle you inhabit, the agreements you've entered, the conventions you are part of, and the era in which you find yourself.

And yet one's philosophical views are bound to be as controversial as one's ethical views. Disagreements in core (and peripheral) philosophical areas are apparently intractable. Empirical evidence hasn't yet been able to solve any major philosophical problem, and any prediction that it someday might is as likely to divide philosophers as any other philosophical question. If intractable disagreement about verdicts and methods is enough to warrant an antirealist diagnosis of an area, then the whole of philosophy must be demoted. That simply is implausible: there really is (or isn't) such a thing as probabilistic causation, numbers without spatio-temporal location, actions that are both free and determined, etc. My say-so doesn't make it so. Neither does anyone else's.

The philosophical stance that denies the existence of nonnatural moral properties is itself the subject of intractable disagreement. If such disagreement is sufficient to undermine the realistic status of the controversial judgments, then the views of the ethical naturalist or moral antirealist cannot be objectively correct. They are either untrue, or are true reports of the attitudes they themselves take toward nonnaturalism, or are noncognitive expressions that reflect their own practical commitments. If they are *any* of those things, then they cannot rationally command the allegiance of their detractors. Nonnaturalists needn't be making any error when rejecting such views.

The alternative is to see our beliefs about such matters as aspiring to, and possibly succeeding in, representing a philosophical reality not of our own making. This reality is constituted by a set of truths whose alethic status is independent of our endorsement of their content. And this despite the presence of intractable philosophical disagreement.

Of course, one might say that were we free of the shortcomings that beset all of us actual enquirers, we would converge on a set of philosophical claims about free will, causation, etc. The disputes that seem to us so intractable would vanish with more information, more efficient and comprehensive application of that information, etc. That may be so. But then we have every reason to render the same verdict in the ethical case. Since ethics is a branch of philosophy, it would be very surprising to come to any other conclusion.

In other words, even if, at the end of the day, there is (much) more disagreement within ethics than there is in science, this is hardly probative evidence for the falsity of nonnaturalism. For there is just as likely to be (much) more disagreement in philosophy generally than there is in science. That doesn't license a verdict of global philosophical antirealism. It certainly doesn't license us in the claim that philosophy is a natural science. So long as it is true (as almost every working philosopher presupposes) that there is an objectively correct view about central philosophical puzzles, then we have just as much reason to accord the same status to ethical matters. We will have our opinions about such matters, but they are ultimately answerable to a truth not of our own making. Things are no different in ethics.

5. Moral disagreement as an epistemic defeater

For any nontrivial moral view one holds, there are bound to be others who disagree with it. This very fact is probably not enough to undermine any epistemic justification one may have for the belief. One might, after all, be unaware of the disagreement, and this ignorance might be nonculpable. Yet what of the ordinary situation, where we realize that our own moral views fail to command universal allegiance? Suppose not only that you know of such disagreement, but that you also rightly believe that your opponents, reasoning correctly from their own incompatible but justified beliefs, will never come over to your side. What does that do to the status of your own beliefs?

As I see it, such awareness does not, by itself, constitute a defeater of one's views. It does not entail that one ought to suspend judgment about what one believes. For one may well think—and this is the usual case—that one has justifying reasons that the other is failing to appreciate. That she is reasoning impeccably from her own starting points does not mean that her beliefs must be true, for her starting points may be way off base. And, as you will see things, they almost certainly are.

Surely it is possible that any defense you offer of your contested views will invoke other beliefs that are as controversial as the ones you are intending to support. In fact, this happens all the time in moral discussions. Perhaps, for many such cases, there is nothing one can do but beg the question. And question-begging arguments never confer justification.

There are two things to say here. First, one's belief might continue to be justified, even if defending it to others has one begging questions. A belief's justification is distinct from an agent's ability to justify it to others. So long as the belief was initially justified, it is possible that its justification survives, despite an agent's inability to advance considerations that an audience finds compelling. (Someone rightly convinced that tomatoes are fruits might be justified in her belief, even if she's unable to bring others around to the idea.) Second, there is excellent reason to believe that the presence of another's incompatible, justified belief doesn't always undermine justification; indeed, there might even be a case for thinking that question-begging arguments can supply positive justification for one's contested beliefs.

We can see this with the help of a series of examples. Suppose that you are engaged in conversation with a principled fanatic. He thinks that the fundamental ethical imperative is to gain power over others; everything else is subsidiary to this primary goal. Any argument you offer for beneficence is bound to be treated as the product of an effective brainwashing. Nothing you can say will convince him. Moreover, suppose that he's not contradicting himself, and isn't making any false empirical claims to support his ultimate principle. In the context of your conversation, you are bound to beg the question.

But you might be justified in your beliefs anyway. For the presence of an intelligent, consistent, and indefatigable opponent does not necessarily undermine a belief that one is otherwise justified in holding. This is a general point. It holds for one's ethical views, but also for perceptual, memorial, and philosophical ones, as well.

To simplify, consider a case in which one's perceptual beliefs later form the basis of a memorial belief. I saw and remember talking to my hated nemesis Smith the moment before he made that fatal misstep that no one else witnessed. I try to convince others of what I have seen, and am met with disbelief. Let's add that my relations with Smith are well known. That others have excellent reason to doubt my word is compatible with my original belief, and its memorial descendant, both being highly justified. In this case, not only do the incompatible, well-justified beliefs of others fail to undermine my justification, but my own question-begging attitudes (e.g. regarding my own innocence in this case) do appear to be enough to constitute positive justification for the beliefs I hold.

We can broaden the picture in an obvious way. Informed, rational, and attentive skeptics, possessed of internally consistent and coherent attitudes, might remain unconvinced by any of our empirical claims. According to this version of the argument from disagreement, that resistance defeats any justification we might have for our empirical beliefs. Though we can't absolutely discount that possibility, the conclusion is so drastic as to call into question the soundness of the argument that generated it. If we assume, as everyone reading this will, that we do have some positively justified empirical beliefs, then, so far as I can tell, it follows that question-begging grounds can confer positive justification. For anything one might cite as evidence on behalf of one's empirical beliefs will surely be regarded as question-begging by the skeptic.

A similar story can be told regarding all of our philosophical beliefs. The most brilliant philosophers, rational, open-minded, and well informed, have failed to agree amongst themselves on just about every key philosophical issue. If pervasive and intractable disagreement signaled an absence of justification, this would mean that none of those philosophers (much less the rest of us) would be at all justified in holding the philosophical views that they (we) do. But this seems false; it's certainly belied by anyone who actually undertakes sincerely to argue philosophically. One who has developed a theoretically sophisticated take on some philosophical issue, coming to grips with deep criticisms and developing novel and integrated positive proposals, is surely justified to some extent in thinking her views correct. Of course such a person will see that some others will fail to be convinced—even some others who are as smart, ingenious, and imaginative as she is. She will recognize her fallibility and appreciate a salient feature of philosophical history—namely, the failure of greater minds to attract even near-unanimity on most of the major points that they had advanced. Still, awareness of this history, and the skepticism of some of her contemporaries, is not enough to force her to suspend judgment on the views that she has so skillfully defended.

I see no reason to register a different verdict for ethics. Deep disagreement there, as elsewhere, should give one pause. It can sap one's confidence, and if it does, then that (but not the disagreement *per se*) may be sufficient to undercut one's justification. But this is no different from the general case. Provided that one brings to a dispute a moral belief that is justified, then exposure to conflicting belief needn't defeat one's justification, even if one is unable to convince an intelligent other of the error of his ways.

The present argument against the epistemic justification of moral belief relies on the following principle (or something very like it):

> (E) If (i) S believes that p, and R believes that not-p, and (ii) S and R know of this disagreement, and (iii) S and R have formed their beliefs in rational and informed ways, then S is not justified in a belief that p, and R is not justified in a belief that not-p.

(E) may be true. But no one could be justified in believing it. (E) itself is the subject of intractable disagreement—there are informed and rational people who endorse it, and equally qualified agents who reject it. By its own lights, then, we must suspend judgment about (E). Having done that, however, we are no longer epistemically forbidden from positively embracing a contested belief, even if our opponents are as smart as we are.

We can reveal another kind of skeptical self-defeat if we renew our emphasis on establishing a parity between ethical investigation and philosophical investigations generally. A familiar skeptical line is that there isn't, really, any adequate evidence that can be called upon to support our ethical opinions. Unlike empirical investigations, we haven't anything tangible that can, at the end of the day, finally settle a disputed moral question. All the sensory evidence at our disposal will underdetermine an ethical verdict. And what's left? Only our emotional responses and our moral convictions, both of which are traceable to accidents of birth and upbringing. Their genesis marks them as unreliable indicators of any truth there might be. But there's nothing else to rely on in ethics. And therefore our moral views lack justification, one and all.

The problem with such an argument should by now be apparent. There is a striking equivalence between the nature and source of our evidence in philosophy, and in ethics. We have no choice but to rely on our intuitions and considered judgments in both. What tells us, for example, that many proposed analyses of knowledge are no good is not some empirical finding that scientists have unearthed. It is instead our conceptual intuitions about counter-examples. If we want to know whether determinism is compatible with free will, we will consult arguments that invariably appeal to our intuitive responses to hypothetical cases. If such convictions and responses have no evidential credibility, then we should have to regard all philosophical beliefs as unjustified. Perhaps they are. But then those of the ethical naturalist, and the moral antirealist, are similarly undone.

6. The causal inefficacy of moral facts

Gilbert Harman (1977: ch. 1) has famously charged that moral facts are causally inert, and are therefore best construed antirealistically. His brief remarks have inspired a minor cottage industry, most of whose workers, it seems to me, are headed in the wrong direction. Rather than try to establish that point with a survey of the literature, I will try for the larger picture, with the aim of arguing that Harman's basic line of attack is misdirected.

Harman doesn't put things in quite this way, but I think his position, and that of many who take his lead, can be accurately captured in the following argument:

1. If something exists, and its existence is best construed realistically, then it must possess independent causal powers.

2. Moral facts possess no independent causal powers.
3. Therefore either moral facts don't exist, or their existence isn't best construed realistically.

Harman himself believes in moral facts, though he regards them as artefacts of social agreements. He is an ethical relativist, not a realist.

Since the argument is valid, any realist must choose either or both of the premises to come in for criticism. I opt for (1), because I suspect that (2) is true. A property has independent causal powers only if its instantiation by itself has causal implications, apart from the instantiation of any other properties it may in an instance depend on or be realized by. I'm not confident that moral facts possess such powers.

I won't try to vindicate my lack of confidence here. If it is misplaced, then so much the better for moral realism. Moral properties would possess independent causal power, and thereby pass the most stringent test for ontological inclusion. But let's instead imagine that my suspicion is correct, and that we are thus placed in what many have considered a worst-case scenario: trying to defend the existence of moral properties, realistically construed, while acknowledging that they are fundamentally different in kind from the properties whose existence is ratified by the natural sciences. If I am right, then such things as a benefactor's generosity, a regime's injustice, a friend's thoughtfulness, are causes (if they are) only by virtue of inheriting the causal powers of the properties that realize them at a time. Any causal power they have is exhausted by that of the subvening properties that fix a situation's moral character. Nothing follows from this admission unless we are also prepared to insist on a causal test of ontological credibility, of the sort espoused in Harman's first premise.

Such a test is powerfully motivated, but is ultimately resistible. This test is an application of Occam's razor, and is responsible for our having pared down our ontology in many sensible ways. We're quite finished with explanations that invoke Osiris or golems or centaurs, and Occam's razor is responsible for that. All that these entities were once invoked to explain can be more parsimoniously explained by relying on facts whose existence is vindicated through scientific confirmation. And such confirmation makes essential reference to a putative entity's causal powers.

So out with the trolls, the ancient pantheon, and the vampires. That's not so bad, is it? Such things aren't required to explain the goings-on in our world. But then, by my admission, neither are moral facts. So, by parity of reasoning, either we keep moral facts, but at the expense of a bloated ontology that implausibly lets these minor supernatural agents sneak back in, or we abolish the lot of them. Why should morality get special treatment here, when, as we all agree, the causal test has done its good work in so many other areas? Very conveniently for me, I don't have the time in this context to provide the full answer to this question.[6] But in lieu of that long story, let me offer a brief reply, and then a longer one that invokes the ethics–philosophy parallel that I have already relied on.

The brief reply: application of the causal test has highly counter-intuitive implications. This is so on two assumptions: first, that only physical properties possess independent causal powers, and second, that at least most of the properties of the special sciences are not identical to, but only supervenient upon, those of physics. From these assumptions, allied with the causal test, it follows that nothing exists but (roughly) atoms and the void. There certainly won't be any such things as atmospheres, rock strata, newts, and dandelions, if we grant that such things are not type-identical to anything referred to in a physics journal. It seems to me that such things do exist, and are multiply realizable by, rather than identical to, particular physical properties. Thus the causal test eliminates too much from our ontology.

Suppose that doesn't faze you—you can live with such a parsimonious ontology, or you don't endorse one of the two assumptions that got us there.[7] Still, we can invoke the ethics–philosophy parallel in the service of a further argument that should worry proponents of the causal test. By way of introduction, we can note that moral facts are a species of *normative fact*. Normative facts are those that tell us what we *ought* to do; they rely on norms, or standards, for conduct within a given realm. Normative facts cause nothing of their own accord.

We can be helped to see this by comparing ethics, not to philosophy as a whole, but to one of its close philosophical cousins. In my opinion, moral facts are *sui generis*, but they are most similar to another kind of normative fact— epistemic facts. Epistemic facts concern what we ought to believe, provided that our beliefs are aimed at the truth. Once one understands the concept of logical validity, then if confronted with a modus ponens argument, one *ought to* believe that it is logically valid. This is a true epistemic principle.

It's also the case that you oughtn't believe things that you have no evidence for, and much evidence against. What does this epistemic truth cause? Nothing. Nor are particular, concrete epistemic duties—duties had by agents at a time—at all independently causally efficacious. Epistemic facts have as their primary function the specification of standards that should or must be met. We can say, if we like, that such standards are descriptive—they describe

---

[6] I try my hand in *Moral Realism*, 98–114.

[7] Beware: arguments for rejecting either assumption may well allow moral facts to pass the causal test (though any sound argument rejecting the second assumption would generate a naturalistic, rather than a nonnaturalistic, moral realism).

the conditions under which agents are (e.g.) appropriately sensitive to evidence, justified in their beliefs, warranted in their views. But, unlike natural scientific principles and facts, such normative standards may be perfectly correct even if they are honored only in the breach. The epistemic requirement that we proportion our beliefs to the evidence can be true even in a world populated wholly by spell-casters and astrologers. The normative facts that specify the conditions under which we ought to believe the truth, or behave morally, lack the ability to explain the workings of the natural order. Our epistemic and moral duties cannot explain why apples fall from trees, why smallpox takes its victims, why leopards have their spots. But they may exist for all that.

Nor is this failure something specific to the moral or epistemological realms. Consider prudential or instrumental duties—those that require us to enhance self-interest or efficiently satisfy our desires. Such normative demands do not explain what goes on in the world. Alternatively, if they are thought, for instance, to be powerful enough to explain why agents act as they do, then surely moral and epistemic requirements are capable of doing so as well. I see no basis for distinguishing the causal powers of any of these normative types from one another.

I don't mean to suggest for a moment that the causal test is useless. Rather, I think we should recognize its limits. The causal test fails as a general ontological test: it doesn't work when applied to the normative realm.

Scientific principles are vindicated, when they are, because they are able to do two closely related things: cite the causes of past events, and accurately predict the nature and occurrence of future events. Their claim to be genuinely explanatory depends almost entirely on their ability to discharge these two tasks.

But moral rules are not like that. We *can* construe rules in this way: Brink, Sturgeon, and others manage this feat.[8] But it's not a very natural way to regard them. Moral principles aren't viewed in the first instance as hypotheses that predict the actions of agents, but rather as requirements that everyone knows will encounter predictive failures. True, moral principles will reliably predict the doings of good and bad agents. But that presupposes the reality of moral properties (goodness and badness), and there's no reason to make such a concession at this stage, especially given the seriousness of antirealist charges, and the proper aim (given a naturalistic vantage point) of beginning from a neutral perspective and relying on the causal test as a way to determine the nature of reality.[9]

---

[8] See e.g. Brink 1989: 182–97, Sturgeon 1984, Boyd 1988, Railton 1986.

[9] So in this respect I think that Harman was wrong to concede to his opponents the existence of moral facts. The proper starting point for an antirealist is one in which we suspend judgment on the existence of such facts, and demand of the realist some positive arguments for believing in them. Harman instead was willing to grant the existence of moral facts, but claimed that even so they possessed no independent causal powers, and so could not be construed realistically.

Yes, we can enshrine moral predicates within true counterfactuals, even (in some cases) counterfactuals of greater generality than those describable at the physical level. But that is no proof of moral realism, as we can do the same for the predicates of etiquette and the civil law, which obviously cannot be construed realistically. Moral principles and facts aren't meant to explain behavior, or anticipate our actions, but rather to *prescribe* how we ought to behave, or *evaluate* states or events. They don't cite the causes of outcomes, but rather indicate what sort of conduct would merit approval, or justify our gratitude, or legitimate some result. Science can't tell us such things.

If I am right, then an allegiance to the causal test entirely eliminates the normative realm. But this is highly implausible. There *are* reasons to believe things, reasons to satisfy one's desires, reasons to look out for oneself. There are also moral duties to aid others and refrain from harming them, even if doing so isn't going to improve one's lot in life. The standards that supply such reasons are not capable of causing anything. Nor, it seems, are the reasons or obligations themselves. (Again, if they are, all the better for moral realists.[10]) If there is any such thing as a genuine reason, the test must fail. Alternatively, if the test is retained, then such reasons must be capable of passing it. And then the causal argument against moral facts evaporates.

Maybe we can have our cake and it eat, too? Why not retain the causal test, allow that normative facts exist, but view them, as Harman does moral facts, as by-products of human choice and election? The causal test is a realist's test. Failure to pass it doesn't mean that a putative fact doesn't exist. It just means that the fact cannot be construed realistically. Normative facts may be like this. If so, we could retain the test, and also retain a global normative antirealism. Perfectly in keeping with the physicalist leanings of so many of our contemporaries.

The animating spirit behind the causal test is the ontological principle that the real is limited to what is scientifically confirmable, and the epistemic principle that we have good reason to believe in something only if it impinges on our experience, or is required in the best explanation of that which does. The causal test obviously supports, and derives support from, both the ontological and the epistemic principle. Yet both principles are dubious. The case for the causal test is considerably diminished once we see why.

The epistemic principle is problematic because it invokes an entity—a good reason—whose existence is not itself scientifically confirmable. It's like saying

---

[10] One natural line of thinking seems mistaken. That is the one that attributes causal power to normative facts by noting that they, as mediated by an agent's beliefs and desires, can explain a great deal of why agents act as they do. That something is *seen by an agent as* (prudentially, epistemically, or morally) obligatory is often enough to get one going. But that sort of mediation undermines the independence of the causal potency that the test requires. (This is one of Crispin Wright's points (1992: 196).)

that God sustains a universe that contains no supernatural beings. There's a kind of internal incoherence here: the claim discounts the existence of the kind of thing that is presupposed by the claim itself.

Further, a belief's being justified is not the sort of thing that impinges on our experience. Nor, seemingly, is reference to its epistemic status required to explain anything that we have ever observed. But then, by the epistemic principle under scrutiny, we have no good reason to think that there is any such thing as the property of being epistemically justified. But if there is no such property, then the principle that implies such a thing cannot itself be justified. And so we can be rid of it.

Here's another way to get to the same result. We needn't make essential reference to this epistemic principle to explain why we see or hear or feel the things we do. Nor, so far as I can see, is any epistemic principle required in the best account of why various observable events have occurred in the world. So if the principle is true, then we lack a good reason for thinking it so. This principle, like normative standards quite generally, seeks to regulate and appraise conduct, rather than to describe its causal antecedents or powers. If that's sufficient to render it unreal, or sufficient to remove any justification we might have for believing it, then it can't rightly be used to constrain our epistemic findings or practices.

And the ontological view? The relevant ontological principle tells us that the only existential truths there are (i.e. truths about what exists) are those that are scientifically confirmed. This is certainly false if we are concerned with science as it stands, as some existential truths have yet to be discovered. Yet the view is no more plausible if we are envisioning the edicts of a perfected natural science. Here's why. Consider this existential claim:

(O)   There are no existential truths other than those ratified by perfected natural sciences.

Either (O) is true or false. If false, let's drop it: our ontology wouldn't then be entirely fixed by the natural sciences. But if it's true, then it must be false: it's self-referentially incoherent. For (O) cannot itself be scientifically confirmed. If it were true, it would be an instance of a nonscientifically confirmable existential truth. Thus either way we go, (O) must be false.

(O) is a thesis from metaphysics, not physics. Philosophers, not natural scientists, are the ones who will end up pronouncing on its merits. This is another application of the general idea that there are specifically philosophical truths that escape the ambit of scientific confirmation. There might be abstract entities, or such a thing as conceptual necessity, justified belief, or goodness. Bring your beakers, your electron microscopes, your calculators and calipers—you'll never find them. You can't abolish such things just because they lack independent causal power, and so escape empirical detection. After all, the principle calling for such abolition isn't itself scientifically confirmable.

In the end, the absence of independent causal power is not a good reason to deny the existence of moral facts, realistically construed. Of course, nothing I've said in this section supplies any argument for thinking that there are such things. I doubt that causal considerations could do that. But undermining their role in antirealist arguments can go some ways towards removing a familiar barrier to justified belief in the sort of nonnaturalism that I find appealing.

7. Conclusion

Once we attend to the fact that ethics is a branch of philosophy, the plausibility of nonnaturalistic moral realism is greatly enhanced. Philosophy is not a natural science. Basic, fundamental philosophical principles are realistic in nature. And central ethical principles are philosophical ones. This combination of claims gives us excellent reason to suppose that fundamental ethical truths are best construed realistically, and nonnaturalistically.

This seems to me to be a very powerful argument that can aid the nonnaturalist realist in replying to a number of perennial criticisms. One such criticism—that persistent, intractable moral disagreement is best explained as antirealists would do—can be met once we avail ourselves of the ethics–philosophy parallel. Moral disagreement shares all structural features with philosophical disagreement generally, and yet a global philosophical antirealism is very implausible. Moral disagreement also fails to provide a strong epistemic defeater for one's own already-justified moral beliefs. Controversial philosophical beliefs might be justifiedly held; things are no different in the specifically moral domain. And the causal inefficacy of moral facts can be admitted without threatening moral realism, since the causal test is too restrictive a standard for ontological credibility. Alternatively, if (contrary to my suspicions) moral facts do manage to pass that test, then retaining the test will entitle moral facts to admission into our ontology.

Once we attend to the fact that ethics is a branch of philosophy, a defense of nonnaturalistic moral realism becomes a bit easier than it otherwise might be. Which is not to say that it's at all easy—the many promissory notes scattered throughout this essay will attest to that. Still, reliance on the ethics–philosophy parallel enables us to plausibly respond to *some* of the critical obstacles to the development of a plausible ethical nonnaturalism. We can hardly hope to vindicate a complex metaethical theory in one fell swoop. We can, if the preceding arguments are any good, manage to dust off a neglected view and show that some of the sources of its unpopularity have been overrated. I hope to have done that here.

References

AUDI, ROBERT (1997). *Moral Knowledge and Ethical Character*. Oxford: Oxford University Press.

—— (1999). 'Self-Evidence,' *Philosophical Perspectives*, 13: 205–26.

—— (2004). *Kantian Intuitionism*. Oxford: Oxford University Press.

AYER, A. J. (1936). *Language, Truth and Logic*. London: Gollancz.

BLACKBURN, SIMON (1993). *Essays in Quasi-Realism*. Oxford: Oxford University Press.

—— (1998). *Ruling Passions*. Oxford: Oxford University Press.

BOYD, RICHARD (1988). 'How to Be a Moral Realist,' in Sayre-McCord (1988).

BRINK, DAVID (1989). *Moral Realism and the Foundations of Ethics*. Cambridge: Cambridge University Press.

COPP, DAVID, and ZIMMERMAN, DAVID, eds. (1984). *Morality, Reason and Truth*. Totowa, NJ: Rowman & Littlefield.

GARNER, RICHARD (1994). *Beyond Morality*. Philadelphia: Temple University Press.

GIBBARD, ALLAN (1990). *Wise Choices, Apt Feelings*. Cambridge, Mass.: Harvard University Press.

HARE, RICHARD (1952). *The Language of Morals*. Oxford: Oxford University Press.

—— (1963). *Freedom and Reason*. Oxford: Oxford University Press.

HARMAN, GILBERT (1977). *The Nature of Morality*. Oxford: Oxford University Press.

JACKSON, FRANK (1998). *From Metaphysics to Ethics*. Oxford: Oxford University Press.

JOYCE, RICHARD (2001). *The Myth of Morality*. Cambridge: Cambridge University Press.

MACKIE, JOHN (1977). *Ethics: Inventing Right and Wrong*. New York: Penguin.

RAILTON, PETER (1986). 'Moral Realism,' *Philosophical Review*, 95: 163–207.

SAYRE-MCCORD, GEOFFREY (ed.) (1988). *Moral Realism*. Ithaca, NY: Cornell University Press.

SKORUPKSI, JOHN (1999). 'Irrealist Cognitivism,' *Ratio*, 12(4): 436–59.

STEVENSON, CHARLES L. (1937). 'The Emotive Meaning of Ethical Terms,' in Stevenson (1963).

—— (1948). 'The Nature of Ethical Disagreement,' in Stevenson (1963).

—— (1963). *Facts and Values*. New Haven: Yale University Press.

STRATTON-LAKE, PHILIP (ed.) (2002). *Ethical Intuitionism: Re-evaluations*. Oxford: Oxford University Press.

STURGEON, NICHOLAS (1984). 'Moral Explanations,' in Copp and Zimmerman (1984).

—— (2003). 'Moore on Ethical Naturalism,' *Ethics*, 113: 528–56.

TIMMONS, MARK (1999). *Morality without Foundations*. Oxford: Oxford University Press.

WRIGHT, CRISPIN (1992). *Truth and Objectivity*. Cambridge, Mass.: Harvard University Press.

11

The Legacy of *Principia*

Judith Jarvis Thomson

I

The influence of G. E. Moore's *Principia Ethica* on twentieth-century moral philosophy is largely due to the attractiveness of a certain argument in it, which came to be known as the open question argument. Let us step back for a moment. Moore thought that the following thesis was obvious and in need of no argument:

(Moore's Premise)   There is such a property as goodness.

Surely there is a property that all and only good things have in common; that is the property goodness.

Here now is the premise of the open question argument:

(OQA Premise)   Whatever natural property NP you fix on, it is an open question whether things that have NP also have goodness.

The conclusion of the argument is:

(OQA Conclusion)   There is no natural property NP such that NP is identical with the property goodness.

It is a very attractive idea that this argument is valid and, indeed, that its premise is true.

Moore, of course, accepted the open question argument and, therefore, rightly, drew the following further conclusion:

(Moore's Conclusion)   The property goodness is a non-natural property.

Alas, the idea that there are non-natural properties looked at best suspect to many of his readers. But how were they to avoid Moore's Conclusion? The readers I will be focusing on accepted the open question argument and therefore had to, and did, reject Moore's Premise.[1]

Then what is done by a person, say Alfred, who says 'A is good'? They thought that if Alfred attributes any property at all to A, then the property he attributes to it is the property goodness. Having agreed that there is no such property, they concluded that Alfred does not attribute a property to A. They therefore concluded that what Alfred says has no truth-value.

They differed, however, in their positive accounts of what Alfred does. I will focus on one of the positive accounts in particular, namely A. J. Ayer's.[2] Ayer held that in saying what he says, Alfred merely expresses—that is, merely displays—a favorable attitude toward A, thus he does no more than he would have done had he instead merely grinned or said 'Hurrah!' in response to A. (See Ayer 1946.)

This idea can helpfully be seen as an idea about why the open question argument succeeds. Thus: it is an open question whether a thing that has NP is good because saying that a thing has NP is not expressing a favorable attitude toward it whereas saying it is good is. I am sure that the fact that the idea can be so seen contributed to its popularity, since what helps to explain the success of an attractive argument inherits attractiveness from it.

What we have so far is a pair of ideas about goodness. They are obviously generalizable, however. First, the open question argument is itself generalizable. Moore had said that for any natural property NP, it is an open question whether things that have NP also have goodness. So similarly, presumably, for badness. And for rightness and wrongness. So similarly for all normative properties. It follows that if there are such properties, they are non-natural properties. That they are is a suspect idea, however. So we had better conclude that there are no normative properties. It follows that one who says a normative sentence does not attribute a normative property to anything. So we had better conclude that one who says a normative sentence attributes no property at all to anything. So we had better conclude that what such a person says has no truth-value. Thus we had better accept:

(No Normative Truth-Value Thesis)   Normative sentences have no truth-values.

---

[1] In recent years, some people who resist Moore's Conclusion have instead accepted Moore's Premise and rejected the open question argument; these people have come to be known as the Cornell realists. See e.g. the papers by Sturgeon and Boyd in Sayre-McCord 1988. I return to them only in n. 14.

[2] I bypass C. L. Stevenson's account, according to which what Alfred says means 'I approve of A; do so as well' (see Stevenson 1944), since Ayer's account still has a following, whereas Stevenson's, I believe, does not.

Then what does a person do who says a normative sentence? We had better accept:

(Expressivism)   What the speaker does is merely to express a favorable or unfavorable attitude—he does no more than he would have done had he merely said 'Hurrah!' or 'Boo!'

This pair of ideas was a major presence throughout twentieth-century moral philosophy. Like them or not, nobody could ignore them. That is the legacy of *Principia*.

II

More precisely, the legacy of *Principia* is the pressure brought to bear by the open question argument, in virtue of which this pair of ideas seemed attractive to their friends and a threat to their enemies, and thus could not be ignored. That pressure continues to be felt, despite the criticism the ideas were subjected to. I will describe only the two objections that have been taken most seriously; both are objections to the No Normative Truth-Value Thesis.

The first was made by Peter Geach. (See Geach 1972: 8.1 and 8.2.) Geach drew attention to the fact that normative sentences appear in what look like truth-functional contexts, such as 'If Hitler is a villain, then we ought not put up a statue to him.' Indeed, they appear in what look like valid arguments, such as:

If Hitler is a villain, then we ought not put up a statue to him.
Hitler is a villain.
Therefore, we ought not put up a statue to him.

But an argument is an ordered set of things with truth-values. If normative sentences have no truth-values, then that is not an argument, and a fortiori it is not a valid argument.

Friends of the No Normative Truth-Value Thesis responded to this objection by recommending that we relax about what an argument might consist in, and allow that a set of things without truth-values might be, well, not strictly speaking a valid argument, but something just as good. (See Blackburn 1984 and Gibbard 1990. Their more recent responses may be found in Blackburn 1998 and Gibbard 2002.) We will return to Geach in the following section.

The second of the two objections emerged from what has come to be called minimalism about truth—minimalism for short. Roughly expressed, minimalism tells us that the results of inserting any declarative sentence in for 'S' in the schema

(T-Schema)   'S' is true if and only if S

are all true.[3] Many people think this idea very plausible. Surely 'Grass is green' is true if and only if grass is green, and so on and on.

Here now is the second objection to the No Normative Truth-Value Thesis. Assume minimalism. The following is obviously true:

(1) 'Hitler is a villain' is a declarative sentence.

From minimalism, we can conclude:

'Hitler is a villain' is true if and only if Hitler is a villain.

No civilized person denies:

(2) Hitler is a villain.

It follows that 'Hitler is a villain' is true and, therefore, has a truth-value. So if minimalism is true, then the No Normative Truth-Value Thesis is false.

Many Expressivists were moved by this argument and, therefore, gave up on the No Normative Truth-Value Thesis—but did not give up on Expressivism. For they pointed to the fact that what entitles us to pass from minimalism to the conclusion that 'Hitler is a villain' is true, and therefore has a truth-value, is the conjunction of (1) and (2); and they said, rightly, that asserting the conjunction of (1) and (2) is entirely consistent with asserting Expressivism. (See, for example, Blackburn 1998 and Timmons 1999.)

But they might have rejected the argument. For they might have drawn attention to the fact that the statement of minimalism that I supplied above won't do at all. It just is not the case that the results of inserting *any* declarative sentence in for 'S' in the T-schema are all true: a sane minimalist imposes constraints on candidate replacements for 'S' beyond that they must be declarative sentences. Thus a candidate must not contain a pronoun, for no sane minimalist wishes to be committed to the truth of ' "I am a Hungarian" is true if and only if I am a Hungarian.' Similarly for all other indexicals, such as demonstratives ('this') and tenses ('will be'). Similarly for 'liar sentences'. Similarly for adjectives like 'big.' 'Alfred is big' is a declarative sentence, contains no indexicals, and is not a liar sentence. Yet no sane minimalist wants

---

[3] Minimalism tells us something else as well, namely that there is no property of being true—the truth of those biconditionals is 'all there is to truth'. I ignore this further claim in the text: I pretend in the text that minimalism tells us only about the T-Schema, or, as the point is sometimes put, that truth is a disquotation device.

to be committed to the truth of ' "Alfred is big" is true if and only if Alfred is big.' Alfred may be a big strawberry but a small piece of fruit. Is Alfred big? There just is no answer to this question, for 'Alfred is big' is semantically incomplete.

It emerges that no set of constraints on replacements for 'S' is strong enough unless it guarantees that a candidate replacement has a truth-value. Thus that the reason why sentences containing indexicals, liar sentences, and sentences whose grammatical predicate is 'is big' are excluded is that, for this or that reason, they lack truth-values.

The fact that the set of constraints on replacements for 'S' must be this strong could have been seen straightway, for the results of making replacements in the T-Schema are themselves true only if what follows 'if and only if' in them itself has a truth-value.[4]

So suppose we instead opt for what might be called constrained minimalism, namely the thesis that the results of inserting any sentence with a truth-value in for 'S' in the T-Schema are all true. There remains a very good question why that is so, but that it is, is plain enough.

But constrained minimalism cannot be thought to provide a reason for thinking that this or that sentence has a truth-value. It can be thought to supply only an account of the conditions under which a sentence—which is independently establishable as having a truth-value—is true. So an Expressivist who wishes to defend the No Normative Truth-Value Thesis can say: your argument that 'Hitler is a villain' has a truth-value relies on the assumption that that sentence is an acceptable replacement for 'S' in the T-Schema. But it is so only if there is sufficient independent reason to think it has a truth-value. So your argument is circular, and not only makes no trouble for Expressivism, it makes no trouble for the No Normative Truth-Value Thesis. (This point was made by Jackson et al. 1994.)

III

In sum, the objection to the No Normative Truth-Value Thesis from minimalism fails because minimalism is false; and an objection to the No Normative Truth-Value Thesis from constrained minimalism fails because it is circular. Let us return to Geach's objection to the No Normative Truth-Value Thesis.

---

[4] This fact obviously makes trouble for the further claim made by minimalists that I pointed to in n. 3. Michael Glanzberg argues in Glanzberg 2002 that that further claim is deeply false.

Geach took it that the fact that normative sentences appear in what look like truth-functional contexts, such as the conditional 'If Hitler is a villain, then we ought not put up a statue to him,' is itself reason to think that those sentences have truth-values. Others pointed to the fact that those sentences appear in non-truth-functional contexts too. 'I believe that—or wonder whether, doubt that, regret that, . . . —Hitler is a villain' are all perfectly respectable sentences. As the point here is sometimes put, normative sentences are embeddable in contexts that might be thought to require sentences that have truth-values.

But Geach drew attention, not merely to complex sentences, but also to the fact that normative sentences appear in what look like valid arguments. The example I gave above certainly looks like a valid argument. But what looks like the explanation of its validity is modus ponens, and that means that the example does not bring out the full strength of Geach's objection. Consider the following:

> All Greeks are villains.
> Hitler is a Greek.
> Therefore, Hitler is a villain.

Surely this is yet another valid argument. The validity of this argument, however, does not turn on the embeddability of normative sentences but, rather, on what is inside the sentences.

The fact is that the normative grammatical predicate 'is a villain' is a logical predicate: it has the inferential role of a predicate.[5] An argument now emerges. From

> (P) 'Is a villain' is a logical predicate,

we may conclude

> (C_1) There is such a property as being a villain.

Therefore,

> (C_2) If Alfred says 'Hitler is a villain,' he thereby attributes a property to Hitler, namely the property 'being a villain.'

Therefore,

> (C_3) What Alfred says has a truth-value, namely true if Hitler has the property and false if he does not.

---

[5] To the best of my knowledge, Paul Horwich is the only minimalist who has taken seriously this fact about normative grammatical predicates like 'is a villain.' See Horwich 1993. Not surprisingly, perhaps, for there is nothing plausibly describable as 'minimal' about the fact that a given expression is a logical predicate.

For this argument to reach (C_3) is for it to yield that the No Normative Truth-Value Thesis is false. For it even to reach (C_2) is for it to yield that Expressivism is false, since according to (C_2), Alfred, who says 'Hitler is a villain,' does do more than Bert, who says 'Boo to Hitler!'—Alfred attributes a property to Hitler and Bert does not.

IV

Does the argument really reach (C_3)? That is, are we really entitled to pass from the fact that a grammatical predicate 'is P' is a logical predicate and, therefore, stands for a property, to the conclusion that 'A is P' has a truth-value? Unfortunately there is reason to think we are not.[6] Michael Glanzberg argues (in Glanzberg 2002) that people who suppose that the fact that 'is P' is a logical predicate warrants the conclusion that 'A is P' has a truth-value will find themselves unavoidably enmeshed in the Liar Paradox. So the argument would need to be enriched by the addition of another premise if it were to reach (C_3), and it is, alas, quite unclear what that new premise should be.

On the other hand, we should be clear that what makes the No Normative Truth-Value Thesis safe from the argument is not the fact that the argument concerns itself with a normative predicate in particular: an analogous argument concerning the non-normative predicate 'is a banana' would have been no more successful. So while an Expressivist who wishes to defend the No Normative Truth-Value Thesis can say 'Fine, the job's done, so far as that objection goes,' he was not the one who did it.

V

Does the argument even reach

(C_2) If Alfred says 'Hitler is a villain,' he thereby attributes a property to Hitler, namely the property 'being a villain'?

If it does, then Expressivism is not safe from it. There is room for an objection to the effect that it does not.

---

[6] A less serious reason to think we are not lies in the fact that 'is a villain' is on any view vague, and on some views, 'Hitler is a villain' lacks a truth-value if Hitler is a borderline-villain. To bypass this objection, we need merely add a further premise to the argument, namely the obvious truth that Hitler is not a borderline-villain.

There are two forms the objection can take: a strong and a weak. In its strong form, it says that there are no properties at all.[7] (Or, perhaps, that there is no sense to be made of the idea that there are such things.) In particular, then, there is no such property as being a villain. A fortiori, the truth of

(P) 'Is a villain' is a logical predicate,

does not justify

(C₁) There is such a property as being a villain,

and so does not justify (C₂).

We can bypass that idea, however, because no Expressivist would offer it as an objection to the argument. Expressivists believe that there is a radical difference between the non-normative and the normative: they believe that there are natural properties, such as being a banana and being red, and that what there aren't, are normative properties such as being a villain.

So perhaps an Expressivist would instead make the objection in its weak form: the fact that 'is P' is a logical predicate justifies the conclusion that 'is P' stands for a property if and only if 'is P' is a non-normative logical predicate. 'Is a banana' and 'is red' are non-normative logical predicates, so they do stand for properties; not so 'is a villain.' Once again, therefore, the truth of (P) does not justify (C₁), and so does not justify (C₂).

Why this restriction to non-normative logical predicates?[8] Here the Expressivist comes into his own: because the use (or function?) of a normative predicate is to express a favorable or unfavorable attitude. (This way of putting the point is common.) Or, more precisely, ... Well, more precisely what? A number of different precisifications are on offer. Let 'is F' be a normative predicate. Precisification (i) says that if a person says 'A is F,' then he expresses— or anyway is rightly taken to express—a favorable or unfavorable attitude toward A. (ii) says that someone who says 'A is F' does not describe A; he evaluates A. (iii) appeals to belief and descends from Hume. It says, first, that one who has the (putative) belief that A is F is thereby motivated to do something, whereas one who has the belief that A is a banana is not thereby motivated to do anything. And it says, second, that there are no beliefs such that the person who

---

[7] There is good reason to reject the objection in its strong form, lying in the plausibility of what might be called minimalism about properties. It obviously won't do to say: if 'is P' is a grammatical predicate, then 'is P' stands for a property. (Compare my first, rough, expression of minimalism about truth.) So let us take constrained minimalism about properties to say: if 'is P' is a logical predicate, then 'is P' stands for a property. What more could it come to for 'is P' to stand for a property than that it is a logical predicate? At a minimum, we can say that a friend of the objection in its strong form has the burden of proof that more is needed.

[8] The consideration mentioned in n. 7 reinforces the idea that the Expressivist who makes this claim has the burden of proof.

has them is thereby motivated to do something. It therefore concludes that there isn't really any such thing as the belief that A is F.

An Expressivist who opts for one of those three ideas must do two things: he must show that his claim is true and then go on to show why his claim should be thought to justify the conclusion that there is no such property as being F. For brevity, I will bypass (i) and (ii); (iii), anyway, is the one I take to be most attractive to most contemporary Expressivists.[9]

It is easy enough to see how a friend of (iii) can get from (iii) to the conclusion that there is no such property as being F. If there were such a property as being F, then nothing would stand in the way of a person's believing that a thing has it. So if there is no such belief, then it follows that there is no such property.

What is not so easy to see is why we should accept (iii) itself. According to the first step taken by friends of (iii), one who has a normative belief (if there are such things) is thereby motivated to do something. This is so often said as for it to seem almost rude to ask: motivate the believer to do *what*? In some cases, the answer all but suggests itself. If I believe that I ought to mow my lawn, then what I am motivated to do is to mow my lawn. If I believe that I ought to pay my taxes, then what I am motivated to do is to pay my taxes.[10] That is because it is perfectly clear in those cases what acting in accord with the belief would consist in. Acting in accord with my belief that I ought to do such and such would consist in doing the such and such; and that is why friends of (iii) would say that what my belief motivates me to do is the such and such.

But what of my other normative beliefs? Such as, for example, my belief that Hitler is a villain? Or worse yet for these purposes, my belief that you ought to mow your lawn? Here it is not at all clear what I am to be thought to be motivated to do by virtue of having the belief. That is because it is not clear what, if anything, acting in accord with these beliefs would consist in.

---

[9] I return briefly to (i) in n. 11. (ii) appears in Moore's post-*Principia* writings, though Moore was markedly more cautious about it than those who later fixed on it have been. In Moore (1942: 591), he said that the idea was not clear, and that '[t]o make it clear it would be necessary to specify the sense of "describe" in question,' and he said he was no more able to do this in 1942 than he had been in 1922, when he first considered the idea. There is a difficulty here, after all, for why should evaluating be thought incompatible with describing? Indeed, why isn't describing as good exactly what evaluating as good consists in?

In an earlier work—Harman and Thomson 1996—I had suggested that accepting (iii) is the mark of the modern Expressivist. The most modern Expressivist, however, evidently prefers something weaker than (iii), namely (iv): there really is such a thing as the belief that A is F, but it is of the quite special sort that Hume pointed to, that is, a belief such that a person who has it is thereby motivated to do something. See n. 12.

I have revised the discussion of (iii) that I presented at the conference in order to meet criticism by Allan Gibbard.

[10] If I have understood him, Allan Gibbard opts for a markedly stronger thesis about first person 'ought-judgments', namely that coming to believe that I ought to do such and such is not merely coming to be motivated to do so, but is actually deciding to do so. See Gibbard 2002. (I think that Simon Blackburn is hinting at the same idea in Blackburn 1998: 70.) For criticism, see Hawthorne 2002.

It may well be supposed that if I believe that Hitler is a villain, then if my town council were to declare a referendum on whether to put up a statue to him, I would be motivated to vote against doing so. Again, if I believe you ought to mow your lawn, then if I came to believe that I was situated as you are, I would be motivated to mow my own lawn. But as things stand now, I do have those beliefs about Hitler and you, but I am not now motivated to do anything at all by them.

Let us borrow a figure from Quine. We can think of a person's normative beliefs at a given time as forming a net—perhaps that the nodes are his normative beliefs and that the strands linking them are either principles of logic that he accepts (for one normative belief may entail another) or statements of fact that he believes true. At the center are his highly abstract and general normative beliefs, such as (perhaps) the Categorical Imperative. Further out are his less abstract, less general normative beliefs, such as that Hitler is a villain and that Jones ought to mow Jones's lawn. Around the edges are his beliefs to the effect that he ought to do this and that he ought to do that.

It is only those beliefs around the edges in respect of which it is perfectly clear what acting in accord with them would consist in. Therefore, it is at most those beliefs around the edges about which it can plausibly be said that the believer is now motivated to do something by virtue of having them—the something being: act in accord with them.

And should we agree that the believer is now so motivated? I believe that I ought to mow my lawn, yet here I sit, feckless as usual in the face of enterprises that require effort. Or I am feeling glum and couldn't care less about returning the library book I know I ought to return now.

The friend of (iii) can certainly ask the following. Suppose we think we have a picture of Alfred's entire normative net. If he is not motivated to do *any* of the things that, according to our picture, he believes he ought to do, then what reason do we have for thinking that our picture is correct? Alfred's saying that it is does not count for much. Indeed, his saying that it is counts for nothing at all if his behavior shows that he is motivated by the normative beliefs around the edges of a quite different net.

There is something right in the offing here, though it would take some delicacy to get the point stated properly; after all, we can hardly want to say that a person's normative beliefs do not survive through his occasional states of deep depression in which nothing matters to him at all. Moreover, there would remain the hard question why it is so, hard because what makes it so is not at all obvious. In particular, explaining what makes it so by appeal to the idea that the nodes of a person's normative net are not really beliefs at all—and therefore that there are no normative properties—is taking a step that, on the face of it, seems utterly unwarranted. For the data remain: the grammatical predicate 'is a villain' and its ilk are logical predicates.

In short, the friend of (iii) can certainly have that the question what a person is motivated to do has an important bearing on what we can plausibly take his normative beliefs to be. But the conclusion the friend of (iii) wishes to reach just does not follow from as weak a claim as that is.[11]

VI

So the idea about belief that we have been looking at does not justify the view that whereas 'is P' stands for a property if it is a non-normative logical predicate, such as 'is a banana,' 'is P' does not stand for a property if it is a normative logical predicate, such as 'is a villain.' And it therefore does not show that an argument from

(P) 'Is a villain' is a logical predicate,

to

(C₁) There is such a property as being a villain,

and therefore to

(C₂) If Alfred says 'Hitler is a villain,' he thereby attributes a property to Hitler, namely the property 'being a villain'

fails to reach its conclusion. But if it does reach its conclusion, then Expressivism is false.

However, there is something else that might be thought to show that that argument fails to reach its conclusion, a something that we glanced at only very briefly in section I. And it may be *this* that is really or ultimately at work in many people who are tempted by Expressivism.

Suppose you accept Moore's open question argument in its most general form. This is, you believe that normative properties generally, if there are any, are non-natural properties. If you grant that (P) entails (C₁), then you are

[11] An Expressivist who opts for precisification (i) may be thought to have an easier time of it with my belief that you ought to mow your lawn than does the Expressivist who opts for (iii). No doubt I need not be motivated by that belief, but don't I anyway have a favorable attitude toward your mowing your lawn? I lack space to expand on this matter, but merely invite the reader to take the following question seriously: *what* favorable attitude? (Blackburn darkly refers to it as 'the attitude that one ought to' in Blackburn 1998: 82.) I make some comments on the ideas in the offing here in Harman and Thomson 1996. The fact that it is hard to see how the Expressivist is to answer the question 'What attitude?' may be what explains why Expressivist writings seem to slither back and forth between (i) and (iii).

committed to the existence of at least one normative, and thus non-natural, property, namely being a villain. But surely it is at best a suspect idea that there are any non-natural properties!

Why is that idea suspect? J. L. Mackie said (in Mackie 1977) that normative properties, if there were such things, would be queer; but that is largely because he was relying on the idea that they would be (objectionably) linked to motivation in the way discussed in the preceding section.

We will look at the sources of this suspicion in the following section. Before doing so, however, I should concede the unfortunate fact that I do not own the term 'Expressivism'. (If I am not mistaken, it was first introduced into philosophy by Allan Gibbard.) I defined it as I did because I believe that twentieth-century Expressivism began as a response to Moore's *Principia* and, indeed, as that quite distinctive response to *Principia*. But it may be that some of our contemporaries who are called, and who would call themselves or allow themselves to be called, Expressivists would not say what I said Expressivists say—it may even be that they would accept (C_2) in particular. But then what exactly do or would they say in response to *Principia*? Each case would have to be examined individually, and I will not try to survey them.[12]

VII

Let us go back to *Principia*. Moore invited his readers to accept:

(Moore's Premise)   There is such a property as goodness.

The open question argument yields:

(OQA Conclusion)   There is no natural property NP such that NP is identical with the property goodness.

[12] I stop for a moment over Simon Blackburn, however, since he is such a puzzling case. He accepts the description of himself as an Expressivist, but his recent Blackburn 1998 leaves it quite unclear what his Expressivism consists in.

On the one hand, he says that 'the expressivist thinks we can say interestingly what is involved for a subject to think that X is good. It is for S to value it, . . .' (p. 50) and that valuing something 'is not to be understood as describing it . . .' (p. 49). Moreover, he says that what we do when we say that something is good or right is this: 'We avow a practical state. "Avowal" here means that we express this state, make it public, or communicate it' (p. 68). He does not mean that we report that we are in the state.

On the other hand, he tells us later that normative sentences have truth-values, and where 'S' is a normative sentence, that we may come to believe that S. As I said in n. 9, the most modern Expressivist evidently prefers (iv) to (iii); I had Blackburn in mind. Indeed, we may find out that S and therefore that there is such a fact as the fact that S (for things do have 'ethical properties'), which is represented by 'S,' and we may therefore come to know that S.

Is there a consistent view held in both of these two hands jointly?

Moore therefore invited his readers to accept:

(Moore's Conclusion)   The property goodness is a non-natural property.

Alas, the idea that there are non-natural properties looked at best suspect to many of his readers. Why so? You would find that idea suspect only if you thought that the natural properties are in a certain way privileged. Which are the natural properties? And what about them privileges them?

It is of interest that Moore himself thought that readers of chapter I, in which he lays out the open question argument, would know perfectly well which the natural properties are, partly because the term was a familiar one, partly from the examples he gave. That he thought this shows itself in the fact that he did not trouble to try to say what a natural property is until chapter II. What he said there is famously unsatisfactory. What was he groping for? In the preface he began to write for a second edition of *Principia*, but never finished, he said that the following indicates the properties he had had in mind: a natural property is a 'property with which it is the business of the natural sciences or Psychology to deal, or which can be completely defined in terms of such' (Moore 1993: 13). And this seems to have been at least roughly the way in which he was understood by the readers of *Principia* that I have been concerned with.

What privileges those properties? Many readers thought: the fact that they alone are the properties whose possession or non-possession one can find out about by the methods of the sciences, namely sense-perception and deduction from sense-perception.[13] Some of them took that fact about the natural properties to entail that they are the only properties: Ayer, for example, who argued as follows: If P is a property that is not a natural property, then attributing P to a thing is asserting a proposition that is not empirically verifiable. But there are no non-empirically verifiable propositions. Therefore there are no non-natural properties. (See Ayer 1946.) That too was famously unsatisfactory, but even those of Moore's readers who rejected Ayer's argument thought it mystery-mongering to say of a putative property that it really is one, though nobody can find out by empirical means whether a thing possesses it.

So they thought that Moore's conclusion had to go, and given the attractiveness of the open question argument, they thought that the best way to get rid of it was to get rid of Moore's Premise.

And isn't there a further, independent, ground for thinking that we should get rid of Moore's Premise? My school's team beats your school's team at

---

[13] Many readers, but very likely not Moore himself, for he thought that although goodness is a non-natural property, it supervenes on natural properties. So it is arguable that what Moore felt really mattered about the natural properties—even at the time of writing *Principia*—was not an epistemological fact about them but instead that one who attributes them to a thing describes it. (See n. 9.)

basketball. 'That's good,' I say. What property could it be thought that I attribute to my team's winning? That it is good for my school? But that is certainly not what people generally attribute to a thing whenever they say 'That's good' of it. Sometimes they are talking about a fountain pen or a watch and are not saying about it that it is good for my school. If we are to think that whenever a person says 'That's good' of a thing he attributes a property, goodness, to the thing, then this seems to be a property without any particular content. So there is something additionally objectionable about Moore's Conclusion, beyond that it commits us to the existence of an epistemologically unsatisfactory property: it commits us to the existence of an epistemologically unsatisfactory property that is also empty.

Two comments are called for. First, this independent ground for thinking that we should get rid of Moore's Premise is entirely right, for there is no property that people attribute to a thing whenever they say 'That's good' of it. The grammatical predicate 'is good' is not a logical predicate; the sentence 'A is good' is semantically incomplete. A person who says 'A is good' attributes something to A only if what he (though not the sentence) means is that A is a good fountain pen or a good dancer or good for use in making cheesecake or good for Jones or England or the tree in his backyard. Just as a person who says 'A is big' attributes something to A only if what he (though not his words) means is that A is a big flea or a big strawberry or a big banana.[14]

This fact emerges in another way. The sentence 'A is a red apple' entails 'A is red and A is an apple,' for 'A is red' (like 'A is an apple') is semantically complete. By contrast, 'A is a good dancer' does not entail 'A is good and A is a dancer'— else 'A is a good dancer and a bad tennis player' would entail 'A is good and A is bad and A is a dancer and A is a tennis player.' 'A is a good dancer' no more entails 'A is good and A is a dancer' than 'A is a big flea' entails 'A is big and A is a flea.' For further discussion, see the Addendum.

One might have thought this an obvious fact, once it had been drawn attention to. But surprisingly enough, it has had almost no impact on normative theorists, some of whom still set themselves—as Moore did in *Principia*—to answer the question which things possess the property goodness, without noticing that if their question is taken literally, the only possible answer to it is 'None.'

In any case, those of Moore's readers who rejected Moore's Premise were entirely right to do so. The mistake that the Expressivists made lay in what they

[14] To the best of my knowledge, it was Peter Geach who first drew attention to this fact about "is good," in Geach 1956. Others who have done so include Ziff 1960, von Wright 1963, Foot 1985, and Thomson 1997. It is because of this fact about "is good" that I have throughout bypassed the Cornell realists—I mentioned them only in footnote 1.

thought had to be concluded, from the falsity of Moore's Premise, about what is done by a person who says 'A is good,' namely that such a person merely displays a favorable attitude toward A—thus that he does no more than he would have done had he merely said 'Hurrah!' in response to A.[15] That was certainly a mistake. A person who says 'A is good' does display a favorable attitude toward A. But he does more than that. He also says that A is a good fountain pen or a good dancer or good for use in making cheesecake or good for Jones or England or the tree in his backyard. If the context in which he says 'A is good' does not tell his hearers which of these things he means, then they simply do not know what he means and have to ask. And what won't do is for him to reply, 'No, no, I didn't mean anything like that, what I meant was only that A is a good thing!'

I have been in the habit of summarizing this point about the predicate 'is good' in the slogan: all goodness is goodness in a way. Nothing is just, simply, good. Though many things are good fountain pens and good dancers and so on and on.

VIII

Something similar holds of 'is right' and 'is wrong.' Nothing is just, simply, right, though many things are right answers to such and such questions or right keys to the front door or right medicines to take to cure a sore throat. Moreover, 'Sherman' is the right answer to the question which general burned Atlanta; it is a wrong answer to the question which general was most admired by Lincoln. In short, all rightness is rightness in a way. (There are obvious differences between 'is right' and 'is good,' but they do not matter for present purposes.)

Similarly for 'is correct' and 'is incorrect.' 'Sherman' is the correct answer to the question which general burned Atlanta; it is an incorrect answer to the question which general was most admired by Lincoln.

What may seem to have been lost sight of is what has been happily called the Imperialism of the Moral. An act might have been good for its agent but morally bad; doesn't that mean that it was on balance bad? An act might have been prudentially right but morally wrong; doesn't that mean that it was on

---

[15] The idea that there is such a property as goodness has had other baleful effects on moral philosophy than that of provoking the response made by Expressivists: I argued in Thomson 2001 that it has caused Consequentialism to seem a more attractive idea than it is. It would be of great interest if those two effects of the idea were connected otherwise than by their joint cause. I do not see how, but it is a striking fact that many Expressivists opt for Consequentialism when they turn their attention from metaethics to normative theory.

balance wrong? If you believe in the Imperialism of the Moral, as I do, you could opt for accounts of 'is good' and 'is wrong' that permit saying these things. But they are not true to usage and not needed. We can make room for the Imperialism of the Moral without them: we can say that where it shows itself is where what is in question is what a person ought to do.

For where what is in question is what a person ought to do, what is in question is what he just, simply, ought to do. Suppose it would be good for a person to do a thing, but his doing the thing would be morally wrong. We do not conclude that he ought in one way to do the thing and ought in another way not to, that ending the matter. When a person asks what he ought to do, what he is asking is what, all things considered, and on balance, he (just, simply) ought to do. The Imperialism of the Moral says: if it would be morally wrong for him to do the thing, then he ought not do it, however good for him his doing it would be. Friends of the Imperialism of the Moral are not committed to thinking that this is true by virtue of the very meanings of the words (which is a wildly implausible idea); they are committed only to its being true.

But I will have to leave 'ought' aside. There are hard, open questions about its logic. And how moral considerations enter into fixing what a person ought to do is too large an issue to enter into here. (I make some suggestions in Thomson 2001: part 2.)

IX

We were looking at the epistemological considerations that led many of Moore's readers to think the natural properties privileged and, therefore, to reject

(Moore's Conclusion)   The property goodness is a non-natural property.

In light of the attractiveness of the open question argument, the readers I have been most concerned with therefore rejected

(Moore's Premise)   There is such a property as goodness.

Indeed, they had an independent ground for rejecting Moore's Premise, since the property goodness, if there were such a property, would have no content. I said that two comments were called for. The first was that they were right to reject Moore's Premise on this independent ground. We should now turn to the second comment.

Once we take seriously that all goodness is goodness in a way and all wrongness wrongness in a way, the boundary between normative properties and natural properties begins to break down. 'Sherman' is the right answer to the question which general burned Atlanta; and its being so consists in the (on any view) natural fact that it was Sherman who burned Atlanta. It may be that of two keys, a large and a small, the large is the right key to the front door; and its being so, if it is, consists in the (on any view) natural fact that it is the large key, not the small, that opens the front door.

The breakdown also shows itself in the case of goodness. One of Moore's paradigm examples of a natural property was being pleasant. (That is because he was particularly concerned to refute normative theories according to which goodness just is pleasantness.) No doubt it is a plausible idea that being pleasant is a natural property. But being pleasant is also a way of being good. You say I really should go see such and such a movie. Why so? You say, 'It's a pleasant little comedy.' In saying it is pleasant you are praising it. Not just giving a ground for praise, but praising.

So also for being interesting, absorbing, thrilling, amusing, elegant, charming, witty. Bert's witty speech at Alfred's funeral might have been a bad funeral oration; but there was anyway something good to be said for it, namely that it was witty. Yet isn't there as much reason to regard these as natural properties as there is to regard being pleasant as a natural property? Some or all of these are 'response-dependent' properties, but that is compatible with their also being natural properties. Many people believe—whether rightly or wrongly—that redness is a response-dependent property; they are not thereby committed to believing that redness is a non-natural property.

No doubt I may not feel like seeing a pleasant little comedy this evening. If so, then your praise of the movie does not motivate me to go see it. And it may be false that I should go see it. But those possibilities are no barrier to the movie's being good in a way. If a thing is a good fountain pen or a good watch or a good car then it is on any view good in a way. That is compatible with its being the case that when I learn that a thing is good in one of those ways I am not thereby motivated to do anything in respect of the thing, and with its being false to think that I should.

X

In sum, I think it very plausible that the attractiveness of Moore's open question argument itself issued from his fixation on, and his invitation to his readers to fix on, the pseudo-property goodness. Of course there is no natural property identical with it! I suspect that if that had been seen for the thoroughly unexciting fact that it is, *Principia* would have had a markedly less powerful impact on twentieth-century moral philosophy than it did.

Addendum

A1. Two further points are worth mention about the analogy Geach draws between 'is good' and 'is big.' First, the former has a much richer range of occurrences than the latter. Whenever a person says 'A is big,' then for some K, what he means is that A is a big K. Not so whenever a person says 'A is good.' It may be that for some K, what a speaker means is that A is a good K. But it may be that what he means is instead that A is good for this or that or that A is good for use in doing this or that and so on and on. 'Good' is the most general evaluative term in English, and we evaluate things, not only as K's, but in other ways too.

A second contrast is more important for moral philosophy. It has been suggested that while it may be that 'A is good' is semantically incomplete, perhaps that is not true of 'A is better than B.' In any case, the fact that 'A is good' is semantically incomplete does not entail that 'A is better than B' is too. Geach's 'is big' is not specially suited to making this point. For suppose that A is tall and skinny, and B is short and fat. Which is bigger? Is that to be settled by comparing their weights? I doubt it. But in any case, 'is tall' would have served Geach's purposes as well as 'is big' did, for whenever a person says 'A is tall,' then for some K, what he means is that A is a tall K. Yet 'A is taller than B' is not semantically incomplete. A person who says 'A is taller than B' does not attribute something to A and B only if what he means is that A is a taller man than B or A is a taller giraffe than B or A is a taller building than B. A person who says 'A is taller than B' does thereby attribute something to A and B, whatever A and B are and whatever he thinks they are—whether both men, both giraffes, one a man and the other a giraffe, and so on.

And if 'A is better than B' is not semantically incomplete, then while the only possible answer to the normative theorist's question 'Which things possess the property goodness?' is 'None,' no such objection can be brought against the question 'Which things stand in the relation betterness to which other things?' (It might pay to make explicit the fact that it would not be possible to get from the comparative back to the non-comparative. It won't do at all to say, for example, that A has the property goodness just in case A stands in the relation betterness to all other things. Or to most other things. Or to many other things.)

But 'A is better than B,' unlike 'A is taller than B,' *is* semantically incomplete. 'A is a taller man than B' entails 'A is taller than B and A and B are men.' By contrast, 'A is a better tennis player than B' does not entail 'A is better than B, and A and B are both tennis players'—else 'A is a better tennis player than B, and B is a better chess player than A' would entail 'A is better than B, and B is better than A, and A and B are tennis players and chess players.'

A2. Geach had contrasted 'is red' with 'is big': 'A is red' is semantically complete; 'A is big' is not. In section VII above, I accepted that 'is red' differs from 'is big' in this way. But in an earlier paper, I had expressed reservations about Geach's choice of predicate to contrast with 'is big.' Michael Zimmerman quotes me as having said in a footnote:

'Red' was not in fact well chosen for Geach's purposes, since 'red' is heavily context dependent: what we ascribe to an apple when we say 'It's red' is different from what we ascribe to the paint in a certain can when we say 'It's red.' Better choices would have been 'visible'... or 'poisonous' or.... (Thomson 1997: 277 n. 5)

And he says:

Now, it seems quite right to say that what's red as far as apples go may not be red as far as paints go. But of course this sort of division can be continued. After all, what's red as far as Macintosh apples go may not be red as far as Red Delicious apples go. And, contrary to what Thomson seems to imply, what's visible or poisonous to x may *not* be visible or poisonous to y. The fact is, *very many* properties are determinable (to some extent) rather than (fully) determinate, including all those just mentioned. (Zimmerman 2001: 22)

And he goes on to use this point to cast doubt on Geach's conclusion about 'is good.' Let us set aside the use Zimmerman makes of the point and merely fix on the predicate 'is red.'

Zimmerman misinterpreted me: what worried me about 'is red' is not what he thinks it was. No doubt I did not make clear enough what it was in the footnote he quotes from.

There are three ideas in the offing here, and I think that it pays to be clear that they differ. There is the fact that (1) redness is a determinable. That is what Zimmerman thinks worried me about Geach's choice of 'is red.' Not so. The contrast Geach drew between 'is red' and 'is big' is not in the least affected by the fact that 'is red' stands for a determinable, and I was certainly not objecting to his contrasting 'is red' with 'is big' on the ground that 'is red' stands for a determinable.

What worried me is what emerges on consideration of the following contrast: (2) for an apple to be red it is enough that its surface be red, whereas for the paint in a certain can to be red, it is required that the paint be red 'all through'. I concluded that there is no such thing as the property redness: there are rather two of them, surface-redness and redness-all-through. And therefore that if someone says 'it's red,' we do not know what he means unless the context tells us which of the two he is attributing to the thing. And therefore that 'is red' is in an important respect similar to 'is big.' I therefore offered alternatives for which a contrast of kind (2) does not arise.

But I should not have been so worried by that contrast. It is worth taking note of because we are thereby reminded that a phenomenon familiar from elsewhere turns up here too. Here is Aristotle's example: healthy people and healthy food. Is there such a thing as *the* property being healthy that healthy people and healthy food share? Here is another: Alfred caused Bert's death and Alfred's shooting of Bert caused Bert's death. Is there such a thing as *the* relation 'causes' that Alfred and Alfred's shooting of Bert both stand in to Bert's death? No, of course not. But the one property 'healthy' is reducible to the other: for something to have the one is for eating it to conduce to the eater's having the other. Similarly, for Alfred to stand in the one to Bert's death is for an act of Alfred's to stand in the other to Bert's death. And so also, I should think, for redness. Surface-redness is presumably fundamental—thus for a thing to have redness-all-through is presumably for every portion of it to have surface-redness. (In light of this reducibility of the one property to the other, it is misleading to say that what we have in these cases is, simply, ambiguity.)

'Is red' remains different from 'is big,' however, and in just the way Geach said it does. 'A is a big flea' does not entail 'A is big and A is a flea.' 'A is a red banana' does entail 'A is red and A is a banana'—despite the fact that if a person says these things, we may not know which of the two properties, surface-redness or redness-all-through, he is attributing to A.

Or so it certainly seems. I said that there are three ideas in the offing here, and according to the third, that is a mistake: 'is red' is exactly like 'is big' in that respect since (3) if Alfred has red hair, then it does not follow that his hair is red! His hair is orange, not red.

Some years ago, Romane Clark recommended construing 'is red' as, like 'is big,' a predicate modifier rather than as a logical predicate. (See Clark 1970, in which he makes suggestions toward a general theory of predicate modifiers.) He said that we should find this idea attractive on the ground that '[a] very red chigger need not be very red at all' (Clark 1970: 334). Not knowing what chiggers look like, I focus instead on red hair.

Concluding that 'is red' is a predicate modifier on such a ground is bringing a big piece of machinery to bear on what must surely be a small local problem. 'Red hair' is not unique in this respect: white people aren't white unless they have been dead for quite a while. But there aren't many such cases. On the other hand, such expressions are of interest, and it might pay to stop for a moment to ask how they should be understood.

Perhaps 'red hair' and 'white people' are metaphors?[16] More precisely, perhaps: unless the context indicates otherwise, a hearer takes them to be metaphors.

---

[16] I thank Catherine Elgin for this idea and for "white people."

For after all, the context might indicate otherwise. If we know that Bert has been wallowing in red paint, we take the child who says 'Look, Bert now has red hair!' literally. This is an attractive idea. Opting for it would explain why we do not normally expect a person's hair to be red when we have been told that he has red hair.

It does not seem entirely satisfactory, however. 'Purple prose' is on any view a metaphor, and we know that for a bit of prose to be purple prose is for it to be wildly exaggerated. Similarly for 'black moods': we know that for a mood to be a black mood is for it to be a state of gloom. We do not supply a color other than purple or black. By contrast, we know that for a person's hair to be red is (normally) for it to be orange, and for a person to be a white person is (normally) for him to be pinko-gray (as Forster put it).

So perhaps 'red hair' and 'white people' are merely stable exaggerations. 'He turned green when he learned that what he just ate was mashed spider.' Well, he didn't, not really. He only went ever so slightly greenish, and that is all you thought had happened when I said what I said. What makes an exaggeration stable is a good question—perhaps of particular interest in the case of 'white people'—but that, I think, may be all that is at work here.

A3. Zimmerman says that in any case, all of the preceding is irrelevant to *Principia*, for what Moore had in mind there was not goodness, but intrinsic goodness. And, Zimmerman says, the fact (supposing it a fact) that there is no such property as goodness is entirely compatible with there being such a property as intrinsic goodness.

Very well, what is intrinsic goodness? We might have taken the term to be intended to refer to non-derivative goodness: the goodness a thing has, but not by virtue of its standing in a suitable relation to (as, for example, its being conducive to) something else that is good. So understood, however, there is no such property if there is no such property as goodness.

So what is it then? Zimmerman says that intrinsic goodness is 'ethical goodness,' where—if I have understood him—for x, y, z, and so on, to possess ethical goodness is for it to be the case that '*there is a moral requirement to favor them* (welcome them, admire them, take satisfaction in them, and so on) *for their own sakes*' (Zimmerman 2001: 24). I mention only one of the difficulties that arise here. If we are morally required to favor x, y, and z, can that be a sheer, self-evident datum? Doesn't it have to be due to their possessing some features in virtue of which we are? And what feature is that? Not goodness, I hope.

In any case, while this idea, or anyway something like it, does turn up in Moore's later writings, I do not find it in *Principia*, which says that 'ought' is analyzable in terms of 'good,' and not the other way round.[17]

---

[17] I thank Tyler Doggett for comments on an earlier draft.

References

AYER, A. J. (1946). *Language, Truth, and Logic*. 2nd edn. London: Gollancz.

BLACKBURN, S. (1984). *Spreading the Word*. Oxford: Oxford University Press.

—— (1998). *Ruling Passions*. Oxford: Oxford University Press.

CLARK, R. (1970). 'Concerning the Logic of Predicate Modifiers'. *Nous*, 4: 311–335.

FOOT, P. (1985). 'Utilitarianism and the Virtues'. *Mind* 94, reprinted in S. Scheffler (ed.), *Consequentialism and its Critics*. Oxford: Oxford University Press.

GEACH. P. T. (1956). 'Good and Evil'. *Analysis*, 17, reprinted in Philippa Foot (ed.), *Theories of Ethics*. Oxford: Oxford University Press, 1967.

—— (1972). *Logic Matters*. Berkeley and Los Angeles: University of California Press.

GIBBARD, A. (1990). *Wise Choices, Apt Feelings*. Cambridge, Mass · Harvard University Press.

—— (2002). 'Normative and Recognitional Concepts'. *Philosophy and Phenomenological Research*, 64: 151–167.

GLANZBERG, M. (2003). 'Minimalism and Paradoxes'. *Synthese*, 135: 13–36.

HARMAN, G., AND THOMSON, J. J. (1996). *Moral Realism and Moral Objectivity*. Oxford: Blackwell.

HAWTHORNE, J. (2002). 'Practical Realism?' *Philosophy and Phenomenological Research*, 64: 169–178.

HORWICH, P. (1993). 'Gibbard's Theory of Norms'. *Philosophy and Public Affairs*, 22: 67–78

JACKSON, F., OPPY, G., AND SMITH, M. (1994). 'Minimalism and Truth Aptness'. *Mind*, 103: 287–302.

MACKIE, J. L. (1977). *Ethics: Inventing Right and Wrong*. New York: Penguin.

MOORE, G. E. (1942). 'A Reply to my Critics'. In P. A. Schilpp (ed.), *The Philosophy of G. E. Moore*. Evanston, Ill.: Northwestern University Press.

—— (1993). *Principia Ethica*, ed. Thomas Baldwin. Cambridge: Cambridge University Press.

PRICHARD, H. A. (1912). 'Does Moral Philosophy Rest on a Mistake?' *Mind*, 21: 21–37.

SAYRE-MCCORD, G., ed. (1988). *Essays on Moral Realism*. Ithaca, NY: Cornell University Press.

STEVENSON, C. L. (1944). *Ethics and Language*. New Haven: Yale University Press.

THOMSON, J. J. (1997). 'The Right and the Good'. *Journal of Philosophy*, 94: 273–298.

—— (2001). *Goodness and Advice*. Princeton: Princeton University Press.

TIMMONS, M. (1999). *Morality without Foundations*. Oxford: Oxford University Press.

VON WRIGHT, G. H. (1963). *The Varieties of Goodness*. London: Routledge & Kegan Paul.

ZIFF, P. (1960). *Semantic Analysis*. Ithaca, NY: Cornell University Press.

ZIMMERMAN, M. J. (2001). *The Nature of Intrinsic Value*. Oxford: Rowman & Littlefield.

12

Cognitivist Expressivism

Terry Horgan and Mark Timmons

Expressivism is a position in metaethics that is a descendant of noncognitivism—a view that was perhaps the dominant metaethical theory for about forty years, between 1935 and 1975.[1] The basic insight of the noncognitivists was that language can play a dynamic as well as a descriptive role in interpersonal interaction, and that moral discourse is a prime example of the dynamic use of language. According to one dominant strain of noncognitivism, *emotivism*, championed by A. J. Ayer and C. L. Stevenson, moral judgments function primarily to express one's feelings about some object of evaluation. In an interpersonal context, such expressions of feeling typically serve the dynamic function of influencing the attitudes of others. The other main variety of noncognitivism, *prescriptivism*, developed by R. M. Hare, took dynamic, imperatival utterances as a model for moral discourse, and thus emphasized the directive, action-guiding element of such discourse. Noncognitivism did come in for its share of criticism, depending on the version under scrutiny, but the bottom line seemed to be that this kind of view appears incompatible with what Allan Gibbard calls the 'objective pretensions' of moral thought and discourse, including the idea that moral judgments seem to be beliefs with assertible, truth-apt content. Emotivists and prescriptivists, because they took moral language to express noncognitive attitudes, were forced to explain away such pretensions. So, for instance, Carnap (1935: 25) held that 'a value statement is nothing else than a command in misleading grammatical form'. But noncognitivist attempts to explain away various deeply embedded features

For their help on this paper, we wish to thank Noell Birondo, Paul Bloomfield, David Chalmers, David Copp, Michael Gill, Uriah Kriegel, Mark Lance, John Tienson, and audiences at the University of Cincinnati, Harvard University, and Wake Forest University.

[1] Ayer's *Language, Truth and Logic* was published in 1936 and contained the first widely influential presentation of a noncognitivist metaethical theory. As Mary Warnock noted in her *Ethics since 1900*, 'It is part of the measure of the importance of [Ayer's] book that no sooner was it published than it seemed that emotivists were everywhere. They had not been converted by the book; it was their creed already' (1960: 84).

of moral thought and discourse have seemed implausible and indeed unnecessary to many moral philosophers.

In the late 1970s and on through the 1990s, some moral philosophers were tempted by moral realism, thinking that with the help of various developments in philosophy of mind and philosophy of language from the 1960s and early 1970s, one could countenance moral properties and facts and yet remain faithful to philosophical naturalism—the dominant metaphysic of the times. Also, metaethical history lately has been returning to its Moorean roots with some moral philosophers boldly defending versions of nonnaturalism.[2] But just as the past 100 years of metaethics has seen realism go and come back again, those working in the tradition of Stevenson and Hare (ourselves included) have devoted time and effort into reviving the spirit, if not the letter, of older noncognitivist positions. Recent work along these lines includes Simon Blackburn's quasi-realism, Gibbard's norm-expressivist view, and our own position, here labeled *cognitivist expressivism*. In some of our previous writings, we have either individually or collaboratively tried to make progress in articulating and defending our view. This paper is another installment in a series of works devoted to this project.

1. Preview of coming attractions

In the days of noncognitivism, the idea that moral judgments are not primarily descriptive of moral properties and facts (nondescriptivism), and the idea that moral judgments do not express beliefs (noncognitivism) were taken to be mutually entailing. Nondescriptivism and noncognitivism were a package deal. And the views *are* mutually entailing if one embraces the following claim, which we call the *semantic assumption*:

> SA   All cognitive content (i.e. belief-eligible, assertible, truth-apt
>   content) is descriptive content. Thus, all genuine beliefs and all
>   genuine assertions purport to represent or describe the world.[3]

The semantic assumption has been widely taken for granted in metaethics; it has framed much of the philosophical debate, and has constrained the range of

---

[2] We have in mind Shafer-Landau (2003) and Audi (2004).

[3] For present purposes we use 'represent' and 'describe' (and their variants) interchangeably. (This use of 'describe' is at work in metaethics when the label 'descriptivism' is deployed; it is wider in scope that the use in which 'descriptive' and 'normative' operate as contrast-terms.) Beliefs and assertions that 'purport to represent or describe the world' include ones with theological content, and can also include ones about abstract entities like numbers; so 'world' does not just mean 'physical world' or 'spatiotemporal world' or 'world of concrete particulars'.

options on the standard menu of competing positions. But this deeply entrenched piece of orthodoxy, we maintain, is false. Its falsity would mean that some metaethical space opens up (potentially anyway) for the combination of nondescriptivism and cognitivism.

We defend just such a view, claiming that although moral judgments are genuine beliefs, their overall content is not descriptive content. Moral judgments count as beliefs, despite being nondescriptive, because they possess enough of the key, generic, phenomenological, and functional features of belief (as well as satisfying the relevant platitudes governing the concept of belief) to qualify as genuine beliefs. We defend the claim that moral judgments are genuine beliefs in section 6 below.

In our previous writings, we have used different labels for our position, sometimes calling it 'assertoric nondescriptivism', sometimes calling it 'nondescriptivist cognitivism'. Gibbard (1990: 7–8) uses the term 'expressivism' to refer to metaethical views that take the primary role of moral judgments to be expressive of attitudes that do not purport to represent or describe some moral reality. So expressivism is committed to nondescriptivism about moral judgments and utterances. Expressivism thus subsumes old-time versions of noncognitivism. But it leaves open the possibility of a cognitivist construal of moral thought and discourse. Because the term 'expressivism' has taken hold, we are here calling our view *cognitivist* expressivism.

Cognitivist expressivism is very similar in spirit to Blackburn's more recent presentation of his quasi-realism—it is a metaethical project that embraces an austere irrealist moral metaphysics and yet attempts, in its semantic construal of moral terms and the concepts, to account for the deeply embedded features of moral thought and discourse. The main differences between our view and Blackburn's have to do with philosophical execution.[4]

In this paper we will not spend time explaining why we reject versions of moral realism, moral constructivism, moral relativism, the error theory, and noncognitivism. We have done that elsewhere.[5] Rather, we plan to articulate and defend our evolving metaethical view in a way that repackages key ideas from our prior writings while also going beyond our previous work in two important respects. First, we will dwell on matters of moral phenomenology— the 'what-it's-like-ness' of experiences involving moral judgment; we will

---

[4] Blackburn (1984: 167–71) refers to any philosophical view that regards the judgments of some discourse as 'expressive' as opposed to descriptive, an 'expressive theory' about that discourse. So his quasi-realism is a form of expressivism. And in more recent writings (1996) he explicitly distances his ethical expressivism from forms of noncognitivism. See also Blackburn (1998).

[5] For a very brief overview of the problems for such theories with references to our other work, see Horgan and Timmons (2005).

argue on one hand that this phenomenology supports the cognitivist contention that moral judgments are genuine beliefs, and on the other hand that such cognitive phenomenology also comports with the denial that the overall content of moral judgments is descriptive. Second, we will offer a more detailed account than we have provided before of how to accommodate certain crucial generic features of the psychological role of belief-states (and corresponding features of the interpersonal role of moral utterances)—features involving the embeddability of moral content within logically complex beliefs and sentences, and inferences employing beliefs and sentences with embedded moral content.

We begin with an insight to be found in G. E. Moore's metaethical reflections and, with Moore's guidance, we then proceed to develop and partially defend our view.

2. Moore on methodology

In *Principia Ethica*, Moore famously defended the idea that goodness is a 'simple, indefinable, unanalysable object of thought' (1903: 72). He also thought that 'real' definitions of terms—definitions that reveal the essential nature of their referent—are possible only when the term to be defined refers to something complex. Since the property of goodness is simple, having no parts, Moore claimed that 'good' cannot be defined.

The most important sense of 'definition' is that in which a definition states what are the parts which invariably compose a certain whole; and in this sense 'good' has no definition because it is simple and has no parts. It is one of those innumerable objects of thought which are themselves incapable of definition, because they are the ultimate terms by reference to which whatever *is* capable of definition must be defined. (1903: 61)

Often, the term 'irreducible' is used in connection with the idea that in some important sense it is not possible to analyze or define fundamental moral concepts and the terms that express them. Put in these terms, Moore thought that because the most fundamental concept in ethics, namely, goodness, refers to something simple, the concept (and the term expressing the concept) is irreducible.[6]

---

[6] It is worth noting that Moore himself thought that talk of what is intrinsically good is equivalent in meaning to talk about what *ought to exist* (1903: 33–4, 68, 166). So, roughly, the kind of reduction Moore was anxious to rebut would involve defining basic moral terms and concepts by using nonmoral terms and concepts.

We do not accept Moore's moral realism, and we do not accept his view that a moral term like 'good' refers to a property. But we do adhere to what we call 'Moore's methodological maxim': moral terms and concepts are irreducible. However, to say this does not mean that that nothing philosophically illuminating can be said about them (in addition to their being irreducible). R. M. Hare, for instance, had quite a lot to say about the semantics of moral terms and concepts, which, if true, is very illuminating. However, in making use of imperatives to understand moral language, Hare insisted that 'it is no part of my purpose to "reduce" moral language to imperatives' (Hare 1952: 2).[7] Rather than offer a reductive analysis of moral terms and concepts which would, in effect, express those terms and concepts in some sort of nonmoral idiom, Hare proposed to understand terms like 'ought' by exploring the 'logical behavior' of these words in ordinary language via similarities between such moral language and imperatives.

Of course, by taking imperative sentences as a model for the 'logical behavior' of moral terms and concepts, Hare did deny in effect that moral judgments are genuine beliefs and that moral utterances are genuine assertions. On his imperatival model, the declarative grammatical form of moral sentences is misleading, since declarative sentences normally are employed to make assertions and to express beliefs. So his metaethical position can be called *weakly* reductive in its use of nonassertoric, nondeclarative, sentences as a model of moral thought and language, even though it eschews the *strongly* reductive claim that moral utterances are synonymous with, or semantically interchangeable with, imperatives.

Like Hare, we propose to explore the meaning of moral terms like 'ought' by considering how such terms function in thought and language. But we plan to give more weight than did Hare to moral thought (as opposed to moral language), and we will give specific emphasis to matters of phenomenology. Also, again like Hare, we will argue that sentences with certain distinctive grammatical features are a useful model for understanding moral thought and discourse (namely, sentences in a specific sort of formal language, described in section 6). But our linguistic model will not be 'reductive' in even weak senses, because it fully accommodates the cognitivist claim that moral judgments are beliefs and moral utterances are assertions. In eschewing any sort of 'reductive' account of moral terms and concepts, we will be respecting Moore's (anti-reductive) methodological maxim.

In articulating and defending our view, we set for ourselves three main tasks that we will proceed to take up in order in the following sections.

Task I: Describe some key generic features of beliefs, and argue that moral judgments exhibit these features.

---

[7] See also Hare 1952: 180–1.

Task II: Explore some key distinctive characteristics of moral judgments
               in particular, as contrasted with ordinary nonmoral beliefs.

Task III: Set forth a theoretical account of belief that simultaneously
               (i) treats moral judgments as genuine beliefs, (ii) treats moral
               judgments as not descriptive in their overall content, (iii) accom-
               modates the key distinctive characteristics of moral judgments in
               a way that renders these features consistent with the claim that
               moral judgments are genuine beliefs, and (iv) accommodates the
               key generic features of belief in a way that is consistent with the
               denial that the overall content of moral beliefs is descriptive.

In the course of pursuing the first two tasks, certain specific challenges will
emerge that will need to be faced in addressing the third task: some of the distinctive features of moral judgments threaten the idea that these judgments are
genuine beliefs, whereas some of the generic features of belief exhibited by
moral judgments threaten the idea that these judgments are nondescriptive in
their overall content. These challenges will be noted as the first two tasks are
pursued, and will be addressed in the course of dealing with the third task.

By completing these tasks we will provide a presumptive case in favor of cognitivist expressivism, but there remain further issues and challenges that our
view must meet. Late in the paper, we consider some of the most pressing of
these, and we briefly explain how our view attempts to meet them.

3. Terminological preliminaries

Before proceeding, it will be useful to make some explicit remarks about matters of terminology. We begin with some observations about our use of 'moral
judgment'. First, we use this term in a metaethically neutral way to refer to those
psychological states whose contents are expressible by a moral sentence. Thus,
calling this sort of state a judgment leaves open whether it is a belief, a desire,
an intention, or some other psychological state. Below we argue that moral
judgments are most plausibly understood as beliefs. Second, like Mandelbaum
(1955: 46), our use of the term is intentionally broad in another way: what we
are calling moral judgments need not be psychologically inferential; they
might be psychologically spontaneous as when one just 'sees' that some action
is obligatory. Third, 'judgment' allows for process/product ambiguity in its
usage, i.e. between an episode of judging and being in the psychological state
resulting from a judging episode. Context should make clear how we are using
the term.

We have been using, and will continue to use, the currently widespread term 'content' in connection with moral judgments and utterances. We discuss content of various kinds: the *overall* content of a judgment or utterance (the content of the 'that'-clause employed to describe the state, or the sentence employed to express it), *cognitive* content (the kind of content that is belief-eligible and truth-apt), *descriptive* content (the kind of content that represents, or constitutes, a way the world might be), and *nondescriptive* content.

Although 'content'-talk is extremely natural and convenient in metaethics and in other branches of philosophy (as was 'meaning' talk in earlier decades), we stress that in relation to cognitivist expressivism, this terminology needs to be taken with a metaphysical grain of salt. On our account, talk of nondescriptive content is to be understood as not really positing any such *items* as overall contents or cognitive contents; likewise for generic talk of overall content and of cognitive content, construed as encompassing nondescriptive as well as descriptive content. (We will take up 'descriptive content' presently.) Rather, such talk is both syncategorematic and pleonastic.

It is *syncategorematic* in the sense that one can use such talk only in a fairly restricted, fairly specific, range of syntactic-grammatical contexts. One can talk about a psychological state or a declarative sentence as 'having cognitive content', about its 'having cognitive content that is not descriptive', and so forth. One can even use definite descriptions like 'the cognitive content of the belief', but only in certain specific kinds of sentential contexts (e.g. contexts like 'The overall content of his belief is that Jones ought to apologize'.) But such talk is not rightly construed as positing some *entity* that *is* a nondescriptive cognitive content. On our picture, there is no such entity.

Generic content-talk is *pleonastic* in this sense: it normally functions as a way of saying something that could pretty much be said some other way (although the other way needn't be outright *synonymous* with the original way). For example, saying that moral judgments, and the utterances expressing them, 'have cognitive content' is often, in effect, a way of saying that the judgments are genuine beliefs and that the utterances are genuine assertions. Likewise, saying that a psychological state has 'overall content' is often, in effect, a way of saying that it is a state describable via a mentalistic characterization employing a 'that'-clause construction.

Although such syncategorematic, pleonastic usage is very convenient, one can employ it as we do to facilitate communication and exposition even if one denies, as we do, that there are any such in-the-world *items* as nondescriptive contents. (Compare: One can sincerely utter the sentence 'He has a loud voice', and this sentence can be true, even though one's usage does not incur any ontological commitment to such in-the-world items as *voices*.) The claim that this terminology is 'ontologically lightweight' will receive theoretical justification from within our own metaethical position, as articulated below.

Talk of *descriptive* content, on the other hand, is a different matter, from our theoretical perspective. In this paper we will assume, at least provisionally, that there *are* such items as descriptive contents—ways the world might be, and or ways that some thing (or things) might be. Below we will invoke two kinds: (i) *propositional* descriptive contents, expressible in English via closed sentences like 'Snow is white', and (ii) *non-propositional* descriptive contents, expressible in quasi-English via open sentences like 'x is white'. We will leave it open how exactly to construe such items metaphysically.[8]

We now proceed to our three tasks.

4. Task I: key generic features of belief

We begin with some prototypical, generic, features of belief—features associated respectively with the phenomenology, the semantic assessability, and the functional role of beliefs. We begin with the former. By 'phenomenology of belief' as used here, we mean to refer to the sort of subjective, what-it-is-like experiential aspect of occurrent beliefs, something that unfortunately has largely been ignored by contemporary philosophers of mind.[9] In making various observations about the phenomenology of belief, we will be discussing ordinary nonmoral descriptive beliefs that most clearly purport to represent or

[8] Perhaps even talk of *descriptive* content ultimately should be construed as pleonastic, syncategorematic, and not ontologically committal. But even if this turns out to be so, such talk is still importantly different metaphysically from talk of nondescriptive content: sentences and psychological states 'with descriptive content' have in-the-world *truth-makers* of some sort, whereas utterances and psychological states 'with nondescriptive content' do not. That difference would need to be respected and reconstructed, within any ontological approach that treats talk of descriptive content as being syncategorematic and pleonastic itself.

[9] That occurrent beliefs have a distinctive phenomenology was recognized by Hume who thought this aspect of beliefs was crucial for understanding the difference between an occurrent belief with a certain content and various nonbelief states having the same content—states such as entertaining without believing. Hume distinguishes between the 'ideas' (roughly contents) and the manner of considering those ideas, and explains:

[B]elief consists not in the nature and order of our ideas, but in the manner of their conception, and in their feeling to the mind. I confess 'tis impossible to explain perfectly this feeling or manner of conception. We make use of words, that express something near it. But its true and proper name is *belief*, which is a term that every one sufficiently understands in common life. And in philosophy we can go no farther, than assert, that it is something *felt* by the mind, which distinguishes the ideas of the judgment from the fictions of imagination. It gives them more force and influence; makes them appear of greater importance; infixes them in the mind; and renders them the governing principles of all our actions. (1739: 629)

Hume, of course, attempts to use the features of force and vivacity to explain the nature of belief. Although we agree with Hume that belief has a distinctive phenomenology, we do not follow him in trying to make sense of this phenomenology (and associated functional role) in terms of force and vivacity.

describe some aspect of the world. But we will also be discussing occurrent moral ought-judgments, calling attention to those phenomenological features that they share with nonmoral descriptive beliefs and which (together with considerations of semantic assessability and functional role) we claim qualify them as genuine beliefs.

The phenomenology of belief

Here, then, is a list of five interrelated features of what we are calling the phenomenology of occurrent belief. This what-it-is-likeness typically involves: (1) psychologically 'coming down' on some issue, in a way that (2) classifies (sometimes spontaneously) some 'object' of focus as falling under some category, where one's classificatory coming down is experienced (3) as involuntary, (4) as a cognitive response to some sort of consideration that is experienced (perhaps peripherally in consciousness) as being a sufficient reason for categorizing as one does, and (5) as a judgment that is apt for assertion and hence is naturally expressible in public language by a sentence in the declarative mood. Each of these elements of phenomenology requires comment.

Occurrent belief involves the experience of 'coming down' on some issue, where this manner of coming down may be preceded by some amount of reflection, as when one is looking up at the October night sky and taking a close look at a very bright celestial object and, after staring for a moment, comes to believe that it is Mars. But very often belief comes about as an automatic response to one's surroundings, as when one catches a glimpse of a passing car while watering the lawn. In this kind of case, by spontaneously and unreflectively taking it to be a car, one spontaneously psychologically comes down with respect to the object-kind instantiated by a moving object passing through one's field of vision.

Turn now to all-things-considered occurrent ought-judgments. One obvious feature of so judging is that one experiences this activity as a matter of psychologically 'coming down' on whatever issue is under consideration. As with descriptive beliefs, coming down with respect to some moral issue may be preceded by deliberation. After listening to various opposing opinions about the morality of same-sex marriages, Jones finds himself accepting the view that such marriages are not morally wrong and that therefore a government ought not to make such unions illegal. Jones, we are supposing, is initially undecided about this issue, but later and in light of reflecting on various facts about same-sex marriages, finds himself 'coming down' on one side of the issue. Of course, many of our moral judgments, like descriptive beliefs, are formed spontaneously: they are triggered immediately in experience. Harman's (1977: 4) famous example of seeing some hoodlums igniting a cat and, without deliberation, coming to think that what they are doing is wrong, is a case in point. In such cases, one's moral judgment is experienced as a fairly unreflective and immediate 'coming down' morally with respect to what one sees. Indeed, here people often talk about just 'seeing' an action as wrong.

Clearly, making decisions and forming intentions are likewise experienced as coming down with respect to some issue. Since intentions are not beliefs (we are supposing), the experience of psychologically coming down is not alone a sufficient phenomenological indicator of belief. The kind of psychological coming down that seems fairly distinctive of belief, as opposed to intention-forming and the like, involves experiencing perceived or contemplated items as falling under categories. Things get *sorted* experientially, when one comes down on a matter in the belief-wise way. In the case of descriptive beliefs, things get sorted experientially into descriptive categories, via category-concepts that purport to represent some worldly object-kind or some property. Likewise, in the case of a moral judgment that some action ought not to be done, a particular act-type or act-token gets sorted experientially into the category of those actions that one is not to perform. We claim that the sorting/categorizing aspect is central to the phenomenology of belief.

Another salient phenomenological feature of beliefs is their involuntariness. One looks out the window and spontaneously and involuntarily believes that the sun is shining. Sometimes reflection precedes one's involuntarily coming down on some issue. After mulling over various bits of evidence concerning a mechanical failure, a trained mechanic involuntarily comes to believe that the failure was due to a faulty oil pump. After inspecting the evidence, she just sees what must have caused the failure. Regarding ought-beliefs, we have already mentioned Harman's case of unreflectively and spontaneously coming to have a moral belief about the hoodlums, as well as a case in which Jones comes to have a belief about same-sex marriages preceded by some amount of reflection.[10]

Related to the involuntariness of beliefs is the fact that they are experienced as possessing a kind of *rational authority*, consisting in their being grounded by *reasons*. In the case of ordinary nonmoral perceptual beliefs about objects and their properties, this experienced authority issues from one's perceptual experiences. In moving my hand across the desk, I feel its smoothness and spontaneously come to believe that it is smooth. The confidence I experience in having this belief is arguably part of the overall experience of occurrently

---

[10] The spontaneity involved in both moral and nonmoral expertise is a major theme in Dewey (1922), and is stressed in Dreyfus and Dreyfus (1990) and Varela (1992).

believing and partly explains why involuntarily psychologically coming down, rather than just entertaining a corresponding hypothesis, is appropriate. Similarly, the experience of morally coming down on some issue includes experiencing this state as possessing a kind of rational authority—an authority grounded in factual considerations that are experienced as rationally grounding one's moral judgment. In matters of morality, it is not 'up to' an individual what to think about some matter of moral concern, just as it is not 'up to' someone what to think about some nonmoral factual matter of concern. Sometimes this feature of phenomenology is put in terms of the idea that judgments of moral obligation have an 'external' authoritative source, just as do nonmoral factual beliefs. It is by dwelling further on the phenomenology of moral authoritativeness that one can begin to distinguish ought-beliefs from nonmoral descriptive beliefs, which, as we shall see, leads to considerations of the distinctive functional role of such beliefs. We save further discussion of these matters for the next section.

Finally, the categorizing manner of psychologically coming down, in occurrent belief, is experienced as a mental affirmation that is *apt for assertion*, and thus is experienced as being naturally and spontaneously expressible in public language by a sentence in the declarative mood.[11] Declarative-mood sentences are the standard public-language vehicles employed for the speech acts of asserting.

To sum up so far: There are a number of phenomenological features characteristic of belief as a distinct state type. These experiential features are possessed by moral judgments, and so there is good prima facie reason for claiming that such judgments are beliefs.

Prima facie, these very features can easily seem to require a construal of moral judgments and moral utterances as being descriptive in their overall content—or at least as *purporting* to be descriptive, even if there are no in-the-world moral properties or facts. How, one might wonder, can one make good sense of the classificatory, involuntary, reason-based, coming-down-ish, phenomenology of moral judgments—including the experience of such judgments as being apt for assertion—except by supposing that their overall content is descriptive in purport? Addressing this challenge will be part of Task III.

Semantic assessability

It is grammatically permissible, and also common in practice, to ascribe truth and falsity to moral judgments and statements. Such judgments and statements thus appear to be *semantically assessable*. Furthermore, truth ascription seems entirely

---

[11] This aspect of belief is a case where the phenomenon we are pointing to is plausibly understood as involving both phenomenological and functional role features.

natural and appropriate, given the belief-ish features of moral phenomenology lately noted. If one definitively 'comes down' on the apartheid issue by finding oneself having formed a judgment expressible as 'Apartheid is wrong', and one expresses this moral judgment by asserting that apartheid is wrong, then one will also think, and will be ready to assert, that it's *true* that apartheid is wrong.

Semantic assessability presents an obvious challenge to moral irrealists: making sense of truth ascription and falsity ascription within a general approach that treats moral judgments, and the declarative sentences expressing them, as having overall content that is not descriptive content. We need to deal persuasively, within our cognitivist expressivism, with the line of thought that says, 'Well, if moral judgments lack descriptive, way-the-world-might-be, content, then their content cannot *correspond* or *fail to correspond* with how things really are; so, such judgments cannot *really* be either true or false, even though people often apply the terms "true" and "false" to them in ordinary discourse'. Addressing this challenge too will be part of Task III.

Functional role

Beliefs are often characterized functionally as being psychological states that combine in distinctive ways with other psychological states to rationally-inferentially yield further content-appropriate states as well as action. This is at least a partial characterization of their typical functional role, which is clearly illustrated in cases where one's belief combines with one's desires leading one to form intentions (assuming that intentions represent a distinct kind of psychological state)—both long term and short term. Intentions in turn lead to action. My desire to eat a taco for lunch together with my belief that Taco del Cielo is around the corner (as well as a host of other content-appropriate beliefs and desires) combine to yield an intention to go to Taco del Cielo in a few minutes.

The *generic* rational-inferential functional role of beliefs is a matter that needs to be approached with some care, in our view. Although *descriptive* beliefs do typically generate intentions and actions only in combination with conative states like desires, *moral* beliefs—if such there be—might very well have somewhat different prototypical functional roles in human mental life. (More on this in section 6.) However, one crucially important and fully generic aspect of the rational-inferential role of beliefs is this:

> The overall content of any given belief can occur as an *embedded content-constituent* of other, logically more complex beliefs; and beliefs with such embedded content-constituents interact with other beliefs to generate new beliefs via logical relations among their contents (specifically, via logical-entailment relations).

We will call this feature *logical embeddability*. A familiar example is the following piece of moral reasoning:

> If it's wrong to steal, then it's wrong to get your little brother to steal.
> It's wrong to steal.
> Therefore, it's wrong to get your little brother to steal.

Logical embeddability has often been posed as a challenge to noncognitivist positions. If what one is really doing in making a moral utterance is something like expressing an attitude of disapproval or issuing a command, then how exactly can one make sense of utterances in which moral content occurs embedded, like the first premise in the argument just above? And how can one make sense of the judgments expressed by such utterances?

Whatever one might think of the prospects for dealing with this challenge within traditional noncognitivism, our own challenge is a different one, namely, to make sense of the relevant, logically complex psychological states as full-fledged *beliefs*, and to make sense of logical-inferential relations involving such beliefs, without supposing that moral belief-content is descriptive content.

This challenge is closely related to the preceding one about semantic evaluability. Inferential connections among beliefs (and among sentences) are normally explained in terms of truth and falsity: if the beliefs that are the premises of an argument are true, then the belief that is the conclusion must be true (in the case of logical entailment) or must be made likely to be true by the premises (in the case of cogent inductive reasoning). Accommodating logical embeddability thus goes hand in glove with accommodating truth-aptness. Yet another burden for Task III.

This completes our first task of exploring the key generic features of belief while at the same time calling attention to the fact that moral judgments exhibit these features. As we have been saying, this creates at least a strong prima facie case for genuine moral belief—while also posing various challenges needing to be addressed by our cognitivist expressivism. We now turn to various phenomenological and associated functional role characteristics that are distinctive of moral judgments, with specific attention to moral ought-judgments. (Hereafter we will explicitly call these judgments *beliefs*.)

5. Task II: the distinctive nature of ought-beliefs

As noted already, beliefs generally, and moral beliefs in particular, are experienced as grounded by a kind of rational authority. Talk of 'rational authority' while suggestive is quite vague, at least so far. But we can begin to illuminate this idea by dwelling further on matters of moral phenomenology.

In characterizing the experienced authority attendant to first-person ought-beliefs, we follow the lead of Maurice Mandelbaum who, in his 1955 *The Phenomenology of Moral Experience*, distinguished what he called 'direct' from 'removed' judgments of moral obligation. Direct moral beliefs (judgments) are first-person ought-beliefs, formed in some context in which the agent experiences a 'felt demand' on her own behavior, while removed ought-beliefs are about what someone else (including one's past self) ought to do or ought to have done. For the time being, we will focus on direct ought-beliefs, making passing references to removed ought-beliefs. Later, in section 8, we will return to the latter type of ought-belief.

Mandelbaum characterizes the felt demand involved in direct moral ought-beliefs as a complex phenomenon involving the experience of an *origin* and a *direction*. In judging that I ought to perform some action—that the action is morally obligatory upon me—I experience a felt demand placed upon my choices and consequent action *issuing from* the circumstances that I confront (at least as I believe them to be). Thus, phenomenologically, one experiences the demand as having an origin that is 'external' to oneself. It is this element of the kind of felt demand characteristic of judgments of moral obligation that distinguishes moral demands from the felt demands that are experienced as having one's own 'internal' desires or preferences as their origin. So, whereas one's own desires may issue forth in a kind of 'internal' felt demand for their satisfaction by the agent who has them, the demandingness associated with a judgment of moral obligation is 'external', coming from, as it were, the morally relevant facts of the circumstances in which one finds oneself on some occasion. This aspect of one's moral experience constitutes, then, the particular manner in which moral ought-judgments are experienced as being grounded in 'objective' reasons. Such reasons are factual considerations confronting the agent that she takes to be morally significant. These considerations are experienced as themselves demanding a certain course of action; they are, as Mandelbaum puts it, the 'origin' in the phenomenology of felt demandingness.

The so-called direction of a felt demand has to do with whom, relative to the judger, the obligation is directed against. In direct ought-judgments, the obligation is directed against the judger herself; this is what Mandelbaum calls a 'reflexive demand'. By contrast, removed judgments of moral obligation are experienced as directed against someone other than the individual making the judgment. This element of the phenomenology of the experience of direct ought-beliefs brings us to issues having to do with their distinctive functional role.

Certain kinds of moral belief—direct ought-beliefs in particular—typically play a motivationally 'hot' functional role in human mental life: they have motivational force in and of themselves, apart from any pre-existing desires or other 'pro-attitudes'. The thought that first-person ought-beliefs are more directly action-oriented than are ordinary nonmoral descriptive beliefs is what inspires various forms of ethical internalism. This thought seems right and important, even though a proper characterization of internalism—one that allows, for instance, for the conceptual possibility of an 'amoralist' with moral beliefs that have no motivational force at all—is a delicate matter.

Also, even though ought-beliefs are typically hot cognitions and thus need not combine with a pre-existing desire in order to provide sufficient motivation to action, a sensible internalism should allow that, at least in atypical cases, such ought-beliefs can work in concert with desire to produce action. Suppose, for instance, that normally Joe's judging that he ought to do something is sufficient to move him to action. However, on some occasions, where Joe is perhaps suffering from mild depression, his having a direct ought-belief will only move him if he has certain content-appropriate desires which serve to provide a supplemental motivational spark strong enough to move Joe to do his duty. Perhaps Joe has a strong desire to maintain a certain self-image, so strong that even in a state of mild depression his focusing on this desire of his, together with his belief that failing to do what he ought would seriously damage his self-image, moves him to act. So, even though direct ought-beliefs have as part of their typical functional role a direct motivational force independent of any pre-existing desires, such psychological states are still capable of combining with prior desires to yield intention and subsequent action.

To sum up: we saw in the previous section that general phenomenological considerations support the claim that moral judgments are genuine beliefs: they involve an involuntary, categorizing, way of psychologically coming down on some issue of moral concern, on the basis of considerations that are experienced as rationally requiring the judgment—where this judgment is experienced as truth-apt and hence as naturally expressed in thought and language by sentences in the declarative mood. Moreover, the overall contents of moral judgments can occur as embedded constituents in logically complex judgments, which then can combine with other judgments to logically-inferentially generate new judgments. These are key generic features of belief. The presumptive case for moral belief is thus strong.

However, moral judgments and, in particular, direct ought-judgments exhibit some distinctive phenomenological and functional role characteristics too; in particular, typically they are motivationally hot. So yet another challenge to be addressed as part of task III is to explain how such judgments, despite sometimes being motivational all by themselves, nonetheless can be full-fledged beliefs. This brings us to our third task—the task of sketching a framework for belief that can accommodate what we have been saying about belief in general and moral belief in particular and which treats moral beliefs as nondescriptive in their overall content.

6. Task III: a framework for belief[12]

Earlier we noted that one deeply entrenched assumption of metaethics and philosophical enquiry generally—the *semantic assumption*, as we call it—is that *all* beliefs are descriptive beliefs. We reject this assumption. Having made our prima facie case for moral belief, we turn now to the task of providing a general framework for understanding belief (and also assertion) which incorporates beliefs (and assertions) whose overall content is not descriptive—i.e. does not purport to represent the world as being a certain way.

Two logically fundamental belief types: is-commitment and ought-commitment

We begin with the logically most basic kinds of belief, leaving embeddability matters until later. On the account we recommend, a belief is a certain kind of *commitment state*—an *affirmatory* commitment—with respect to a descriptive content that we call the belief's *core* descriptive content. There are two logically fundamental belief types: *is*-commitment with respect to a core descriptive content, and *ought*-commitment with respect to a core descriptive content. For example, the belief that *it is the case that Bush is US president*, and the belief that *it ought to be the case that Bush is US president*, are respectively an is-commitment and ought-commitment vis-à-vis the same core descriptive content, namely, *that Bush is US president*. (In the case of the ought-commitment, the core descriptive content, *that Bush is US president*, differs from the belief's overall content, *that it ought to be the case that Bush is US president*; and this overall content is not itself descriptive. In the case of the is-commitment, on the other hand, the core descriptive content coincides with the overall content, namely, *that Bush is US president*.[13])

---

[12] This and the following two sections derive partly, but with significant refinements, from sections I and III–V of Horgan and Timmons (2000*a*).

[13] The 'that'-clause 'that Bush is US President' expresses a *way the world might be*, as does the 'that'-clause 'that Gore is US president'. Neither clause says that the world *is* the way expressed (or that the world *ought* to be the way expressed), because 'that'-clauses by themselves don't have assertoric force.

These two species of belief, involving two distinct ways of mentally affirming a core descriptive content, are both *sui generis*: neither type of mental state is reducible to the other, and neither type is reducible to some kind of nonbelief state such as an attitude of approval or a mental state appropriately expressible via an imperative sentence. The way to understand the nature of the beliefs we are calling ought-commitments is not by trying to reduce them to something else, but rather by delineating their key features—both the generic features they share in common with descriptive beliefs (is-commitments), and the distinctive features that set them apart from descriptive beliefs. This is just what we have lately been doing, in the course of addressing Task I and Task II.

Recall that Task III was formulated as follows: Set forth a theoretical account of belief that simultaneously (i) treats moral judgments as genuine beliefs, (ii) treats moral judgments as not descriptive in their overall content, (iii) accommodates the key distinctive characteristics of moral judgments in a way that renders these features consistent with the claim that moral judgments are genuine beliefs, and (iv) accommodates the key generic features of belief in a way that is consistent with the denial that the overall content of moral beliefs is descriptive. Part (i) is addressed by what we have just said, in conjunction with our treatment of Task I in section 4 above: a moral judgment is an ought-commitment with respect to a core descriptive content, and ought-commitments are a species of belief because they possess the key generic features of belief described in section 4.

Concerning part (ii), the crucial point is that ought-commitment is a fundamentally different kind of affirmatory mental stance toward a core descriptive content than is-commitment. An ought-commitment is not a mental state whose overall content is descriptive, representing a way the world might be; hence it is not a state of mentally affirming that the world *is* such a descriptively represented way. To construe moral beliefs in this manner is to mistakenly assimilate them to descriptive beliefs, i.e. to is-commitments. Rather, an ought-commitment is a *distinct* kind of mental affirmation vis-à-vis a core descriptive content. Although there is a certain temptation to assimilate ought-commitments to nonbelief states of the sort expressible linguistically by nondeclarative utterances like 'That Bush is US president, boo!', or 'US citizens, do not elect Bush as US president!', this temptation should be resisted—and can be, once one gives up the semantic assumption. Ought-commitment is a *sui generis* type of mental state, while also being an irreducible species of belief. Although the overall content of ought-commitments is nondescriptive, nevertheless these states exhibit the key generic features that qualify them as beliefs.

Concerning part (iii), the motivationally 'hot' psychological role typically played by first-person ought-judgments now gets smoothly accommodated.

Although this feature makes trouble for the idea that moral judgments are beliefs insofar as one assumes that all beliefs have overall content that is descriptive, it makes no trouble at all for us, because our framework rejects the semantic assumption SA and treats ought-commitments as a distinctive species of belief whose overall content is nondescriptive. Motivational hotness is an important aspect of what *constitutes* ought-commitment in typical cases—although we think that an adequate moral psychology also should allow for cases in which the typical motivational force of moral belief is outweighed, or suppressed, or even silenced altogether by other psychological states of the agent.

Part (iv) of Task III will require more extensive treatment. We will segment the discussion into several subsections that address respectively the three challenges noted earlier in discussing Tasks I and II: accommodating the phenomenology of belief, accommodating truth-aptness, and accommodating the key generic functional-role feature of belief, namely, inferential embeddability.

Accommodating the phenomenology of belief

In section 4 we described some key generic phenomenological features of belief, and we argued that moral judgments exhibit these features. Is the possession of these characteristics consistent with the contention that moral judgments are ought-commitments whose overall content is nondescriptive?

Indeed it is. One can experience an occurrent ought-commitment as an involuntary, classificatory, coming-down state vis-à-vis some descriptive content, even though the overall content of this state is not descriptive. The phenomenologically classificatory aspect of this coming-down state, expressible in language via moral terminology (e.g. via 'ought'), need not be a matter of experiencing oneself to be mentally attributing some putatively in-the-world moral *property* to some act, agent, or state of affairs. Rather, it can perfectly well be the experiential manifestation of the specific *mode of affirmatory commitment* that the agent now instantiates with respect to the given descriptive content—namely, ought-commitment.

Likewise, an occurrent ought-commitment can be based psychologically upon descriptive considerations that are experienced as *rationally grounding* this commitment state independently of the morally judging agent's pre-existing desires, even though the overall content of the commitment-state is not descriptive.

Furthermore, an occurrent ought-commitment can be experienced as apt for assertion by virtue of its involuntarily classificatory phenomenology and its experienced authority, despite not being descriptive in its overall content.

So, since the declarative grammatical mood is the appropriate linguistic vehicle for assertion, and since a sincere assertion is normally a belief-expressing speech act, it is no surprise that occurrent ought-commitments are experienced as psychological states appropriately expressible linguistically via declarative sentences.

In short, the generic phenomenological features in virtue of which moral judgments count as beliefs can perfectly well be present even if, as we maintain, moral beliefs are ought-commitments whose overall content is nondescriptive. These phenomenological features do not, in and of themselves, build descriptivity into moral judgment.

It remains possible even so, however, that the phenomenology of moral judgment does include descriptivity, even though the phenomenological features described in section 4 do not *themselves* entail it. That is, it remains possible that the full what-it's-like of classificatory coming-down, in moral judgment, includes the experience of *predicating a putative in-the-world moral property*. Well, does it in fact include such an experiential dimension?

Introspection, we submit, yields no ready or obvious answer to this question. Moral belief is experientially much like descriptive belief, to be sure: both kinds of state involve the experience of involuntary, classificatory, coming-down that is based upon considerations as grounding-reasons. But beyond this patent and powerful phenomenological similarity in the two kinds of belief, can one also detect introspectively that moral belief is clearly like—or clearly *unlike*—descriptive belief with respect to descriptivity *per se*? It seems not, either way. Rather, the presence or absence of descriptivity as an aspect of the phenomenology of moral belief is a subtle question about which introspection does not deliver a confident judgment.

This being so, wider theoretical considerations weigh in on the matter. For one thing, there is no particular reason why moral phenomenology *should* include descriptivity, given its functional role in human cognitive economy and given the sociological role of moral discourse in human social intercourse. On the contrary: since there are powerful theoretical reasons for denying the existence of in-the-world moral properties and facts, the presence of descriptivity within moral phenomenology would constitute a built-in experiential *error* with respect to the nature of external reality. Since descriptivity would be a gratuitous and erroneous aspect of moral phenomenology, probably it is not really an aspect of moral phenomenology at all.

Another theoretical consideration in support of this conclusion is the fact that first-person moral judgments typically are motivationally hot, despite qualifying as genuine beliefs. Descriptivity, though, would not comport smoothly with this distinctive motivational role. Why should a belief concerning putative in-the-world facts of any kind, qua *factual* belief, be intrinsically motivating? Surely it comports better with the motivational role of moral judgments to say that they are beliefs of a different, *non-factual*, kind: namely, non-descriptive ought-commitments.

These theoretical considerations are not conclusive, admittedly. The question whether moral phenomenology includes an aspect of descriptivity strikes us as ultimately empirical—albeit an issue whose investigation would need to be methodologically very subtle, and might well need to incorporate especially careful introspection. But meanwhile, two key points need emphasis.

First, we take it that the dialectical burden is on those who would claim that moral phenomenology *does* include descriptivity; they need to make a case for this claim, given that simple introspection delivers no clear verdict either way.

Second, even if it should turn out that descriptivity is indeed an aspect of moral phenomenology, this would not be terribly damaging to our metaethical position. Although we would then be forced to claim that there is an erroneous *element* in moral phenomenology, this would not undercut our contention that moral judgments already qualify as beliefs anyway, for reasons independent of their descriptivity—the reasons set out earlier in this paper. Nor would it undercut our claim that moral judgments are a distinctive species of belief, namely, ought-commitments. Qua ought-commitments, moral judgments would be a *sui generis* kind of belief already, even if they turned out *also* to be erroneous is-commitments that mistakenly predicate putative in-the-world moral properties. And they would still play a crucial and legitimate action-guiding role in human psychology.[14]

One final point. Moral phenomenology may very well be susceptible to influence by higher-order beliefs about the nature of morality itself. Certainly many people believe that there are objective moral facts—a belief that can easily be instilled, for instance, through the persistent intertwining of religious

---

[14] J. L. Mackie's version of error theory is much more philosophically problematic than would be the kind of error theory just described, because Mackie in effect construed moral judgments as being *only* descriptive beliefs whose contents involve putatively in-the-world moral properties. If that's all there is to being a moral belief, and if there are no such properties, then it becomes hard to see why moral thought and moral discourse are not so hugely mistaken that they should be abandoned altogether. But if moral beliefs are also ought-commitments with respect to core descriptive contents, then moral beliefs and moral assertions have important, legitimate, and indeed indispensable psychological and sociological roles to play even if they also include an erroneous aspect of descriptivity.

Also worth noting is that moral realists too could accept our contention that moral judgments are ought-commitments, and could accept that ought-commitments are a distinctive, *sui generis* species of belief. A moral realist could claim that a moral judgment is *both* an is-commitment with respect to its overall content *and* an ought-commitment with respect to its core descriptive content. This approach would have the advantage, for moral realists, of allowing them to acknowledge the internalist aspects of moral judgment. For further discussion of this theme, with explicit attention to the reasons for preferring our own cognitivist expressivism to such a view, see Horgan and Timmons (2000*a*), especially section V.

instruction with moral education. For those who believe (perhaps only implicitly) in objective moral facts, there may well arise a derivative kind of moral phenomenology—induced by the interaction of this higher-order belief with the more universal aspects of moral experience—that does include descriptivity. But even if such erroneous moral phenomenology sometimes occurs by virtue of the permeating effects of false beliefs about the metaphysics of morals, we contend that the more fundamental, more universal, kind of moral experience does not include an aspect of phenomenological descriptivity.

Accommodating semantic assessability

The concepts of belief, assertion, and truth are interconnected by a battery of platitudes. For example, to sincerely assert some claim is to express one's belief regarding that claim; to believe a claim is to take that claim to be true; and so forth. Since, on our view, moral judgments are genuine beliefs and moral utterances are genuine assertions, our position must be able to make sense of attributions of truth and falsity to moral judgments and utterances. Since we advocate a robust form of irrealism in ethics, we claim there are no in-the-world moral facts that could serve as truth-makers for moral beliefs and assertions. Moreover, since we are nondescriptivists about moral thought and discourse, we claim that moral beliefs and assertions lack overall descriptive content and so we maintain that they are not in the business of purporting to represent or describe the world: we are not error theorists. So the challenge for us is to make sense of truth in ethics.

Our fundamental contention, in addressing this challenge, is that truth ascriptions to statements and judgments with moral content are *morally engaged* semantic appraisals—i.e. appraisals in which semantic evaluation is 'fused' with moral evaluation. These truth ascriptions thus are not *descriptive*, because the overall content of the first-order judgments and utterances to which they are applied is not descriptive. That the notion of truth should be employable in a nondescriptive, morally engaged way is to be expected (given our irrealist construal of moral concepts), since ordinary uses of the truth predicate normally operate in accordance with schema T. Since first-order moral judgments and utterances have overall content that is not descriptive, the accompanying truth ascriptions governed by schema T inherit this same feature.

Although the point just made suffices to accommodate semantic assessability within our cognitivist expressivist position, we think there is quite a lot more to say about the notion of truth in general and about its various uses with respect to matters moral. Here we will briefly sketch some further views of ours on these matters that are developed at greater length elsewhere (cf. Horgan 2001 and other papers cited therein; Horgan and Timmons 2002, 2006; Timmons 1999: ch. 4). We mention these additional claims partly because we think they speak to various potential concerns regarding our position, and partly because we think they smoothly situate the morally engaged form of truth-ascription within an independently plausible general conception of how the notion of truth operates.

First, although in many contexts it is appropriate to employ the truth pre-dicate in a morally engaged way in which one's truth ascriptions run in tandem with one's first-order moral beliefs and assertions, there are also contexts in which it instead becomes appropriate to engage in morally *detached* semantic assessment. Under this usage, truth is a matter of correspondence to the world, and falsity is a matter of noncorrespondence: a judgment or assertion is true or false if and only if it has objective truth conditions, and otherwise it lacks truth value. (It is true if the world satisfies those truth conditions—this is correspondence—and it is false if the world fails to satisfy them—noncorrespondence.) When the notion of truth is being employed in the morally detached, correspondence-requiring manner, the proper thing to say about moral judgments and assertions is that they are neither true nor false.

Second, first-order moral judgments and assertions, and likewise morally engaged truth ascriptions, are typically *categorical* in content. Although they are made from within a morally engaged stance in which one brings one's own moral standards to bear, they are not implicitly relativized to those standards themselves. Relativism, about first-order moral claims and/or about truth ascriptions to such claims, seriously misconstrues their content. In effect, relat-ivism of this sort conflates morally engaged and morally detached usage, by mistakenly treating engaged usage as a form of detached usage that incorp-orates implicit relativization to some specific set of moral standards.

Third, we advocate a general approach to concept–world and language–world relations, and to the notion of truth, that we call *contextual semantics*. Some leading ideas are these. (1) Truth is *semantically correct affirmability*, under contextually operative semantic standards; falsity is semantically correct deniability, under such standards. (2) Numerous concepts and terms, includ-ing the concept of truth itself, are governed by contextually variable semantic standards of correct affirmability/deniability—where contextual variation can occur not only across different subject matters, but even within thought or discourse about a specific subject matter (e.g. morals). (3) Sometimes the contextually operative semantic standards are *tight*, i.e. these standards con-spire with how things are in the world to render a given judgment or statement correctly affirmable or correctly deniable. (4) Thought and discourse governed by semantically tight standards is descriptive. (5) Uses of the truth predicate (and the falsity predicate) governed by semantically tight standards express correspondence (or noncorrespondence) to the world. (6) Sometimes the contextually operative semantic standards are not tight. (7) Thought and discourse governed by semantically non-tight standards is nondescriptive in its overall content. (8) Uses of the truth predicate (and the falsity predicate) governed by non-tight standards do not express correspondence or (or noncorrespondence) to the world; when applied to moral thought and discourse, such truth ascriptions are fused semantic/normative appraisals.[15]

Fourth, given the general framework of contextual semantics, it would be far too crude to say that the detached and the engaged forms of semantic appraisal involve 'different concepts of truth' or 'different meanings of the word "true"'. Contextual variation in operative semantic standards, both at the first-order level and at the level of truth ascription, is a much more subtle matter. The same concept and the same meaning *persist* across such variation despite identity-preserving changes from one context to another, in something like the way a single person persists through time even while undergoing identity-preserving changes.

Logical embedding: accommodating the generic functional role of belief

How is logical embedding to be explained, within cognitivist expressivism? We will now sketch the leading ideas of the account we recommend. We provide further elaboration of technical details, plus further commentary, in the Appendix.

Suppose that an agent, Tom, has a logically complex belief—say, the belief that *either Dick is cheerful or Harry ought to apologize*. This belief does not

---

[15] Another key thesis of contextual semantics is that tight semantic standards often operate in such a way that a statement can be correctly affirmable under such standards—i.e. true—even though there are no in-the-world objects or properties answering directly to the statement's singular terms, predicates, or unnegated existential quantifications. Such *indirect* correspondence, as we call it, does involve in-the-world truth-makers (and falsity-makers), but the truth-making conditions need not include items in the world answering directly to the given statement's referential apparatus. (For instance, the statement 'Mozart composed 27 piano concertos' can be true even if the objectively correct ontology does not include such items as piano concertos.) Indirect correspondence is very important with respect to the ontological commitments of statements governed by tight semantic standards. But for present purposes it is secondary, because we claim that the semantic standards at work in the engaged use of moral concepts are non-tight; this means that moral statements lack even the *indirect* kind of correspondence (or noncorrespondence) to reality. For a treatment of truth and objectivity with substantial similarity to our own contextual semantics, see Wright (1992). Wright, however, seriously flirts with the idea of reducing truth to an idealized form of *epistemically* warranted affirmability that he calls 'superassertibility', whereas we maintain that semantically correct affirmability cannot be reduced to any form of epistemically warranted affirmability however idealized (cf. Horgan 1995, 1996).

contain an 'embedded is-commitment' or an 'embedded ought-commitment', whatever those might be. In holding this belief, Tom is not is-committed to the content *that Dick is cheerful*, and is not ought-committed to the content *that Harry apologizes*. Rather, the belief state is a *logically complex commitment state*, one that obtains with respect to these core descriptive contents jointly. It is a *disjunctive* commitment state.

Crucial and essential to such a logically complex commitment state, on the view we are here suggesting, is its distinctive *constitutive inferential role* in the cognitive economy of a cognitive agent (insofar as the agent does not exhibit lapses in logical competence). Such a state is one that is poised to interact with other potential beliefs to inferentially generate yet further beliefs that are inferentially 'in the offing.' For instance, if Tom occurrently has the disjunctive belief about Dick and Harry, and Tom also occurrently has the belief that Dick is not cheerful, these two beliefs together should inferentially generate (insofar as Tom does not exhibit a rationality failure) the occurrent belief that Harry ought to apologize. (Note that such inferential processes have a phenomenological aspect too; there is *something that it's like* to consciously recognize such logical connections, and there is something that it is like for such inferences to occur in conscious experience.) The constitutive inferential role of logically complex beliefs also includes combining with other beliefs to yield certain *implicit*, logically grounded, further commitment states—even if these remain implicit and perhaps fail to be psychologically operative in the agent.

Constitutive inferential role is a matter of logical consequence relations among various beliefs. So we need to provide a way of construing the logical consequence relation among belief-commitments of the various kinds: is-commitments, ought-commitments, and logically complex commitments. We will do so in three steps: first, describing a formal language whose logical syntax overtly models the various types of belief-commitment posited by our account; second, providing formal semantics for sentences of this language, including a definition of the relation of logical consequence; and third, explaining how this formal semantics comports with our above-described treatment of the semantic assessability of moral beliefs and assertions. (This three-step account is sketched in this section and then developed more fully in the Appendix.)

Step 1. The formal language we propose employs two affirmatory-force operators, I[ ] and O[ ], whose respective analogues in English are the constructions 'It is the case...' and 'It ought to be the case...' The familiar atomic formulas of predicate logic here are construed not as sentences but rather as *closed non-sentential formulas*. The natural analogues in English are 'that'-clauses. So, for example, letting Pb symbolize 'that Bush is US president', the formal sentence I[Pb] says *It is the case that Bush is US president*, whereas O[Pb] says *It ought to be the case that Bush is US president.* Grammatically, the operators I[ ] and O[ ] are thus sentence-forming (and more generally, sentential *formula* forming) operators.

Logically complex non-sentential formulas, including open ones containing free variable-occurrences, are constructable within the formal language in the standard ways described in predicate logic. Because they all are *nonsentential* formulas, however, the closed ones (i.e. those without free variable-occurrences) are not sentences. A sentence (or open sentential formula) results from application of the syntactic operation of *inserting* a nonsentential formula into the bracketed slot of I[ ] or O[ ]. For example, letting 'Fx' symbolize 'x is a Fraternity member' and and 'Gx' symbolize 'x takes out the Garbage', the formal version of the sentence *It ought to be the case that some fraternity member takes out the garbage* results from insertion of the closed nonsentential formula (∃x)(Fx & Gx) into the bracketed slot of the operator O[ ], to yield the sentence O[(∃x)(Fx & Gx)]. Although nonsentential formulas that can be inserted into the bracketed slots of the operators I[ ] and O[ ] can be arbitrarily complex, they all have *descriptive* content (insofar as the formal language is semantically interpreted). Closed nonsentential formulas have *propositional* descriptive content, and open ones have *non-propositional* descriptive content.

Turn now to logically complex commitment-types, like the disjunctive one involved in Tom's belief that *either Dick is cheerful or Harry ought to apologize.* Within the formal language, such logically complex commitments are explicitly reflected by complex *sentence-forming operators*, which are built from the primitive operators I[ ] and O[ ] by way of operator-forming connectives and operator-forming quantifiers. For vividness, we use different symbols for these connectives and quantifiers than for the connectives and quantifers that are used to construct logically complex nonsentential formulas; we also use boldface for all these operator-forming connectives and quantifiers. There is a whole hierarchy of logically complex commitment-types, corresponding to the various logically complex sentence-forming operators.

For instance, Tom's disjunctive belief that *either Dick is cheerful or Harry ought to apologize* involves a logically complex commitment-type expressible by the complex, disjunctive, sentence-forming operator (I[ ] **o** O[ ]). If the closed nonsentential formulas 'Cd' and 'Ah' respectively symbolize *that Dick is cheerful* and *that Harry apologizes*, then Tom's disjunctive belief about Dick and Harry is formally expressible by the sentence that results from respectively inserting these formulas into the operator's respective slots, thus: (I[Cd] **o** O[Ah]). Ontologically, Tom's belief is a logically complex commitment-state of type (I[ ] **o** O[ ]), with respect to the pair of propositional contents *that Dick is cheerful* and *that Harry apologizes.*

For an example of a complex operator with quantification, suppose that Tom believes that *there is a specific fraternity member who ought to take out the garbage.* This belief involves a logically complex, quantificational, commitment-type whose structure is reflected by the sentence-forming operator $(\Sigma)(I[\ ] \wedge O[\ ])$. A formal sentence expressing Tom's belief results from inserting a variable into the existential-quantificational slot of this complex operator and inserting open sentential formulas into the operator's bracketed slots, thus: $(\Sigma x)(I[Fx] \wedge O[Gx])$. Ontologically, Tom's belief is a logically complex commitment-state of type $(\Sigma)(I[\ ] \wedge O[\ ])$, with respect to the pair of non-propositional descriptive contents *that x is a fraternity member* and *that x takes out the garbage.*

Step 2. In the Appendix we employ the idea of a *valuation*, i.e. an assignment of the truth values T and F to some (but not necessarily all) of the sentences and closed nonsentential formulas of the formal language, and we then use this idea to define the relation of logical consequence.

Step 3. Nothing in the formal semantics set forth in the Appendix requires that the notion of truth employed in the definition of valuation be understood as operating in the morally detached 'correspondence' manner. On the contrary, insofar as the formal language is construed as an interpreted language rather than an uninterpreted formal calculus, the truth values assigned to sentences by a given valuation can perfectly well be those that reflect a given agent's morally *engaged* truth assessments. (These run in tandem with the agent's morally engaged first-order beliefs, in accordance with schema T.) Thus, the definition of logical consequence in the Appendix can likewise be understood as reflecting logical relations among an agent's various morally engaged beliefs (including logically complex beliefs), and as also reflecting the implicit belief-commitments logically generated by these beliefs.

The notion of valuation is defined so as to allow for valuations in which certain sentences and/or nonsentential formulas are assigned neither T nor F. This is because, insofar as a valuation reflects a given agent's nonmoral and moral beliefs, certain sentences might be ones whose overall content the agent holds neither true nor false (even when using the truth predicate in a morally engaged way), but instead is agnostic about.

On the other hand, there will also be a valuation that assigns truth values in accordance with a morally detached correspondence-usage of 'true', and that furthermore assigns truth and falsity based on whether or not a given sentence actually corresponds to how things are or not (rather than on the basis of any particular agent's *beliefs*). In such a valuation, all sentences of the form O[A] will be assigned neither T nor F.

In short: In the formal language we have described, there is a hierarchy of sentence-forming operators with logical structures that explicitly reflect the various kinds of commitment, both simple and logically complex, that constitute distinct types of belief. The nonsentential formulas, corresponding to 'that'-clauses in natural language, have descriptive content but not assertoric force. A sentence, constructed by inserting the respective members of a sequence of nonsentential formulas into the respective bracketed slots of a sentence-forming operator (and inserting suitable variables into the respective quantificational slots, to bind all free variable-occurrences in the inserted formulas), reflects the ontological structure of the belief it expresses: the belief is a certain type of commitment-state with respect to a sequence of propositional or non-propositional descriptive contents—where the commitment-type is expressed by the relevant sentence-forming operator, and the respective descriptive contents are expressed by the closed and/or open nonsentential formulas inserted into this operator's respective bracketed slots. The notion of a valu-ation—a logically permissible assignment of the truth values T and F—can be defined for this formal language, and the relation of logical consequence can be defined using this notion. This definition of logical consequence comports well with the contention that truth ascription to sentences whose overall con-tent is nondescriptive is a matter of morally engaged semantic evaluation in which the evaluator's moral and semantic standards are fused. The definition of logical consequence thereby comports well with cognitivist expressivism.

In addressing Task III, we have described belief as *affirmatory commitment* with respect to one or several core descriptive contents. There are two logically fundamental belief-types: is-commitment and ought-commitment. Although an ought-commitment with respect to a core descriptive content is indeed a species of belief, its overall content is nondescriptive; nevertheless, it does have the involuntary, classificatory, coming-down phenomenology that is distinct-ive of occurrent beliefs. Truth ascription to beliefs and assertions with moral content is a morally engaged fusion of moral and semantic evaluation, and thus comports with the fact that moral content is not descriptive. There are also logically complex belief-types: kinds of affirmatory commitment expressible by logically complex sentence-forming operators in the formal language we have proposed as modeling the ontological structure of beliefs. Beliefs bear log-ical consequence relations to one another, whether or not they have overall content that is descriptive.[16]

We have mainly been dwelling on matters of moral psychology, arguing that moral judgments are beliefs whose overall content is nondescriptive. Similar points can be made about moral utterances. These are assertoric speech acts

---

[16] In the Appendix we explain how the descriptive/nondescriptive distinction applies to beliefs involving logically complex commitments, and to the sentences expressing such beliefs.

that play a distinctive sociolinguistic role—a role in interpersonal dynamics. An assertion, we claim, is best understood as a *stance-taking* speech act, an act through which one overtly comes down on some issue and thereby expresses an is-commitment, or an ought-commitment, or a logically complex commitment with respect to one or more core descriptive contents. In so doing one positions oneself within the context of sociolinguistic interaction, vis-à-vis the core content(s). A stance is therefore an orientation that one occupies in an interpersonal situation. An ought-stance in particular is typically an action-guiding stance with respect to some core descriptive content. Some ought-stances are more directly action-guiding than others, but they are all distinctively action-oriented—just as removed ought-beliefs are still tied to action, although less directly so than direct ought-beliefs. Moreover, just as moral beliefs typically involve a responsiveness to reasons, so engaging in a moral stance-taking speech act normally involves occupying a sociolinguistic role involving the preparedness to *give* reasons for one's moral stance on some issue. For instance, by asserting that Jones ought not to lie to his neighbor, one thereby takes a moral stance in which one signals one's willingness to engage in interpersonal reason-giving with respect to one's own ought-commitment, and to defend one's commitment against objections, or else give up one's commitment.

So sincere utterances of declarative sentences with moral content are speech acts of assertion, even though the overall content of such sentences is not descriptive. Of course, sincere utterances of sentences with descriptive overall content are assertions too. But it should be noted that token descriptive sentences also can be construed as making *belief-independent* assertions (as we will call them)—i.e. assertions that are independent of any specific asserter(s). For instance, an inscription on a subway wall of the sentence 'There are no weapons of mass destruction in Iraq!' asserts—in and of itself, apart from its author(s)— that there are no weapons of mass destruction in Iraq. According to cognitivist expressivism, however, sentence tokens whose overall content is not descriptive cannot rightly be construed as making belief-independent assertions. If an inscription of 'Abortion ought to be outlawed!' is written on a subway wall, then it can be correctly regarded as an assertion only insofar as one interprets it as expressing an ought-commitment of some person(s), known or unknown.

7. More on methodology

Having completed our three main tasks in setting out our metaethical view, let us pause to reflect a bit more on matters of metaethical methodology. Then, following this section, we will briefly consider various additional tasks that a view like ours must eventually tackle.

Recall from section 2 that we take a page from Moore in refusing to 'reduce' moral thought and discourse to any other type of discourse. We can now be more explicit in explaining what we are refusing to do and in explaining what we think can be done by way of illuminating such thought and discourse.

First, we refuse to set forth truth conditions for moral beliefs and assertions except, of course, non-substantive ones such as, for example, 'Slavery is wrong' is true if and only if slavery is wrong. The typical expectation in giving some sort of semantically illuminating set of truth conditions for a form of statement is (in effect) to set forth a set of non-trivial substantive truth-makers for such claims. On our view, it is a mistake to suppose that there are substantive truth-makers for moral beliefs and assertions; our view is robustly irrealist in this respect.

Second, we refuse to engage in any sort of paraphrase of moral 'ought' judgments that would effectively 'reduce' them to some other type of judgment, or to some combination of those. We have in mind any sort of 'analysis' that would construe an 'ought' judgment of the form 'S ought to do A' as equivalent in meaning to (say): 'S, do A!' directed toward oneself or another. We also eschew any *weakly* reductive strategies, such as those that treat certain nondeclarative linguistic constructions (e.g. imperative sentences) as *models* for moral thought and discourse—models that supposedly provide semantic and metaphysical illumination without necessarily yielding translations or paraphrases.

But these denials do not mean that we are quietists about the possibility of illuminating the meaning of moral thought and discourse. Like Hare, quoted earlier in section 2, we think that proper illumination comes from understanding the distinctive point and purpose of moral 'ought' judgments in moral thought and discourse as well as their associated phenomenology. So, there is a methodological component to our brand of cognitivist expressivism that we may formulate as follows:

> Moral thought and language does not admit of any kind of semantic 'reduction'; rather it is *sui generis*. Moreover, a proper understanding of such thought and discourse involves understanding the distinctive phenomenology and associated functional roles of such psychological states and sociolinguistic speech acts.

In articulating the key elements of our view, we have been illustrating our Moorean nonreductive methodology.

8. Remaining tasks—brief progress report

There is a battery of challenges that any view like ours must meet. In the remainder of this paper we can only indicate our current thinking about how to go about addressing some of these; dealing with them fully will have to be left as remaining tasks. The challenges we have in mind concern: (1) extending our account of direct ought-beliefs to other types of moral belief, (2) moral progress, (3) reasons, (4) moral seriousness, (5) lingering adherence to the descriptivist conception of belief. We now proceed to take them up in order.

Extending the account

In order to fully defend cognitivist expressivism, we need to extend our account of direct ought-beliefs to encompass removed ought-beliefs, beliefs about value (goodness), and moral beliefs that employ 'thick' moral concepts such as benevolence, courage, and malice. For present purposes, we will only consider removed ought-beliefs, again following the lead of Mandelbaum.

According to Mandelbaum, removed judgments of moral obligation, like direct judgments, are a response to one's experiencing some action as 'fitting' vis-à-vis the circumstances confronting an agent. But as distinct from direct judgments, removed judgments are: (1) made from a third person, spectator's point of view, (2) typically expressed by sentences of the form 'S ought to do/have done A' (where 'S' might refer to one's past self as well as to another person), and (3) are connected with an agent's motivation relatively indirectly and are thus further removed from an agent's motivation to act accordingly.

Phenomenologically, and in contrast to direct judgments, there is obviously no felt reflexive demand, upon the individual engaged in this kind of judging, to perform or not perform the action whose performance or avoidance is judged to be obligatory. However, such judgments often ground attitudes of disinterested approval or disapproval toward the action being evaluated. Here is how Mandelbaum describes this basic contrast:

Removed moral judgments, as we have seen, involve attitudes which may be denominated as 'selfless' or 'detached'; they are 'contemplative' rather than being states of the self. On the other hand, in a direct moral judgment the element of reflexive demand evokes emotion; this emotion, like fear or anger, is experienced as a state of the self and is directly related to action. Thus, the stirredupness and pressure which are present in direct moral judgments have no counterpart in removed moral judgments. In the latter we approve or disapprove, or we may feel admiration, disgust, contempt, or loathing; but even when these stronger affective states are present they appear as by-products of our acts of moral apprehension, and not as direct manifestations of what are experienced to be motivational forces. (1955: 127)

So with removed 'ought' judgments, in contrast to direct ought-commitments, the element of felt reflexive demand is absent and thus the motivational role of the judgment differs from direct moral judgments.[17]

So, direct and removed ought-beliefs differ in that beliefs of the former type involve a felt reflexive demand whose role is directly action-guiding, whereas the latter type of belief lacks these characteristics. Further exploration of the distinctive phenomenology and functional role of these types of commitment-state cannot be undertaken here. Nevertheless, both types of ought-commitment state are genuine beliefs—they both involve involuntarily coming down on some matter of moral concern, and they both are typically grounded in reasons and thus possess a kind of felt authority.

Moral progress

For a metaethical descriptivist-realist, intellectual moral progress is made when one's moral beliefs come to better approximate the moral facts. For a descriptivist-constructivist, intellectual moral progress is made when one's moral beliefs come to better accord with the moral norms that would be accepted by individuals under certain idealized conditions. Indeed, for a cultural moral relativist, there can be individual moral progress in the sense that one's moral beliefs come to better approximate the moral norms (either actual or ideal, depending on the version of relativism) of her culture. But if moral belief and assertion are not to be understood as purporting to describe or represent substantive moral facts, then how can one make sense of genuine moral progress? Furthermore, if there is no metaphysical anchor for moral thought and discourse, then why take it seriously, why not construe moral dispute and discussion as being more like disputes over fashion in clothes and matters of taste generally?

These challenges focus on our irrealist moral metaphysics, and we consider them to be among the most difficult for any robust moral irrealist. Here, then, is an indication of how we would respond to these challenges, though they certainly deserve more attention than it is possible to give them here.

On our view, moral progress is not to be understood as a matter of bringing one's beliefs into closer proximity to some realm of moral facts. Instead, we propose thinking of moral progress as something to be judged from within a

---

[17] However, this is not to say that removed moral judgments do not have an important tie to motivation. Hare (1952), for instance, maintained that because moral judgments are grounded in reasons and thus commit one to a moral principle which expresses those reasons, in making a removed moral judgment, one is committing oneself to act in a certain way were one to face the circumstances in which the agent being judged is placed. In this way such judgments are at least indirectly action-guiding.

committed moral outlook: when one makes judgments about moral improvement, one does so from an engaged moral perspective. So, for example, in judging that one's current view about the morality of euthanasia is better (more correct) than one's former view about this issue, one is not simply registering the fact that one's view on this matter has changed—mere change is not equivalent to progress! Rather, one is making, based on what one experiences as an improved understanding of the morally relevant aspects of euthanasia (including various types of cases this practice covers), a moral judgment—a judgment backed by reasons. In other words, judgments about moral progress are morally engaged themselves, to be understood according to the general metaethical picture we have been sketching.

Reasons

According to our characterization of moral beliefs, such commitment-states are typically grounded in what one experiences as reasons for the belief or assertion in question. We are irrealists about moral properties and facts, but what about moral reasons? Is our view committed to realism about moral reasons? If it is, then our overall metaphysical view countenances normative properties and facts—properties and facts having to do with reasons. But then, why be irrealists about normative properties and facts such as goodness and rightness? On the other hand, if we are reasons irrealists, how do we propose to make sense of such claims as, 'The fact that her lie was motivated by pecuniary self-interest is a reason for concluding that her lie was wrong'?

Here, we embrace the spirit if not the letter of C. L. Stevenson's way of dealing with this issue on behalf of his version of noncognitivism. According to Stevenson, claims about some nonmoral fact R constituting a reason for or against some moral judgment are themselves moral claims made from within a morally engaged outlook. Here is how Stevenson put the point:

So, the general situation is this: when we claim that the factual reason, R, if true, would justify or help to justify the evaluative conclusion, E, we are in effect making another value judgment, E', of our own—the latter serving to evaluate the situation that we shall have if the facts of the case include those that R purports to describe. (1963: 89)

Thus, an enquiry into those nonmoral factual considerations that serve as good reasons for accepting or denying moral statements is what moral thinking is all about. And various normative moral theories have been proposed (versions of consequentialism, deontology, virtue ethics, and so forth) in answer to questions about reasons in ethics. Moral reasons claims, then, express substantive moral beliefs and are themselves to be understood (depending on the type of reasons claim in question) in the general manner set forth in our version of cognitivist expressivism.

Moral seriousness

How, on our view, can sense be made of the fact that people take their moral views with utter seriousness? If there are no moral facts to which our moral beliefs and assertions must answer, then why care so much about morality?

In response, we think that the sort of challenge being posed is best construed as a *moral* challenge: why *ought* people to take their moral views seriously? And the appropriate response is to give moral reasons—reasons that, for instance, will likely appeal to the important role that morality plays in people's lives. Such moral reasons are not hard to find. And here again, our understanding of the challenge is to take it as appropriately dealt with from within an engaged moral outlook.

Beliefs as descriptive

A final challenge worth mentioning will come from those who continue to embrace the semantic assumption we described in section 1, and who insist that genuine, full-fledged *beliefs* must be psychological states whose overall content is descriptive.

We have two points to make in response. First, we have offered a battery of *arguments* supporting both the claim that moral judgments are genuine beliefs and the claim that the overall content of a moral judgment is nondescriptive, and we have offered *responses* to various challenges that such a position faces. Given these arguments and responses, there is a substantial burden of proof upon those who wish to insist nonetheless that real beliefs must be descriptive. The fact that the semantic assumption has traditionally been so widely accepted does not alone suffice to justify its acceptance.

Second, even if it should turn out that genuine beliefs really must be descriptive in their overall content, a variant of our cognitivist expressivism would still be available, and would constitute a significantly novel, nontraditional, version of noncognitivism. This variant position, which might be called *quasi-cognitivist expressivism*,[18] would deny that ought-commitments are a species of belief, but otherwise it would look very much like our own view. It would embrace the claims (1) that these states are *sui generis* and irreducible, (2) that they share with beliefs certain key phenomenological features involving involuntary, reason-based, classificatory 'coming-down' on an issue, (3) that they are subject

---

[18] This label was suggested by Uriah Kriegel.

to morally engaged semantic assessment, and (4) that there are logical consequence relations among (i) ought-commitments, (ii) beliefs whose over-all content is descriptive, and (iii) logically complex commitment-states.

In section 2 we pointed out that traditional forms of noncognitivism are at least *weakly* reductive, by virtue of their reliance on certain nondeclarative grammatical constructions (e.g. universal imperatives) as providing a putative model of moral discourse—even though some prominent advocates of such theories (e.g. Hare) repudiated the kind of *strong* reductionism that asserts the outright synonymy or semantic equivalence of moral utterances with such nondeclarative utterances. Quasi-cognitivist expressivism, on the other hand, is not reductive even in the weak sense, because it shares with our own position a reliance on certain *declarative* grammatical constructions as providing a model of moral discourse and of the ontological structure of moral judg-ments—namely, sentences containing the ought-operator O[ ], in the formal language we have described. Eschewing weak reductionism is thus another important respect in which the fallback view we call quasi-cognitivist expres-sivism is similar to our own position and is different from traditional forms of noncognitivism.

9. Conclusion

We have covered quite a lot of ground, sketching a general phenomenology of belief, developing a general framework of belief (and assertion) that treats some beliefs and assertions as having overall content that is not descriptive, and argu-ing that there is reason to construe moral beliefs and assertions as nondescript-ive. A cognitivist version of expressivism thus emerged. After saying a bit more about our methodology, we concluded by considering a battery of likely chal-lenges often raised against expressivist views in metaethics, and briefly explained how our view answers them. We maintain that our brand of cognit-ivist expressivism is superior to its metaethical competitors and is well worth developing further.[19]

Appendix

We here describe in detail the formal language we propose, with sentences whose syntactic structure models the ontological structures that we claim are possessed by

---

[19] Our further explorations will be recorded in our works in progress, *Moral Phenomenology and Moral Theory* and *Expressivism's Progress.*

various kinds of belief. We also set forth formal semantics for this language, including a definition of the logical consequence relation. We then add a number of observations by way of commentary.

Syntax

Primitive symbols

Non-boldface: name letters, predicate letters, individual variables, connectives $\sim$, $\vee$, &, $\supset$, $\equiv$, quantifier symbols $\forall$ and $\exists$, parentheses, commas.

Boldface: operator symbols **I**, **O**, **Bel**, connectives $\neg$, **o**, $\wedge$, $\rightarrow$, $\leftrightarrow$, quantifier symbols **Π** and **Σ**, parentheses, brackets.

Non-sentential formulas (nsf's):

If P is an n-ary predicate letter or a complex n-ary predicate, and $T_1, \ldots, T_n$ are terms (not necessarily distinct) each of which is a name letter or a variable, then $PT_1, \ldots, T_n$ is a nonsentential formula. (Complex n-ary predicates are defined below.)

If A is a nonsentential formula and X is a variable, then $\sim$A, $(\forall X)A$, and $(\exists X)A$ are nonsentential formulas.

If A and B are nonsentential formulas, then so are $(A \vee B)$, $(A \,\&\, B)$, $(A \supset B)$, and $(A \equiv B)$.

Nothing else is a nonsentential formula.

If A is a nonsentential formula with no free variable-occurrences, then it is **closed**. Otherwise it is **open**.

Sentential-formula forming operators (sff operators):

I[ ] and **O**[ ] are sff operators. (The slots in these operators are *bracketed* slots.)

If **Ω** is an sff operator, then $\neg$ **Ω**, **(Π)Ω**, and **(Σ)Ω** are sff operators. (The indicated slots are *quantificational* slots.)

If **Ω** and **Δ** are sff operators, then so are **(Ω o Δ)**, **(Ω ∧ Δ)**, **(Ω → Δ)**, and **(Ω ↔ Δ)**.

Nothing else is an sff operator.

Sentential formulas:

If **Ω** is an sff operator containing n quantificational slots and m bracketed slots, and Q is a sequence of n variables (not necessarily distinct), and *F* is a sequence of m non-sentential formulas (not necessarily distinct), then **Ω**//(Q, *F*) is a sentential formula. (Notation: **Ω**//(Q, *F*) is the expression obtained by inserting the respective elements of Q into the respective left-to-right quantificational slots in **Ω** and inserting the respective elements of *F* into the respective left-to-right bracketed slots in **Ω**.)

Nothing else is a sentential formula.

A sentential formula containing no free variable-occurrences is a **sentence**.

Predicate-forming-operator forming operators (pfo forming operators):

> **Bel**[ ] is a pfo forming operator.
>
> **Bel**( )[ ] is a pfo forming operator.
>
> Nothing else is a pfo forming operator.

Predicate-forming operators (pfo's):

> If Ω is a sff operator, then **Bel**$[\Omega]$ and **Bel**( )$[\Omega]$ are predicate-forming operators.
>
> Nothing else is a predicate-forming operator.

Complex predicates:

> If $\Omega///(Q, F)$ is a sentence, then **Bel**$[\Omega]///(Q, F)$ is a complex 1-place predicate.
>
> If $\Omega//(Q, F)$ is a sentential formula containing free occurrences of all and only the distinct variables $X_1, \ldots, X_n$, then **Bel**$(X_1, \ldots, X_n)[\Omega]//(Q, F)$ is a complex $(n + 1)$-ary predicate. (The operator **Bel**( )[ ] binds the initial occurrences of $X_1, \ldots, X_n$ in **Bel**$(X_1, \ldots, X_n)[\Omega]//(Q, F)$, and also binds all occurrences of these variables that are free within $\Omega//(Q, F)$.)
>
> Nothing else is a complex predicate.

Semantics

A ***nonsentential valuation* N** is an assignment of the truth values T and F to some (but not necessarily all) closed non-sentential formulas, in conformity with the following conditions.

> No closed nonsentential formula is assigned both T and F by **N**.
>
> If A is a closed nonsentential formula, then
>
> > **N** assigns T to A iff **N** assigns F to $\sim$A.
> >
> > **N** assigns F to A iff **N** assigns T to $\sim$A. (So **N** assigns neither T nor F to A iff **N** assigns neither T nor F to $\sim$A.)
>
> If A and B are closed nonsentential formulas, then
>
> > **N** assigns T to (A $\vee$ B) iff either **N** assigns T to A or **N** assigns T to B.
> >
> > **N** assigns F to (A $\vee$ B) iff **N** assigns F to both A and B.
> >
> > **N** assigns T to (A & B) iff **N** assigns T to both A and B.
> >
> > **N** assigns F to (A & B) iff either **N** assigns F to A or **N** assigns F to B.
> >
> > **N** assigns T to (A $\supset$ B) iff either **N** assigns F to A or **N** assigns T to B.
> >
> > **N** assigns F to (A $\supset$ B) iff **N** assigns T to A and **N** assigns F to B.
> >
> > **N** assigns T to (A $\equiv$ B) iff either **N** assigns T to both A and B or **N** assigns F to both A and B.

N assigns F to (A ≡ B) iff either **N** assigns T to A and F to B, or **N** assigns F to A and T to B.

If A is a nonsentential formula in which the only free variable-occurrences are occurrences of X, then

N assigns T to (∀X)A iff for every name letter N, **N** assigns T to A(X/N). (Notation: A(X/N) is the result of replacing every free occurrence of X in A by N.)

N assigns F to (∀X)A iff for some name letter N, **N** assigns F to A(X/N).

N assigns T to (∃X)A iff for some name letter N, **N** assigns T to A(X/N).

N assigns F to (∃X)A iff for every name letter N, **N** assigns F to A(X/N).

A closed nonsentential formula A is a *nonsentential consequence* of a set of closed nonsentential formulas {B₁,...,Bₙ} iff (1) every nonsentential valuation that assigns T to each of B₁,...Bₙ also assigns T to A, and (2) every nonsentential valuation that does not assign F to any of B₁,...Bₙ also does not assign F to A.

A *valuation* **V** is a pair < **N, S**> such that **N** (the *nonsentential element* of **V**) is a nonsentential valuation and **S** (the *sentential element* of **V**) is an assignment of truth values to some (but not necessarily all) sentences in conformity with the following conditions:

No sentence is assigned both T and F by **S**.

If A is a closed nonsentential formula, then

S assigns T to the sentence I[A] iff **N** assigns T to A.

S assigns F to the sentence I[A] iff **N** assigns F to A.

S assigns T to the sentence O[A] only if for every closed nonsentential formula B that is a nonsentential consequence of A, **S** assigns T to O[B].

S assigns F to the sentence O[A] only if for every closed nonsentential formula B such that A is a nonsentential consequence of B, **S** assigns F to O[B].

If $\Omega//(Q, F)$ is a sentence, then

S assigns T to ¬$\Omega//(Q, F)$ iff **S** assigns F to $\Omega//(Q, F)$.

S assigns F to ¬$\Omega//(Q, F)$ iff **S** assigns T to $\Omega//(Q, F)$.

If $\Omega//(Q_1, F_1)$ and $\Delta//(Q_2, F_2)$ are sentences, then

S assigns T to $(\Omega \circ \Delta)//(Q_1, F_1, Q_2, F_2)$ iff either **S** assigns T to $\Omega//(Q_1, F_1)$ or **S** assigns T to $\Delta//(Q_2, F_2)$. (Notation: $(\Omega \circ \Delta)//(Q_1, F_1, Q_2, F_2)$ is the expression obtained by inserting the respective elements of Q_1 and F_1 into the respective quantificational and bracketed slots of the Ω segment of $(\Omega \circ \Delta)$, and likewise inserting the respective elements of Q_2 and F_2 into the slots of the Δ segment of $(\Omega \circ \Delta)$.)

S assigns F to $(\Omega \circ \Delta)//(Q_1, F_1, Q_2, F_2)$ iff **S** assigns F to both $\Omega//(Q_1, F_1)$ and $\Delta//(Q_2, F_2)$.

S assigns T to $(\Omega \wedge \Delta)//(Q_1, F_1, Q_2, F_2)$ iff **S** assigns T to both $\Omega//(Q_1, F_1,)$ and $\Delta//(Q_2, F_2)$.

S assigns F to $(\Omega \wedge \Delta)//(Q_1, F_1, Q_2, F_2)$ iff either S assigns F to $\Omega//(Q_1, F_1)$ or S assigns F to $\Delta//Q_2, F_2)$.

S assigns T to $(\Omega \rightarrow \Delta)//(Q_1, F_1, Q_2, F_2)$ iff either **S** assigns F to $\Omega//(Q_1, F_1)$ or **S** assigns T to $\Delta//Q_2, F_2)$.

S assigns F to $(\Omega \rightarrow \Delta)//(Q_1, F_1, Q_2, F_2)$ iff **S** assigns T to $\Omega //(Q_1, F_1)$ and **S** assigns F to $\Delta//(Q_2, F_2)$.

S assigns T to $(\Omega \leftrightarrow \Delta)//(Q_1, F_1, Q_2, F_2)$ iff either **S** assigns T to both $\Omega //(Q_1, F_1)$ and $\Delta//(Q_2, F_2)$ or **S** assigns F to both $\Omega //(Q_1, F_1)$ and $\Delta//(Q_2, F_2)$.

S assigns F to $(\Omega \leftrightarrow \Delta)//(Q_1, F_1, Q_2, F_2)$ iff either **S** assigns T to $\Omega //(Q_1, F_1)$ and F to $\Delta//(Q_2, F_2)$ or **S** assigns F to $\Omega //(Q_1, F_1)$ and T to $\Delta//(Q_2, F_2)$.

If X is a variable and $\Omega//(Q, F)$ is a sentential formula in which the only free variable-occurrences are occurrences of X, then

S assigns T to $(\Pi X)\Omega//(Q, F)$ iff for each name letter N, **S** assigns T to $\Omega//(Q, F)///(X/N)$. (Notation: $\Omega//(Q, F)///(X/N)$ is the expression obtained from $\Omega//(Q, F)$ by replacing all free occurrences of the variable X by the name letter N.)

S assigns F to $(\Pi X)\Omega//(Q, F)$ iff for some name letter N, **S** assigns F to $\Omega//(Q, F)///(X/N)$.

S assigns T to $(\Sigma X)\Omega//(Q, F)$ iff for some name letter N, **S** assigns T to $\Omega//(Q, F)///(X/N)$.

S assigns F to $(\Sigma X)\Omega//(Q, F)$ iff for each name letter N, S assigns F to $\Omega//(Q, F)///(X/N)$.

A valuation **V** *assigns* T (or F) to a sentence or nonsentential formula Φ iff either the sentential element or the nonsentential element of **V** assigns T (or F) to Φ.

A valuation is *complete* iff it assigns T or F to every closed nonsentential formula and every sentence. Otherwise it is *partial*.

A sentence or closed nonsentential formula *A* is a *logical consequence* of a set of sentences or closed nonsentential formulas $\{B_1, \ldots, B_n\}$ iff (1) every valuation that assigns T to each of $B_1, \ldots, B_n$ also assigns T to *A*, and (2) every valuation that does not assign F to any of $B_1, \ldots B_n$ also does not assign F to *A*.

Commentary

1. We can now state how the descriptive/nondescriptive distinction applies to sentences generally, including sentences constructed by insertion of nonsentential formulas (nsf's) into logically complex sentence-forming operators. A sentence *A* has descriptive overall content just in case there is a partial valuation **V** such that (1) for every closed nsf B, **V** assigns neither T nor F to O[B], and (2) **V** assigns T or F to *A*. The idea is that there is some valuation that assigns a truth value to the sentence *A* while also assigning no truth value to any ought-sentence.

2. The semantics involves a substitutional rather than objectual treatment of the quantifiers. This is for simplicity, but one could instead formulate the semantics model-theoretically with an objectual construal of the quantifiers, rather than the truth-theoretic way with substituational quantifiers.

3. Truth values are assigned by a valuation not only to sentences but also to closed nsf's, because the latter too have propositional descriptive content and hence can be true or false. Likewise in English, a that-clause can be true or false.

4. As explained already, some sentences can be assigned neither T nor F by a valuation. Falsity conditions thus needed to be built into the notion of valuation, rather than a stipulation that F is assigned to any sentence or closed nsf not assigned T.

5. We depart from familiar approaches to formal semantics, which construe a valuation as an assignment of truth values just to the logically simplest sentences and then define 'truth in a valuation' recursively. This is because we take it that not all sentences have their truth values uniquely determined by the truth values assigned by a valuation to logically simpler ones. For instance, suppose that for every name symbol N, a valuation **V** assigns F to the sentence O[GN], where 'Gx' symbolizes 'that x takes out the garbage'. Such a valuation might yet assign either T or F to the sentence O[(∃x)Gx]. Even though no particular individual is such that *he/she* ought to take out the garbage, perhaps nonetheless it ought to be the case that *somebody* takes out the garbage; or perhaps not. Logically, both possibilities remain open.

6. The fundamental semantic principles governing the operator I[ ] are the ones saying that a valuation assigns T (or F) to I[A] iff it assigns T (or F) to A. The idea is that a given descriptive content should be assigned the same truth value by a valuation as is assigned to the sentence that makes an is-the-case assertion with respect to that content. As we pointed out in addressing semantic assessability in section 6, a valuation can serve either of two roles: first, reflecting an agent's beliefs, and second, describing the truth values the sentences possess when they are construed as belief-independent assertions. Consider these two construals of a valuation, in turn. First, if an agent is is-committed with respect to the content expressed by A, i.e. has a belief of type I[ ] with respect to A, then a valuation reflecting the agent's beliefs will assign T both to A itself and to I[A]. Second, if sentences of the type I[ ] are being construed as making *belief-independent assertions* (rather than belief-expressive assertions), then again a sentence I[A] should be assigned T by **V** just in case **V** also assigns T to A itself. If a certain descriptive content is true under a valuation, then so is the sentence that is-asserts that content; and conversely.

7. The fundamental semantic principles governing the operator O[ ] are the ones saying that **V** assigns T to O[A] only if for every B that is a nonsentential consequence of A, **V** assigns T to O[B]; and that **V** assigns F to O[A] only if for every B such that A is a nonsentential consequence of B, **V** assigns F to O[B]. It is because these are *if/then* constraints, rather than biconditionals, that the truth values assigned by a valuation to statements of the type O[A] are not uniquely determined by the truth values assigned to logically simpler statements. For instance, if for every N, **V** assigns F to O[FN], then **V** may assign either T or F to O[(∃x)Fx]. (See the example in comment 5 above.)

8. The fundamental semantic principles governing the operator **O**[ ] are quite weak. One could consider strengthening them in various ways, even while retaining their *if/then* form. But we doubt that there is adequate theoretical motivation for doing so. Also, a general reason to avoid stronger principles is the need to avoid various well-known deontic paradoxes. Consider, for instance, this candidate semantic principle: If **V** assigns T to both **O**[A] and **O**[(A ⊃ B)], then **V** assigns T to **O**[B]. Building this closure principle into the formal semantics would allow the generation of the 'contrary to duty imperative paradox.' Suppose, for example, that Andy steals the money, that he ought to be punished for doing so, but that he is otherwise undeserving of punishment. Letting 'Sa' and 'Pa' respectively symbolize 'that Andy steals the money' and 'that Andy is punished', these four claims are all true: **O**[Pa], **O**[~Sa], **O**[(~Sa ⊃ ~Pa)], (**O**[~Pa] →¬(**O**[Pa]). Given the closure principle under consideration, these claims would jointly entail the contradiction (**O**[Pa] ∧ ¬(**O**[Pa]).

9. Iteration of the operator symbols **I** and **O** and is not permitted in this formal language, as we have specified its syntax. Allowing iteration of **I** would be entirely pointless, as far as we can tell. If desired, however, one could permit iteration of **O** by modifying the syntax to say that if **Ω** is an sff operator then so is **OΩ**. (One might also modify the formal semantics too, to lay down certain constraints on how a valuation's assignment of T or F to a sentence of type **OΩ** must be related to the truth values the valuation assigns to various other sentences. Alternatively, one might not build in any such constraints; perhaps logic alone—or anyway, *nonmodal* logic alone—does not impose any formal constraints upon the iteration of 'ought'.) Although it is not obvious that moral thought and moral discourse really need iterated 'ought' constructions, a prima facie case can be made for this claim. Suppose, for instance, that Andy has stolen the money, and let 'Sa' and 'Pa' respectively symbolize 'that Andy steals the money' and 'that Andy is punished'. Arguably, although **O**[Pa] is true, **OO**[~Pa] is also true (because **O**[~Sa & ~Pa] is true).

10. Suppose that a sentence is constructed (by insertion of nonsentential formulas, plus perhaps insertion of variables and prefixing of quantifiers) from a *logically complex* sentential-formula forming operator, rather than being constructed directly from either of the logically simple sff's **I**[ ] or **O**[ ]. The assertoric force of such a sentence is borne by the *entire logically complex sff operator*, and not by its *proper constituents*. Likewise, for a belief expressed by such a sentence, the belief's affirmatory force is borne by the entire logically complex commitment-type of which the belief is an instance. For example, letting 'Cd' and 'Ah' respectively symbolize 'that Dick is cheerful' and 'that Harry apologizes', the assertoric force of the disjunctive sentence (**I**[Cd] o **O**[Ah]) is borne by the entire operator (**I**[ ] o **O**[ ]) from which this sentence is constructed, and not by either of this operator's proper constituents **I**[ ] or **O**[ ]. Likewise, the affirmatory force of the *belief* that either Dick is cheerful or Harry ought to apologize is borne by the entire logically complex commitment-type of which this belief is an instance—a commitment-type expressed by the complex operator (**I**[ ] o **O**[ ]).

11. In the definition of a valuation, the clauses governing logically complex sentential formulas work semantically exactly the same way they would work if these

sentential formulas were constructed syntactically in the more familiar manner—namely, directly from logically simpler sentential formulas via connectives and quantifiers (rather than by insertion of nsf's into the slots of logically complex operators). But it bears reiteration that the purpose of our own syntactic construction rules is this: the syntactic structure of the sentences thereby reflects the ontological structure (on our account) of the relevant beliefs expressible by these sentences. The key point to appreciate is that formal semantics does not *mandate* construing logically complex sentences as being built up syntactically in ways familiar from standard symbolic logic; on the contrary, the logical syntax can perfectly well be as we have specified.

12. The formal semantics is naturally construed as yielding two complementary classes of logical relations, applicable to two distinct domains of relata. First is the domain of *propositions* and *nonsentential formulas*. A proposition can be construed as a *set of ways the world might be*, and is expressible linguistically by a closed nonsentential formula. (Such a formula *expresses* the proposition without *asserting* it.) Propositions, and the closed nonsentential formulas that are their linguistic vehicles, bear logical relations to one another characterizable in terms of the notion of a nonsentential valuation—notably, the relation of nonsentential consequence. Second is the domain of *beliefs*, *assertions*, and *sentences*—with sentences being the linguistic vehicles for expressing beliefs and for making assertions. Beliefs, assertions, and sentences bear logical relations to one another (notably the relation of sentential consequence) characterizable in terms of the notion of valuation. Not all beliefs and assertions are ones whose overall content is *propositional* content; this is reflected in the fact that the notion of valuation is broader than that of nonsentential valuation.

13. Consider beliefs of logically complex type—i.e. beliefs other than those belonging to the two logically simple commitment-types, is-commitments and ought-commitments. For any belief B of logically complex type: if B is descriptive (and thus is expressible by a descriptive sentence —cf. comment 1), then B is logically equivalent to some belief B* that is a logically simple is-commitment (and thus is expressible by a descriptive sentence constructed by inserting some closed nonsentential formula into a single occurrence of the operator 'I[ ]'). Take, for instance, the belief that *either it is the case that Dick is cheerful or it is the case that Harry apologizes*, expressible symbolically via the descriptive sentence (I[Cd] o I[Ah]). This belief is logically equivalent to the belief that *it is the case that either Dick is cheerful or Harry apologizes*, expressible symbolically via the descriptive sentence I[(Cd v Ah)]. The former belief is a commitment of logically complex type (I[ ] o I[ ]) with respect to the pair of descriptive contents *that Dick is cheerful* and *that Harry apologizes*, whereas the latter belief is a logically simple is-commitment with respect to the logically complex descriptive content *that either Dick is cheerful or Harry apologizes*.

14. For any belief B of logically complex type: if B is *not* descriptive (i.e. is not expressible by a descriptive sentence), then B is *not* logically equivalent to any is-commitment. Take, for example, the belief that *either it is the case that Dick is cheerful or it ought to be the case that Harry apologizes*, expressible symbolically via the sentence (I[Cd] v O[Ah]). This belief, which is a commitment of logically complex type

(I[ ] **v** O[ ]) with respect to the pair of descriptive contents expressed respectively by the nonsentential closed formulas 'Cd' and 'Ah', is not logically equivalent to any is-commitment whatever.

15. The asymmetry revealed in points 13 and 14 is to be expected, given our irrealism about the ontology of morals: an is-commitment (or an ought-commitment) can only obtain with respect to a *way the world might be*, and according to our moral irrealism, only *descriptive* that-clauses express genuine ways the world might be. (All closed nonsentential formulas of the formal language correspond to *descriptive* that-clauses of natural language.)

16. The formal language includes belief-attributing predicates. Once again, we have specified the syntax so that these constructions too reflect, in their syntactic structure, the ontological structure of the beliefs they attribute. For each kind of commitment-state that is a type of belief, including the logically complex ones, there is a predicate-forming operator whose structure mirrors that belief-type. A belief-attributing predicate expressing a specific belief is constructed by inserting, into the operator's bracketed slots, nsf's expressing the respective descriptive contents that are the descriptive-content relata of the given belief. For instance, Tom's belief that *either Dick is cheerful or Harry ought to apologize* involves a commitment-type expressed by the predicate-forming operator **Bel**[(I[ ] **o** O[ ])]. Letting 'Cd' and 'Ah' respectively symbolize 'that Dick is cheerful' and 'that Harry apologizes', a formal predicate expressing Tom's belief-property is obtained by inserting into the operator's respective bracketed slots the closed sentential formulas expressing the two propositional-content relata of the belief, thus: **Bel**[(I[Cd] **o** O[Ah])]. So, letting 't' refer to Tom, the logically complex nonsentential formula *that Tom believes that either Dick is cheerful or Harry ought to apologize* is symbolized this way: **Bel**[(I[Cd] **o** O[Ah])]t. Likewise, Tom's belief that that *there is a specific fraternity member who ought to take out the garbage* involves a commitment-type expressed by the predicate-forming operator **Bel**[(Σ)(I[ ] $\wedge$ O[ ])]. A formal predicate expressing the belief-property is obtained by inserting a variable into the operator's quantificational slot and inserting into its bracketed slots open sentential formulas expressing the two non-propositional descriptive-content relata of the belief: **Bel**[(Σx)(I[Fx] $\wedge$ O[Gx])]. Thus, the nonsentential formula *that Tom believes that there is a specific fraternity member who ought to take out garbage* becomes: **Bel**[(Σx)(I[Fx] $\wedge$ O[Gx])]t.

17. The point of the belief-attributing predicates employing the variable-binding operator **Bel**( )[ ] is to accommodate 'de re' belief constructions, in addition to de dicto ones. So, letting 'r' and 'o' refer to Ralph and Ortcutt respectively and letting 'S' symbolize 'is a spy', the de dicto belief predicate 'believes that Ortcutt is a spy' is symbolized as **Bel**[I[So]], and the de dicto nonsentential formula *that Ralph believes that Ortcutt is a spy* is symbolized as **Bel**[I[So]]r—whereas the de re belief predicate 'believes of Ortcutt that he is a spy' is symbolized as **Bel**(x)[I[Sx]]o, and the de re nonsentential formula *that Ralph believes of Ortcutt that he is a spy* is symbolized as **Bel**(x)[I[Sx]]o, r.

18. Our treatment of the logical syntax of de dicto and de re belief predicates is adapted from a proposal of Quine (1960, 1970), further discussed and developed in

Horgan (1989). Quine, though, construed his approach as a way of dispensing with so-called 'propositional objects' of belief, whereas here we are instead construing beliefs as relations linking a believer to one or more descriptive contents—namely, the contents expressed by the nonsentential-formulas that get inserted into the bracketed slots of the complex predicate-forming operator expressing a particular belief-type. Thus, Ralph's de dicto belief is a relation between Ralph and the propositional descriptive content expressed by 'that Ortcutt is a spy'; and Ralph's de re belief is a relation linking both Ortcutt and Ralph to the nonpropositional descriptive content expressed by 'that x is a spy'.

19. Our account of morality-involving beliefs—both logically simple ought-commitments and logically complex commitments like those of the logical type expressed by the predicate-forming operator **Bel**[(I[ ] o O[ ])]—is extendable in a fairly natural way to other kinds of morality-involving psychological states too. Consider, for instance, the state *entertaining that* either Dick is cheerful or Harry ought to apologize. This can be construed as 'hypothetically trying on' the state of *believing* that either Dick is cheerful or Harry ought to apologize. Ontologically, it is a logically complex attitude type with respect the pair of core descriptive contents *that Dick is cheerful* and *that Harry apologizes*. And this attitude type can be expressed within the formal language in an ontologically perspicuous way by introducing the predicate-forming-operator forming operators **Ent**[ ] and **Ent**( )[ ], analogous to the belief operators **Bel**[ ] and **Bel**( )[ ]. Or consider the state *suspecting that* either Dick is cheerful or Harry ought to apologize. Ontologically, this too is a state of 'hypothetically trying on' the corresponding belief, but with an accompanying disposition to *embrace* that belief. On the general picture we are here advocating, logically complex psychological attitudes of entertaining, suspecting, doubting, fearing, etc. all are ways of 'hypothetically trying on' a logically complex belief—and hence all can be accommodated by fairly natural extensions of the ontological/syntactic/semantic treatment we recommend for logically complex, morality-involving, beliefs.

References

AUDI, R. (2004). *The Good in the Right: A Theory of Intuition and Intrinsic Value.* Princeton: Princeton University Press.

AYER, A. J. (1936). *Language, Truth and Logic.* 2nd edn. New York: Dover.

BLACKBURN, S. (1984). *Spreading the Word.* Oxford: Oxford University Press.

—— (1996). 'Securing the Nots'. In W. Sinnott-Armstrong and M. Timmons (eds.), *Moral Knowledge? New Readings in Moral Epistemology.* New York: Oxford University Press.

—— (1998). *Ruling Passions.* Oxford: Oxford University Press.

CARNAP, R. (1935). *Philosophy and Logical Syntax.* London: Kegan Paul, Trench, Trubner & Co.

DEWEY, J. (1922). *Human Nature and Conduct.* Carbondale: Southern Illinois University Press.

DREYFUS, H., and DREYFUS, S. (1990). 'What is Morality: A Phenomenological Account of the Development of Ethical Expertise'. In D. Rassmussen (ed.), *Universalism vs. Communitarianism.* Cambridge, Mass.: MIT Press.

GIBBARD, ALLAN (1990). *Wise Choices, Apt Feelings.* Cambridge, Mass.: Harvard University Press.

HARE, R. M. (1952). *The Language of Morals.* Oxford: Oxford University Press.

HARMAN, G. (1977). *The Nature of Morality.* Oxford: Oxford University Press.

HORGAN, T. (1989). 'Attitudinatives'. *Linguistics and Philosophy*, 12: 133–65.

—— (1995). 'Critical Study: Crispin Wright, *Truth and Objectivity*'. *Nous*, 29: 127–38.

—— (1996). 'The Perils of Epistemic Reductionism'. *Philosophy and Phenomenological Research*, 56: 891–7.

—— (2001). 'Contextual Semantics and Metaphysical Realism: Truth as Indirect Correspondence'. In M. Lynch (ed.), *The Nature of Truth: Classic and Contemporary Perspectives.* Cambridge, Mass.: MIT Press.

—— and TIMMONS, M. (2000a). 'Nondescriptivist Cognitivism: Framework for a New Metaethic'. *Philosophical Papers*, 29: 121–53.

—— —— (2000b). 'Copping Out on Moral Twin Earth'. *Synthese*, 124: 139–52.

—— —— (2002). 'Conceptual Relativity and Metaphysical Realism'. *Philosophical Issues*, 12: 74–96.

—— —— (2005). 'Morality without Moral Facts'. In J. Dreier (ed.), *Contemporary Debates in Moral Theory.* Oxford: Blackwell Publishers.

—— —— (2006). 'Expressivism, Yes! Relativism, No!' In R. Shafer-Landau (ed.), *Oxford Studies in Metaethics.* Oxford: Oxford University Press.

HUME, D. (1739). *A Treatise of Human Nature.* Oxford: Oxford University Press.

MANDELBAUM, M. (1955). *The Phenomenology of Moral Experience.* Glenco, Ill.: The Free Press.

MOORE, G. E. (1903). *Principia Ethica.* Cambridge: Cambridge University Press.

QUINE, W. V. (1960). *Word and Object.* Cambridge, Mass.: MIT Press.

—— (1970). *Philosophy of Logic.* Englewood Cliffs, NJ: Prentice-Hall.

SHAFER-LANDAU, R. (2003). *Moral Realism: A Defense.* Oxford: Oxford University Press.

STEVENSON, C. L. (1963). *Facts and Values.* New Haven: Yale University Press.

TIMMONS, M. (1999). *Morality without Foundations: A Defense of Ethical Contextualism.* New York: Oxford University Press.

VARELA, F. (1992). *Ethical Know-How.* Stanford, Calif.: Stanford University Press.

WARNOCK, M. (1960). *Ethics since 1900.* London: Oxford University Press.

WRIGHT, D. (1992). *Truth and Objectivity.* Cambridge, Mass.: Harvard University Press.

13

Truth and the Expressing in Expressivism

Stephen Barker

0. Introduction

In the beginning expressivism—otherwise known as emotivism—was the thesis that utterances of value-sentences are mere expressions of desire and that consequently they are not genuine assertions that manifest genuine beliefs or judgements, or are open to truth evaluation.[1] This first wave of expressivism was a highly revisionist doctrine, since value-statements really appear to have all these features. Latter-day, or new wave, expressivism renounces this revisionism. Its essence is distilled in the following claim:

> In asserting a value-sentence, then at least with respect to the value-content of that utterance, the speaker is not *reporting* any fact—natural or non-natural—but is rather *expressing* a motivational state of some kind. Thus value-sentences, at least with respect to their value-content, are not made true by reality.[2]

In short, the essence of new wave expressivism is rejection of the principle that all truth-apt sentences have truth-makers—parts of reality that make them true. Somehow, motivational states are part of the content of value-sentence utterances, but the latter are not reports about the possession of such states by speakers.

Clearly some discourse is reportive and subject to truth-making. For example, true logically simple sentences, like *Snowy is black*, are, it seems, made true by reality; a dog's being black. So within the domain of truth accessible discourse there is, if new wave expressivism is right, a division between

---

[1] A paradigm first-wave expressivist is Ayer (1946). Blackburn (1984) is a more recent proponent. See Hale (2002) and van Roojen (1996), for criticisms of Blackburn's theory. Gibbard (1990) portrays himself as an expressivist, but it is not clear at all that he is. See Koelbel (2002).

[2] I make the proviso about value-content because expressivism is consistent with the position that value-sentences have dual contents; reportive non-value-content and expressive value-content. See Hare (1952).

reportive and expressive assertion. But what is *expressing* in the expressivist's required sense?[3]

I think there is a broad set of ideas that the reporting/expressing distinction might be understood as the distinction between representational and non-representational discourse. A programme that sets out to realize this idea is the *Minimalist Programme* or **MP**:

MP (Minimalist Programme)

A: Truth-aptness and truth are to be understood minimally. Truth-apt discourse is discourse meeting certain syntactic and use-conditions. The essence of our concept of truth is given by our commitment to affirm all instance of the T-schema: *'S' is true iff S* (or it is given by this commitment and avowal of certain further minimal norms).

B: Some areas of discourse meeting the above conditions for truth-aptness involve contents that, because of additional facts about assertoric practice, function as representations. Other areas meeting the same conditions for truth-aptness involve contents that do not function as representations.

C: Both representational and non-representational truth-apt discourse is equally truth-apt. Because truth is defined minimally and not linked essentially to representation in any substantial sense, the truth-maker principle is not generally valid. Value-sentences are instances of this kind of discourse: truth-apt but lacking truth-makers.

Price (1990), Wright (1992), Blackburn (1998), Horgan and Timmons (2000) are examples of theorists carrying out **MP** in different ways. Wright does not equate his treatment of value-sentences with expressivism, but that is, in part, because he takes expressivism to be first wave, revisionist expressivism. For Horgan and Timmons the emphasis is on beliefs and judgements either possessing or not possessing representational content, and only secondarily on sentences possessing such content.

Does **MP** represent the right form for second wave expressivism? I don't think so. One doubt is that **MP** buys into minimalism about truth and the T-schema. I argue in Barker (2003) that the T-schema is not valid. Natural languages contain conventional implicature operators like, 'even', 'but', 'nevertheless', 'therefore', and 'if'. These operators are non-truth-conditional.

---

[3] The word 'expressing' has a technical use in this paper, that suited for the value-expressivist's needs. I will not be considering expressing in the sense that expletives or utterances of thanks express emotion or assertions express beliefs.

Languages containing conventional implicatures are ones where the truth-predicate lacks the disquotational property. For example, take the two sentences:

(1) 'Even Mother Teresa was pious' is true.

(2) Even Mother Teresa was pious.

If minimalism about truth is right, then (1) and (2) have the same linguistic-rule-based commitments. However, the rule-based commitment of (2) and (1) differ: (2)'s is to (2)'s truth and its implicature content being satisfied; (1)'s is to (2)'s truth only. Now, implicature-operators like 'even' embed in logical compounds and semantically interact with sentential operators. Thus *'Even Mother Teresa was pious' is true if and only if even Mother Teresa was pious* is a well-formed instance of the T-schema. But the formal, rule-based ground for this instance of the T-schema is not one we accept since its right-hand and left-hand sides differ with respect to rule-based commitments. If so, not all instances of the T-schema are correct, and consequently, minimalism about truth must be rejected.

I don't expect people to take this argument seriously, partly because its conclusion disputes a principle long held as a part of philosophical lore. Also its appeal to linguistic facts is non-standard. So I will not press it here. I have another objection to **MP**. The second objection is that the division between the representational and non-representational is flawed since discourse is essentially representational. In uttering sentences we are just in the business of representing how things are, either with the world, or with ourselves. The representational/non-representational distinction then cannot ground the reporting/expressing distinction. I cannot defend this strong claim here, but I can argue for a weaker one that is just as damaging: two utterances can be equally representational but one is reportive and the other expressive. Consider the sentences:

(3) I believe strongly that it is raining.

(4) It is probably raining.

(3) involves a report about the speaker U herself possessing a credence state, namely $[C(It's\ raining) = high]$. We judge (3) true if and only if we think U has this state. (4) is not a report of a credence state but an *expression* of one.[4] We judge (4) true if and only if we think it probable that it is raining, that is, if and only if we have the credence state. However, utterances of (3) and (4) by U are

---

[4] See Barker (2004) for some detailed argument that (4) cannot be construed as a report about an objective probability or a subjective state.

representational in the same way. As uttered by U, both sentences involve U representing her possession of the credence state. Both (3) and (4) are signs of that state. In each case, audiences take away the information that U has [C(*It's raining*) is high]. (3) and (4) have the same assertability conditions for the speaker. There is a rule-based regularity that it is permissible for U to utter either when she believes that she has [C(*It's raining*) is high]. In short, they have the same representational content. But they differ in truth-conditions. One reports a state and is true if and only if U has [C(*It's raining*) is high]. The other does not.

I think a similar line of argument can be applied to value-sentences, assuming expressivism about value. Analogous to (3) and (4), we shall find sentence pairs, the first of which— the analogue of (3)   is used to report possession of a motivational state Δ, and has the form 'I have Δ', and the second—the analogue of (4)—is a sentence *V* used to express possession of Δ. Both sentences will have the representational content that U has Δ. But one is reportive and the other expressive.

To conclude, expressive discourse is not non-representational discourse; **MP** can't be right. I don't expect the reader to be convinced by this argument. Nevertheless, let us suppose it is correct. Where would the project of expressivism about value go from here if it was? Let us suppose that discourse is essentially representational. It might seem that making that admission would be fatal to expressivism, because it would mean that something like the semantic conception of truth or **SCT** would be correct:

SCT: Truth-bearers are sentences with representational content.

If **SCT** were correct, truth would be correct representation, and the truth-maker principle would generally hold, blocking expressivism. In fact, the admission that discourse is representational does not commit us to **SCT** at all. We can deny that truth is essentially about representation by proposing that it is not merely representation; truth-bearers are sentences with representational content *used in a certain way*. More precisely, my thought is the pragmatic concept of truth or **PCT**:

PCT: The truth-bearers are sentences with representational content that are also used with an assertoric purpose.

On this conception, truth-bearers are assertions, and assertions are sentences carrying representational content *used* with a certain assertoric communicative purpose. That purpose, as will be revealed, is one of defending a commitment property: a cognitive or conative state that the speaker is in. Assertions are exercises in defending commitment properties. Assertions come in varieties: *reportive* and *expressive*. The distinction between reportive and expressive assertions is not that between representational and non-representational discourse—as MP—would suggest, but between sentences with representational content used with one assertoric communicative purpose as opposed to another.

In this conception of truth-bearers, truth-claims are not *reports* about representation of or correspondence to mind-independent reality, or *reports* about coherence, peer agreement, or possession of the disquotational property, but *expressions* of a kind of intersubjective agreement about the instantiation of the commitment properties associated with assertions. Reportive and expressive assertions are both capable of genuine truth, in precisely the same sense. Nevertheless, true reportive assertions correspond to, and are made true by, reality whereas this doesn't hold for true expressive assertions.

In sections 1 to 3 below, I sketch the basic idea. In section 4, I lay out the conception of normativity and objectivity. In section 5, I explain the case of value-sentences and provide thereby a new framework for expressivism about value.

1. Preliminaries: assertion

We are supposing that all discourse is representational. In giving George an order to jump, I represent how things are—I desire George to jump. In asserting that I want George to jump I represent how things are—I desire George to jump. But why is my second utterance truth-apt but not the first? Because the second involves assertion? But what is assertion? Assertion cannot simply be uttering sentences intending to represent how things are, for the same goes on in orders—this is just repeating the point about representation.

Appeals to truth and belief won't help us identify assertions either. Assertions cannot be analysed simply as acts of uttering sentences with intentions to utter truths, because we need to know what a truth-apt sentence is. We cannot analyse assertions as acts in which speakers express their beliefs, since speakers express beliefs in other illocutionary acts.[5]

What then is the peculiar activity that we call assertion? Assertion is a kind of *stance taking* (Alston 2000 and Horgan and Timmons 2000). I interpret this

---

[5] Brandom (1983) contends that U asserts that *S* iff (i) U undertakes to justify *S*, if asked to, and (ii) permits speakers to use *S* as a premise in arguments. But one can make a case that orders meet both conditions. Re (i), audiences can challenge the correctness of an order. Re (ii), one can certainly make inferences based on orders, e.g. inferring that Fred is sick from the order to cure him. Of course, one might object that we cannot write up *Cure Fred! So he is sick*, as an argument. But why not, given that we can make inferences based on orders? I think we provide an answer to this question through a prior account of assertion.

idea in the following way. To make a stance is to defend turf. The turf is a cognitive or conative state of some kind possessed by the speaker. Assertion involves (potentially) intersubjective engagement: acceptance, dispute, dialogue with another about what is *defended*. In asserting that Snowy is black, I defend a belief, but we could also say, I defend a commitment to representing the world as being a certain way, namely, that Snowy the dog is black. My audience will engage with me, and agree with my assertion, if they too defend the same kind of thing: they defend a commitment to representing things thus and so. An audience H judges my assertion correct/true if and only if she is willing to defend that kind of turf. In short, assertion is to defend a commitment, and judgement of truth is to express in some way that that commitment is accepted.

How does this help us distinguish orders from assertions? In orders and assertions speakers represent how things are. The difference is in purpose. In assertions, speakers defend a commitment to a cognitive/conative state, whereas in orders they are not defending anything. Assertions are democratic; they are a form of stance-taking dialogue. Orders are autocratic. In an order, a speaker represents how things are—that they desire an audience to do such and such—where the speaker's purpose is that the audience recognize this desire. That's it. There is no invitation to dispute defence of commitment to that desire. The speaker is not defending anything. In contrast, assertions are about defence. The truth-predicate is used to express acceptance of what the speaker defends. That's why orders are not truth-apt! This is despite the fact that in both assertion and ordering, discourse is representational.

Communicative purposes then enable us to isolate truth-apt discourse within the sphere of representational discourse. It also allows us to distinguish the reportive from the expressive within the sphere of the truth-apt, that is, within the sphere of assertions. Consider (3) and (4). In uttering (3), the speaker U defends a commitment to representing the world as one in which she has [C(*It's raining*) is high]. An audience H judges (3) true if and only if she, H, accepts the commitment. But what of (4)? In uttering (4), U is not defending a representational intention. She is defending something else. We can see what by looking at how a potential audience H truth-accesses U's utterance. H does not judge (4) true if and only if she thinks U has the state [C(*It's raining*) is high], but if and only if she, H, thinks she, H, has the state. If so we can conclude that what U defends in uttering (4) is acceptance of [C(*It's raining*) is high].

The difference between reportive and expressive assertions is then this: in reportive assertions speakers defend commitments to representational intentions; in expressive assertions speakers defend commitments to states—such as credence states—whose possession they have in fact represented. This accords with the schema **PCT** outlined above. In illocutionary acts, be they orders, reportive or expressive assertions, speakers represent how things are. What distinguishes the illocutionary acts from each other is purpose. Truth is pragmatic in that it is not a semantic property like representation; the truth-bearers are assertions: representational acts used with a specific kind of purpose.

2. The Pragmatic conception of truth (**PCT**)

To get this account up and running we need more details about assertion and semantic content. First, assertion and some finessing. I have spoken of illocutionary acts in terms of representing and intentions to represent. But the reality is more subtle. We really need to talk of speakers *advertising* intentions to represent. By *advertising intentions* I mean that U intentionally engages in the behaviour characteristic of a person who, following certain rules, has the intentions. So in uttering 'Snowy is black' U advertises an intention to represent how things are, that a fact of a certain form obtains. Advertising is the common element in sincere, insincere, and fictional assertion. If U sincerely asserts that Snowy is black, U really has the fact-representing intention she advertises. If U is lying, then she lacks the intention she advertises, but intends her audience to believe she has it. And if U is engaging in fictional make-believe, she lacks the intention she advertises, and intends her audience to recognize this fact.

The first component of an assertion then involves uttering a sentence and advertising a fact-representing intention. But assertion involves more than representation. It also involves a communicative purpose of defending a commitment to a property. This again involves advertising. In asserting a speaker advertises an intention to defend a certain cognitive or conative property—call it Π—and in fact really has that intention. So an assertion has the form:

Assertion: (i) U utters *S* and advertises intentions:
  (*a*) to represent a fact of the form $<P>$; and
  (*b*) to defend commitment to a property Π.
  (ii) U possesses the intention (*ib*).

So in reporting that Snowy is black, U utters a sentence, say 'Snowy is black', advertises an intention (*a*) to represent a fact $<$snowy, black$>$ and (*b*) to defend a commitment to intending to represent the obtaining of that fact. That U has this communicative purpose is indicated, conventionally, in the case of simple sentences like 'Snowy is black', by the indicative mood of the sentence.

Whether the assertion is a reportive or an expressive assertion depends on what Π is. The assertion about Snowy is a case where Π is a representational intention. But if the assertion is expressive, Π may be a cognitive or conative property like having a belief or a subjective probability state, or an intending or desiring something. For example, we can now give the official analysis of the assertions of (3) and (4), given in section 1, which are, respectively, a report and expression of a mental state:

P1: (i) U utters 'I believe strongly that it is raining' advertising intentions:
> (*a*) to represent a fact of the form $<$U has [C(*It's raining*) is high]$>$;
> (*b*) to defend commitment to the representational intention in (*a*).

    (ii) U has the intention in (*ib*).

P2: (i) U utters 'It is probably raining' advertising intentions:
> (*a*) to represent a fact of the form $<$U has [C(*It's raining*) is high]$>$;
> (*b*) to defend commitment to [C(*It's raining*) is high].

    (ii) U has the intention in (*ib*).

In both **P1** and **P2**, U produces a sentence with the same representational content—U performs the act (*a*) of uttering a sentence advertising an intention to represent a fact concerning acceptance of a credence state. What differs in **P1** and **P2** are the advertised communicative intentions. In **P1**, it is the property of defending the representational intention displayed, the (*a*)-intention. In **P2**, it is the defence of the commitment to the probability state represented.

That difference in communicative intention means that (3) and (4) have different truth-conditions for an audience. In uttering (3), U performs **P1**, defending a representational-intention. H accepts U's utterance, judges it true, just in case H accepts commitment to that representational intention in her own case, i.e. just in case H believes U has the probability state. In uttering (4), U performs **P2**, defending commitment to a subjective probability state. H accepts U's utterance, judges it true, just in case H accepts the property U defends, that is, the probability state: [C(*It's raining*) is high]. In short, the different truth-conditions of (3) and (4), that differing applicability conditions of the truth-predicate, are determined by the distinct communicative intentions associated with them.

We are now in a position to answer the question: what is a truth-bearer? Just what truth-bearers amount to is elicited by considering a dialogue (5),

(5) Smith: It's probably raining.

      Jones: True. It's probably raining.

Smith and Jones are in agreement about a truth. But what is the object of which they both predicate truth?[6] According to **PCT**, the truth-bearer is an assertion-type defined by a commitment property. That type is **P2**, where 'U' is treated as a variable. Both Smith and Jones are in agreement about instantiating the property, [C(*It's raining*) is high]. But this also translates into agreement about a truth. Both are disposed to perform instances of **P2**, which is an assertion-type. In short, the thought that both contemplate, and of which they predicate truth, is defined by this assertion-type and this commitment property. Truth-bearers are identified not by propositions—states of affairs—but by commitment properties.

How does the truth-predicate function here? Utterance of '*S* is true' is not a report that one agrees with one's interlocutors; that would be to introduce a kind of relativism. Nor is it a report that *S* has a certain property such as correspondence with reality, being believed-by-such-and-such-group, cohering with some system of beliefs, or even the disquotational property.[7] Rather, the truth-predicate is used to express commitment to accepting certain commitment properties Π pertaining to an assertion. In uttering '*S* is true', U expressively asserts her commitment to accepting the Π-property pertaining to assertion of '*S*'. That is:

True: (i)   U utters '*S* is true' advertising intentions:

           (*a*)   to represent a fact of the form $<$U accepts the commitment property of assertion of *S*$>$;

           (*b*)   to defend commitment to the state in (*a*), that is, accepting the commitment property of assertion of *S*.

     (ii)   U has the intention (*ib*).

According to this theory, true sentences are not necessarily made true by reality. They will be, if the assertion judged true is reportive, but not if the judged assertion is expressive. In both cases, the truth-predicate functions in the same way: as the expressive predicate described here.

---

    [6] According to **SCT**, the semantic concept of truth described in section 0, the truth-bearer is a sentence with representational content. No truth-bearer in this sense can be found for (5), since there is no state of affairs in the world that both speakers are representing. See Barker (2004: ch. 1.2).

    [7] Since, as already suggested, the truth-predicate lacks the disquotational property. See Barker (2003) for the argument.

3. Objectivity, defence, and naturalism

The key component of this account is *defending*, but I have said little about it. I now offer an account of it. U defends a commitment to Π just in case U dialectically engages with her audience. This occurs when:

(i) H recognizes that U has Π; and

(ii) H either accepts, confirms, or disputes a commitment to Π in her own case.

In (ii), *dispute* means either rejection or doubt. So in assertion U intends to get H to believe that she accepts Π and for H to respond by confirmation, acceptance, doubt, or rejection.[8]

It might be thought that commitment, acceptance, and rejection are normative states. They are internally connected to having reasons. So expressivism about value or subjective probability statements rests on a prior normativity: that of reason. Even if this were so, it would not undermine the project of expressivism about moral and aesthetic value, and expressivism about probability statements or, say, *if*-sentences. But in fact there is no intrinsic normativity built into these states.

In Barker (2004), I give naturalistic treatments of acceptance, rejection, and commitment. Underpinning the capacity to form speech-acts is a natural system of representation with simple cognitive and conative states. That system comprises logically simple representational states, laws regulating relations between such states, dispositions and propensities to token representations, constraints on not tokening them, etc. The system itself does not contain thoughts of the kind that are realized through use of natural language sentences, since the system is not intersubjective. Thoughts, as we know them, are communicative: they feature communicative intentions. This pre-linguistic system is the precondition for having such intentions.

In terms of this system, being committed to Π is just a cognitive state, to the effect that given normal functioning of the system it would produce instantiation of Π as one of its states. Rejection is an attitude in which U is not disposed to instantiate Π where, in addition, U is constrained, by internal cognitive conditions, to cease all epistemic search procedures for justifying that commitment. A state of doubt is one that is neither acceptance nor rejection.

---

[8] Perhaps the claim that in assertion U *intends* to get H to believe U accepts Π is too strong. A better approximation might be that U *hopes* that H will believe that she accepts Π. Can one assert something without any interest at all that any audience responds? I suggest not. If a depressed Robinson Crusoe soliloquizes, indifferent to the attention of anyone else, he still hopes to get things right by his own lights. He monitors his own speech. The producer hopes to satisfy the monitor, both being, in this case, within the same speaker.

In saying these states are natural I am not proposing a reduction of cognitive norms to natural facts about agents. No such reduction is possible. Rather I am saying there are natural facts about cognitive systems to which we have normative attitudes. The normative attitude is simply the fact that we are prepared to defend the cognitive regularities that in fact we instantiate. In asserting that Snowy is black, U displays herself as committed to representing a certain fact. Her commitment, which is simply a dispositional state, is open to scrutiny, in the sense that the cognitive laws that produce it can in turn be defended. Hence we find a kind of boot strapping; U defends acceptance of Π through her cognitive and inferential dispositions. That defence has normative force because of U's disposition to defend these cognitive states and inferential dispositions in turn, and so on.

Another way of putting this is in terms of reason. Acceptance, rejection, etc. are intimately connected to possession of reasons; one accepts Π because one has a reason, say, accepting Π'. In the expressive framework proposed here, the normativity of reason is itself expressively analysed. That is, assertions of sentences R, below,

R: Accepting Π is a reason for accepting Π'

are assertions where we express commitment to certain cognitive regularities of the form: instantiating Π' is a causal ground for instantiating Π. So, assertions of R have the structure:

R: (i)   U utters R and advertises intentions:
          (*a*)   to represent a fact of the form <For U, instantiating Π' is a causal ground for instantiating Π>; and
          (*b*)   to defend commitment to a property in (*a*).
       (ii)   U possesses the intention (*ib*).

An audience H will judge an assertion of R true if and only if she herself experiences the cognitive causal law as something compelling in her case; she instantiates the state. Thus an assertion of R is not a claim that certain causal law holds for certain cognitive systems—that is a crude and untenable naturalistic reduction—but is an expressive assertion in which such a state is defended.

In short, the intersubjective engagement of defence presupposes that agents embody certain natural regularities in their cognitive and conative systems. These regularities must be reasons—they must have normative rightness—but their having such status just resides in the fact that *normative assent* is always possible with respect to them. This means that we are disposed to defend the cognitive/conative regularities through intersubjective engagement. Of course, we cannot defend every regularity of our system in one go.

The **PCT**-account uses the intersubjectivity of defence to underpin normativity and objective truth. But it might seem that it cannot be right. What of the lone thinker, Robinson Crusoe, who does not engage with any one? Crusoe makes assertions to himself that are objectively true. But Crusoe is not engaged intersubjectively with others. Of course, we can allow that Crusoe monitors his own speech. However, in describing Crusoe, we, as authors of a certain fiction, take up a stance towards our fictional creation. If we think that Crusoe has said something true it is because we express a commitment to the Π-property he defends.

Another objection to the **PCT**-account is that it over-intellectualizes assertion. In assertion U intends, tries to bring it about, that H recognizes her possession of the state, and either accepts or disputes it. It might seem that this is a rather complex intention, and a higher-level intention at that. In advertising an intention to defend Π, U intends to engage in the behaviour characteristic of a speaker who intends that H recognize that U accepts Π. But, this, I suggest, is ultimately just causal complexity. Speakers do not need explicit theories themselves about what they are doing any more than they need a theory of grammar. So there is no over-intellectualization.

4. Embedding and belief

According to **PCT**, truth-bearers are assertion-types or tokens. This entails that unasserted sentences—though fully contentful—don't have truth-values. But is that plausible?[9] There are three reasons to think not. (*a*)In locutions of the form 'It is true that *S*' we assert truth of something, but one might claim it is unasserted. (*b*)The sentences embedded in logical compounds like negations and disjunctions have truth-values, but are unasserted. (*c*) Generally what is believed is open to truth-evaluation, but it's not an assertion.

I deal with these objections in turn. Clearly assertions don't embed. What embeds is something prior to assertion. In uttering *S* embedded, U performs component (i) of the illocutionary act of assertion: the act of advertising intentions to represent and defend. That U so advertises is a conventional matter. U advertises these intentions, but of course lacks them. I call this act of advertising intentions *proto-assertion*. It is proto-assertions that embed in constructions like 'It is true that…' and logical compounds. Although falling short of a full-fledged assertion, proto-assertions, nevertheless, determinately indicate assertions. So with respect to objection (*a*), my reply is that in 'It is true that *S*' U performs a proto-assertion with *S*, but 'that *S*' denotes an assertion-type

---

[9] One piece of evidence that non-asserted declarative sentences are not truth-apt is the fact that declarative sentences used to perform orders are not truth-apt. See Barker (2004: ch. 1.2).

corresponding to this proto-assertion. We predicate truth of this assertion-type. With respect to objection (*b*), I say that in a compound 'It is not the case that *S*' U performs a proto-assertion with *S* and the whole is judged true just in case the corresponding assertion-type is judged false. And so on.

According to **PCT**, truth-bearers are assertion-types and assertions are either reportive or expressive. Are then logical compounds reportive or expressive assertions? I propose treating them as expressive assertions. Thus in uttering 'It is not the case that *S*' U expresses a commitment to rejection of the Π-property of A(*S*), the assertion of *S*. That is,

Neg: (i) U utters 'It is not that the case that *S*' U performs a proto-assertion of *S*, and in addition advertises intentions:

    (*a*) to represent a fact of the form $<$U rejects Π of A(S)$>$; and

    (*b*) to defend commitment to a property: rejection of Π of A(S).

  (ii) U possesses the intention (*ib*).

Disjunction can likewise be characterized. In uttering 'either S_1 or S_2', U expresses her rejection of commitment to rejecting both disjuncts, S_1 and S_2.

As expressive assertions, logically complex assertion are evaluated with respect to truth or falsity just as other expressive assertions are. An audience H employs the truth- or falsity-predicates to express her acceptance, or rejection, of the commitment states U expresses. Such sentences lack special truth-makers. So for example, negations are not made true by negative facts, disjunctions by disjunctive facts, etc.

The third objection (*c*) given above is that beliefs can be truth-apt but are not assertion-types. In reply, I emphasize that beliefs and judgements are not entities that lie behind assertions, as wholly distinct from them. Judgement just is assertion. Thus what I call assertions may be private affairs involving purely internal episodes—sentences in the head or word qualia—associated with intentions. I reject the view of assertions as public and relatively superficial manifestations of underlying states that are the real cognitive action.

Secondly, I note that there are belief-attributions that are best explained as cases where the object of belief is an assertion-type. Take attribution of probabilistic beliefs—as in 'Jones believes that it is probably raining.' Jones is related to a content. That content, I suggest, is simply the expressive assertion-type, given in **P2**. There is no other candidate.

It is not my claim here, however, that belief-objects are always and essentially assertion-types. As already noted, underpinning an ability to perform assertions—verbal judgements—is a natural cognitive/conative representational system. Some of the states of this system are logically simple belief-like representational states. I call these doxastic tracking states. Perhaps non-verbal creatures unequipped to perform illocutionary acts have such states as what are essentially belief-states with non-linguistic objects. They have doxastic tracking states. However, doxastic tracking states are not truth-apt. Truth is not the property of correctly representing reality.

What is believing when its object is an assertion-type? Is it a disposition to sincerely assert? An objection to this is that people can sincerely assert that *S* even though all other evidence indicates that they believe not-*S*. There are two ways to go here. First, we can propose that the speaker has contradictory beliefs. She believes that *S*, based on verbal production, and consciously, and she believes that *not-S* unconsciously, based on behaviour. An alternative is that we put stronger conditions on belief: it is not merely being disposed to perform an assertion sincerely, it is also required that the underpinning doxastic grounds in fact commit U to assertion.

5. Value

That completes my sketch of **PCT** and a theory of expressive discourse that is an alternative to **MP**.[10] We now turn to value-sentences. My hypothesis is that the concept of *expressing* articulated in the last few sections is precisely the notion of expression required for the value expressivist. Consider ought-statements like (6) on a deontic reading:

(6) Bill ought to confess.

If we were objectivists about value, we might treat utterance of (6) as a report about a putative special fact of value. Expressivism rejects this analysis; utterance of (6) is an expression of attitude. We can now give a linguistic model of what that is. Utterance of (6) is, I submit, an expressive assertion with a structure analogous to P2 above, the structure of a subjective probability statement. The only difference is that the state that U is expressing is a desire state rather than an epistemic state. So the assertion-type corresponding to (6) is something like:

VO: (i) U utters 'T ought to Φ' advertising intentions:
         (*a*) to represent a fact of the form $<$U approves of *T*'s Φ-ing$>$; and
         (*b*) to defend commitment to approval of T's Φ-ing.
    (ii) U has the intention in (*ib*).

---

[10] See Barker 2004 for a detailed treatment of **PCT**, and especially the issue of compositionality.

Evidently, the kind of approval that U is defending is of the special ethical kind. It is an approval based on the judgement that certain kinds of properties are instantiated, ones we identify as ethically relevant. An expressivist treatment of value needs to provide some kind of account of what sorts of properties these are—that would be a theory of what distinguishes moral attitudes from other kinds. I won't attempt to provide any such account here.

On the current view, 'T ought to Φ' has the content of 'It is desirable that T Φs' or 'It is preferable that T Φs,' where these sentences are used in expressive assertions in exactly the same sense. It is quite consistent with this theory that U asserts, 'I do not want to do Φ, but I ought to do Φ.' U simply has conflicting desires about Φ-ing. Φ-ing has properties which make it desirable but also undesirable, where those properties that make it desirable are properties that stimulate moral attitudes.

In the case of ethical musts, such as 'Fred must not kill Jane,' it seems that the attitude expressed is stronger than desire or preference. Perhaps the state defended in 'Fred must Φ' is something more like:

(7) [x would be shocked, horrified, filled with deep disapproval, etc., if Fred were not to Φ]

Ethical 'may' as in 'Fred may/is permitted to Φ', are cases in which U expresses her rejection of any commitment to desiring that Fred not Φ or her rejection of a state like (7). States of desire can be rejected since there are rational connections between belief and desire sets and desires. (More of that in a moment.)

Truth and objectivity

The **PCT**-analysis applied to value-sentences enables us to explain how value-sentences, assuming value-expressivism, are truth-apt, but have no truth-makers. Assertion of value-sentences is guided by subjective states, but they are not reports about those states or any facts in the world that might have given rise to them. Consider the dialogue (8):

(8) Smith: Bill ought to confess.
Jones: True. Bill ought to confess.

Let us assume **VO** above. Smith and Jones in (8) defend approval states about Bill's confessing. They are not merely reporting their own states; their utterances are not true by virtue of the obtaining of those states of approval—there is no subjectivist relativism here. In fact, their utterances are not true by virtue of anything. The common truth-bearer about whose truth Jones and Smith agree upon is the assertion-type whose commitment property is possession of the state of desiring that Bill confesses. Both Smith and Jones accept this Π-property. Jones's judgement of truth is his expression of acceptance of that Π-property. Our truth judgement as third parties is expression of acceptance of the Π-property; or if we judge the assertion false, our falsity judgement is an expression of rejection of that Π-property.

I submit that PCT-account, applied to value-statements, can explain the objectivity that attends ought-statements. That objectivity resides in the facts that: (*a*) what ought to be, or may be, etc., is not a matter of desire; (*b*) the truth of value-sentences is something that we can debate; (*c*) where there is disagreement we can talk of error. These three aspects of objectivity are captured by PCT as follows. According to the PCT-account, subjects' possessing desires doesn't make ought/must/may-statements true. Rather the truth of value-statements is established through defence of motivational Π-properties, that is, through, potentially, rational dispute. Participants in such intersubjective engagement are often prepared to stand by their commitments. It is not an arbitrary matter what subjects desire or prefer. Given U disapproves of lying, U, as a result, disapproves of Fred's lying. The former is a reason for the latter. The normativity of reasons, as already noted in section 3, resides in our expressed commitment to acceptance/instantiation of causal laws in our cognitve/conative systems. So, in the present case, U's cognitive/conative system instantiates the following causal law:

(9) (Π') Disapproval of lying causes (Π) disapproval of Fred's lying.

So U's defence of disapproval of Fred's action is grounded by her instantiation of (9) and the state of disapproving of lying. The normative force of this defence derives from the fact that U is prepared to defend these states in turn. That is, the PCT-analysis does not attempt to reduce normativity to causal regularity, but rather to the intersubjective engagement of defending cognitive/conative states that may involve causal regularities.

This account presupposes that motivational states can be defended, that is, accepted, and rejected, etc. For this to be possible in PCT's terms, all that is required is transitional laws like (9) and states, like disapproval of lying, that can be instantiated or not, or which, in the case of rejection, are states that U's system is disposed not to instantiate, given certain constraints. These are essentially the same basic conditions that underpin defence of properties in the case of non-value-assertions. PCT countenances no difference as such between the truth of logical compounds, such as 'There are no hippos in this room', and moral truths such as 'Hippos ought not to be treated cruelly'. Both have equal status to be called real, objective truths.

Note the objectivity of moral truth does not require convergence. It is not built into the possibility of objective moral truth that there is agreement with a community of moral judges. Moral truth can be essentially contested—there is no guarantee that there is agreement to be had out there. What we have instead is openness to contestation, and dialectical engagement. Value-assertions are challenges to a potential other to debate. Because 'is true' is not a descriptive predicate, with the content 'believed by my peers', a speaker cannot isolate herself in her own community—immune from critique from others outside that community. Rather the moral judge is open to challenge because built into making any judgement at all is the act of taking a stance. In short, we don't have a descriptive, static conception of truth—truth as a kind of achievement of correspondence or agreement—but a dynamic conception of truth. A judgement of moral truth is an expression of acceptance of a certain conative, or related, property, potentially defendable by some agent. But this, as we have seen, is essentially the same story with all truth.[11]

Embedding, validity, and belief

The possibility of objective moral truth is one dimension of the semantics of moral statements. A second important dimension to moral truth is embedding and validity. The **PCT**-account has no problems treating embedded value-sentences. Consider a conditional like (10):

(10) If Bill did it, he ought to confess.

Utterance of (10) expresses commitment to belief that the assertability for U of the antecedent, given background beliefs, is a reason for accepting the assertability for U of the consequent. We include as a background belief, say, that people who do wrong ought to confess, and the denotation of 'it' in (10) was a wrong.

The validity of arguments like (11) below is perfectly explicable:

(11) If Bill did it, he ought to confess. Bill did it. Therefore, he ought to confess.

Validity falls out straightforwardly in terms of truth—assuming that *if*-sentences are truth-apt. We can say that an argument is valid if and only if any valuation *V* of its premises that renders them true, will render its conclusion true. By *valuation* I mean a set of judgements of truth and falsity of the logically simple

---

[11] How do we think of isolated moral agents like Robinson Crusoe? As we did for the agent isolated in general. Moral judges don't need audiences as such. To say something true is not constituted by being in agreement with anyone else. (It is not constituted by anything, in fact.) In imaging Crusoe we assess the truth of his moral utterances, which is to say, we express commitment to the motivational Π-properties he defends or not.

sentences of the language concerned, with logically complex sentence receiving values as a consequence, given their meanings, of this assignment.

In section 4, I argued that assertion-types are the principal objects of belief. In the moral case, the object of belief is an expressive assertion-type. In the case in which U believes that Bill ought to confess, the assertion-type has the structure of **VO**. U's moral belief-state is a commitment to this assertion-type, one in which U defends a motivation state: approving of Bill's confessing. The moral belief-state is then, effectively, a disposition to defend a motivational state. It is not the motivational state itself.

'Good' and thick ethical terms

Sentences with modal auxiliaries such as 'ought', 'must', and 'may', etc. are not the only kinds of ethical value-sentences. There are non-modal value-sentences such as 'T is good' or 'T is right'. One might attempt to treat these as corresponding to assertion-types of exactly the same kind as ought-sentences. In other words, 'T is good' is like '*S* is true'; they are used in expressive assertions. What, however, of thick ethical terms, such as *courageous* or *generous*?

In Barker (2000), I propose an implicature theory of value that is applied to thick evaluative assertions. According to it, value-sentences such as 'T is courageous' have a *said*-content, which is a factual assertion about T possessing a certain property *G*; and an implicature that U is committed to approving of things that have *G*. Such value-assertions have the same structure as utterances of 'Even T is *G*', which feature the implicature operator 'even'. This sentence has a said-content that T is *G* and an implicature about the relative unlikeliness of T being *G*. So, 'T is courageous' has the form:

C: If U asserts the sentence 'T is courageous' then U intends to denote by 'courageous' a property *F*: being such as not to flee in situations of adversity, etc, and:

   (i) U reportively asserts that T is *F*;

   (ii) U implicates that U is committed to approval of *F*-things.

This theory is expressivist because value-content is non-reported content, albeit the value-assertion as a whole has a reportive, non-value component.

Implicature is a form of pragmatic presupposition. So in asserting that T is courageous, U communicates that approval of *F*-things is to be taken for granted by her audience. This means that H judges U's utterance correct if and only if she, H, judges that T has *F* and she, H, approves of *F*-things.[12]

---

[12] In fact, in Barker (2000) I supply a similar dual-content theory for 'good'.

To fully develop this account we need to explain what implicature is as form of non-truth-conditional content, embedding, and validity—I do this in Barker (2003, 2004) using the **PCT**-framework.

Summary

In this paper I have presented an alternative framework for understanding new wave value expressivism, which fully embraces the truth-aptness of value-sentences. I argued that the Minimalist approach, **MP**, which attempts to analyse expressing in terms of non-representational discourse, is not tenable. According to the alternative I defend, **PCT**—the pragmatic conception of truth—truth-bearers are assertions, which come in two kinds, reportive and expressive. This theory can be supplemented with an implicature account, which applies to thick ethical terms.

References

ALSTON, W. (2000). *Illocutionary Acts & Sentence Meaning*. Ithaca, NY: Cornell.

AYER, A. J. (1946). *Language, Truth and Logic*. 2nd edn. London: Victor Gollancz.

BARKER, S. (2000). 'Is Value Content a Component of Conventional Implicature?' *Analysis*, 60/3: 268–79.

—— (2003). 'Truth and Conventional Implicature'. *Mind*, 112: 1–31.

—— (2004). *Renewing Meaning*. Oxford: Clarendon Press.

BLACKBURN, S. (1998). *Ruling Passions*. Oxford: Clarendon Press.

BRANDOM, R. (1983). 'Asserting', *Nous*, 17: 637–50.

GIBBARD, A. (1990). *Wise Choices, Apt Feelings*. Cambridge, Mass.: Harvard University Press.

HALE, B. (2002). 'Can arboreal knotwork help Blackburn out of Frege's abyss?' *Philosophy and Phenomenological Research*, 65: 144–9.

HARE, R. (1952). *The Language of Morals*. Oxford: Oxford University Press.

HORGAN, T., and TIMMONS, M. (2000). 'Nondescriptivist Cognitivism: Framework for a New Metaethic', *Philosophical Papers*, 29: 121–53.

KOELBEL, MAX, (2002). *Truth without Objectivity*. London: Routledge.

PRICE, H. (1990). 'Why "not"?' *Mind*, 99: 221–38.

VAN ROOJEN, M. (1996). 'Expressivism and Irrationality'. *Philosophical Review*, 105: 311–35.

WRIGHT, C. (1998). *Truth and Objectivity*. Cambridge, Mass.: Harvard University Press.

14

Normative Properties

Allan Gibbard

When the young G. E. Moore chose the title of his first book, *Principia Ethica*, roughly a hundred years ago, he was of course emulating Newton. And like anyone who hopes to develop a systematic treatment of ethics, he first needed to explain what questions he would be addressing. On this he found himself to be in a minority of two, along with his old teacher Henry Sidgwick, whose personality and lectures Moore had found dull back in his student days a decade earlier.[1] Sidgwick was the only other writer who recognized that the basic concept of ethics is indefinable, so that no full explanation of ethical questions in terms drawn entirely from outside ethics can be given.[2] 'What definition can we give of "ought", "right", and other terms expressing the same fundamental notion?' asked Sidgwick. 'To this I should answer that the notion which these terms have in common is too elementary to admit of any formal definition.'[3] The century of metaethics we now celebrate, though, begins with Moore, not with Sidgwick in 1874. That's not because all of Moore's arguments for the indefinability claim were sharply different from Sidgwick's. It's not because Moore, any more than Sidgwick, meant the indefinability thesis to be the centerpiece of his work; for both men it was a preliminary. But Moore was vivid where Sidgwick was dull, and he not only attacked specific alternatives but gave arguments intended to drive the thesis home in general.

Moore stressed the distinction in ethics between questions of meaning and questions of substance, and thereby gave rise to a tradition in analytic philosophy of separating the two parts of ethical theory: the metatheory and the substantive, normative part. Some philosophers have rejected the distinction; some Kantians, for instance, think that if you get the metatheory right, substantive ethical conclusions fall out as some kind of consequence, so that metaethics and substantive ethics are not really separate. Then too, anyone who rejects Sidgwick's and Moore's indefinability claim and thinks that ethical terms

---

[1] Moore, 'An Autobiography,' 16.   [2] Moore, *Principia Ethica*, 17.
[3] Sidgwick, *Methods of Ethics*, I. iii . 3, p. 32.

can be given analytic, naturalistic definitions thinks that the two putative subdivisions are not really separate. Those who reject any systematic distinction between questions of meaning and questions of substance might likewise reject a sharp, separate subject of metaethics. Still, in the analytic tradition, the distinction between substantive ethics and metaethics has been tenacious, and even philosophers who doubt it keep falling back into enquiries that seem recognizably metaethical. Highlighting a hundred years of metaethics since Moore's book, then, is entirely appropriate.

The subject that came to be known as metaethics fits awkwardly into philosophical subdivisions. Its central questions concern meanings and concepts, and how to treat these in general is a question not for the peripheral subfield of philosophy that ethics is, but for the 'core areas'; these are questions for the philosophy of language and philosophy of mind, along with metaphysics and epistemology. The dual nature of metaethics suited Moore himself perfectly: Moore had a novel ethical vision to propound, with its organic wholes in place of hedonism and its stress on the value of taking pleasure in true beauty and true friendship. A correct metaethics, he thought, would clear the way to a correct ethics. He also joined Russell to revolutionize English philosophy in the core areas. Since Moore, metaethics has been driven both by people who want to do ethics and by philosophers of the core areas, who ask whether ethics poses any special problems for their philosophies—for theories of concepts, properties, and the like. Ayer, for instance, found philosophical ethics a nuisance, since it threatened to offer a counterexample to the verifiability criterion of meaning.[4] Stevenson worked on metaethics, he told Frankena, because he wanted a subject that Wittgenstein wasn't working on;[5] he developed a view he had found in a one-page passage of Ogden and Richards on the meaning of meaning.[6] He and Ayer eventually converged on a view that included elements drawn from each of them.[7] Those in our recognized canon of the greatest philosophers ever, Plato, Aristotle, Hume, and Kant, all worked seriously both on core areas and on ethics, including what we'd now call metaethics, and their ethical and core area theories are of a piece with each other. We recently sadly lost the great David Lewis, whose interests centered on the core areas but whose work in ethics, metaethics, and social philosophy fills a volume.[8] Metaethics by now is a subject that brings together two tribes of philosophers: specialists in

---

[4] Ayer, *Language, Truth and Logic*, ch. 6.   [5] This is my memory of what Frankena told us.

[6] Ogden and Richards, *The Meaning of Meaning*, 125. Stevenson reproduces the passage at the start of *Ethics and Language*, and in 'The Emotive Meaning of Ethical Terms,' he calls it 'the source of the ideas embodied in this paper' (23).

[7] See Stevenson, *Facts and Values*, 210–14, and Ayer, *Language, Truth and Logic*, 2nd edn. (1946). I thank Kevin Toh for clarifying changes in Stevenson's thought.

[8] Lewis, *Papers in Ethics and Social Philosophy*.

ethics and specialists in the 'core areas.' Since most of us can't do both with a specialist's degree of sophistication, this makes for tensions. The ideal in metaethics must be to combine experience and sensitivity in both areas.

Indeed in recent decades, aspects of ethics have begun to enter the core areas. The special features of ethical concepts that Moore stressed are not, many of us now think, special to narrow morality, with its stress on right and wrong, the morally admirable and the blameworthy. We do of course need to understand the concepts of narrow morality, to wield them effectively or to criticize them (as do Nietzsche and Bernard Williams[9]). But part of what's special about morality is that it operates in the 'space of reasons;' it concerns justification and oughts. So, broadly speaking, does epistemology, with its focus on what we have reason to believe. The same goes for questions about sentiments or feelings: what we have reason to admire or be ashamed of. The term 'normative' is central to much current philosophical discussion. There's no agreement on what this technical term in our discipline is to mean, but it involves, in a phrase drawn from Sellars, being somehow 'fraught with ought.' And in recent decades, it has been claimed—even proclaimed as an established finding—that the concept of meaning is normative. It has been held that the concept of mental content is normative, the concept, that is, of what a person is thinking; thus, for instance, the predicate 'thinks that snow is white' is, according to some, a normative concept. So not only is metaethics, in some ways, a branch of core area philosophy, with all the privileges and duties pertaining thereto. Crucial parts of the core areas now become branches of metaethics, more or less. What's crucially puzzling in metaethics extends to the puzzling topic of normative concepts in general. That makes for a broader subject matter, the metatheory of normativity, covering concepts of justified belief and justified feelings. The metatheory of meaning and of mental content, the 'meaning of meaning,' will, if some philosophers are right, be a part of all this. If so, then substantive theory of meaning and mental content are branches of a broad subject, substantive normative theory. Ethics and metaethics expand to take in most all of philosophy.

I won't explore in this paper whether, in some important sense, meaning indeed is 'normative.' Some philosophers argue that it is and some that it isn't.[10] I do think that normativity in general is an intelligible topic, worthy of

---

[9] Nietzsche, *The Genealogy of Morals*; Williams, *Ethics and the Limits of Philosophy*.

[10] Kripke's words on p. 58 of *Wittgenstein on Rules* at least suggest a view that the concept of meaning and the concept of what a person is thinking are normative concepts. McDowell endorses such a view in 'Wittgenstein on Following a Rule,' 336. Brandom makes such a view central to his theory of thought and language in *Making it Explicit*. I propose an interpretation of such claims in 'Meaning and Normativity.' For criticisms of such claims, see Horwich, *Meaning*, ch. 8, and Millar, 'Normativity of Meaning.'

study, and I have a hypothesis on what it involves. In advance of establishing what normativity consists in, we can characterize it in a theory-light way that allows for competing theories of its nature. Suppose Moore is right that the concepts of good, morally ought, and the like have some important feature that the empirical concepts of science and everyday life don't share. And suppose later philosophers are right that this puzzling feature is shared by a wider class of concepts that somehow involve reasons or being 'fraught with ought.' Then if there is some special, problematic feature that all these concepts share, our technical term for it is 'normativity'. If there isn't any such crucial, distinctive feature, then there's no such special topic of study as normativity. If there is such a feature, then this theory-light characterization tells us what competing theories of normativity are at odds over: what the special, problematic feature is that concepts of reasons and oughts and other concepts that seem laden with these all distinctively share.[11]

If there is such a distinctive thing as normativity in this sense, then we'd expect metaethical enquiries to go in two directions. One is to develop, refine, and criticize metatheories of normativity in general. The other is to enquire into moral and ethical concepts in particular: within the broad field of normativity, we can ask, what's special about ethics? These two broad areas of enquiry must speak to each other: if ethics is a special branch of normative enquiry, then a correct theory of the nature of ethics must fit with a correct theory of the normative in general, and ethics will provide a crucial test case for any theory of how normativity in general works. But the two flavors of enquiry will be quite different. Developing metanormative theory must involve, ideally, a close collaboration of thinkers from different subdisciplinary backgrounds, ethics and the core areas. Asking what's special about ethics within the normative in general, on the other hand, should lead to centrally ethical concerns.

In this paper, I grapple with normative concepts in general. I myself have a view on how normative concepts work,[12] and in this paper I consider one crucial aspect of the view. The view draws on resources from the classic non-cognitivists Ayer and Stevenson, but it ends up with theses that sound highly 'realistic' and metaphysical. There is a property, I say, that constitutes being what one ought to do. This property is, in a broad sense, a natural property. Concepts are another matter: normative concepts are distinct from

---

[11] I propose this theory-light characterization in 'Meaning and Normativity,' 97.

[12] My new book *Thinking How to Live* develops the aspects of my view that this paper explores further. My 'Normative and Recognitional Concepts' was largely drawn from the manuscript of that book, and contains some of its central contentions. See also my 'Reply to Hawthorne' and 'Knowing What to Do, Seeing What to Do.' My *Wise Choices* presents the main aspects of the view and is broader in its concerns, but on the issues in this paper it says far less than does *Thinking How to Live*.

naturalistic concepts; on this score Moore was quite right. But normative and naturalistic concepts signify properties of the same kinds; indeed a normative and a naturalistic concept might signify the very same property. What's distinctly normative, then, is not properties but concepts. It is this set of claims about normative properties—that they exist and are, in a broad sense, natural—that I scrutinize here.

1. The thesis and the argument for it

I distinguish concepts and properties. The property of being water turns out just to be the property of being H_2O, consisting of molecules made up in a certain way. The concepts, though, are different; it came as a discovery that water is H_2O, and people could intelligibly disagree on whether it is—whereas disagreement on whether water is water would be baffling. Moore's arguments for non-naturalism harped on such possibilities of intelligible disagreement, and what arguments of this kind show, as with water and H_2O, is not a difference of properties but of concepts. Moore himself insisted that what he called '*the* good' is a natural object of thought; it is the natural property that all and only good things must always have. We could emend Moore, then, to say that whereas the *concept* of being good is distinct from any naturalistic concept—from concepts fit for empirical science and its everyday counterparts—the *property* of being good is a natural property, a property for which we could have a naturalistic concept. Moore thought that this property involves complex organic wholes, but his chapter I arguments in *Principia Ethica* were not the ones he thought established this. The doctrine of organic wholes, as we would now say, is a substantive ethical claim, not a conclusion of his metaethical arguments. An ethical hedonist, for instance, would be mistaken but might be intelligible, thought Moore. On the emended Moore-like picture I am proposing, such a metaethically unconfused hedonist would think that the concepts are different but the properties are the same. The property of being good just *is* the property of being pleasant.

Any being capable of action, I claim, is committed to a view with this structure—not that being good is being pleasant, but that *some* natural property is the property of being good, whether or not we know what property it is. To show how the argument for this works, I switch from *good* to *ought*. (Good, on my view, is a composite concept: to be good is to be desirable, such that it ought to be desired.) The starting point of the argument owes much to Ayer: we say what the word 'ought' means not directly, but by saying what is to *think* or *believe* that a person ought to do something. What is it, say, to think that one ought to leave a building if the fire alarm rings? To think this, I propose, is to plan for a contingency. I think, 'Jack ought to leave the building,' and accepting this amounts to adopting a contingency plan: a plan to leave the building in the contingency of being in Jack's exact circumstances. Now this is something on which we can agree or disagree; there is such a thing as *disagreement in plan*. You and I, in other words, can disagree on what to do in Jack's plight. And this possibility of disagreement in plan leads to all the metaphysical-sounding things that I want to say.

What, then, of more complex normative claims? That is the crucial 'Frege–Geach' worry for 'expressivistic' theories, theories in the spirit of Ayer and Stevenson. Take, for instance, a disjunctive claim,

Jack is engaged in some matter of life and death or he ought to leave the building.

Now if we can make sense of disagreement in plan, then we can offer a general account of what such complex normative claims amount to. We elicit the content of this claim by mapping what agreeing or disagreeing with it amounts to. To do this, take an onlooker who is *fully decided*: she has a view as to how the world is naturalistically and has a full contingency plan for living—or at least one full enough to cover purposes at hand. I'm decided enough to agree or disagree with this claim if I'm settled on two matters: the naturalistic matter of whether life or death hinges on what Jack is doing and the planning matter of whether to leave the building if faced with his plight. The onlooker disagrees with this claim just in case she both (i) thinks that Jack isn't engaged in a matter of life and death, and (ii) plans not to leave the building if faced with his plight. The content of the claim, then, amounts to which decided states it disagrees with, to which possibilities it rules out.

Now for the claim of Natural Constitution, the claim I explore in this paper. *Some broadly natural property constitutes being what one ought to do*—that is the claim. Any planner whatsoever is committed to this claim, I argue. Here is the proof, quickly sketched[13]: Imagine first an onlooker who is decided enough to agree or disagree with any normative claim whatsoever. Fantastically, she has what we might call a *hyperplan*: a full contingency plan for living, which covers any situation a person might conceivably be in. Now a full plan for a circumstance must be couched in terms that are empirical or naturalistic. A plan, say, simply to do whatever is best would be no plan at all, until it was supplemented with directions for recognizing what's best. Infinitely, then, we could put this onlooker's hyperplan in naturalistic terms: it runs, 'In circumstance C_1, do A_1; in circumstance C_2 do A_2;' and so on. According to this onlooker, then, there is

---

[13] See my *Thinking How to Live* (forthcoming), ch. 5.

a property that constitutes being what one ought to do—namely this one: being act A_1 in circumstance C_1, or act A_2 in circumstance C_2, and so on. The terms in this infinite disjunction are all couched naturalistically. Infinite disjunctions of natural properties are 'natural' in a broad sense. This onlooker, then, accepts Natural Constitution: that there is some broadly natural property that constitutes being what one ought to do.[14]

Most of us, of course, aren't hyperdecided on what to do and how things stand. But here is a principle that applies to the rest of us too. Suppose there's something I'd accept no matter how I filled out my views, so long as I didn't change my mind about anything. I'm undecided, imagine, whether the temperature this afternoon will be in the high 80s or low 90s Fahrenheit. Any way of filling out my views without changing my mind then involves thinking it will be hot. And so, we can conclude, I'm already committed to the claim that it will be hot this afternoon. This principle applies to the claim of Natural Constitution. Any way I might fill out my plans for living completely without changing my mind about anything would bring me to accept Natural Constitution. I'd think that there is a broadly natural property that constitutes being what one ought to do, because I'd have a view on what that property is. And so Natural Constitution is a claim to which I'm already committed.

I now make a transcendental move and voice the claim to which I am committed: *Some broadly natural property constitutes being what one ought to do.*

This quick argument needs far more elucidation and exploration that I can give it here. In this paper, though, I explore just one set of questions it raises— questions I don't get far enough into in my new book *Thinking How to Live.*

2. Too many properties?

The proof I just sketched assumes a particular kind of conception of what a property is. Any full contingency plan for living, I supposed, amounts to the plan always to do whatever act has a certain property. The proof goes through if a 'possible worlds' conception of properties is correct, a model-theoretic conception. A property, on this conception, is a function of a particular kind. A *world-to-extension* function, let's say, is one whose domain is the set of all

---

[14] Moore's own arguments concerned a broader class of properties than the strictly natural. He thought they applied not only to natural objects of thought but to supernatural and metaphysical ones too; he thought he had refuted the possibility of a supernatural definition of good or a metaphysical one. Perhaps we should use a term like 'factual property' to cover all of these—but that wouldn't fit a minimalist reading of 'fact'. For more discussion of this, see my 'Reply to Hawthorne'; on minimalism for 'truth' and 'fact', see Horwich, *Truth.*

possible worlds, and which assigns to each possible world a set of entities in that world. The proof I offered works so long as a property is just a world-to-extension function. Or alternatively, I could have made a slightly weaker assumption: that properties correspond one-to-one with world-to-extension functions. A full contingency plan determines, for each possible world, a set of occasions for action along with the act the plan prescribes for that occasion. It thus assigns to each world a set of occasion-act pairs—and thus, on the possible world's conception of a property, determines a property of occasion-act pairs.

Now trivially, any property is characterized by a world-to-extension function. Redness is characterized by the function that assigns, to each possible world, the set of entities in that world that are red in that world. In general, on this pattern, any property P, we can say, is characterised by the world-to-extension function that assigns, to each world w, the set of entities in w that have property P in w. My argument for Natural Constitution depended, though, on a controversial assumption that goes the other way around: that every world-to-extension function characterizes some property. I supposed too that no world-to-extension function characterizes more than one property.

I help myself freely to possible worlds, and I follow Stalnaker in thinking that such talk is innocuous. A possible world is a way things might have been—a way that is fully determinate.[15] So the world-to-extension function for 'red' is the function that assigns, to each determinate way things might have been, the set of all entities that would have existed and would have been red had things been that way.

Given my assumptions, the property that constitutes being what one ought to do is natural in the following sense. A *natural world*, we can say, is a completely determinate way that things might have been so far as basic natural properties go. Given any natural world, there is a set of acts open in that world. (Think of an open act as consisting in an occasion for action and one of the alternatives open to the agent on that occasion.) Then there's a world-to-extension function defined as follows: to each natural world, it assigns the set of all acts open in that world which an agent ought to perform. In other words, to each determinate way things might have been naturalistically, it assigns the set of all acts that would, if the things had been that way, be open to someone and be what that person ought to do. Suppose then, as I did, that any world-to-extension function corresponds to a unique property. With natural worlds in question, this property is broadly natural in this sense: the worlds are ways things might have been naturalistically, and the identity of the property is fixed by natural aspects of how things would have been had they been that way.

---

[15] Stalnaker, 'Possible Worlds.'

Indeed Natural Constitution in no way depends on my expressivistic starting point. The principle holds so long as what one ought to do supervenes on the natural properties of the situation, in this sense: in two possible situations, what an agent ought to do differs only if situations differ in some natural feature.[16] The point of the proof is that expressivism mimics a normative realism like Moore's in this regard: from expressivism follows the supervenience of the normative on the natural, and from this supervenience follows Natural Constitution.

This view of properties as world-to-extension functions, though, is probably a minority view among metaphysicians who think about such matters. In a way, the view may be too indiscriminate: it allows the wildest infinite disjunction of properties to count as a property. In another way, it may be too restrictive, for it doesn't allow that there could be necessarily equivalent properties that are distinct, such as being triangular and being trilateral.

I need to enquire, then, what happens if we question the assumption that properties are world-to-extension functions—or at least correspond to them one to one.

3. Plans that coincide with properties

The assumptions on which my argument depended, recall, were two: that (i) for each world-to-extension function there is a property that it characterizes, and (ii) no world-to-extension function characterizes more than one property. This second assumption is, in other words, that necessarily equivalent properties are identical. Properties are necessarily equivalent just in case, no matter how things had been, they would have been coextensional, that is, possessed by the same set of things. I'll explore the issue as follows: Take first any contingency plan that does *coincide* with a property, in the sense that some property N satisfies this condition:

> for any possible occasion for action and any act open on that occasion, the plan prescribes that act for that occasion just in case the act has property N.

I'll urge—though with misgivings—that it's then idle to think anything but that being what one ought to do consists in having property N. I'll then turn to assumption (i) and argue that we should be liberal with our attributions of properties, allowing every world-to-extension function to characterize a

---

[16] Of the many species of 'supervenience' that have been distinguished in the literature, this is roughly 'strong supervenience' in Kim's sense, *Supervenience and Mind*, 149–56; he adds a vague dependence requirement that seems to be met.

property. My exploration, at the end of the paper, will arrive at an issue that has been central to recent ethical theory and can be formulated independently of the metaphysical questions I am asking about properties.

Suppose for now that assumption (i) fails, in that not every hyperplan coincides with a property. Consider, though, any hyperplan that does so coincide; it directs all and only those acts that have a certain property N. Someone who adopts this hyperplan, I'll suggest, should accept that being what one ought to do consists in having property N. She should consider the property of being what one ought to do just to *be* property N.

Without loss of generality, we could take some particular hyperplan that coincides with a property and ask what lessons generalize. Consider the hyperplan of a universal hedonist and the property of maximizing net pleasure in the universe. Shouldn't she claim that the property of being what one ought to do just is the property of prospectively maximizing net happiness in the universe— of being *unihedonic*, as I'll say? Look again to our familiar paradigm of property identity, water and H_2O. The property of being water is the property of being H_2O—why say this? Natural properties, we can say, are properties open to empirical investigation; they seem to earn their keep in empirically based causal explanations.[17] Being H_2O is a matter of chemical structure, with two hydrogen atoms bonded to an oxygen atom. Having this structure turns out to explain the manifest phenomena we more familiarly explain wielding the concept water. Thus we say that being water turns out to consist in being H_2O—that one property is in play, and molecular theory explains its nature. The property identity helps explain many things about water: why, for instance, passing an electric current through water produces two gases with distinct properties.

Take now the property of being pleasant. It figures in causal explanations; pleasure helps to explain, for instance, why we eat chocolate. It's for reasons like this that being pleasant counts as a natural property, if commonsense psychology has its explanations right. Now explaining why things *do* happen as they do is quite different from explaining why people *ought* to do some things and not others. (That's a truism that falls out from my account of the concept of ought: explaining why one ought to do something is just explaining why to do it; this kind of explanation figures in deciding to do it or not.) So if properties somehow earn their keep in explanations, won't different classes of properties figure in these fundamentally different kinds of explanations?

---

[17] This distinction between concepts and properties stems from Putnam, 'On Properties'; he contrasts 'predicates' or 'concepts' with 'physical properties' or 'physical magnitudes'—although he does not mean to confine the distinction to physics in any narrow sense. He stresses the role of properties in what I would call causal-explanatory theories.

A concept like being pleasant, to be sure, figures in both kinds of explanation: People *do* eat chocolate because it is pleasant, and because chocolate is pleasant, other things equal we *ought* to eat it. But the puzzling claim here is the fundamental one: that other things equal, we ought to do what brings pleasure. Will explaining this require two separate kinds of properties, natural ones like being pleasant and normative ones like being what one ought to do?

The universal hedonist explains why to do things in terms of pleasure: once it is shown that an act maximizes net pleasure in the universe, his explanation of why to do it comes to an end. What explanatory purpose could he then serve by saying that two distinct properties are in play? On a parallel with the case of water and H_2O, he can instead treat this as a case of property identity. He thereby achieves a kind of explanatory power that parallels the explanatory power of thinking that being water and being H_2O are one and the same property. In both cases, that's where explanation comes to an end. In both cases, the identity can be intelligibly rejected by those who reject the consequent explanations. In the one case, the explanations are causal/empirical, and in the other case they are explanations of why to do some things and not others. Pleasure figures in explaining, causally, why people do things, and it figures too, according to the hedonist, in explaining why to do things. In either case, no explanatory purpose would be served by supposing an extra property. A further property of being what one ought to do would add nothing to the explanation of why to eat chocolate; the identity claim itself works as the start of the explanation.

Anti-hedonists, to be sure, will insist that more than one property is in play. They will deny that the property of being what one ought to do is the property of maximizing net pleasure in the universe. The universal hedonist can then be asked why we should accept his claim of property identity. But that parallels the case with water and H_2O: the opponent of molecular theory denies the property identity, and the proponent can be challenged on why we should accept it. As long as a universal hedonist doesn't change his mind, though, he can still put his view as follows: 'Being what one ought to do consists in maximizing net pleasure in the universe. The properties are one and the same, and that explains, at base, why to do the things we ought to do. The concepts are distinct, and that explains why, nevertheless, my opponent's view is intelligible.'

I now turn to a worry I don't know how to quell. Do the things I have said extend to any contingency plan whatsoever that coincides with a property? Philosophers who think that necessarily equivalent properties may be distinct cite cases like being triangular and having three sides.[18] Perhaps

---

[18] See, for instance, Sober, 'Why Logically Equivalent Predicates May Pick out Different Properties.'

explaining the properties of triangles demands believing in both these
properties and believing them distinct. Of course neither of these properties
plausibly enters into basic explanations of why to do things, but imagine
someone with a bizarre view of how to live: one ought at base, this person
thinks, to accumulate triangles. The question might then arise, for this person, what property of triangles explains, at base, why we ought to accumulate
them. Ought we to accumulate them because they have three angles or
because they have three sides? If the latter, then trilaterality, not triangularity,
is what explains why we ought to do things. Perhaps we should then say this:
It's a property involving trilaterality, not triangularity, that constitutes being
what one ought to do.

On this particular, bizarre view of how to live, necessarily coextensional
properties are sometimes distinct, but still, there's a natural property that being
what one ought to do consists in. Still, once we admit that a natural property
might be necessarily coextensional with oughtness without explaining
which things we ought to do, we seem to allow this possibility: there's a natural
property that's necessarily coextensive with oughtness, but an act's having that
property doesn't explain why we ought to do it—and indeed no property
explains why one ought to do the things one ought to do.

The triangularity/trilaterality example suggests that properties have structure, with complex properties somehow composed of simpler properties and
structures. How a view of properties as structured might work for properties
like being alive or being overjoyed might seem baffling—what is their
structure? Suppose, though, that such a view is nonetheless right.[19] Then to
establish that there is a property of being what one ought to do, we would have
to establish something like the following: when we ask why to do a thing, there
is a general answer with a structure of the kind that characterizes properties.
The argument I have given establishes no such thing.

Perhaps, however, another kind of argument could. We have an ideal of
ultimately correct reasoning on what to do and why; what would such reasoning be like? If hedonists are right, the answer is straightforward, whereas if
some pluralists are right, good reasoning on what to do can always be further
refined, so that the ideal right answer must be unlimited in its refinement. But
this ideal right answer will have a structure—even if it is infinite. That, then,
we might try saying, will be the structure of the property of being what one
ought to do.

---

[19] Putnam, in 'On Properties' (313–15), proposes a way of treating such properties as second-order,
functional properties.

4. A property for each function?

Normative pluralists maintain the thesis, sometimes, that no single property always explains why to do those things we ought to do. Sometimes we ought to do something because it's keeping a promise at a small loss in general happiness, sometimes because it's crucial to one's self-development and requires breaking only a minor promise—and so on. Perhaps some such way as this is the best way to put the views of a pluralist like Ross or of a current particularist.[20] Trivially, there's a world-to-extension function that characterizes ought. But why think it characterizes any single property at all?

My argument for Natural Constitution assumed such a liberal conception of properties as to make the answer trivial: any world-to-extension function whatsoever, I took it, characterizes a property. Many philosophers, though, are more sparing with the properties they countenance. Certainly if my assumptions are right, then most properties are wild: they are unfamiliar, and in terms of elementary properties and relations, they can be characterized only in ways that are infinite. They don't figure in causal explanations. Shouldn't we be cautious when it comes to believing in properties? And shouldn't we be especially careful in calling properties 'natural,' even in the broadest sense?

These considerations should indeed bear some weight in our thinking. We need to ask, though, whether any alternative conception of a natural property could answer these worries without introducing others. Will a more restrictive conception of natural properties allow the familiar candidates we need but still rule out *being what one ought to do* as a natural property?

Fundamentally, let's assume, the causal patterns of the world stem from elementary entities that have elementary properties and stand in elementary relations to each other. These are the basic natural entities, properties, and relations. (I'll from now on drop talk of 'relations' and include them in my talk of 'properties.') These can't, though, be the entities and properties that figure in everyday explanations: We explain the length of a shadow by the tallness of the tree that casts it, damage to a house by the severity of a storm, and chocolate-eating by cravings and expectations of pleasure. If tallness, severity, and expecting count as properties, they somehow come down to elementary properties of elementary entities, but not in a way we can specify in detail. We can talk loosely of 'higher order' or 'emergent' properties, but how is such talk to be understood? How do properties like these relate to elementary things and properties and somehow 'emerge' from them?

---

[20] See Ross, *The Right and the Good*; Hooker and Little, *Moral Particularism*; Dancy, *Ethics without Principles* (2004).

Candidate answers come in at least two possible flavors. One is the flavor I have been offering: the systematic, model-theoretic one. This offers us a plethora of non-elementary properties, though most of them are of little or no explanatory importance. The other is a thinner flavor: according to these views, 'wild disjunctions' of properties, when they explain nothing, are not properties at all.

Now my puzzle with the latter kind of view is that many properties of great explanatory importance could be presented as wild disjunctions: sex and parenthood among sexually reproducing organisms, for instance, and even some of the properties that physics studies—being a solid body or a coupled harmonic oscillator. Coupled harmonic oscillators may be electronic or mechanical; solid bodies can be composed of many different materials bonded in a variety of ways. Or consider being yellow (in the sense in which dandelion petals are yellow): from the point of view of pure physics, the property of being yellow is wildly gerrymandered; it consists of a miscellaneous assortment of reflectances a surface can have. But when human beings enter the picture, being yellow can help explain much: why, say, the child hands you the second block from the left when you say, 'Give me the yellow one.' The property exists independent of us: there were yellow flowers before there were people and would have been if our species had never evolved. What depends on our species is the explanatory importance of color, not color itself.[21]

Being a property presents itself as an all-or-nothing matter, whereas explanatory importance is a matter of degrees. If what makes for being a natural property is helping in causal explanations of things that happen, then since helping comes in degrees, there will be degrees of qualifying as a natural property. Why not say instead that there are degrees of naturalistic importance? The contrast shouldn't be between properties and non-properties but between degrees of importance in explaining events in the world.

Think again of color. Beings on a planet of Alpha Centauri have, perhaps, a visual system as discriminating as ours, but one that differentiates classes of reflectances that are quite unlike colors such as yellow. Their responses aren't explained by colors, then, but by a different set of properties that reflectances can have. Like colors with us, those properties existed before the centaurs (as I'll call them), and like colors, they would be of zero explanatory importance had the centaurs never evolved. Moreover, an indefinite number of such classifications must have equal claim to fix properties—properties that, in most cases, are of no explanatory importance at all because no species sensitive to that

---

[21] This view of color is sketched in my 'Visible Properties of Human Interest Only.'

classification has ever evolved. We seem forced to allow many more properties than figure in explaining anything.

I conclude, tentatively, that we should accept a plethora of properties in the universe, all but a small proportion of which have little or no explanatory importance, either causal or normative. The possible worlds, model-theoretic view of properties lets us do this.

5. Causal-explanatory importance

There remains a question that can be couched independently of the metaphysical issues involved in the claim of Natural Constitution: Do normatively significant properties figure significantly in causal explanations? Or in deference to those who reject the view of properties that I appealed to in deriving Natural Constitution, here is the question put more cautiously: Take any important normative concept, such as Moore's concept of an intrinsically good state of affairs. Is there a causally significant property, we can ask, such that being good is necessarily equivalent to having that property? Is there, in other words, a causally significant property N such that no matter what the natural world were like, all and only good happenings would have property N?

Hedonists think that there is such a property, the property of being pleasant on balance. They think that no matter how things went in the universe, all and only states of affairs with more pleasure than displeasure in them would be intrinsically good on balance. Now pleasure figures in causal explanations, and being pleasant counts as a natural property if anything with a close bearing on ethics does. That leaves open the question of quasi-metaphysics, as we might call it, that I have been discussing: whether if hedonists are right on how to live, then there is such a thing as the property of being good and it is the property of being pleasant. But whatever the answer is to this, still, if universal hedonists are right, we can truly say this: There is a natural property, a property of causal-explanatory importance, the having of which is necessarily equivalent to being good.

Moore himself rejected substantive hedonism. Goodness involves organic wholes, he thought; that a pleasure stems, say, from contemplating something ugly can vitiate the claim that a state of affairs is good. Most current ethical theorists likewise reject ethical hedonism, and many think that ethical judgment requires a refined sensibility that stymies codification. All this raises the possibility that nothing equivalent to goodness plays a significant causal role in our lives. There is of course a world-to-extension function that characterizes being good, and this function is 'natural' at least in the sense of being infinitely constructible from clearly natural materials. But whether or not it characterizes a property and does so uniquely—the issues I have been addressing—perhaps it fails to characterize anything of causal-explanatory significance. Good happenings do, of course, have their effects, just as acts performed by red-haired girls on Wednesday have their effects. Perhaps, though, being good as such has nothing to do with explaining these effects.

If we think this to be so, we'll be skeptics of a kind; we'll be skeptical of the importance of good and evil, justice and injustice themselves, in the causal explanations of history and social science.[22] Can we accept such a picture of how the world works causally, though, and not become normative skeptics? I paint normative skepticism as a state we'd be hard pressed to achieve: so long as we come to views on what to do, we are committed to there being normative truths and falsehoods, and so long as we place some faith in our own plans, we ascribe to ourselves some capacity to know these truths, or some of them— fallibly and imperfectly though it be. Still, isn't coming to know a causal process? And so if we are to know that a state of affairs is good, mustn't goodness somehow figure in the causal story of how we come to believe as we do?

Whether we plausibly count as responsive to goodness in our ethical judgments may be in part an empirical question. It turns out that we are less responsive to what's better than we might have imagined: ethical judgments of alternative policies in dealing with an epidemic, for instance, may respond to whether the results are described in terms of lives lost or lives saved—even when the two descriptions are logically equivalent.[23] Our first responses to these cases, then, can't all be veridical: we don't reliably respond to a policy's being right with a judgment that it's right. Once we note this systematic discrepancy in our judgments, though, we can revise our plans and work them toward consistency. True, so long as we know our plans to be inconsistent, we can't reasonably think ourselves fully accurate judges of how to respond to such dilemmas. But as we work to resolve our plans' inconsistencies, we can think ourselves increasingly responsive to goodness. In the limit as we refine our judgments, we can think, the goodness of a state of affairs causes us to think it good.

These reflections suggest a more sophisticated argument that goodness, rightness, being the thing to do and the like go to causally explain things that happen. Planning itself, we can say, supposes that there is such a possible state as being a competent judge of what to do. This state might include, among other

---

[22] Sturgeon hypothesizes such a significant causal role for moral properties in 'Moral Explanations'; Joshua Cohen argues for the plausibility of such explanations in 'The Arc of the Moral Universe.'

[23] Tversky and Kahneman, 'Framing of Decisions and the Psychology of Choice,' 453.

things, correcting for systematic biases and inconsistencies in unreflective human judgments. Imagine, then, we did achieve ideal competence as normative judges. Then goodness would have causal efficacy: we'd be responsive to it. Goodness (or something necessarily equivalent to goodness) would then figure in the causal explanation of our responses.

Does this line of reasoning show that goodness—or something equivalent— is a property with causal-explanatory significance? I have laid out a mere hint of an argument, which leaves many issues to be sorted through. One flaw, though, looks damning: We are asking whether being good and the like fig- ure significantly in causal explanations of how the world works. We have now said that it would so figure if there were ideally competent judges of goodness. We are committed to the possibility of ideally competent judges of goodness, let's agree, just by being planners. That, however, doesn't establish that there in fact are any ideally competent judges. It doesn't, then, establish that goodness enters into causal explanations of anything that really happens in the world.

Take, after all, any world-to-extension function f, no matter how irrelevant it is to anything of significance in explaining our judgments and social phenomena. There is a possible state of finding something good, when one contemplates a way the world might be, if and only if it is in the extension that the function f assigns to that world. We might try arguing, then, that the function f characterizes a causally significant property because it *would* if there *were* an f-responsive judge in the world. But such an argument would clearly be fallacious. That a property would be causally significant if things were different fails to establish that the property is causally significant in actuality, as things are. And this fallacious argument takes exactly the same form as the argument I proposed for the causal significance of goodness.

The state of being an ideally competent normative judge is, of course, of great normative significance: such a person would be the one to consult and defer to in planning how to lead one's life. And planning coherently must be hostage to regarding oneself as at least on the right track as a normative judge— for if I thought that I wasn't in the least a competent judge of what to do, how could I coherently follow through on the judgments I make? Perhaps this requirement on planning commits us, somehow, to constraints on what being the thing to do consists in. Perhaps it shows that the property can't be too wild and infinitely arbitrary; perhaps it even shows that the property must be causally significant in human affairs. I haven't found an argument that it does, but I regard the issue as unsettled. This question arises from the way of analyz- ing normative concepts that I am proposing, and finding an answer to it would be an important advance in normative theory.

References

AYER, A. J., *Language, Truth and Logic*. London: Victor Gollancz, 1936; 2nd edn. 1946.

BRANDOM, ROBERT, *Making it Explicit*. Cambridge, Mass.: Harvard University Press, 1994.

COHEN, JOSHUA, 'The Arc of the Moral Universe.' *Philosophy and Public Affairs*, 26/2 (1997): 91–134.

DANCY, JONATHAN, *Ethics without Principles*. Oxford: Clarendon Press, 2004.

GIBBARD, ALLAN, 'Knowing What to Do, Seeing What to Do,' in Philip Stratton-Lake (ed.), *Ethical Intuitionism: Re-evaluations*. Oxford: Clarendon Press, 2002.

—— 'Meaning and Normativity.' In *Philosophical Issues*, 5: *Truth and Rationality*, ed. Enrique Villanueva. Atascadero, Calif.: Ridgeview Publishing Co., 1994; 95–115.

—— 'Normative and Recognitional Concepts.' *Philosophy and Phenomenological Research*, 64/1 (2002): 151–67.

—— 'Reply to Hawthorne.' *Philosophy and Phenomenological Research*, 64/1 (2002): 179–83.

—— *Thinking How to Live*. Cambridge, Mass.: Harvard University Press, forthcoming.

—— 'Visible Properties of Human Interest Only.' In *Philosophical Issues*, 7: *Perception*, ed. Enrique Villanueva. Atascadero, Calif.: Ridgeview Publishing Co., 1996: 199–208.

—— *Wise Choices, Apt Feelings*. Cambridge, Mass.: Harvard University Press, 1990.

HOOKER, BRAD, and LITTLE, MARGARET (eds.), *Moral Particularism*. Oxford: Oxford University Press, 2000.

HORWICH, PAUL, *Meaning*. Oxford: Clarendon Press, 1998.

—— *Truth*. Oxford: Oxford University Press. 2nd edn. 1998.

KIM, JAEGWON, *Supervenience and Mind: Selected Philosophical Essays*. Cambridge: Cambridge University Press, 1993.

KRIPKE, SAUL, *Wittgenstein on Rules and Private Language*. Cambridge, Mass.: Harvard University Press, 1982.

LEWIS, DAVID K., *Papers in Ethics and Social Philosophy*. Cambridge: Cambridge University Press, 2000.

McDOWELL, JOHN, 'Wittgenstein on Following a Rule.' *Synthese*, 58 (1984): 325–63.

MILLAR, ALAN, 'The Normativity of Meaning.' In Anthony O'Hear (ed.), *Logic, Thought and Language*. Cambridge: Cambridge University Press, 2002: 57–73.

MOORE, G. E., *Principia Ethica*. Cambridge: Cambridge University Press, 1903.

—— 'An Autobiography.' In Paul Arthur Schilpp (ed.), *The Philosophy of G. E. Moore*. LaSalle, Ill.: Open Court, 1942.

NIETZSCHE, FRIEDRICH, *Zur Genealogie der Moralen*, trans. as *On the Genealogy of Morals*, Walter Kaufmann and R. J. Hollingdale. New York: Vintage Books, 1967.

OGDEN, C. K., and RICHARDS, I. A, *The Meaning of Meaning*. New York: Harcourt Brace, 1923.

PUTNAM, HILARY, 'On Properties.' *Mathematics, Matter and Method: Philosophical Papers*, vol. i. Cambridge: Cambridge University Press, 1975: 305–22.

ROSS, W. D., *The Right and the Good*. Oxford: Clarendon Press, 1930.

SCHILPP, PAUL ARTHUR (ed.), *The Philosophy of G. E. Moore*. La Salle, Ill.: Open Court, 1942.

SIDGWICK, HENRY, *The Methods of Ethics*, 7th edn. London: Macmillan, 1907.

SOBER, E., 'Why Logically Equivalent Predicates May Pick out Different Properties.' *American Philosophical Quarterly*, 19 (1982): 183–9.

STALNAKER, ROBERT, 'Possible Worlds.' *Nous*, 10 (1976): 65–75.

STEVENSON, CHARLES L., 'The Emotive Meaning of Ethical Terms.' *Mind*, 46 (1937): 14–31.

—— *Ethics and Language*. New Haven: Yale University Press, 1944.

—— *Facts and Values: Studies in Ethical Analysis*. New Haven: Yale University Press, 1963.

STURGEON, NICHOLAS L., 'Moral Explanations.' In David Copp and David Zimmerman (eds.), *Morality, Reason and Truth*. Totowa, NJ: Rowman & Allanheld, 1985: 49–78.

TVERSKY, AMOS, and KAHNEMAN, DANIEL, 'The Framing of Decisions and the Psychology of Choice.' *Science*, 211 (1981): 453–8.

WILLIAMS, BERNARD, *Ethics and the Limits of Philosophy*. Cambridge, Mass.: Harvard University Press, 1985.

15

Moral Intuitionism Meets Empirical Psychology

Walter Sinnott-Armstrong

...if this be all, where is his ethics? The position he is maintaining is merely a psychological one.

(Moore 1903: § 11, 11)[1]

G. E. Moore's diatribe against the naturalistic fallacy in 1903 set the stage for most of twentieth-century moral philosophy. The main protagonists over the next sixty years were intuitionists and emotivists, both of whom were convinced by Moore that empirical science is irrelevant to moral philosophy and common moral beliefs. Even in the 1970s and 1980s, when a wider array of moral theories entered the scene and applied ethics became popular, few moral philosophers paid much attention to developments in biology and psychology.

This isolation must end. Moral philosophers cannot continue to ignore developments in psychology, brain science, and biology. Of course, philosophers need to be careful when they draw lessons from empirical research. As Moore and his followers argued, we should not jump straight from descriptive premises in psychology or biology to positive moral conclusions or normative conclusions in moral epistemology. That would be a fallacy.[2] Nonetheless, psychology can still affect moral philosophy in indirect ways. That is what I want to illustrate here. I will trace an indirect path from empirical premises to a normative conclusion

For comments on drafts and oral presentations, I thank Robert Audi, Paul Bloomfield, George Pappas, Bernard Gert, Terry Horgan, Don Loeb, James Moor, Matthew Nudds, Diana Raffman, John Skorupski, Roy Sorensen, and others in audiences at the Ohio State University, the University of Connecticut, the University of Vermont, the University of Nebraska at Lincoln, and the University of Edinburgh.

[1] Here Moore was discussing the claim that the object of desire is not pleasure, but his charge against naturalism extended much further.

[2] Although some such arguments are formally valid. See my 2000: 159–74. I add the qualification 'positive' because 'Bertie and Madeleine are dead' might entail 'It is not the case that Bertie ought to marry Madeleine.'

in moral epistemology. In particular, I will argue that some recent research in psychology and brain science undermines moral intuitionism.

1. What is moral intuitionism?

Some philosophers define moral intuitionism as the structural view that there are many moral values or requirements with no systematic unification or ranking. Other philosophers see moral intuitionism as the metaphysical view that moral properties are non-natural. Neither of these views concerns me here. I mention them only to set them aside.

The kind of moral intuitionism that is my target here is a position in moral epistemology, which is general epistemology applied to moral beliefs. The deepest challenge in moral epistemology, as in general epistemology, is raised by a skeptical regress argument: Someone is justified in believing something only if the believer has a reason that is expressible in an inference with premises that the believer is already justified in believing. This requires a chain of inferences that must continue infinitely, close into a circle, or stop arbitrarily. Academic skeptics reject all three options and conclude that there is no way for anyone to be justified in believing anything. The same regress arises for moral beliefs (cf. Sinnott-Armstrong 1996: 9–14; 2002a).

The simplest way to stop this regress is simply to stop. If a believer can work back to a premise that the believer is justified in believing without being able to infer that premise from anything else, then there is no new premise to justify, so the regress goes no further. That is how foundationalists stop the regress in general epistemology. Moral intuitionists apply foundationalism to moral beliefs as a way to stop the skeptical regress regarding moral beliefs.

The motivation behind moral intuitionism is not always to stop the skeptical regress,[3] but that use of moral intuitionism is common and is what concerns us here, so we can use it to decide among possible definitions of moral intuitionism. What we need to define is the weakest version of moral intuitionism

---

[3] As George Pappas reminded me, part of foundationalism can be separated from the denial of skepticism. Foundationalists can be skeptics if foundationalism claims only that a believer is justified in a belief only if the belief is either non-inferentially justified or inferable from non-inferentially justified beliefs. Non-skeptical foundationalists merely add that some beliefs are justified. Analogously, moral intuitionism could be seen as a claim about the structure of justification separate from any denial of skepticism. Nonetheless, I will define moral intuitionism to include the denial of moral skepticism because almost all actual moral intuitionists do deny skepticism and because I am concerned with whether moral intuitionism can succeed as a response to skepticism.

that is strong enough to solve the regress problem that would lead to moral skepticism. Here it is:

> Moral intuitionism is the claim that some people are adequately epistemically justified in holding some moral beliefs independently of whether those people are able to infer those moral beliefs from any other beliefs.[4]

Several features of this definition are worth highlighting.

So defined, moral intuitionism is not about knowledge. It is about justified belief. This makes it normative. Psychologists sometimes define intuitionism as a descriptive claim about the nature and origins of moral beliefs (see Haidt 2001). Such descriptive claims are not intended to stop the skeptical regress; so they do not concern me here.

More specifically, the defining claim of moral intuitionism is about what is *epistemically* justified because moral skeptics win if the only justification for holding moral beliefs is that those belief states have beneficial practical effects. Similarly, moral skeptics win if some moral beliefs are inadequately justified but none is *adequately* justified, that is, justified strongly enough that the believer ought to believe it as opposed to denying it or suspending belief.[5] Accordingly, I will henceforth use 'justified' as shorthand for 'adequately epistemically justified'.

To say that moral believers are justified independently of an inferential ability is just to say that they would be justified even if they lacked that ability, that is, even if they were not able to infer those beliefs from any other beliefs. This independence claim can hold even when moral believers are able to infer those moral beliefs from other beliefs as long as they do not need that inferential ability to be justified.[6] This notion of need will become prominent later.

---

[4] Although I define moral intuitionism in terms of 'some' believers and 'some' moral beliefs, all actual moral intuitionists claim that a significant group of believers and beliefs can be justified non-inferentially. It also might seem odd that a theory counts as moral intuitionism on my definition if it holds that some beliefs based on testimony are justified independently of any inference or inferential ability. However, my arguments will apply to such views, so I see no pressing need to complicate my definition so as to avoid these problems.

[5] I will discuss pro tanto justifiedness in responses to objections below. For more detail on kinds of justifiedness, see my 2002*b*: 17–25.

[6] Compare Ross 1930: 29: 'without any need of proof'. (Since not all inferences are proofs, and Ross does not mention abilities, he might not deny the need for an inferential ability.) Contrast Moore (1903: 77), who sees moral intuitions as unprovable. Moore's stronger claim is not needed to stop the skeptical regress. Notice also that opponents of moral intuitionism, who claim that an inferential ability is *necessary*, do not have to claim that any inferential ability is *sufficient* to make any moral belief justified. At least the moral belief must also be *based on* the inferential ability. Other necessary conditions might also have to be met. Opponents of moral intuitionism can hold that an inferential ability is needed without specifying what, if anything, else is needed and, so, without specifying what is sufficient for justified moral belief.

I infer a belief when I go through a reasoning process of which the belief is the (or a) conclusion and other beliefs are premises. A believer is able to draw such an inference when the believer has enough information to go through a reasoning process that results in this belief if he had enough incentive and time to do so. This ability does not require self-consciousness or reflection about the beliefs or abilities. All that is needed, other than general intelligence, is for the requisite information to be encoded appropriately in the believer's brain at the time of belief.[7]

Some moral intuitionists claim only that certain moral beliefs are justified independently of any actual inference. However, that weak moral intuitionism is not enough to stop the skeptical regress. Even if whether certain moral beliefs are justified does not depend on any actual inference, it still might depend on the believer's ability to infer them from other beliefs. The ability to draw an inference cannot make a belief justified if beliefs in the inference's premises are not themselves justified. This requirement is enough to restart a skeptical regress. Thus, to meet the skeptical challenge, moral intuitionists must make the strong claim that some moral believers are adequately epistemically justified in holding some moral beliefs independently of any ability to infer the moral belief from any other belief.[8] So that's what they claim.

Although this claim is strong, it has many defenders. Rational intuitionists see basic moral beliefs as analogous to beliefs in mathematical axioms, which are taken to be justified independently of inference. Moral sense theorists assimilate particular moral beliefs to perceptual beliefs, which are supposed to be justified independently of inference. More recently, reliabilists hold that any belief is justified if it results from a reliable process, regardless of whether that process has anything to do with any inference. I group these views together under my broad definition of moral intuitionism because my arguments will apply to them all.

Under my definition, there are at least two ways to deny moral intuitionism. Moral intuitionists claim that some moral believers would be justified even if they did not have any ability to infer their moral beliefs from any other beliefs. Some opponents object that moral beliefs always depend on some inference or inferential ability. However, the evidence (cf. Haidt 2001) strongly suggests

---

[7] The relevant notion of ability, then, is not the same as when I am able to become justified in believing that there are ten coins in my pocket because I could take them out of my pocket and count them. To have an ability of the relevant kind, I must be able to infer the belief from other beliefs that I already have without gaining any new information. I hope that it is also clear that, when I write about needing 'an inferential ability', I am not referring to a general ability to draw just any old inference, or any inference of a certain form. What is at issue is the ability to infer the specific moral belief from other beliefs.

[8] The stronger claim is also needed for moral intuitionism to contrast with its traditional opponent, moral coherentism, since coherentists do not claim that believers must actually draw inferences in order to be justified.

that people often have moral beliefs that do not result from any actual inference. It is harder to tell whether any moral beliefs are independent of any ability to infer. Nonetheless, I will grant for the sake of argument that some moral beliefs are spontaneous in the sense that they are independent of any inference or inferential ability.

Other opponents of moral intuitionism deny that moral believers are ever justified in holding such spontaneous moral beliefs if they lack certain inferential abilities. This conclusion follows if inferential abilities are always needed for a moral believer to be justified. That is what I will try to show.

2. When is confirmation needed?

We cannot answer this question directly. If a moral intuitionist baldly asserts that we do not need inferential abilities to back up our spontaneous moral beliefs, then this assertion begs the question. Similarly, if a critic of moral intuitionism baldly asserts that we do need inferential abilities to back up our spontaneous moral beliefs, then this assertion also begs the question. Neither side can win so easily. We need a less direct method.

One alternative uses analogies to non-moral beliefs. This path is fraught with peril, but it might be the only way to go. What this approach does is appeal to non-moral cases to develop principles of epistemic need and then later apply those principles back to moral beliefs. Let's try it.

I will formulate my principles in terms of when confirmation is needed, but they do not claim that the believer needs to go through any process of confirming the belief. The point, instead, is only that some confirmation needs to be available at least implicitly as information stored somehow in the believer that gives the believer an ability to infer the belief from some other beliefs.[9] The question is when some such confirmation is needed in non-moral cases.

Suppose that I listen to my daughter in a piano competition. I judge that she played great and her rival was mediocre. Am I justified in trusting my judgment? Not if all I can say is, 'Her performance sounded better to me.' I am too biased for such immediate reactions alone to count as evidence. I still might be justified, if I am able to specify laudable features of her performance, or if I know that others agree, but some confirmation seems needed. Generalizing,

Principle 1: confirmation is needed for a believer to be justified when the believer is partial.

---

[9] Confirmation need not always be evidence, since I want confirmation to include defeator defeaters, that is, reasons to discount what would otherwise keep a belief from being justified.

This principle also applies to direct perceptual judgments, such as when I believe that my daughter played middle C at just the right time in the midst of her piece. This partly explains why we prefer umpires, referees, and judges not to be parents of competitors. Even reliabilists can admit this principle because partiality often creates unreliability.

Second, imagine that each of us adds a column of figures, and I get one sum, but you get a different sum. Maybe I would be justified in believing that I am right if you were my child and I was helping you with your homework. However, if you are just as good at arithmetic as I am, then, when we get different answers, we need to check again to find out who made a mistake before either of us can be justified in believing that his or her answer is the correct one. We owe each other that much epistemic respect. The best explanation of this natural reaction seems to be

> Principle 2: confirmation is needed for a believer to be justified when people disagree with no independent reason to prefer one belief or believer to the other.

This principle also applies when the person on the sidewalk looks like Tom Cruise to me but not to you. If I have no reason to believe that I am better than you at this identification, then I am not justified in believing that your belief is incorrect or that mine is correct.

A third principle concerns emotions. When people get very angry, for example, they tend to overlook relevant facts. They often do not notice excuses or apologies by the person who made them angry. We should not generalize to all emotions, but we can still endorse something like this:

> Principle 3: confirmation is needed for a believer to be justified when the believer is emotional in a way that clouds judgment.

This explains why jurors are dismissed from a case that would make them too emotional. This principle applies even if their emotions do not bias them towards either side, so it is distinct from Principle 1, regarding partiality.

Next consider illusions. At least three kinds are relevant here. First, some illusions are due to context. Objects look larger when they are next to smaller objects, and they look smaller when they are next to larger objects. Since our estimates of their sizes are affected by their surroundings, we are not justified in trusting our estimates until we check their sizes in other circumstances or by other methods.

A second group of illusions arises from generalizations. For example, an oval that is shaded on top looks concave, but an oval that is shaded on the bottom looks convex. The explanation seems to be that our cognitive apparatus evolved in circumstances where the light usually came from above, which would produce a shadow on the top of a concave oval (such as a cave opening) and on the bottom of a convex oval (such as an egg). Since we often overextend generalizations like this, we are not justified in trusting beliefs that depend on such generalizations until we check to determine whether our circumstances are exceptional.

The third kind of illusion involves heuristics, which are quick and simple decision procedures. In a passage with a thousand words, how many seven-letter words have the form '_ _ _ in _'? How many seven-letter words have the form '_ _ _ ing'? Most people estimate more words have the latter form, although that is impossible, since every word of the form '_ _ _ ing' also has the form '_ _ _ in _'. Why do people make this simple mistake? They seem to test how likely something is by trying to imagine examples and guessing high if they easily think of lots of examples. This is called the availability heuristic (Kahneman *et al.* 1982). Most people easily produce words that end in 'ing', but they have more trouble coming up with words that end in 'in _' because they do not think of putting 'g' in the last place. In cases like this, the availability heuristic is misleading. Accordingly, they do not seem adequately epistemically justified in trusting beliefs based on such heuristics until they check on whether they are in circumstances where the heuristics work.

This quick survey of three common kinds of illusion suggests

Principle 4: confirmation is needed for a believer to be justified when the circumstances are conducive to illusion.

This principle would apply as well to many other kinds of illusions.

A fifth and final principle considers the source of a belief. If you believe that George Washington never told a lie, and if this belief comes from a legend spread by Washington's allies to gain power, then you are not justified in believing the legend, though it still might be true. Even if you believe only that Washington was unusually honest, this belief might be a lingering effect of this childhood story, and then its origin makes this belief need confirmation. The point can be generalized into something like

Principle 5: confirmation is needed for a believer to be justified when the belief arises from an unreliable or disreputable source.

This principle also explains why we do not view people as justified in beliefs based only on prejudice and stereotypes.

These five principles, although distinct, complement each other. When a belief is partial, controversial, emotional, subject to illusion, and explicable by dubious sources, then all of these principles apply. In such cases, they work together to make it even clearer that confirmation is needed for justified belief. Even if not all of these principles apply, the more that do apply, the clearer it will be that there is more need for more confirmation. We might think of this as a sixth principle.

I do not claim that these principles are precise or that my list is complete.[10] What I do claim is that these principles or some close relatives seem plausible to most people and are assumed in our shared epistemic practices. I also claim that they make sense because they pick out features that are correlated with reliability and other epistemic values.

Most importantly, I claim that these principles apply in all areas of belief. My illustrations include beliefs about arithmetic, language, history, identity, value, sound, size, and shape, but the same principles apply in scientific research, religion, and so on. The main question here is whether they apply to moral beliefs. Admittedly, morality might be a special case where these principles do not apply. However, unless someone can point to a relevant difference between these other areas and moral beliefs, it seems only fair to apply these same standards to moral beliefs when asking whether moral beliefs are justified. So that's what I will do.

3. When are moral beliefs justified?

Some of these principles can be applied only with the help of empirical research. Others are easier to apply. Let's start with the easy ones.

Partiality

Principle 1 says that partiality adds a need for confirmation. But what is partiality? A judge is often called partial when the judge's self-interest is affected by the outcome of the case. However, if the judge's self-interest does not influence the judge's decision, so the judge would have made the same decision if the judge's self-interest had not been involved, then it is natural to say that the judge's decision is not partial, even if the judge is partial. Analogously, believers can be called partial whenever their beliefs affect their self-interest either directly or indirectly (by affecting the interests of people whom they care about). Beliefs are then partial only when the believer's self-interest influences whether the believer holds that belief. Thus, a partial believer can hold an

---

[10] One additional principle might claim that confirmation is needed when errors are costly. This principle applies to moral beliefs insofar as moral errors are costly.

impartial belief (or can hold it impartially) if the believer has an interest in holding the belief, but that interest does not influence whether the believer holds that belief.

Partiality of a belief can't be all that triggers Principle 1. To see why, recall the examples that motivated Principle 1. Because I am biased in favor of my daughter, even after watching her play in the piano competition, I need confirmation to be justified in believing that my daughter played better than her rival. Maybe my interest in her victory did not influence my assessment, but the danger of such influence is enough to create a need for confirmation. Admittedly, if I can rule out such influence, then I can be justified in believing that my daughter played better, but the only way to rule out such influence involves independent confirmation. Thus, confirmation seems needed when the believer is partial, even if the believer is not actually influenced by that partiality, so the belief is not partial. Since confirmation is also needed when the belief is partial, Principle 1 requires confirmation when either the believer or the belief is partial.

To apply this principle to moral beliefs, we need to determine whether moral beliefs affect our self-interest either directly or indirectly. The answer seems clear: Moral beliefs affect us all. It can be very expensive to believe that we are morally required to help the needy, but it can be even more expensive if others do not believe that they are morally required to help us when we are in need. It can also cost a lot to believe that we have to tell the truth or to keep a promise. And all of us know or should know that, if killing, stealing, lying, cheating, and promise-breaking were generally seen as morally permitted, then we would be more likely to get hurt by others doing such acts. Life would be more 'solitary, poor, nasty, brutish, and short', as Hobbes put it. Moreover, if an individual did not see such acts as immoral, then he or she would be more likely to do them and then to be punished in various ways—'if not by law, by the opinion of his fellow creatures', as Mill said. Special interests also arise in special cases: Women and men know or should know that, if abortion is not seen as morally permissible, then they, their friends, or their daughters will be more likely to suffer more. Moral beliefs about affirmative action affect the interests of the preferred groups and also the non-preferred groups. And so on. Indeed, on many views, what makes an issue moral in nature is that interests are significantly affected by the judged actions. Since moral beliefs about actions affect those actions, our moral beliefs themselves affect our interests at least indirectly. Finally, social groups often form around and then solidify moral beliefs (cf. Chen and Tetlock *et al.* as discussed in Haidt 2001). People who believe that homosexuality is immoral find it harder to get along with homosexuals and easier to get along with homophobes. Conversely, people who believe that homosexuality is not immoral find it harder to get along with homophobes and easier to get along with homosexuals. Some might try to fake moral beliefs in order to get along, but few of us are good enough actors, and those who believe that homosexuality is immoral usually also believe that they ought not to pretend otherwise in order to get along with homosexuals. Thus, our moral beliefs affect our social options as well as our actions.

Many moral beliefs might seem to have no effect on us. If I believe that it was immoral for Brutus to stab Caesar, this moral belief by itself will not change my social options or rule out any acts that I could do today. Still, given universaliz-ability, my judgment of Brutus seems to depend on a principle that does apply in other cases where my self-interest is involved more directly. Arguments from analogy also might force me to take a moral stand that affects my interests Thus, any moral belief can affect my self-interest indirectly.

Because our moral beliefs affect our self-interest so often in so many ways at least indirectly, we cannot be justified in assuming that any of us is ever fully impartial as a moral believer. Even if our self-interest is not involved in some exceptional case, we still need a reason to believe that our self-interest is not affected in that case, since we know or should know that such effects are very common and often hidden. The facts that partiality is so common in this area and so difficult to detect in ourselves are what create a need for confirmation of all moral beliefs, according to Principle 1.

Disagreement

Principle 2 says that disagreement creates a need for confirmation. Many people seem to think that this principle is easy to apply to moral beliefs because moral disagreement is pervasive. In their view, people from different cultures, time periods, social classes, and genders disagree about a wide variety of particular moral judgments and general moral principles.

Actually, the extent of moral disagreement is not obvious. One reason is that people who seem to disagree are often judging different actions or using differ-ent concepts. Also, many apparently moral disagreements are really factual, since those who seem to disagree morally would agree in their moral judgments if they agreed about the facts.

Still, straightening out concepts and non-moral facts seems unlikely to resolve all apparently moral disagreements. One reason is that people often express different moral beliefs about hypothetical cases where all of the facts are stipulated, so these moral believers seem to accept the same non-moral facts. Admittedly, descriptions of these situations usually leave out important facts, and moral believers might interpret the hypothetical cases in light of different background beliefs. But there still seem to be lots of cases where all relevant non-moral facts are agreed upon without leading to agreement in moral belief.

This claim is supported by a study in which Jana Schaich Borg and I surveyed fifty-two undergraduates at Dartmouth College, using thirty-six scenarios, including the well-known side-track and fat-man trolley cases. In both cases, five people tied to a track will be killed by a runaway trolley if you do nothing, and the only way to save the five is to kill one other person.[11] In the side-track version, you can save the five only by pulling a lever to divert the trolley onto a side-track where it will run over one victim. In the fat-man variation, you can save the five only by pushing a fat man in front of the trolley so that his body will stop the trolley before it hits the five. In two rounds, 35 per cent then 43 per cent of our subjects said that it would be wrong to divert the trolley onto the side-track. When the same scenario was described with more vivid language, 61 per cent then 45 per cent judged diversion wrong in the two rounds. In contrast, 76 per cent in the first round then 88 per cent in the second round judged it wrong to push the fat man. (Interestingly, there were still 35 per cent in the first round and 18 per cent in the second round who said that they would push the fat man.) These percentages did not change much with more vivid language. Thus, we found significant disagreement about the very cases that philosophers often cite to support their theories.[12]

There is, admittedly, more agreement about other cases: Would it be wrong to push the fat man in front of the trolley just because you are angry at him for beating you at golf when killing him will not save or help anyone else? I hope and expect that 100 per cent would answer, 'Yes.' But what would that show? The universality of moral beliefs about cases like this one could hardly be used to justify any moral theory or any controversial moral belief.[13] Such cases cannot get moral intuitionists all that they seem to want.[14]

Moral intuitionists might respond that all they claim is that *some* moral beliefs are non-inferentially justified. One case seems enough to establish that

[11] These cases originate from Foot 1967. If such cases seem unrealistic, see the real case at www.cnn.com/2003/US/West/06/21/train.derail.ap/index.html.

[12] For more evidence of disagreement, see Haidt *et al.* 1993.

[13] Compare Descartes's 'I think,' which is nowhere near enough to ground science. Notice also that I am talking about actual moral beliefs, not possible moral beliefs. There might be an infinite number of possible moral beliefs that would garner agreement from everyone who understands them. However, there still might be a high rate of disagreement among the actual moral beliefs that people bother to form. That is what matters when we ask whether our actual moral beliefs are justified.

[14] Some intuitionists might claim agreement on qualified general principles, such as that it is morally wrong to kill anyone in a protected class without an adequate reason. Of course, those who accept this formula still disagree about which class is protected and which reasons are adequate. Similarly, although many people (today!) agree that all moral agents deserve respect, different people count different acts as violating that rule by showing disrespect. It is not clear whether to count agreement on such indeterminate formulas as real moral agreement. See Snare 1980.

claim. However, the fact that there is so much disagreement in other cases affects the epistemology of cases where there is no disagreement. Compare a box with one hundred thermometers. We know that many of them don't work, but we are not sure how many. If we pick one thermometer arbitrarily from the box, and it reads 77 degrees, then we are not justified in believing that the temperature really is 77 degrees, even if we were in fact lucky enough to pick a thermometer that works. Of course, if we confirm that this thermometer works, such as by testing it against other thermometers, then we can use it to form justified beliefs, but we cannot be justified in trusting it before we confirm that it works.[15] Similarly, if we know that many moral intuitions are unreliable because others hold conflicting intuitions, then we are not justified in trusting a particular moral intuition without some reason to believe that it is one of the reliable ones. If we know that everyone agrees with that particular moral intuition, then we might have reason to trust it. But that is just because the known agreement provides confirmation, so it does not undermine the point that some confirmation is needed, as Principle 2 claims.

Emotion

Next consider Principle 3, which says that emotions that cloud judgment create a need for confirmation. It is hard to tell whether this principle applies to moral beliefs. Philosophers and others have argued for millennia about whether moral beliefs are based on emotion or on reason. They also argue about which emotions, if any, cloud judgment. How can we resolve these debates? Luckily, some recent empirical studies suggest an answer.

Haidt and his group have been accumulating an impressive body of behavioral evidence for what they call the social intuitionist model:

This model suggests that moral judgment is much like aesthetic judgment: we see an action or hear a story and we have an instant feeling of approval or disapproval. These feelings are best thought of as affect-laden intuitions, as they appear suddenly and effortlessly in consciousness, with an affective valence (good or bad), but without any feeling of having gone through any steps of searching, weighing evidence or inferring a conclusion. (Greene and Haidt 2002: 517)[16]

---

[15] According to Bayesians, if the temperature feels to us as if it is about 70 degrees, so we start with that assumption, then the fact that this thermometer reads 77 degrees should make us move our estimate towards 77 degrees. How much our estimate should increase depends on our prior assumption about how many thermometers work. This might make it seem as if the thermometer reading can lead to justified belief. However, if our initial estimates (about temperature and the percentage of working thermometers) are unjustified, then I doubt that one reading can ground justified belief. Besides, many of us do not form any of the initial estimates that are needed to start Bayesian reasoning.

[16] See also Haidt 2001. Of course, many other judgments cause emotional reactions 'suddenly and effortlessly'. But Haidt argues that emotions drive or constitute moral judgments rather than being effects of those judgments.

Haidt's behavioral evidence dovetails nicely with independent brain studies. Moll's group found that brain tissue associated with emotions becomes more activated when subjects think about simple sentences with moral content (e.g. 'They hung an innocent') than when they think about similar sentences without moral content (e.g. 'Stones are made of water') (Moll *et al.* 2001) or disgusting non-moral sentences (e.g. 'He licked the dirty toilet') (Moll *et al.* 2002*a*).[17] Similar results were found with pictures in place of sentences (Moll *et al.* 2002*b*).

Studies by Joshua Greene and his colleagues are even more fascinating because they distinguish kinds of moral beliefs (2001).[18] Greene's group scanned brains of subjects while they considered what was appropriate in three kinds of dilemmas: non-moral dilemmas, personal moral dilemmas, and impersonal moral dilemmas. A moral dilemma is personal if and only if one of its options is likely to cause serious harm to a particular person other than by deflecting an existing threat onto a different party (Greene and Haidt 2002: 519). A standard personal moral dilemma is the fat-man trolley case. A paradigm impersonal moral dilemma is the side-track trolley case. These different moral cases stimulated different parts of the brain. While considering appropriate action in impersonal dilemmas, subjects showed significant activation in brain areas associated with working memory but no significant activation in areas associated with emotion. In contrast, while considering appropriate action in personal dilemmas, subjects showed significant activation in brain areas associated with emotion and under-activation (below the resting baseline) in areas associated with working memory. It is not obvious what to make of these results. Brain scientists do not know how to interpret under-activation in general. Nonetheless, one natural speculation is this: When asked about pushing the fat man, subjects react, 'That's so horrible that I can't even think about it.' Emotions stop subjects from considering the many factors in these examples. If this interpretation is correct, then many pervasive and fundamental moral beliefs result from emotions that cloud judgment.[19]

Some moral intuitionists might argue that there is no need to consider anything else when the proposed action is the intentional killing of an innocent fat man. It might even be counterproductive to consider additional factors, since they might lead one away from the correct belief. Such responses,

[17] It would be interesting to test reactions to negations, such as 'They did not hang an innocent' and 'He did not lick the dirty toilet.'

[18] This article also reports timing studies that confirm the different roles of emotion in different moral beliefs.

[19] Philosophers should notice that what Greene calls 'personal dilemmas' include most proposed counterexamples to consequentialism. If those intuitions are unjustified, then Greene's study might help consequentialists defend their moral theory, even if other intuitions are not affected.

however, assume that it is morally wrong to push the fat man, so they beg the question here. When asking whether a moral belief is justified, we should not assume that the only relevant factors are those that would be relevant if the belief were true. Ridiculous moral beliefs could be defended if that method worked.

Still, moral intuitionism is hardly refuted by these experiments because Greene's results must be replicated and interpreted much more carefully. (Some initial replication can be found in Greene 2004.) All I can say now is that such brain studies seem to provide some evidence that many moral judgments result from emotions that cloud judgment.

Additional evidence comes from Wheatley and Haidt (2005). They gave participants the post-hypnotic suggestion that they would feel a pang of disgust whenever they saw either the word 'take' or the word 'often'. Participants were later asked to make moral judgments about six stories designed to elicit mild to moderate disgust. When a story contained the word that elicited disgust in a participant, that participant was more likely to express stronger moral condemnation of acts in the story. Moral judgments were then affected by elements of the story that could not determine the accuracy or acceptability of those moral judgments. In that sense, emotions clouded their judgment. Because independently caused emotions can distort moral beliefs in such ways, moral believers need confirmation in order to be justified in holding their moral beliefs.

Illusions

To apply Principle 4 to moral beliefs, we again need empirical research, but this time in cognitive science rather than brain science. I mentioned three kinds of illusions that should be considered separately.

The first kind of illusion occurs when appearances and beliefs depend on context. An interesting recent example comes from Peter Unger, who found that the order in which options are presented affects beliefs about whether a given option is morally wrong. He also claims that people's moral beliefs about a certain option depend on whether that option is presented as part of a pair or, instead, as part of a series that includes additional options intermediate between the original pair (Unger 1996: 88–94).[20] Since order and intermediate options

---

[20] Unfortunately, Unger does not describe the method or precise results of his informal survey, so there is room for more careful empirical work to test his claims. Some philosophical support comes from moral paradoxes, which often arise through the mechanisms that Unger describes. One example is the mere addition paradox of Parfit 1984, in which B seems worse than A when the two are compared directly, but it seems not worse than A when Parfit interjects A+ and Divided B as options intermediate between A and B.

are not morally relevant factors that could affect the moral wrongness of the judged option, the fact that moral beliefs are affected by these factors shows that moral beliefs are unreliable in such cases. That is why confirmation is needed. One still might confirm one's moral belief by reconsidering the issue in several contexts over time to see whether one's moral belief remains stable, but that is just a way of seeking confirmation, so it does not undermine my point that confirmation is needed.

The second kind of illusion arises from overgeneralization. Such illusions also affect moral beliefs. Jonathan Baron even argues that all 'nonconsequentialist principles arise from overgeneralizing rules that are consistent with consequentialism in a limited set of cases' (1994: 1). But one need not accept consequentialism in order to admit that many people condemn defensible lying, harming, and love-making because they apply generalizations to exceptional cases. We probably disagree about which moral beliefs are overgeneralizations, but we should agree that many people overgeneralize in ways that create illusions of moral wrongness. In any such case, the moral believer could argue that this case is not an exception to the generalization, but, as before, that is just a way of seeking confirmation, so it does not undermine my point that this kind of illusion creates a need for confirmation.

Heuristics, which are quick and simple decision procedures, also create illusions in morality. One reason is that many moral beliefs depend on consequences and probabilities, for which we often lack adequate evidence, and then we have to guess these probabilities. Such guesses are notoriously distorted by the availability heuristic, the representative heuristic, and so on.[21] Even when moral beliefs do not depend on probability assessments, moral beliefs are affected by the so-called 'I agree with people I like' heuristic (cf. Chaiken and Lord, Ross, and Lepper as discussed by Haidt 2001). When people whom we like express moral beliefs, we tend to go along and form the same belief. When people whom we dislike oppose our moral beliefs, we tend to hold on to them in spite of contrary arguments. This heuristic often works fine, but it fails in enough cases to create a need for confirmation.

In addition to these three kinds of illusions, moral beliefs also seem subject to framing effects, which were explored by Kahneman and Tversky (1979). In one famous experiment, they asked some subjects this question:

Imagine that the U.S. is preparing for an outbreak of an unusual Asian disease which is expected to kill 600 people. Two alternative programs to fight the disease, A and B, have been proposed. Assume that the exact scientific estimates of the consequences of

---

[21] Kahneman *et al.* 1982. Lackey 1986: 634, suggests how such heuristics might explain conflicting moral intuitions about nuclear deterrence.

the programs are as follows: If program A is adopted, 200 people will be saved. If program B is adopted, there is a 1/3 probability that 600 people will be saved, and a 2/3 probability that no people will be saved. Which program would you choose?

The same story was told to a second group of subjects, but these subjects had to choose between these programs:

If program C is adopted, 400 people will die. If program D is adopted, there is a 1/3 probability that nobody will die and a 2/3 probability that 600 will die.

It should be obvious that programs A and C are equivalent, as are programs B and D. However, most subjects who chose between A and B favored A, but most subjects who chose between C and D favored D. More generally, subjects were risk averse when results were described in positive terms (such as 'lives saved') but risk seeking when results were described in negative terms (such as 'lives lost' or 'people who die').

The question in this experiment was about choices rather than moral wrongness. Still, the subjects were not told how the policies affect them personally, so their choices seem to result from beliefs about which program is morally right or wrong. If so, the subjects had different moral beliefs about programs A and C and about programs B and D. The only difference within each pair is how the programs are framed or described. Thus, descriptions seem to affect moral beliefs. Descriptions cannot affect what is really morally right or wrong. Hence, these results suggest that such moral beliefs are unreliable.

Moral intuitionists could claim that moral intuitions are still reliable when subjects have consistent beliefs after considering all relevant descriptions. But then moral believers would need to know that their beliefs are consistent and that they are aware of all relevant descriptions before they could be justified in holding moral beliefs. Framing effects distort moral beliefs in so many cases that moral believers need confirmation for any particular moral belief.

To see how deeply this point cuts, consider Warren Quinn's argument for the traditional doctrine of doing and allowing, which claims that stronger moral justification is needed for killing than for letting die. In support of this general doctrine, Quinn appeals to moral intuitions of specific cases:

In Rescue I, we can save either five people in danger of drowning at one place or a single person in danger of drowning somewhere else. We cannot save all six. In Rescue II, we can save the five only by driving over and thereby killing someone who (for an unspecified reason) is trapped on the road. If we do not undertake the rescue, the trapped person can later be freed. (1993: 152)

Most people judge that saving the five is morally wrong in Rescue II but not in Rescue I. Why do they react this way? Quinn assumes that these different intuitions result from the difference between killing and letting die or, more generally, doing and allowing harm. However, Tamara Horowitz uses a different distinction (between gains and losses) and a different theory (prospect theory) to develop an alternative explanation of Quinn's moral intuitions:

> In deciding whether to kill the person or leave the person alone, one thinks of the person's being alive as the status quo and chooses this as the neutral outcome. Killing the person is regarded as a negative deviation.... But in deciding to save a person who would otherwise die, the person being dead is the status quo and is selected as the neutral outcome. So saving the person is a positive deviation.... (1998: 153)

The point is that we tend to reject options that cause definite negative deviations from the status quo. That explains why subjects rejected program C but did not reject program A in the Asian disease case (despite the equivalence between those programs). It also explains why we think that it is morally wrong to 'kill' in Rescue II but is not morally wrong to 'not save' in Rescue I, since killing causes a definite negative deviation from the status quo. This explanation clearly hinges on what is taken to be the status quo, which in turn depends on how the options are described. Quinn's story about Rescue I describes the people as already 'in danger of drowning', whereas the trapped person in Rescue II can 'later be freed' if not for our 'killing' him. These descriptions affect our choice of the neutral starting point. As in the Asian disease cases, our choice of the neutral starting point then affects our moral intuitions. Horowitz adds, 'I do not see why anyone would think the distinction [that explains our reactions to Quinn's rescue cases] is morally significant, but perhaps there is some argument I have not thought of. If the distinction is not morally significant, then Quinn's thought experiments do not support one moral theory over against another' (1998: 155).

Admittedly, Horowitz's explanation does not imply that Quinn's moral intuitions are false or incoherent, as in the Asian disease case. It does not even establish that his moral intuitions are arbitrary. As Mark van Roojen says, 'Nothing in the example shows anything wrong with treating losses from a neutral baseline differently from gains. Such reasoning might well be appropriate where framing proceeds in a reasonable manner' (1999).[22] Nonetheless, the framing also 'might well' *not* be reasonable, so the epistemological dilemma remains: If there is no reason to choose one baseline over the other, then our moral intuitions seem arbitrary and unjustified. If there is a reason to choose one baseline over the other, then either we have access to that reason or we do not. If we have access to the reason, then we are able to draw an inference from

---

[22] Van Roojen might admit that Horowitz's argument undermines moral intuitionism, since he defends a method of reflective equilibrium that is coherentist rather than foundationalist.

that reason to justify our moral belief. If we do not have access to that reason, then we do not seem justified in our moral belief. Because framing effects so often lead to incoherence and error, we cannot be justified in trusting a moral intuition that relies on framing effects unless we at least can be aware that this intuition is one where the baseline is reasonable. So Horowitz's explanation creates serious trouble for moral intuitionism whenever framing effects could explain our moral intuitions.

The doctrine of doing and allowing is not an isolated case. It affects many prominent issues and is strongly believed by many philosophers and common people, who do not seem to be able to infer it from any other beliefs. If moral intuitions are unjustified in this case, doubts should arise about a wide range of other moral intuitions as well.

Origins

Some previous principles look at origins of individual moral beliefs, but Principle 5 considers the social origins of shared moral beliefs. The two issues are related insofar as many of our moral beliefs result from training and social interaction.

Specifically, Principle 5 claims that problematic social origins create a need for confirmation. To apply this principle, we need to ask whether moral beliefs have problematic social origins. The social origins of moral beliefs might be problematic in two ways. First, moral beliefs might be caused by factors that are unrelated with the truth of those beliefs. Second, the origins of moral beliefs might be immoral according to those moral beliefs. I will focus on the latter case.

Are the origins of our moral intuitions immoral by their own lights? Friedrich Nietzsche suggests as much when he argues that Christian morality results from slaves cleverly overcoming their superiors by re-evaluating values. Insofar as Christian morality condemns such subterfuge and self-promotion, Christian morality condemns its own origins, if Nietzsche is correct (Nietzsche 1966).[23] Similarly, Michel Foucault argues at length that moral beliefs express or result from social power relations. Yet these moral beliefs themselves seem to condemn the very kind of power that leads to these beliefs. But I don't want to rely on Nietzsche or Foucault, at least not in this context, so I will consider Gilbert Harman's explanation of the common moral belief that harming someone is much worse than failing to helping someone in need:

whereas everyone would benefit equally from a conventional practice of trying not to harm each other, some people would benefit considerably more than others from a

---

[23] I am not, of course, endorsing Nietzsche's speculations.

convention to help those who needed help. The rich and powerful do not need much help and are often in the best position to give it; so, if a strong principle of mutual aid were adopted, they would gain little and lose a great deal, because they would end up doing most of the helping and would receive little in return. On the other hand, the poor and the weak might refuse to agree to a principle of non-interference or non-injury unless they also reached some agreement on mutual aid. We would therefore expect a compromise [that] would involve a strong principle of non-injury and a weaker principle of mutual aid—which is just what we now have. (1977: 110; cf. Scheffler 1982: 113)

Remember also that rich and powerful people have always controlled the church, the media, and culture, which in turn affect most people's moral beliefs. In this context, Harman's claim is that the self-interest of the rich and powerful in making everyone believe that harming is worse than failing to help can explain why so many people believe that harming is worse than failing to help. But our moral beliefs also seem to condemn such self-serving indoctrination by the rich and powerful, since morality is supposed to consider everyone's interests equally. Thus, if Harman is correct, morality condemns its own origins, as Nietzsche and Foucault claimed.

The point is not that such moral views are internally inconsistent, self-condemning, or even self-defeating. The point is only that there are grounds for doubt when beliefs come from disreputable sources. Defenders of such moral beliefs must admit that the sources of their beliefs are disreputable if Harman's explanation is accurate. Then they need additional support for their beliefs beyond the mere fact that those beliefs seem correct to them.

These speculations about the origins of moral beliefs are mere armchair psychology. Perhaps more support could be obtained from the literature on sociobiology or evolutionary psychology. Still, these explanations are likely to remain very controversial. Luckily, I don't need to prove them here. I claim only that these undermining accounts are live possibilities. They seem plausible to many people and have not been refuted.

That would not be enough if I were arguing for the falsehood of a certain moral belief, such as Christian morality (from Nietzsche) or the prevalence of non-injury over mutual aid (from Harman). However, I am not drawing any substantive moral conclusion. To do so would commit a genetic fallacy, but my argument is different. My point lies in moral epistemology, and I reach it indirectly. If these disreputable origins are live possibilities, then moral believers need some independent confirmation that their beliefs are not distorted by such disreputable origins. This need for independent confirmation then undermines moral intuitionism.

Togetherness

Don't forget that Principles 1–5 complement each other. If I am right, moral beliefs are partial, controversial, emotional, subject to illusion, and explicable by dubious sources, so all of the principles apply. However, even if not all but only several of them apply, these principles still work together to make it clear that confirmation is needed for justified moral belief. That undermines moral intuitionism. It also shows how empirical research can be indirectly relevant to normative moral epistemology.

4. Objections

None of my arguments is conclusive, so opponents can object at several points. Here I cannot respond to every objection or to any objection thoroughly. But I will quickly run through the most formidable objections.

Confirmation

One common objection is that, even if some confirmation is needed, that does not show that any inference is needed. If we can confirm color beliefs just by looking again in different light, perhaps we can confirm moral beliefs simply by reflecting on the moral issue again in a different mood without involving any substantive moral principle from which we infer our moral belief.

I grant that confirmation does not require an actual inference. To avoid the skeptical regress, however, moral intuitionists must deny more than the need for an actual inference. They must deny the need for any ability to infer the moral belief. It is hard to see how you could confirm a moral belief without gaining information that makes you able to draw some kind of inference to the moral belief. Even if you just think about the moral issue several times in different moods, after such rethinking you have all the information you need for a simple inference like this:

> I hold this moral belief after reflecting on the issue several times in different moods.
>
> If I hold a moral belief after reflecting on the issue several times in different moods, then it is usually true.
>
> So, probably, this moral belief is true.

Admittedly, this inference is not a deductive proof. Nor does it infer the moral belief from a more general substantive moral principle. But no specific kind of inference is needed. Any kind of inference can lead to a skeptical regress, so moral intuitionists have to deny dependence on any kind of inference or ability to infer. And an ability to draw the above kind of inference is needed, since, if the moral believer does not believe its premises (or something like them), then it is hard to see why the moral believer is justified in holding the moral belief.

At this point, externalists (including reliabilists) sometimes accuse me of confusing whether a belief is justified with whether the believer knows that it is justified. I plead innocent. I do not assume that justified believers must know or be justified in believing (or even be able to know or be justified in believing) that they are justified. I claim only that justified moral believers must be able to infer their moral beliefs from something. Some externalists still deny this, but their denial is implausible, as I have argued elsewhere (Sinnott-Armstrong 2002*b*). Besides, most externalists are mainly concerned about non-moral beliefs, including perceptual beliefs. Principles 1–5 do not apply to perceptual beliefs in the same way as to moral beliefs. Most perceptual beliefs are not partial, controversial, emotional, or explicable by dubious sources. Perceptual illusions are common, but they are normally easier to detect than moral illusions, and they do not affect anything as widespread and fundamental as the doctrine of doing and allowing. Consequently, externalism and reliabilism might work for perceptual beliefs even if, as I have argued, moral beliefs need confirmation of a kind that requires an inferential ability.[24]

Children

This response leads to another objection. It might seem too strict to require an inferential ability because then young children cannot have justified moral beliefs, since they cannot formulate the needed inferences.

I love children. I grant that they can have justified beliefs in other areas, such as beliefs about food and toys. However, it is not as clear that very young children (say, 1–3 years old) can be justified in holding moral beliefs. After all, young children often base their normative beliefs on fear of punishment. If someone believes that stealing is wrong just because he believes that he is likely to get punished if he steals, then it is not even clear that the belief is a moral belief. It might be purely prudential. Instead of fear, the basis for some young children's moral beliefs might be deference to authorities (or peers). But if children accept their parents' word that an act is wrong without any idea of what makes that act wrong, then these children might not believe that the act is wrong *morally*, since they might not believe that there is any specifically

---

[24] I do not claim that moral judgments are the only ones that need confirmation according to Principles 1–5. Several of these principles also apply to beliefs about what is prudent, rational, wise, and beautiful.

moral reason not to do the act. Moreover, authorities can make someone justified only if she is justified in trusting those authorities. Maybe young children are justified in trusting their parents, for example. But then they can infer:

My parents are trustworthy.

My parents tell me that I shouldn't pull my sister's hair.

Therefore, I shouldn't pull my sister's hair.

If a young child is not able to draw any inference like this, then this child does not seem justified (even if her parents are trustworthy and even if her belief is true). Those who think otherwise are too soft on their kids.

Ignorance

Another objection claims that, if a moral believer could not know that moral beliefs are subject to controversy, partiality, illusion, and so on, then that moral believer does not need to guard against these problems by getting confirmation. Children and some adults (such as isolated medieval peasants) might have no way of discovering such problems for moral beliefs. They certainly lack access to the psychological research that I cited. So maybe these moral believers do not need confirmation for their moral beliefs.

This objection confuses two claims. To call a believer unjustified is often to criticize that believer. Such criticism seems misplaced when the believer is not responsible for any epistemic failures. Believers are not responsible when they have no way of knowing that their beliefs are problematic. Thus, if children and medieval peasants cannot know that moral beliefs are problematic, it seems odd to call them unjustified.

In contrast, to say that a believer is not justified is not to criticize the believer. It is only to withhold the praise of calling the believer justified. There is nothing unfair about withholding praise when a believer is not responsible. Thus, even if children and medieval peasants are not responsible for their epistemic failures, that does not undermine my claim that they are not justified in their moral beliefs.

Moreover, even if children and medieval peasants were justified in their moral beliefs, that would not save moral intuitionists or my readers from the need for confirmation. Moral intuitionists and my readers are neither children nor medieval peasants. They are modern educated adults. Modern educated adults can know that moral beliefs are problematic in the ways that I outlined (at least if they have read this far). So my readers and other modern adults need confirmation for moral beliefs, regardless of what you think about other people.

Moral intuitionists might seem to avoid this point if they claim only that some moral believers are justified. However, moral intuitionists always include themselves among those who are justified. Similarly, I assume that my readers want to know whether they themselves are justified moral believers. If it turns out that the only moral believers who are justified without confirmation are children, medieval peasants, and others who are ignorant of the empirical research in this paper, then it is not so great to be justified.

Defeasibility

Some moral intuitionists accuse me of forgetting that a moral believer can be defeasibly justified without being adequately justified. Again, I plead innocent.

To say that a moral believer is defeasibly justified is to say that the believer would be justified in the absence of any defeater. Defeaters come in two kinds. An overriding defeater of a belief provides a reason to believe that the belief is false. For example, if one newspaper predicts rain tomorrow, but a more reliable newspaper predicts clear skies, then the latter prediction overrides the former, even if I still have some reason to believe the former. In contrast, an undermining defeater takes the force out of a reason without providing any reason to believe the opposite. If I find out that the newspaper that predicts rain based its prediction on a crystal ball, then this new information keeps the prediction from making me justified in believing that it will rain, but the new information does not make me justified in believing that it will *not* rain, since a crystal ball is just as likely to lead to a true prediction. When my justification is undermined completely in this way, I have no reason left for believing that it will rain or that it will not rain.

The factors in Principles 1–5 cannot be overriding defeaters, since they do not provide any reason to believe the moral belief is false. Even when moral beliefs are partial, controversial, emotional, subject to illusion, and due to disreputable sources, that does not show that those beliefs are false. Thus, the factors in Principles 1–5 seem to be undermining defeaters. That suggests that we have no reason to trust our spontaneous moral beliefs before confirmation. Admittedly, some defeaters might not completely undermine a justification. They might leave some weaker reason that makes believers partially justified. However, the manifold underminers in Principles 1–5 add up, so that it is hard to see why there is any reason left to hold spontaneous moral beliefs without confirmation.

Moreover, I am not just talking about *possible* underminers. I argued in section 3 that the underminers in Principles 1–5 actually exist for many moral beliefs. Actual moral believers are partial and emotional. They actually do disagree often. Cultures actually are disreputable in ways that affect moral beliefs. There is even empirical evidence for actual widespread illusions in morality.

Moral intuitionists can still say that spontaneous moral believers are prima facie justified if that means only that they would be adequately justified if their moral beliefs were not undermined by the factors in Principles 1–5. This counterfactual claim is compatible with their actually not being justified at all, but only appearing to be justified. They might have no real reason for belief but only the misleading appearance of a reason (as with the newspaper's rain prediction based on a crystal ball). In contrast, to call a believer pro tanto justified is to indicate some actual positive epistemic force that is not cancelled or undermined even if it is overridden. If the factors in Principles 1 5 are underminers, as I argued, then spontaneous moral believers are not even pro tanto justified. At most they misleadingly appear to be justified when they are not really justified at all.

Besides, even if moral intuitions were pro tanto justified independently of any inferential ability, this status would not make them adequately justified. As I said, skeptics win if no moral belief is adequately justified. So moral intuitionists cannot rest easy with the claim that moral intuitions are merely pro tanto justified.

Some

Many opponents object that, even if Principles 1–5 apply to some moral beliefs, they do not apply to all moral beliefs. As I admitted, some moral beliefs are not controversial. For example, almost everyone (except moral nihilists) agrees that it is morally wrong to push the fat man in front of the trolley just because you are angry with him for beating you in a game. Such cases also do not seem due to context, heuristics, overgeneralization, or framing effects. Still, such moral believers are partial and emotional (as Greene's experiments suggested). So Principles 1 and 3 do seem to create a need for confirmation even in such clear cases.

Furthermore, if very many moral beliefs need confirmation, the others cannot be immune from this need. To see why, compare a country with lots of barn façades that look just like real barns when viewed from the road (Goldman 1976). If someone looks only from the road, then he is not justified in believing that what he sees is a real barn, at least if he should know about the barn façades. The barn façades are analogous to situations that produce distorted moral beliefs. Since such distortions are so common, morality is a land of fake barns. In such areas, confirmation is needed for each justified belief, even for those beliefs formed in front of real barns. Analogously, confirmation is needed for each spontaneous moral belief, even when the common distorting factors are absent. We need to get off the road and look closer. At least when we should know that moral beliefs in general are so often subject to distortion, we cannot be justified in trusting any moral belief until we confirm that it is an exception to the rule that most moral beliefs are problematic. So moral intuitionists cannot claim that any moral believers are justified without confirmation.

This point can be presented as a dilemma: If a moral believer is an educated modern adult, then she should know that many moral beliefs are problematic in the ways indicated by Principles 1–5. She either knows or does not know that her moral belief is an exception to the trend. If she does not know this, she should accept a significant probability that her belief is problematic. Then she cannot be justified without confirmation. Alternatively, if she does know that her moral belief is exceptionally reliable, then she has enough information to draw an inference like this: My moral belief is exceptionally reliable. Exceptionally reliable beliefs are probably true. Therefore, my belief is (probably) true. If this moral believer does not have the information in these premises, then it is hard to see why we should call her justified. So, either way, moral intuitionism fails.

Skepticism

A common objection is that my argument leads to general skepticism, since every inference has premises, so the demand for an inference cannot always be met. However, my argument does not generalize so easily. If my belief that a pen is in front of me is not subject to disagreement or illusions and has no disreputable sources, and if I am neither partial nor emotional about pens, then I might be justified in holding that non-moral belief without being able to support it with any inference. Thus, my argument against moral intuitionism does not lead to general skepticism.

My argument still might seem to lead to moral skepticism. If so, and if moral skepticism is unacceptable, then something must be wrong with my argument. However, my argument does not by itself lead to moral skepticism. My thesis is not that spontaneous moral beliefs are not justified, but only that they are not justified non-inferentially because they need confirmation. Such confirmation still might be possible somehow. Even if moral intuitionism is rejected, there are other non-skeptical methods in moral epistemology, including coherentism, contractarianism, contractualism, contextualism, and naturalism (Sinnott-Armstrong 1996: 31–41). Moral skepticism arises only after all of these other approaches fall. So my argument does not by itself support moral skepticism.

Besides, even if these other approaches also fail, so my argument plays a role in a larger argument for moral skepticism, that does not show that anything is wrong with my argument, unless one assumes that moral skepticism is unacceptable. Why assume that? I accept a limited Pyrrhonian version of moral skepticism. So I, at least, will not be dismayed if my argument takes one step in that direction.[25]

Anyway, my goal here has not been to argue for moral skepticism. My goal has been to argue against moral intuitionism. More generally, I tried to show one way in which empirical research in psychology and brain science might be relevant to normative moral epistemology. If I succeeded in that enterprise, I will happily leave moral skepticism for another occasion.

References

Baron, J. (1994). 'Nonconsequentialist Decisions'. *Behavioral and Brain Sciences*, 17: 1–42.

Foot, Philippa (1967). 'The Problem of Abortion and the Doctrine of Double Effect'. *Oxford Review*, 5: 5–15.

Goldman, A. (1976). 'Discrimination and Perceptual Knowledge'. *Journal of Philosophy*, 73: 771–91.

Greene, J., *et al.* (2001). 'An fMRI Investigation of Emotional Engagement in Moral Judgment'. *Science*, 293: 2105–8.

—— and Haidt, J. (2002). 'How (and Where) does Moral Judgment Work?' *Trends in Cognitive Science*, 6: 517–23.

—— *et al.* (2004). 'The Neural Bases of Cognitive Conflict and Control in Moral Judgment.' *Neuron*, 44: 389–400.

Haidt, J. (2001). 'The Emotional Dog and its Rational Tail: A Social Intuitionist Approach to Moral Judgment'. *Psychological Review*, 108: 814–34.

—— *et al.* (1993). 'Affect, Culture, and Morality, or is it Wrong to Eat Your Dog?' *Journal of Personality and Social Psychology*, 65: 613–28.

Harman, G. (1977). *The Nature of Morality*. New York: Oxford University Press.

Horowitz, T. (1998). 'Philosophical Intuitions and Psychological Theory'. In M. DePaul and W. Ramsey (eds.), *Rethinking Intuition: The Psychology of Intuition and its Role in Philosophical Inquiry*. Lanham, Md.: Rowman & Littlefield.

---

[25] See Sinnott–Armstrong 2006. My version of Pyrrhonism denies that any particular contrast class is the relevant one in the sense that believers need to rule out all alternatives in that class in order to be justified without qualification. That view might seem to conflict with my claim here that moral beliefs need inferential confirmation. However, there might be no need to rule out any particular contrast class, even if there is a need to give evidence of a certain kind.

KAHNEMAN, D., SLOVIC, P., and TVERSKY, A. (eds.) (1982). *Judgment under Uncertainty: Heuristics and Biases*. Cambridge: Cambridge University Press.

—— and TVERSKY, A. (1979). 'Prospect Theory: An Analysis of Decision under Risk'. *Econometrica*, 47/2: 263–92.

LACKEY, D. (1986). 'Taking Risk Seriously'. *Journal of Philosophy*, 83: 633–40.

MOLL, J., *et al.* (2001). 'Frontopolar and Anterior Temporal Cortex Activation in a Moral Judgment Task: Preliminary Functional MRI results in Normal Subjects'. *Arq. Neuropsiquiatr*, 59: 657–64.

—— *et al.* (2002*a*). 'Functional Networks in Emotional Moral and Nonmoral Social Judgments'. *Neuroimage*, 16: 696–703.

—— *et al.* (2002*b*). 'The Neural Correlates of Moral Sensitivity: A Functional Magnetic Resonance Imaging Investigation of Basic and Moral Emotions'. *Journal of Neuroscience*, 22: 2730–6.

MOORE, G. E. (1903). *Principia Ethica*. Cambridge: Cambridge University Press.

NIETZSCHE, F. (1966). *Genealogy of Morals*. In *Basic Writings of Nietzsche*, ed. and trans. W. Kaufmann. New York: Random House.

PARFIT, D. (1984). *Reasons and Persons*. Oxford: Clarendon Press.

QUINN, W. (1993). 'Actions, Intentions, and Consequences: The Doctrine of Doing and Allowing', repr. in *Morality and Action*. New York: Cambridge University Press.

ROSS, W. D. (1930). *The Right and the Good*. Oxford: Oxford University Press.

SCHEFFLER, S. (1982). *The Rejection of Consequentialism*. Oxford: Clarendon Press.

SINNOTT-ARMSTRONG, W. (1996). 'Moral Skepticism and Justification'. In W. Sinnott-Armstrong and M. Timmons (eds.), *Moral Knowledge?* New York: Oxford University Press.

—— (2000). 'From "Is" to "Ought" in Moral Epistemology'. *Argumentation*, 14: 159–74.

—— (2002*a*). 'Moral Skepticism', in Edward N. Zalta (ed.), *The Stanford Encyclopedia of Philosophy* (Summer 2002 edn.), **http://plato.stanford.edu/archives/sum2002/entries/skepticism-moral/**.

—— (2002*b*). 'Moral Relativity and Intuitionism'. *Philosophical Issues*, Realism and Relativism, 12: 305–28.

—— (2006). Moral Skepticism. New York: Oxford University Press.

SNARE, F. (1980). 'The Diversity of Morals'. *Mind*, 89: 353–69.

UNGER, P. (1996). *Living High and Letting Die*. New York: Oxford University Press.

VAN ROOJEN, M. (1999). 'Reflective Moral Equilibrium and Psychological Theory'. *Ethics*, 109: 846–57.

WHEATLEY, T., and HAIDT, J. (2005). 'The Wisdom of Repugnance: Hypnotically-Induced Disgust Makes Moral Judgments More Severe' (unpublished manuscript, University of Virginia).

16

Ethics Dehumanized

Panayot Butchvarov

1. Ethics and anthropology

It is too early to judge how twentieth-century philosophy ended, but its beginning was remarkable. Both Moore's *Principia Ethica* and Russell's *Principles of Mathematics* appeared in 1903, the first volume of Husserl's *Logical Investigations* in 1900–1, and four of William James's major philosophical books in 1902–9. There was not a significant difference, except in style and temperament, between Anglo-American and European philosophers. The analytic/continental schism came much later. Both Russell and Husserl began as mathematicians. Moore wrote in the preface of *Principia* that his ethics was closest to Brentano's. Russell studied and discussed Frege and Meinong in detail. James was admired in Britain and in Europe, influenced Husserl and Wittgenstein, and was the subject of articles by Moore and Russell.

The present occasion is devoted to Moore's *Principia* and what his heirs in analytic ethics accomplished. But we must not neglect the rest of its historical context, the important, often illuminating, similarities Moore's ethics bears to the views not only of Brentano but also of his close associates Russell and Wittgenstein, as well as of predecessors such as Plato and Kant and his immediate successors H. A. Prichard and W. D. Ross. The relation of analytic ethics to Moore's book rested largely on his thesis in chapter I that the property good is indefinable. Yet Moore made clear he had no interest in what he called verbal and the tradition calls nominal definitions. They are the business of lexicography, he wrote. But it is just such definitions that analytic philosophers sought, sometimes calling them analyses. The most familiar example comes from analytic epistemology, not ethics: the definitions of 'S knows that p' in the 1960s, 1970s, and early 1980s. They were not even lexicographic definitions, which record lexical fact and are tested by empirical investigation of speech and writing. Rather, they recorded *impressions* of lexical fact, and were tested by the author's 'intuition' of what would or would not be said in some hypothetical situation, called a 'counterexample' if it did not fit the intuition. The question 'How do I know what one would say in that situation, given that I am not in it?' was usually ignored. For it could be answered properly only by appealing to what I and, especially, others have said in relevant situations, and this would be to appeal to lexical fact. Even the *Oxford English Dictionary* is valuable mainly for the examples of usage it lists, not the definitions it distills from them.

The kind of definition Moore did seek was an account of the constitution of the thing, *res*, that is defined. It was closer to what the tradition calls real definition, though it gave not the genus and differentia but the parts of the thing. Such a definition can be called an analysis, in a sense reasonably similar to that employed in chemistry. In later years analyses were offered mainly of facts and propositions, which were taken to be nonlinguistic entities categorially different from those chemistry analyzes. Their analysis was intended to reveal logical form and, for this reason, was called logical analysis. It was in such analyses that analytic philosophy took root, beginning in 1905 with Russell's theory of definite descriptions and culminating in Moore's claim two decades later, in 'A Defense of Common Sense,' that he knew the proposition 'This is a hand' to be true but did not know how to analyze it. In *Principia*, however, his example was the definition of a horse and consisted of an anatomical inventory. Our example might be the account of water as H_2O. Moore in effect agreed with Kant that 'in matters of morality it is always real definitions that must be sought.'[1]

Despite its inattention to what he meant by 'definition,' analytic ethics did begin and develop in relation to Moore's ethics, though by way of sustained disagreement, not agreement. Discussions of *Principia* seldom ventured beyond chapter I, which alone was included in most anthologies. Usually ignored were the crucial preface, where Moore explained what he meant by 'intuition' and 'self-evidence' and, thus, what anyone calling him an intuitionist and a foundationalist ought to mean. Also usually ignored were the beginning of chapter II, where he explained what he meant by 'natural' and 'nonnatural,' thus what anyone calling his ethics nonnaturalist ought to mean, and chapter V, where he explained his theory of right on the basis of the theory in chapter I.

By 'intuitions,' Moore wrote, he meant self-evident propositions, and 'nothing whatever as to the manner or origin of our cognition of them.' And a self-evident proposition, he explained, is one that is evident but not by virtue of inference from other propositions. He did not say what he meant by 'evident,' perhaps thinking it unnecessary. A proposition is evident, of course, if it is, or can readily be, seen to be true, either literally or metaphorically. Therefore, it

---

[1] Immanuel Kant, *Logic*, trans. Robert S. Hartman and Wolfgang Schwartz (New York: Dover, 1974), 144.

may also be said to be known, in the serious and traditional sense of 'know.' The noun 'evidence,' as used in court or in the lab, has a wider meaning, but the same root. Moore used 'self-evident' for the propositions stating 'what kind of things ought to exist for their own sakes,' that is, are intrinsically good.

As to the meaning he attached to calling something 'natural,' he wrote he meant that the thing is in time. Thus a paradigm of a *nonnatural* thing would be a number, an abstract entity. The mere fact that a thing falls outside the subject matter of physics does not make it nonnatural. For example, irreducibly mental states would be in time and thus natural. If we said that a natural thing is one belonging in the province of the natural sciences, as Moore himself did on occasion, we would need a noncircular account of what is meant by calling a science natural, as he doubtless was aware and so did not offer this as his definition of 'natural.' The fact is that the distinction between the natural and the nonnatural did not play a central role in his book, though the phrase 'naturalistic fallacy' of course did. As Moore made clear in the also ignored chapter IV, which was devoted to what he called metaphysical ethics, even ethical theories concerned with the 'supersensible' committed the fallacy. The fallacy was just that of confusing two things: the property good and some other property.

In chapter I Moore held that the property good is nonnatural and simple, therefore (given his account of definition) indefinable, that almost all earlier ethical theories had committed the naturalistic fallacy of confusing it with another property, and that they could be refuted with the so-called open question argument, which in effect encouraged the reader to pay close attention to the property such a theory confuses with the property good in order to see that they are two properties, not one. But his contemporaries in the Society of Apostles and the Bloomsbury Circle, who included Russell, Keynes, and Virginia Woolf, found more important not these metaphilosophical generalities but the substantive views, defended in chapter VI, that personal affection (love, friendship) and aesthetic appreciation (contemplation of beauty, in art and in natural objects, human and nonhuman) are the greatest goods. In contrast with Kant's position, it is they that for Moore were the Ideal. And it is they that prompted Keynes to rate Moore higher even than Plato. That chapter, too, has been ignored in analytic ethics, which has focused instead on the preliminary discussions in chapter I, especially the objectivity of value it took Moore to be defending there. But, in a recent book, Brian Hutchinson points out that 'Moore never even entertained doubts about the objectivity of value.' Hutchinson acknowledges that for us this may be 'a mystery difficult to fathom,' but wisely suggests that the mystery 'is to be savored rather than solved.'[2]

---

[2] Brian Hutchinson, *G. E. Moore's Ethical Theory: Resistance and Reconciliation* (New York: Cambridge University Press, 2001).

While the central tenet of Moore's theory of good was that it is a simple, indefinable, and nonnatural property, the central tenet of his theory of right was that duty is the action that 'will cause more good to exist in the Universe than any possible alternative,'[3] the action that 'is *the* best thing to do,' that 'together with its consequences presents a greater sum of intrinsic value than any possible alternatives,' either because it 'itself has greater intrinsic value than any alternative' or because 'the balance of intrinsic value' of its consequences does, so that 'more good or less evil will exist in the world' if it is adopted (*Principia Ethica*, 76–7). Of course, the action need not do so on a grand scale. To think that it must, or even could, would be human conceit of cosmic proportion. And 'cause' or 'produce' should be understood broadly in the sense of 'contribute,' since the action might be the best thing to do because of its own goodness or its organic relationships. Moore's was an ideal utilitarianism, which unlike Bentham's, Mill's, and Sidgwick's presupposed a theory of good that placed no limits on what items might enjoy intrinsic goodness, thus allowing that some may be actions.

Moore's theory of right may be called *cosmological*. It tells us that we ought to do what would be best, *all* things in the universe considered. It accords with Aquinas's first principle of natural law: 'Good is to be done and promoted, and evil is to be avoided.'[4] It does imply, as Moore noted, that justice is not to be done if the heavens should fall—unless, he wryly added, 'by the doing of justice the Universe gains more than it loses by the falling of the heavens' (*Principia Ethica*, 197). The ethical views of Russell and Wittgenstein, the other two founders of analytic philosophy, were also nonnaturalist and cosmological. But, with the exception of Prichard, a thinker of unsurpassed acuity, and Ross, whose terminology and distinctions we still find indispensable, later Anglo-American ethics diverged in both respects. They are related. If ethics is naturalistic, then it is not likely to be cosmological. And if it is cosmological, then it is not likely to be naturalistic.

Naturalistic ethics is almost certainly ethics humanized, a sort of anthropology: it is about humans, not cats or bats. So it is not cosmological. Not only does it ignore the good of the universe, it ignores that of gods, angels, and extraterrestrials, if there are any, and usually also that of rivers, plants, and even nonhuman animals. Thus it lacks the supreme generality and abstraction distinctive of philosophy and probably alone justifying its existence alongside the other cognitive disciplines. A cosmological ethics can be expected, of course, to have application to humans, just as chemistry and mathematics do. But this makes none of them about humans.

---

[3] G. E. Moore, *Principia Ethica*, 2nd edn. (Cambridge: Cambridge University Press, 1993), 198.
[4] Thomas Aquinas, *Summa Theologica*, Part Two, Question 94, Article 2.

To be sure, we all feel what Cora Diamond calls the 'heart-breaking specialness' of the human.[5] We all are human, enormously interested in ourselves and in other humans, especially those we love or hate. It seems unfriendly, indecent, inhumane to suggest that our ethics should be dehumanized, that it should not be about us. Many demand that even space research be funded only if it leads to cures for our diseases. But we are not the center of the universe, much as we crave center stage. As Russell insisted, man does not have 'the cosmic significance assigned to him by traditional philosophers.' Man only has cosmic vanity. To think that philosophy should be about us is like thinking that astronomy should be about us. If this was not evident in the past, perhaps the reason was the belief that, though God did see to it that all things he created were good, he created only man in his own image.

Of course, there is a special, deep, and often misunderstood sense in which humans may be cosmically central, namely, that leading to views such as Kant's transcendental idealism and its recent versions in Goodman and Putnam. They rest on the virtual tautology that how we perceive and understand (conceive of) the world, and thus the world itself as perceived and understood, depend on our faculties of perception and understanding (conception). It does not follow that there is nothing else. As Kant remarked, we can at least think of things in themselves, for the notion of such things is not self-contradictory.[6] If we denied that we can, we would be committing ourselves to a peculiar sort of epistemic creationism. Nevertheless, in that special sense, Kant, Putnam, and Goodman may be said to have humanized even astronomy. But they did not hold that astronomy is about humans. Although for Kant 'the ultimate end of the pure use of our reason' was ethical, he resolved to '[keep] as close as possible to the transcendental and [to set] aside entirely what might . . . be psychological, i.e., empirical' (*Critique of Pure Reason*, A 797/825–A 801/B 829), since 'the metaphysic of ethics is really the pure morality, which is not grounded on any anthropology' (A 841/42–B 869–70).

Ethics humanized thus is unphilosophical. It also lacks competence. Quine, who took up the case for epistemology naturalized, in effect epistemology humanized, often mentioned the role in cognition of 'surface irritations' but wisely left the study of those irritations to neurology. In both epistemology humanized and ethics humanized, we would be frivolous to compete with the sciences specializing in humans, their cognitive functions and capacities, or

---

[5] Cora Diamond, *The Realistic Spirit: Wittgenstein, Philosophy and the Mind* (Cambridge, Mass.: MIT Press, 1991), 352.

[6] Immanuel Kant, *Critique of Pure Reason*, trans. Paul Guyer and Allen W. Wood (Cambridge. Cambridge University Press, 1998), B xxviii.

their ways of acting and well-being.[7] If humans are natural objects, a species of animal, we can hardly expect to have special philosophical knowledge of them, just as we can hardly expect to have special philosophical knowledge of stars or bats. Accounts of human well-being and searches for the best explanation of human conduct do not belong in philosophy departments, just as accounts of human anatomy and human evolution do not. My point does not depend on a narrow use of the words 'natural' and 'science.' If mental states are not reducible to physical states, there could still be a natural science of them, in Moore's sense of 'natural' and the traditional sense of 'science' in which history and political geography are social sciences. In fact there was such a science in Moore's time, namely, the largely introspective psychology of James, Wundt, and Titchener. My point does depend, however, on taking *competence* seriously, whether in forensic pathology and medieval history—or in ethics and epistemology. Genuine competence requires serious training, for example, in chemical analysis or parsing Latin. Nothing analogous with respect to humans occurs in philosophy seminar rooms. If employed in hospitals, medical ethicists are expected to learn some medicine. The reason is that their concern is properly with humans, and it is naturalistic in Quine's sense of being continuous with natural science. They are often invaluable, not because they know something physicians do not, but because they are Socratic—they ask questions physicians do not.

We need not go to hospitals for examples. How to achieve happiness, in the ordinary sense, recognized by both Kant and Mill, of enjoyment or satisfaction of our needs and desires, has been a stock question in ethics, with Epicurus and even Plato offering much advice; but arguably the invention of aspirin and contraceptives, tractors and pesticides, air conditioning and spreadsheets, answered it better. This is especially evident in politics. In Buddhist ethics, sadly but realistically, suffering seems the primary concern, not pleasure, as in Western ethics. Indian Benthamites hoping to learn from Americans how to reduce suffering presumably go to American colleges of agriculture and schools of public health, not to American philosophy departments.

One may ask, indignantly, what about loftier goods, not Bentham's perhaps but certainly Plato's and Kant's, such as justice, authenticity, salvation? Especially in India, a deeply religious country, they are often thought far more important. But these loftier goods call for nonanthropological, nonzoological, considerations. Of course, philosophers who avow allegiance to naturalistic ethics do write about some of them, at least about justice, not about gustatory delights. Do they think they have access to human nature that zoologists lack?

---

[7] Cf. my 'Epistemology Dehumanized,' in Quentin Smith (ed.), *Epistemology: New Essays* (Oxford: Oxford University Press, forthcoming).

Of course, they do not. Long ago, they took the conceptual turn. They adopted a view of ethics far removed from both naturalism and nonnaturalism: ethics as a 'conceptual,' not 'factual,' discipline. This allowed them to avoid both commitment to nonnatural facts and responsibility for competence about natural facts. Such ethics may be called analytic in the metaphorical sense in which we do speak of analyzing concepts. And it may be called 'naturalistic' in the secondhand sense that it analyzes ethical concepts by referring only to properties it deems 'natural' or at least to properties 'supervenient' on such properties (see below, section 3). Conceptual analysis was the descendant of the seventeenth-century 'new way of ideas,' which philosophers took in search for a place not already occupied by Copernicus and Galileo. They chose as their subject matter the human 'mind' and its 'ideas,' at that time unexplored by other disciplines, and wrote books such as 'An Essay Concerning Human Understanding,' 'A Treatise Concerning the Principles of Human Knowledge,' and 'A Treatise of Human Nature.' But if concepts are in nature—presumably in human languages or human brains—conceptual analysis remains a part of anthropology, in the broad but literal sense of this word. Concepts, so understood, also lie outside philosophers' competence today: there are linguistics and the lexicography that through painstaking research produces dictionaries like the *OED*, and there are the rapidly growing brain sciences. Philosophers have no more special competence in human languages or brains than earlier they had in human minds or the solar system. On the other hand, if concepts are *not* in nature, then Moore's venture into the nonnatural at least was straightforward.

It also, unlike conceptual analysis, was not dated, though its critics relish calling it 'obsolete.' Like the seventeenth-century way of ideas, conceptual analysis has been out of date since 1787 when Kant pointed out that our business is not merely to analyze concepts but to extend our knowledge (*Critique of Pure Reason*, B 18). It has been out of date since 1951 when Quine pointed out that 'meaning is what essence becomes when it is divorced from the object of reference and wedded to the word.'[8] Like the seventeenth-century way of ideas, the twentieth-century 'way of concepts' inherited its rationale from the medievals' concern with essences, but left out the grounding of essences in things, which the medievals had taken for granted. Without such grounding the rationale is opaque, even if we say, in often unwitting imitation of Wittgenstein, that our concern is with how language or discourse 'works.' What special qualifications do philosophers have for research in the workings of language? To be sure, because of their interests, sometimes they do have a

---

[8] W. V. O. Quine, 'Two Dogmas of Empiricism,' *Philosophical Review*, 60 (1951): 20–43.

better ear than professional lexicographers for the nuances of some segments of speech. J. L. Austin's work half a century ago is an example. But, as Austin vigorously argued, having such an ear is not a substitute for empirical knowledge.

Research in concepts or meanings, or in the 'workings of our language,' calls for the competence of linguists, philologists, and lexicographers, today also of neurologists, even computer scientists. It requires meticulous empirical descriptions and fruitful, empirically verifiable hypotheses, not definitions or 'iff' statements. If concepts are brain states, to focus on definitions of them would be alien to neurology, just as such a focus would be to the other sciences. That water is H_2O was a discovery of chemistry, not a definition, lexical or stipulative, and it concerned a substance, not a concept. And if concepts are meanings or uses of words, to attempt to capture them in definitions would be alien even to current philosophy of language, owing to the three trail-blazing developments in it half a century ago. The first was Quine's already mentioned attack on appeals to meanings. It is widely accepted today, but usually only pro forma. Phrases such as 'conceptual question,' 'conceptual content,' and 'conceptual connection' still abound in the literature. The second development, also widely accepted just pro forma, was Wittgenstein's relentless argument in the *Philosophical Investigations*, posthumously published shortly after Quine's article, that words are not used in accordance with necessary and sufficient conditions. He gave 'game' as an example, but the argument applies also to 'good,' 'right,' 'reason,' 'know,' 'exist,' and other denizens of the philosopher's lexicon, which, like 'game,' are everyday words, not technical terms introduced as abbreviations of multi-clause descriptions. The third development was Chomsky's linguistics, announced four years later. It marked a striking advance by stressing the biological, largely inherited, core of linguistic competence and urging the use in the study of language of the standard methods of scientific research.

The project of defining knowledge, which I gave as an example of conceptual analysis, was already dated at its birth in the late 1950s, when Ayer's *Problem of Knowledge* and Chisholm's *Perceiving* appeared. A paper by Edmund Gettier, a student of Wittgenstein's disciple Norman Malcolm, made this evident in the early 1960s. Few of those who wrote the thousands of pages devoted to it seemed aware that, whatever its author's intentions, the paper called not for greater diligence, sophistication, or imagination in pursuing the project but for its abandonment. Thirty years earlier Wittgenstein had written: 'If I was asked what knowledge is, I would list items of knowledge and add "and suchlike." There is no common element to be found in all of them, because there isn't one.'[9]

---

[9] MS 302, 'Diktat für Schlick' 1931–3. Quoted by David Stern, 'Sociology of Science, Rule Following and Forms of Life,' in M. Heidelberger and F. Stadler (eds.) *History of Philosophy and Science* (Dordrecht: Kluwer, 2002), 347.

Like post-Gettier analytic epistemology, post-Moorean analytic ethics was unfazed by misgivings such as Kant's, Quine's, and Wittgenstein's. It clung to conceptual analysis, and thus, despite its professions, was really neither naturalistic nor nonnaturalistic. It went through several stages. The first began in Vienna, soon after the publication of Wittgenstein's *Tractatus Logico-Philosophicus* and with some personal involvement by him. Ethical statements were rejected as nonsense, or at least as lacking cognitive sense. The subtlety of Wittgenstein's verbally similar position, however, was missed altogether. The second was to offer a positive characterization: they are expressions of emotion. But the rich literature already in existence on the emotions in psychology (from James to Arnold) and in phenomenology (from Meinong to Sartre) was ignored, though it seemed to show that they are not, as the emotivists thought, self-contained subjective episodes, Humean 'impressions of reflexion,' but intentional states, directed upon objects, with character dependent on that of their objects, and thus in principle cognitive. The third stage, probably motivated by the experience of the Second World War, which made both the outright rejection and the emotivist interpretation of moral statements seem jejune, was to suppose that they express a special 'moral point of view,' something psychologically as genuine as emotion but less subjective, and that their function is to guide, not goad. In effect, it was to deny them a full-fledged, unqualified cognitive status, yet concede that their function is not merely imperative or exclamatory. Taken for granted in all three stages was that the job of ethics is to describe the meanings or uses of moral words, or the content of moral concepts, or the features and workings of moral discourse. We cannot give people what really interests them, namely, an ethics that says what they should do, Moore's heirs held, but we can give them an ethics that says what they mean—a 'metaethics.' This was the message even in the more recent fallback positions of projectionist antirealism and supervenience realism, where the focus remained metaethical, not substantive. Few worried that the very idea of telling people what they mean seemed paradoxical—except perhaps to psychoanalysts.

2. The good and the world

By taking the conceptual turn analytic ethics did not provide a genuine alternative to ethics humanized. Its new, 'conceptual,' subject matter was either specious, or genuine but beyond its competence. The alternative provided by Moore remained. Let us return to some of its details. I suggested that the place in it of the indefinability and nonnaturalness of the property good was relatively minor, given his explanation of what he meant. Less familiar is that Moore proposed a criterion, a test, for determining whether something has that property: 'the method of isolation.' It consisted in asking whether a world, a *whole* world, which contains the thing but otherwise is just like a world that lacks it, would be better (*Principia Ethica*, 135–6, 143–7, 236–8, 245–7). The two worlds might be wholly inanimate and considered even, as Moore said, 'apart from any possible contemplation . . . by human beings.' He applied the criterion to the intrinsic goodness of beauty, in opposition to Sidgwick's contention that nothing 'appears to possess this quality of goodness out of relation to human existence, or at least to some consciousness or feeling' (133).

The method of isolation implies important similarities of Moore's views to Kant's and Wittgenstein's, which are seldom noticed. I am not suggesting historical connections, though as a student Moore did study Kant assiduously, even attending a course on him in Germany, and Wittgenstein, who had read *Principia* and heard Moore's lectures at Cambridge (but liked neither—he found them repetitious), went camping with him in Norway, presumably discussing not just logic and the Norwegian landscape. Similarities between major philosophers are especially enlightening when their views are reached independently. Kant, Moore, and Wittgenstein shared a dehumanized conception of ethics despite their fundamental differences in most other respects.[10]

In Moore's case that conception was rooted in his method of isolation, in his conviction that, contrary to Sidgwick, the focal good is that of the *world*, not that of the human or sentient parts of it, and that it is independent even of *possible* human consciousness. This conviction led to his ideal utilitarianism. It also led to his principle of organic wholes: 'the value of a whole may be different from the sum of the values of its parts' (*Principia Ethica*, 40). For the method of isolation suggests that the world itself is an organic whole. The goodness of a thing *overall*, we may say, is a function of (1) its intrinsic goodness, determined by the method of isolation, (2) the intrinsic goodness of the totality of its consequences, which are determined, insofar as this is possible, empirically, and (3) its noncausal contribution to the intrinsic goodness of the organic wholes, including the world, of which it is a part, which also are determined, insofar as this is possible, empirically. The overall goodness of a particular item, whether an action or not, depends thus on the actual or possible goodness of the whole world, the 'universe.'

I believe that the usual objections to Moore's theory of a nonnatural property good are no more properly motivated or philosophically astute than

---

[10] I discuss Wittgenstein's view in detail in 'Saying and Showing the Good,' in Heather Dyke (ed.), *Time and Ethics* (Dordrecht: Kluwer Academic Publishers, 2003).

the objections to Plato's theory of forms as a commitment to a 'heaven' or as growth of a philosophical 'beard.' But more to the point here is that even if good were a natural property, *right* would remain nonnatural if it is understood in terms of good. For, so understood, it would still involve reference to all the consequences of an action and all the organic wholes of which it is a part—to all space and time, to the whole world. Scrupulous moral thought sets no time or place beyond which it cares not what happens. Some Americans do care about the floods in Bangladesh, and many people, wherever they may be, care about the climate on earth a century from now. Authentic environmentalists do not say that when humans become extinct, whales and prairie grass might just as well. Many believe honesty would be owed to, and expected of, also gods, angels, and extraterrestrials, should they exist. But these totalities of consequences and organic wholes, indeed the world itself, might not be natural objects. They would not be natural in Moore's precise sense if they are not in time, even if they consist only of things that are in time. But they might not be natural also in a larger sense. Wittgenstein held that, although sentences about such totalities *show* what is higher, they *say* nothing.

At a meeting of the Apostles in 1912 Wittgenstein heard Moore's paper 'Is Conversion Possible?' which Moore had first read to them in 1900 while working on *Principia*. That Moore read the paper again suggests he had not abandoned its ideas. Moral conversion, he said, 'is not unlike religious conversion,' even though it 'is not necessarily connected with any religious ideas.' It is 'both a great good in itself and it secures all other goods which depend on one's own mind alone.... You see "life steadily and whole" and can feel neither desire nor fear of what you see to be bad in it.'[11] We may note that in 1903, when *Principia* was published, Bertrand Russell had written: 'Man's true freedom ... [lies] in the determination to worship only the God created by our own love of the good,'[12] and that in 1914, after (but probably not because of) two years of intense discussions with Wittgenstein, he attributed to 'the ethical work of Spinoza ... the very highest significance,' as 'an indication of some new way of feeling towards life and the world.'[13] This new way of feeling, Russell added, lay outside the scope of 'the scientific method.'

At about the same time, Wittgenstein wrote in his *Notebooks*: 'To believe in a God means to understand the question about the meaning of life ... to see that the facts of the world are not the end of the matter ... to see that life has a meaning.'[14]

[11] Tom Reagan, *Bloomsbury's Prophet* (Philadelphia: Temple University Press, 1986), 144.
[12] Bertrand Russell, 'A Free Man's Worship,' in *Mysticism and Logic* (London: Allen & Unwin, 1917), 50.
[13] Bertrand Russell, 'Scientific Method in Philosophy,' in *Mysticism and Logic*, 109.
[14] Ludwig Wittgenstein, *Notebooks, 1914–1916*, trans. G. E. M. Anscombe (Oxford: Blackwell, 1961), 74.

And later, in the *Tractatus*: 'The sense [*Sinn*] of the world must lie outside the world. In the world . . . no value exists. . . . If there is any value that does have value, it must lie outside the whole sphere of what happens and is the case. For all that happens and is the case is accidental' (6.41).[15] The sense (or meaning) of the world is not something *in* the world because it is the sense of the *whole* world. It constitutes '[t]he solution of the riddle of life in space and time,' but that solution 'lies outside space and time' (6.4312). Later, in 1929, Wittgenstein explained: 'What is good is also divine. Queer as it sounds, that sums up my ethics. Only something supernatural can express the Supernatural.'[16] And elsewhere, also in 1929: '[Attributions of] absolute value are nonsensical but their nonsensicality [is] their very essence. [A]ll I wanted to do with [those attributions] was to go beyond the world and that is to say beyond significant language.'[17] He meant, however, not that the attributions are gibberish, but only that they are not logical pictures, in the sense required by his rather exacting theory of meaning.

What Wittgenstein called the riddle of life presumably concerns the sense or meaning of life, and this has been a central topic in serious ethics. To ask about ultimate value is to ask about the meaning of life, what makes life worth living. And the meaning of life does involve the meaning of the world. One who asks about the meaning of one's life does sometimes phrase the question as asking about 'the sense of it all.' Life can hardly be fully meaningful in a meaningless world. Indeed, that the world exists at all, that there is something rather than nothing, may be the ultimate object of joy (or sorrow) and certainly of wonder (6.44). But to ask about the sense of the world requires, as Wittgenstein put it, 'view[ing] the world sub specie aeterni,' even 'feeling the world as a limited whole,' which, he wrote, is something 'mystical' (6.45). Ethics does ask what makes life good, but 'the good life is the world seen *sub specie aeternitatis*' (*Notebooks*, 83e). Realization of value, whether goodness or rightness, does not consist in the occurrence in the world of some particular event or events, but in the world itself being different, at its limits, in its waxing and waning as a whole (6.43). However, all this can only show itself. For there cannot be ethical propositions. The reason is not that, as Wittgenstein's early followers thought, there is nothing for such propositions to be about, but that what they purport to say cannot be *said*, in the precise sense that it cannot be pictured, not even 'logically.' It is 'the higher,' which can only be *shown* (6.42).

[15] Ludwig Wittgenstein, *Tractatus Logico-Philosophicus*, trans. D. F. Pears and B. F. McGuinness (London: Routledge, 1972). References use the decimal system in the original.

[16] Ludwig Wittgenstein, *Culture and Value*, ed. G. H. von Wright, trans. Peter Winch (Chicago: University of Chicago Press, 1980), 3e.

[17] Ludwig Wittgenstein, *Philosophical Occasions 1912–1951* (Indianapolis: Hackett, 1993), 40, 44.

Why is this so? Even if we refrain from calling the world mystical, we should acknowledge that it is mysterious. The reason is logical, not mawkish or cabbalistic. It is not that the world is too big or too unlike what we take it to be. Not its size or content, but its logical/ontological category, or rather its failing to fall in any category, is what makes it mysterious. This is why genuine propositions about it, and thus ethical propositions, are impossible. We may say that the world is *everything*, but this would only acknowledge its peculiarity. For to speak of *everything* is to employ the predicate 'is a thing' or 'is a fact,' depending on whether we think the world is the totality of things or of facts. Both predicates, Wittgenstein noted, express only formal concepts, corresponding to formal or internal properties, and thus the sentences in which they occur say nothing, though they show much. '[T]he variable name "x" is the proper sign for the pseudo-concept object,' he wrote. This is why 'it is nonsensical to speak of the *total number of objects*.' And he added: 'The same applies to the words "complex", "fact", "function", "number", etc. They all signify formal concepts and are represented in conceptual notation [only] by variables...'(4.1272).

The concept of a *world* also is formal and thus unsuited for any 'saying,' though available for 'showing,' because it involves the formal concept of fact (the world is the totality of *facts*). But it is formal for yet another reason: it involves the formal concept of generality (the world is the *totality* of facts). An important, especially relevant to this paper, application of the distinction between saying and showing was Wittgenstein's attempt to avoid both naive realism and superficial antirealism with respect to the account of general propositions. A general proposition does not assert an irreducibly general fact that is 'out there in the objective world,' as Russell held in his *Lectures on Logical Atomism*.[18] But neither is it reducible to the conjunction of its singular instances, as (following Frege) Russell showed in that same work.

Wittgenstein rejected both realism and antirealism regarding general propositions by proposing a remarkably original and sophisticated third alternative. In a 1919 letter to Russell, which replied to Russell's objection that in an account of a general proposition in terms of elementary (i.e. singular) propositions 'It is necessary also to be given the proposition that all elementary propositions are given,' he wrote: 'There is no such proposition! That all elementary propositions are given is *shown* by there being none having an elementary sense which is not given.'[19] There is no such proposition, presumably,

[18] Bertrand Russell, *The Philosophy of Logical Atomism* (Chicago: Open Court, 1996), 103.

[19] *Notebooks*, 130. See also *Letters to Russell, Keynes and Moore*, ed. G. H. von Wright (Ithaca, NY: Cornell University Press, 1974), 73. In *Principia Mathematica* (Part I, Summary), an elementary proposition is defined as one that 'contains no reference to any totality.'

because 'proposition,' and thus also 'elementary proposition,' belong on
Wittgenstein's list of words signifying formal concepts. To be sure, he wrote
that all propositions are truth-functions of elementary propositions (*Tractatus*,
5), implying that general propositions are truth-functions of their elementary
instances. He thus acknowledged what makes the antirealist position regarding
generality plausible. But he also wrote that the concept 'all' is not a truth-function
(5.521), thus acknowledging what makes the realist position plausible.
Presumably, his reason was that, as Frege and Russell had shown, a general
proposition is not a molecular proposition: its singular instances are not components of it. 'It is surely clear,' Frege wrote, 'that when anyone uses the sentence "all men are mortal" he does not want to assert something about some
Chief Akpanya, of whom perhaps he has never heard.'[20] And Russell pointed
out that 'in order to arrive [by "complete induction"] at the general proposition
"All men are mortal", you must already have the general proposition "All men
are among those I have enumerated." '[21] The quantifier 'all' does not gather its
singular instances in the way the paradigm truth functions, namely, the
propositional connectives, gather the propositions they connect. The horse-
shoe requires two propositions—an antecedent and a consequent—however
complex they may be. The quantifier requires only a propositional function.[22]

The realism/antirealism debate, in metaphysics and logic as well as in ethics,
must be bypassed wherever it involves putative statements employing formal
concepts about the totality of things or of facts, that is, about the world. If
ethics involves such statements, as Wittgenstein held, then both moral realism
and moral antirealism are to be rejected. Ethical statements both *say* nothing
and *show* something. The controversy between moral realism and moral antirealism is thus a special case of the controversy between metaphysical realism
and metaphysical antirealism. Insofar as the latter concerns the world, namely,
its reality or nature apart from our cognition of it, neither alternative can be
stated properly. Thus we do not face the stark choice between them.[23]
Antirealism is usually a negative position, merely denying the reality of whatever
items are in question, and today usually asserting that with respect to them
'language is all there is.' This is why it is deeply unsatisfactory, whether in metaphysics or in ethics. Wittgenstein's distinction between saying and showing

---

[20] Peter Geach, and Max Black (eds.), *Translations from the Philosophical Writings of Gottlob Frege*
(Oxford: Blackwell, 1970), 83.

[21] Bertrand Russell, *The Philosophy of Logical Atomism* (Chicago: Open Court, 1996), 101.

[22] In the first edition of *Principia Mathematica* we find: 'Our judgment that all men are mortal collects
together a number of elementary judgments. It is not, however, composed of these, since, e.g., the fact that
Socrates is mortal is not part of what we assert . . .' (Cambridge: Cambridge University Press, 1964), 45.

[23] In *Skepticism about the External World* (New York: Oxford University Press, 1998), I argue for an
analogous conclusion in epistemology regarding the existence of bodies, of an 'external world.'

offered an alternative to antirealism that did not constitute a return to realism, to the equally unsatisfactory acceptance of the items in question as unqualifiedly 'out there.' It is often dismissed as obscurantist. Tough-minded philosophers ask, How can there be things that only show themselves? But the question misses the point of the distinction. It is an alternative to both realism and antirealism. What only shows itself is not part of reality. But neither is it unreal, like Hamlet, the golden mountain, or the round square.[24]

Contrary to received opinion, Wittgenstein's distinction between saying and showing is reasonably clear. What can be said is what can be pictured, at least logically. What can only be shown is what the picturing involves but cannot itself be pictured—not even by a 'meta-picture.' Consider the statement 'Socrates is white.' It does *say* something. What it says can even be pictured literally, not just logically. But the putative statement 'Socrates is an individual,' in the sense 'individual' has in logic, says nothing. Yet it is not gibberish. Nor is it 'metalinguistic,' i.e. asserting that 'Socrates' is an individual constant, just as 'Socrates is white' is not about 'Socrates.' 'Socrates is an individual' *shows* something about the very individual it purports to be about. It shows the logical category to which the individual belongs, and a logical category is ontologically and cognitively much 'higher' than color. 'Socrates is an individual' presupposes what it purports to say, its having sense depends on its being true. You can picture an individual's being white but not its being an individual—as is obvious in the case of literal pictures, e.g. paintings. You can use color to picture a face, but you cannot picture the color—you can put a splash of it on a canvas, but as Nelson Goodman pointed out this would be a sample, not a picture, of the color, even if the canvas is touted as a 'painting.'

Wittgenstein's distinction between saying and showing was thus a natural consequence of his picture theory of meaning. And, again contrary to received opinion, this theory is also reasonably clear, indeed familiar in the history of philosophy. It was a descendant of the traditional theories according to which meaning depends on the presence in the mind of 'ideas,' 'representations,' sometimes explicitly held to be 'mental images,' even 'copies,' of what is meant. And the idea that a representation need not be literal is standard in present-day accounts, neurological or computational, of cognitive states as involving representations. Wittgenstein's picture theory of meaning is no more questionable than such theories and accounts. Of course, it also is no less questionable, as in his later works he himself argued.

---

[24] See my 'Metaphysical Realism and Logical Nonrealism,' in Richard Gale (ed.), *Blackwell Guide to Metaphysics* (Oxford: Blackwell, 2002), 282–302.

As we saw, Moore also held that ethics involves reference to the world as a whole. For this reason and in this sense, he might have agreed with Wittgenstein that, like logic, ethics is transcendental, that it concerns the limits of the world, not its contents (*Tractatus*, 6.13, 6.421). Such a view of ethics was not novel. For Plato the philosophic life culminated in a glimpse of the Form of the Good, which he held to be indescribable. Aquinas placed Good in the company of Being, One, Truth, and Beauty, the so-called transcendentals, which were said to range across the categories, that is, the highest genera, and thus to lack even the status of categories of things in the world, much less the status of things. In philosophical theology God was described as a being of infinite goodness that is the source and measure of all other goodness, earthly and unearthly. And Kant, as if using words from the *Tractatus*, held that, unlike what he called practical anthropology, moral thought is concerned not with what happens but with what ought to happen, even if it never happens (*Critique of Pure Reason*, A 802/B 830). The 'supersensible' was as central to Kant's ethics as the 'nonnatural' was to Moore's and the 'supernatural' to Wittgenstein's.

Kant gave 'Thou shalt not lie' as an example of an imperative of duty, but promptly explained that it 'does not apply to men only, as if other rational beings had no need to observe it.' For 'the ground of obligation here must not be sought in the nature of man or in the circumstances in which he is placed,' Kant wrote, and he urged that 'it is a matter of the utmost necessity to work out for once a pure moral philosophy completely cleansed of everything that can only be empirical and appropriate to anthropology.'[25] Kant's distinction between what happens and what ought to happen was in tune with Wittgenstein's distinction between saying and showing. If ethics is not about what happens or is the case, yet truth is correspondence to what is the case, then ethics contains no truths. Kant did not explicitly draw this conclusion, but Wittgenstein did. The logical positivists also drew it, attacked Moore with it, but misunderstood it.

Whether we ourselves should draw it depends on how circumspect we are in wielding the notion of truth. That truth is correspondence (*Übereinstimming*, 'agreement,' in Kant's terminology) to fact is a truism of common sense, but as a philosophical theory it is too crude for ethics, as well as for logic and mathematics, indeed, for the reasons mentioned earlier, even for ordinary general statements. Wittgenstein saw this, perhaps Kant also did, and Moore might have seen it, at least in the case of statements predicating goodness overall, had he considered the matter. To be sure, all three accepted the truism. But Kant

---

[25] Immanuel Kant, *Groundwork of the Metaphysics of Morals*, trans. H. J. Paton (New York: Harper & Row, 1964), 57.

called it a 'mere verbal explanation' (*Logic*, 55), a nominal definition (*Namenklärung*) that proffers no criterion of truth (*Critique of Pure Reason*, A 58/B 72), and, paving the way to Hegel, he held that the proper and sufficient criterion of empirical truth presupposes the idea of the systematic unity of nature (ibid., A 651/B 679). There were no Russellian facts for Kant, or anything else not already epistemic and thus, by implication, alethic, to which judgments might correspond if they were to be called true without circularity. It is not our cognition that must conform (*richten*) to objects; rather, objects must conform to our cognition (ibid., p. xvi). Wittgenstein also endorsed a correspondence view of truth, but only for impossibly impoverished sentences about configurations of simple objects of which no example could be given, not for the sentences of logic, mathematics, ethics, or even everyday discourse. Moore discussed the nature of truth extensively but inconclusively in lectures delivered in 1910–11 and not published in his lifetime. He wrote that 'to say that a belief is true is to say that it corresponds to a fact,'[26] that this means that 'the fact to which it refers is, or has being' (ibid. 267), but also that the notion of a fact itself can be understood as standing for what corresponds to true belief (ibid. 298), and he acknowledged that the truth of conditional statements did not seem to fit the account at all (ibid. 268). Moore, too, seemed confident about the definition of truth as correspondence only if understood as merely nominal.

The moral, however, is not that we should accept ordinary noncognitivism or stampede into a coherentist or some other standard theory of truth, but that we should recognize that the ways of knowledge and truth are not neat and tidy. A doctor's orders are neither true nor false, but their legitimacy and authority are cognitive through-and-through. The reason, of course, is that their ground is taken to be cognitive. Religious and theological thought often rests the authority of the will of God on his omniscience. But a sophisticated theology can also hold that it is grounded nonepistemically in God's status as our creator. It is in this latter way, presumably, that the authority of what Kant called practical reason (*Vernunft*) and his description of ethical judgments as both imperatives (*Imperative*) and cognitions (*Erkenntnisse*) should be understood.[27] We may call ethical judgments 'valid' instead of 'true,' as Kant often did, just as we may describe both the doctor's orders and the propositions grounding them as valid, though only the latter as true. Or we may follow Nelson Goodman and just use 'right' for both. Goodman's antirealism ('irrealism') closely resembled

---

[26] G. E. Moore, *Some Main Problems of Philosophy* (London: Allen & Unwin, 1953), 277.

[27] Immanuel Kant, *Critique of Practical Reason*, trans. Lewis White Beck (Indianapolis: Bobbs-Merrill, 1956), 68.

Kant's transcendental idealism. And Kant's ethics cannot be detached from his transcendental idealism, the first two sections of the *Groundwork* from the third. If we cannot understand his transcendental idealism, then we cannot understand the moral yet nonepistemic authority of a noumenal self, but we should be clear that nothing merely human can enjoy such authority. The autonomy Kant thought essential to morality required membership in the intelligible, not just the sensible, world.[28]

3. The right and the good

It is often asked whether a dehumanized ethics such as Moore's could be 'relevant' to action. The question is as ancient as Aristotle's complaints about Plato's Form of the Good. But it is ambiguous. It may be asking (1) whether Moore's property good can bear a relation to the rightness of actions, (2) whether one can be motivated to action by it, (3) whether one can be motivated by cognitive states of which it is an object, by itself or as a constituent of states of affairs, or (4) whether there can be such cognitive states in the first place.

The connection between good and right cannot be just happenstantial, but neither can it be trivially definitional. In *Principia Ethica* Moore did define duty as 'that action, which will cause more good to exist in the Universe than any possible alternative' (198), but he also described what 'is good in itself or has intrinsic value' as what 'ought to exist for its own sake' (34). In *Ethics* he repeated that 'it is always our duty to do what will have the best possible consequences,' but denied that this is 'a mere tautology.'[29] And in the preface to the second edition of *Principia* he wrote that he had used 'good' in a sense that bears an 'extremely important relation to the conceptions of "right" and "wrong"' (4). While Kant did not allow for a concept of moral good that is independent of the concept of right, he did take for granted the independence of the general concept of good. He held that 'all imperatives ... say that something would be good to do or leave undone' (*Groundwork*, 81), that 'the necessary object of a will which is determined by [the moral law],' as 'given to it a priori,' is 'the highest good' (*Critique of Practical Reason*, 4), and that 'It is the concepts of the good and evil which first determine an object for the will' (ibid. 70). As John Rawls remarks, 'the priority of right ... does not mean that

---

[28] 'The causality of [actions which can be done by disregarding all desires and incitements of sense] lies in man as intelligence and in the laws of such effects and actions as accord with the principles of an intelligible world ... [H]e is there his proper self only as an intelligence (while as a human being he is merely an appearance of himself) ...' (*Groundwork*, 125).

[29] G. E. Moore, *Ethics* (Oxford: Oxford University Press, 1912), 73.

Kant's moral doctrine includes no conception of the good, nor does it mean that the conceptions used are somewhat deduced from a previously specified concept of right.... No moral doctrine can do without one or more conceptions of the good.'[30]

The idea of being motivated to action by Moore's property good indeed does have doubtful coherence, but only because the idea of being motivated by any property may be incoherent for purely logical, not ethical or psychological, reasons. Dyadic relations do not hold between individuals and properties. But it is not incoherent to ask whether one can be motivated by cognitive states that have that property or states of affairs involving it as object. Would such cognitive states be 'reason-giving'? Would they be 'action-guiding'? This question is difficult to answer because the specialists in such matters, namely, psychologists working on motivation, still know too little, probably because they cannot engage in serious experimentation with human subjects, while philosophers engage only in speculation. When Hume announced that reason is and ought to be the slave of the passions, we may ask how he knew all this, how he knew that it is their slave, whatever we think of his adding that it ought be. Perhaps he could be excused for thinking that the 'passions' are discoverable through introspection. But his own views should have kept him from thinking that their being motives, i.e. their *motivating*, could be so discovered. Nevertheless, there have been advances in genuine, scientific psychology. The preoccupation with 'primary drives' seems to have ended. There is growing recognition of the spontaneity of the young child's artistic and play behavior, the importance of surprise for its cognitive development, its preference for the novel, the presence, even in nonhuman animals, of curiosity, a tendency to explore, a desire to know for the sake of knowing. Progress has been made away from the egoism and hedonism presupposed by most so-called 'rationality' theories.[31] The genetic basis of motives like empathy is readily acknowledged. Chomsky accepts Plato's thesis in the *Meno* about the innateness of much of our knowledge.

Can there be cognitive states of which the property good, or a state of affairs that includes it as constituent, is the object? Those who give a negative answer usually rely on causal or quasi-causal metaphysical and epistemological theories, accepted, if not because they seem 'scientific,' then because of thought-experiments about what we would or would not 'say.' They ask, 'Would you say that S knows (perceives, sees, is aware of) x if x bears no relation to S?' And then they ignore the obvious answer, 'No, I would not, but x does bear a relation to

---

[30] John Rawls, *Lectures on the History of Moral Philosophy* (Cambridge, Mass.: Harvard University Press, 2000), 231.

[31] Cf. Philip Kitcher, 'The Evolution of Human Altruism,' *Journal of Philosophy*, 90 (1993): 497–516.

S, that of being known by S,' in favor of unobvious answers, as if the right answer could not be the obvious one. They think they understand the nature of causality better than they understand the nature of knowledge and would deny even the cognitive status of arithmetic, a paradigm of unquestionable knowledge, if it is taken to be about numbers. They would find a mathematician's intellectual life as inexplicable as the mathematician's moral life when understood in Moore's way, if arithmetic turned out to be about numbers.

Elsewhere I have suggested that the property good, described by Plato as blinding, by Moore as nonnatural, and by Wittgenstein as unsayable, is best considered a generic property, though one on the highest level of generality.[32] It is the genus to which Moore's personal affection and aesthetic appreciation, Aristotle's eudaimonia, Mill's pleasure, and other goods reasonably proposed by reasonable people belong as species. This is why we cannot 'see' it in the way we see a shade of yellow. But then neither can we see even Color in that way, though Color is a generic property on an incomparably lower level of generality. We might say (though Wittgenstein did not) that Goodness only shows itself in its species, just as Color only shows itself in yellow, red, blue, etc., and is not seen as a separate property additional to them. We might also say that the genus supervenes on its species, and thus provide the idea of supervenience with content that avoids reliance on an otherwise puzzling relation such as 'determination.'

Whether or not this suggestion is right, the theorists denying that we can have cognitive access to Moore's property good need to pay more attention to the epistemological and metaphysical details. Their epistemology is open, of course, to the familiar objection to externalism, namely, that it cannot answer the skeptic, although finding such an answer was the *raison d'être* of modern epistemology. But they also ignore, or require us to count as unintelligible, Kantian accounts of cognition, which even if we do not accept we ought to be able to understand and respect. According to Kant, Putnam, Goodman, and many others, though as a fact in the world human cognition is a zoological matter, and thus subject to the demands of scientific causal explanation, the world itself is comprehensible only as an object of a cognition that is not zoological.

The theorists also owe us answers to numerous metaphysical questions, such as those explored in detail by David Armstrong[33] and Evan Fales.[34] The first, of course, is 'What is causation?' They cannot just revert to Hume and in effect beg the question against Moore by saying that causation is constant conjunction in

---

[32] I do so in *Skepticism in Ethics* (Bloomington: Indiana University Press, 1989).

[33] David M. Armstrong, *Universals and Scientific Realism* (Cambridge: Cambridge University Press, 1978).   [34] Evan Fales, *Causality and Universals* (London: Routledge, 1990).

time, even if 'nomological.' Is it then, as Armstrong and Fales hold, a relation of universals, properties, or at least based on one? But are properties universals in the first place, or are they rather particulars, tropes, or perhaps both, as Moore in fact held?[35] How would the arguments against Moore read in the case of each possibility? Fales argues that there must be properties we can identify independently of their causal powers if a vicious infinite regress is to be avoidable. His examples are the properties characterizing the content of sense perception, though his ultimate concern is with the identification of properties in physics (*Causality and Universals*, 221–4). But if some properties can be identified or known without reference to their causal powers, so might Moore's property good, whether or not it has causal powers. If our theorists deny this on the ground that it is nonnatural, then they must revisit the distinction between natural and nonnatural properties and give a serious, detailed account of it. Is a property nonnatural because it is not in time, as Moore held? What is it for a property to be in time? Would they say, in a vicious circle, that to be in time is to have causal powers? Moreover, since a property, natural or nonnatural, enters in causal relations only indirectly, as a constituent of states of affairs, we would need to be told a great deal about the nature of states of affairs and how and what properties might be constituents of them. For example, can a state of affairs that is in time and part of the causal order have a nonnatural property as a constituent? The latter would not itself be in time and enter in causal relations, but is not this the case with all properties?

Yet another question the theorists need to consider is whether there are uninstantiated properties. If there are, do they have causal powers? Are moral properties, even though real, uninstantiated? If they have no causal powers, is this so just because they are uninstantiated? Being an angel perhaps has no causal powers, but is this true of being a circle, as this property, though never instantiated, must be understood at Michelin and Goodyear? Is Moore's property good like that of being an angel or like that of being a circle, or is it rather like the shape of my pen? And if the latter, is it also, like it, a specific property, or a generic property, like Shape, or a transcendental and thus not even generic? Perhaps generic properties as such have no causal powers but their species do. A tire's having shape helps no car roll but its being round does. A traffic light's being colored stops no driver but its being red sometimes does. Are Moore's ideal goods, personal affection and aesthetic appreciation, species of goodness, as I suggested? Do *they* have causal powers? If they do but their genus, goodness, does not, is this so because the latter is a nonnatural property or just because it is a generic one, like Shape or Color? Or are Moore's ideal goods

[35] G. E. Moore, "Identity," *Proceedings of the Aristotelian Society*, NS 1, (1900–1).

uninstantiated properties, mere ideals? If so, can mere ideals—moral, political, religious—have causal powers? If they cannot, how are we to understand our striving and sometimes dying because of them?

Of course, I shall not attempt answers to these questions here, but answers are needed, detailed and carefully worked out, if we are to take seriously the complaint that Moore's property good is irrelevant to action. Appeals to 'naturalism' or 'the scientific point of view,' let alone to our 'intuitions,' are not enough. Without such answers, the complaint might be like the seventeenth-century natural philosophers' complaint that Newton appealed to occult and immaterial gravitational forces, rather than to intelligible and robust bumping, or H A Prichard's complaint that Einstein's theory of relativity was unintelligible. How a body could 'motivate' another body at a distance without the help of intervening bodies was incomprehensible to the natural philosophers, and Prichard could not visualize a non-Euclidean space. Some of Moore's heirs have been unable to comprehend or visualize the property good as doing any pushing or pulling.

So, I shall ignore the metaphysical and epistemological concerns behind the usual questions about the relevance of Moore's ethics. But a different question does arise. It is both legitimate and deep. By requiring reference to the whole world in judgments of duty, Moore could tell us nothing specific about how we ought to act in any particular situation, just as Wittgenstein could not. This is why Moore virtually admitted that his theory of right was profoundly skeptical. There might be an action we ought to do, but we could not know which or what it is. In view of the mind-boggling range of its consequences and organic relationships, 'throughout an infinite future' (*Principia Ethica*, 202), even probability statements about them could not be seriously made. According to Wittgenstein, we could not make genuine statements about them at all, since this would require reference to totalities determined by formal properties. For both Moore and Wittgenstein, radical moral skepticism seemed inevitable, though in Moore's case the reasons were empirical, while in Wittgenstein's they were logical.

But Moore's moral skepticism does not lead to amoralism. Ideal utilitarianism is not mere consequentialism. An action may be intrinsically good even if it ought not to be done, even if it did not make the world better. In Ross's terminology, if not meaning, it may be a prima facie duty even if not an actual duty. This is why respect for the good, for Aquinas's first principle of natural law, may continue to inform the ideal utilitarian's actions. Such respect would be akin to love, whether practical or pathological, not to calculation. This love can have as its object only the intrinsic goodness of the action, its being a prima facie duty, not its being an actual duty. Only a part of a world, not a whole world, can be loved.

I am not suggesting an inference, surely specious, from the intrinsic goodness of an action to its rightness. No claim is made that the former makes the latter 'probable,' even to a tiny degree, or that it 'justifies' or is a 'reason' for the action. In Hutcheson's useful terminology, if not meaning, it is at most an 'exciting reason'—not a 'justifying reason,' i.e. an item one may appeal to in reasoning, what Kant called *Grund* and Moore called evidence. What I am suggesting is that if in acting one is motivated and guided only by respect for the good, and only the intrinsic goodness of an action is intellectually visible, then one is motivated and guided only by respect for the intrinsic goodness of the action. One has no knowledge of the totality of its consequences and organic relationships, indeed not even a genuine conception of it. Thus, qua agent, the ideal utilitarian can only be a deontologist, not a consequentialist. This is why Moore's ideal utilitarianism was not inimical to moral common sense, which views with distaste the spirit of calculation consequentialism cultivates. The ideal utilitarian has no 'justifying reasons' but plenty of 'exciting reasons' for doing good particular actions without guile: their plain goodness. Thus Moore's dehumanized ethics may be seen as the marriage—of love, not convenience—of the two great ways of moral thinking: the utilitarian and the deontological.

INDEX

Note to readers
Because G. E. Moore and his works are discussed throughout the text, an entry for Moore would not be useful and is not included. To find discussion of Moore and his works readers should search for relevant subject entries, e.g., organic unity; goodness, whether simple property; etc.